LANGUAGE IN SOCIETY

American English

Language in Society

GENERAL EDITOR
Peter Trudgill, Chair of English Linguistics, University of Fribourg

ADVISORY EDITORS
J. K. Chambers, Professor of Linguistics, University of Toronto
Ralph Fasold, Professor of Linguistics, Georgetown University
William Labov, Professor of Linguistics, University of Pennsylvania
Lesley Milroy, Professor of Linguistics, University of Michigan, Ann Arbor

American English

Dialects and Variation

Walt Wolfram
and
Natalie Schilling-Estes

Blackwell
Publishing

© 1998 by Walt Wolfram and Natalie Schilling-Estes
Parts of this book are based on *Dialects and American English* (Prentice Hall, 1991).

350 Main Street, Malden, MA 02148-5020, USA
108 Cowley Road, Oxford OX4 1JF, UK
550 Swanston Street, Carlton, Victoria 3053, Australia

The right of Walt Wolfram and Natalie Schilling-Estes to be identified as the Authors
of this Work has been asserted in accordance with the UK Copyright, Designs, and
Patents Act 1988.

First published 1998 by Blackwell Publishing Ltd
Reprinted 1998, 1999, 2000, 2001, 2002, 2003, 2004

Library of Congress Cataloging-in-Publication Data

Wolfram, Walt, 1941–
    American English : dialects and variation / Walt Wolfram and Natalie Schilling-
Estes.
        p.   cm. – (Language in society; 25)
    Includes bibliographical references and index.
    ISBN 0–631–20486–5 (hardcover : alk. paper). – ISBN 0–631–20487–3 (pbk. : alk.
paper)
    1. English language-Dialects-United States. 2. English language–Variation–United
States. 3. Americanisms. I. Schilling-Estes, Natalie. II. Title. III. Series: Language
in society (Oxford, England); 25.
PE2841.W63   1998
427'.973–dc21   97–37242
                                                                                          CIP

A catalogue record for this title is available from the British Library.

Set in 10.5 on 12 pt Ehrhardt
by Graphicraft Typesetters Ltd, Hong Kong
Printed and bound in the United Kingdom
by MPG Books Ltd, Bodmin, Cornwall

For further information on
Blackwell Publishing, visit our website:
http://www.blackwellpublishing.com

Contents

Figures

Tables

Series Editor's Preface

Perhaps now is the time to confess that the Language in Society series has always had as one of its secret ambitions the signing up of all the major, significant players in the arena of world sociolinguistics. With the addition of Walt Wolfram to our team, this dream has come one step closer to being achieved, since we now have on our side one of the veterans from the original squad of young scholars who contributed to that first large-scale flowering of American sociolinguistics in the early 1970s, to which many aspects of work in modern sociolinguistics owe so much. That Walt Wolfram has been joined in the authoring of this book by one of the most energetic and gifted scholars from the latest generation of American sociolinguists, Natalie Schilling-Estes, is a source of additional excitement and satisfaction.

The book is very much, as is only appropriate when working with dialectology, a data-based work, with a great deal of the data being – as is typical of practicing sociolinguists – the authors' own, but it is also a ground-breaking work full of important new theoretical contributions and insights. The book is obviously aimed primarily at an American audience, but it will also be of very considerable importance and interest indeed outside the United States. Not only will it be essential for any non-American concerned to learn more about American English; it will also be vital reading for scholars with theoretical interests in historical linguistics, new-dialect formation, variation theory, language and gender, African American Vernacular English, creolization, and many other issues, as well as for practitioners involved in issues to do with mother-tongue education, speech therapy, and dialectological research itself. There is nothing quite like the writings on dialectology of linguists who have been out there and done the fieldwork with real live human beings and analyzed the data themselves. And there are very few dialectologists who have done as much of this type of work – and used the results of their work to do their best to improve the lot of the communities from which they have obtained their data – as these authors.

Peter Trudgill

Preface

Dialects are fascinating to people from a wide range of backgrounds. Some are interested in the topic simply because it piques a natural curiosity about how different groups of people talk. Others feel that information about dialects may be relevant to an allied field of study, while still others are interested in dialect variation as a specialized concentration in linguistics or sociolinguistics. Given the diverse backgrounds and interests of students who end up in a course on dialects, the challenge is to fashion a text that can meet the needs of this varied audience without compromising the inherent complexity of the subject matter. In our opinion, this course of study should combine an informed approach to the nature of dialect variation, descriptive and explanatory detail about dialects, and a discussion of the broader socioeducational implications of dialect diversity. Confronting this challenge has led to the current version of a textbook on dialects and American English. This text has its origins in Wolfram and Fasold's *The Study of Social Dialects* (1974) and Wolfram's *Dialects and American English* (1991). But this is more than a simple revision of the latter text, thanks in large part to the addition of Natalie Schilling-Estes as a co-author. The text contains a completely new chapter on the history of American English dialects (chapter 4) and several drastically reworked chapters, including chapter 2 (Why Do Languages Have Dialects?), chapter 7 (Gender and Language Variation), and chapter 8 (Dialects and Style). We have also integrated research from our extensive studies of rural, post-insular dialects in the Southeast United States which were initiated in the 1990s.

Throughout the book, we have attempted to keep the diverse nature of the audience in mind, so that the text is readable and relevant for students in English, education, speech and language pathology, cultural anthropology, sociology, and psychology, as well as the various branches of linguistic studies. A number of texts are marketed with such broad-based claims; we hope that this will be one of those rare cases where the actual text matches introductory promises. We have tried to keep technical linguistic terminology to a minimum, even with respect to phonetics. For convenience only, we have included a skeletal phonetics chart for readers (see pp. xvi–xvii); it should be used with the understanding that much phonetic detail is eliminated. In particular, many aspects of vowel pronunciation could have been included, but we have worked under the assumption that most readers will not have an extensive background in phonetics. We apologize to those who find our discussion of phonetic detail somewhat frustrating because they have a solid background in phonetics.

We have also tried to avoid linguistic formalism. From our perspective, underlying principles of variation are much more significant than their formal representation. There are, however, times when technical terms are needed to convey essential constructs in the field. To help readers in this regard, a glossary of technical terms has been provided. Students also should be aided by exercises which are incorporated into the text at relevant points.

We have made an honest attempt to write a text for the range of students who take various "courses on dialects" rather than our professional colleagues who may wish to scrutinize our current state of sociolinguistic erudition. The text should be appropriate for both upper level undergraduate and graduate students.

Conceptually, the text is divided into four major sections. The first three chapters introduce students to basic notions about the nature of dialectal variation. The next chapter, chapter 4, gives an overview of the history and development of American English dialects. Chapters 5 through 9 offer a descriptive account of some of the major factors accounting for variation in American English, including region, status, ethnicity, gender, and style; this section introduces students to the systematic nature of language variation (chapter 9). We tried to balance the approach of traditional dialectology with the advances of variation studies while avoiding the technicalities of quantitative analysis. The final section, chapters 10 and 11, considers the applications of dialect study. We focus on dialects and education but also discuss ways in which researchers can work collaboratively with communities from which they gather data for dialect study.

An updated summary appendix of diagnostic grammatical and phonological structures is included as a convenient reference for readers. The appendix shows an admitted bias in favor of socially significant structures over regionally significant ones, although some regional patterns are included.

The list of people to whom we are indebted starts with the first author's initial teacher in linguistics as an undergraduate student, Roger W. Shuy, and extends to our most recent classes of students at North Carolina State University, Stanford University, and the Linguistic Institute of the Linguistic Society of America. We have been fortunate enough to associate with a group of people who have taught us that professional colleagues can also be good friends: Carolyn Adger, Guy Bailey, Robert Bayley, Allen Bell, John Baugh, Janet Bing, Charles Boberg, Ron Butters, Adrianne Cheek, Donna Christian, Connie Eble, Penny Eckert, Ralph Fasold, Janet Fuller, Matt Gordon, Gregory Guy, Kirk Hazen, Dave Herman, Brian Joseph, Scott Kiesling, Craig Melchert,

Howard Mims, Miriam Meyerhoff, Michael Montgomery, Naomi Nagy, Bill Labov, Ceil Lucas, Joy Peyton, Shana Poplack, Dennis Preston, John Rickford, Edgar Schneider, Roger Shuy, Sali Tagliamonte, Erik Thomas, Peter Trudgill, Dick Tucker, Fay Vaughn-Cooke, Tracey Weldon, and Keli Yerian, among many others who should have been named as well. Thanks for your support and friendship. This cast of characters has made academic inquiry much more fun than we ever thought it could be. If students reading this text can just catch a little bit of the excitement that academic inquiry in a real-world context can actually bring, we will be greatly satisfied.

Special thanks are due to those who read and commented on particular chapters covered by their specialized areas of research expertise, including Allen Bell, Janet Bing, Penny Eckert, Bill Kretzschmar, Michael Montgomery, Erik Thomas, and Tracey Weldon. Our greatest indebtedness is reserved for our spouses, Marge Wolfram and Chris Estes. They have given the most – in time, patience, and unfailing encouragement and support throughout this and all of our varied sociolinguistic ventures.

Walt Wolfram, William C. Friday Professor
North Carolina State University

Natalie Schilling-Estes
Stanford University and Old Dominion University

Phonetic Symbols

Consonants

Symbol	Key Words	Phonetic Description
[p]	*pit, spit, tip*	voiceless bilabial stop
[b]	*bat, rabbit, rib*	voiced bilabial stop
[t]	*tip, stop, put*	voiceless alveolar stop
[d]	*doom, under, bud*	voiced alveolar stop
[D]	*butter, buddy*	voiced alveolar flap
[k]	*cap, skate, bake*	voiceless velar stop
[g]	*go, buggy, bag*	voiced velar stop
[ʔ]	*bottle, button* (in some dialects)	voiceless glottal stop
[f]	*fee, after, laugh*	voiceless labiodental fricative
[v]	*vote, over, love*	voiced labiodental fricative
[θ]	*thought, ether, both*	voiceless interdental fricative
[ð]	*the, mother, smooth*	voiced interdental fricative
[s]	*so, fasten, bus*	voiceless alveolar sibilant
[z]	*zoo, lazy, fuzz*	voiced alveolar sibilant
[š]	*shoe, nation, bush*	voiceless palatal sibilant
[ž]	*measure, closure*	voiced palatal sibilant
[h]	*hat, behind*	voiceless glottal fricative
[č]	*chew, pitcher, church*	voiceless palatal affricate
[ǰ]	*judge, ranger, dodge*	voiced palatal affricate
[m]	*my, mommy, bum*	bilabial nasal
[n]	*no, funny, run*	alveolar nasal
[ŋ]	*singer, long*	velar nasal
[l]	*look, bully, call*	lateral
[r]	*run, bury, car*	retroflex
[w]	*way, quack*	labiovelar glide
[y]	*yes, feud*	palatal glide

Vowels

Symbol	Key Words	Phonetic Description
[i]	*beet, leap*	high front tense
[ɪ]	*bit, rip*	high front lax
[e]	*bait, grade*	mid front tense
[ɛ]	*bet, step*	mid front lax
[æ]	*cap, bat*	low front tense
[ə]	*about, afford*	mid central tense
[ʌ]	*shut, was*	mid central lax
[a]	*father, stop*	low central
[u]	*boot, through*	high back tense
[ʊ]	*book, put*	high back lax
[o]	*no, toe*	mid back tense
[ɔ]	*oral, taught*	low back tense
[au]	*crowd, bout*	low central backing diphthong
[aɪ]	*buy, lie*	low central fronting diphthong
[ɔɪ]	*boy, coin*	low back fronting diphthong
[ɚ]	*mother, bird*	mid central retroflex

1

The Reality of Dialects

Most of us have had the experience of sitting in a public place and eavesdropping on conversations around us. As a matter of etiquette, we politely pretend to be preoccupied with the magazine or paper sitting on our lap, but we listen intently to people around us. And we form impressions of them, based not only on the topic of conversation, but on how they are discussing the topic. In fact, there's a good chance that the most critical part of our impression comes from *how* the people are talking rather than *what* they are discussing. We make judgments about regional background, social status, ethnicity, and a host of other social characteristics based simply on the kind of language people are using. On those occasions when we get to check out our initial reactions, we are not surprised when many of our first impressions turn out to be relatively accurate.

We also have similar kinds of reactions in telephone conversations, as we try to associate a set of characteristics with an unidentified speaker in order to make claims such as, "It sounds like a salesperson of some type" or "It sounds like the auto mechanic." In fact, it is surprising how little conversation it takes to draw conclusions about a speaker's background – a sentence, a phrase, or even a word is often adequate to trigger a regional, social, or ethnic classification.

Assessments of a complex set of social characteristics based on language differences are as inevitable as the kinds of judgments we make when we find out where people live, what their occupations are, where they went to school, and who their friends are. In fact, there are some who feel that language differences serve as the single most reliable indicator of social position in our society. When we live a certain way, we are expected to match that lifestyle with our talk. And when we don't match people's expectations of how we should talk, the incongruity between words and behavior is itself a lively topic for conversation.

Language differences seem to be unavoidable in a society composed of a variety of social groups. In a broader context, of course, we must note that the inevitability of these differences is hardly peculiar to American society; any civilization with social and geographical dispersion can be expected to reveal language diversity, or "dialect differences." These differences are a fact of life. Like other "facts of life," our understanding of dialects has been passed on to us with a peculiar mixture of fact and fantasy.

1.1   Defining Dialect

Given the widespread awareness of language differences in our society, just about everyone has some notion of what the term "dialect" refers to. However, the technical use of the term in linguistics is different from its popular definition in some important, but sometimes subtle ways. Professional students of language typically use the term DIALECT as a neutral label to refer to any variety of a language which is shared by a group of speakers. Languages are invariably manifested through their dialects, and to speak a language is to speak some dialect of that language. In this technical usage, there are no particular social or attitudinal evaluations of the term – that is, there are no "good" or "bad" dialects; dialect is simply how we refer to any language variety that typifies a group of speakers within a language. The particular social factors which correlate with dialect diversity may range from simple geography to the complex notion of cultural identity. Furthermore, it is important to understand that socially favored, or "standard," varieties constitute dialects every bit as much as those varieties spoken by isolated, socially disfavored groups whose language differences are socially stigmatized. The technical definition of dialect simply as a variety of a language typical of a given group of speakers is not rigorous and precise, but it is a sufficient starting point in discussing language variation.

1.2   Dialect: The Popular Viewpoint

Although linguists accept a loosely defined technical definition of dialect, happily arguing about what language features belong to a particular dialect or how two dialects differ, non-specialists tend to use "dialect" in a somewhat different sense. At first glance, the differences between popular and technical uses seem inconsequential, but closer inspection reveals that its popular uses carry connotations that give insight into how dialect differences are viewed in our society. Consider, for example, some commonly held beliefs about dialects demonstrated by popular uses of this term in the following quotes:

(1)   "We went to the Outer Banks of North Carolina for a vacation and the people there sure do speak a dialect."

(2) "I know we speak a dialect in the mountains, but it's a very colorful way of speaking."
(3) "The kids in that neighborhood don't really speak English; they speak a dialect."
(4) "The kids in this school all seem to speak the dialect."

In one popular use, the term "dialect" refers simply to those who speak differently from oneself (Quote 1 above). When the authors of this book were children, growing up in Philadelphia, Pennsylvania, and the Eastern Shore of Maryland, respectively, they didn't necessarily realize that they spoke dialects; it was speakers from other areas who spoke dialects. Of course, we came to realize that this perception could be a two-way street when we attended college in different states and classmates pointed out particular features of our "dialect." When we think about it, we have to admit that the perception that only other people speak dialects is somewhat provincial and ethnocentric, as one group's customary way of speaking turns out to be another group's language peculiarity.

In another common use, the term "dialect" refers to those varieties of English whose features have, for one reason or another, become widely recognized throughout American society (Quote 2). Society at large recognizes a "southern drawl" or a "Boston accent." In other words, if the variety contains some features that are generally acknowledged and commented on by the society as a whole, then it may be recognized as a dialect even by the speakers themselves. If someone keeps telling you that you speak a dialect, after a while, you start to believe that you do. Thus, native New Yorkers often believe that they speak a dialect, because the dialect has become a topic of widespread public comment in American society. Similarly, speakers of an Appalachian dialect might recognize that they speak a dialect because of the caricatures and comments that so often appear in the media. On the other hand, the same perception does not hold true of middle-class residents of Ohio whose speech does not receive the same popular attention. This perception is, of course, simply an extension of the view that attaches the dialect label to some language varieties while excusing others from this designation.

In the most extreme case (Quote 3), dialect is used to refer to a kind of deficient or "corrupted" English. In this case, dialect is perceived as an imperfect attempt to speak "correct" or "proper" English. If, for example, members of a socially disfavored group utter a phrase such as *three mile* instead of the standard English *three miles* or *Her ears be itching* instead of *Her ears itch*, it is assumed that they have attempted to produce the standard English sentence but simply failed. The result is incorrectly perceived as a "deviant" or "deficient" form of English. Based upon the careful examination of such language structures however, dialectologists take the position that dialects are *not* deviant forms of language, but simply different systems, with distinct subsets of language patterns. When we talk about language patterning, we are referring to the fact that language features are distributed in systematic and orderly ways rather than used randomly. That is, for any given language feature, there are contexts in which the form is used and contexts in which it is not used.

Exercise 1

An Exercise in Dialect Patterning

In historically isolated rural dialects of the United States, particularly in Southern Appalachia, some words that end in *-ing* can take an *a-*, pronounced as *uh*, attached to the beginning of the word (Wolfram 1980, 1988). We call this the *a-* prefix because it attaches to the front of the *-ing* word. The language pattern or "rule" for this form allows the *a-* to attach to some words but not to others. In this exercise, you will figure out this fairly complicated rule by looking at the kinds of *-ing* words *a-* can and cannot attach to. You will do this using your inner feelings about language. These inner feelings, called INTUITIONS, tell us where we *can* and *cannot* use certain features. As linguists trying to describe this dialect, our task is to figure out the reason for these inner feelings and to state the exact patterns that characterize the dialect.

Look at the sentence pairs in **List A** and decide which sentence in each pair sounds better with an *a-* prefix. For example, in the first sentence pair, does it sound better to say *A-building is hard work* or *He was a-building a house*? For each sentence pair, just choose one sentence that sounds better with the *a-*.

List A: Sentence pairs for a- prefixing
1 a _____ Building is hard work.
   b _____ She was building a house.
2 a _____ He likes hunting.
   b _____ He went hunting.
3 a _____ The child was charming the adults.
   b _____ The child was very charming.
4 a _____ He kept shocking the children.
   b _____ The store was shocking.
5 a _____ They thought fishing was easy.
   b _____ They were fishing this morning.
6 a _____ The fishing is still good here.
   b _____ They go fishing less now.

Examine each of the sentence pairs in terms of the choices for the *a-* prefix and answer the following questions.

- Do you think there is some pattern that guided your choice of an answer? You can tell if there is a definite pattern by checking with other people who did the same exercise on their own.
- Do you think that the pattern might be related to parts of speech? To answer this, see if there are any parts of speech where you *cannot* use the *a-* prefix. Look at *-ing* forms that function as verbs and compare those with *-ing* forms that operate as nouns or adjectives. For example, look at the use of *charming* as a verb and adjective in sentence 3.

The first step in figuring out the pattern for the *a-* prefix is related to the part of speech of the *-ing* word. Now let's look at another difference related to prepositions such as *from* and *by*. Based on the sentence pairs in **List B**, say whether or not the *a-* form can be used after a preposition. Use the same technique you used for **List A**. Select the sentence that sounds better for each sentence pair and say whether it is the sentence with or without the preposition.

List B: A further detail for a- patterning
1   a   _____   They make money by building houses.
    b   _____   They make money building houses.
2   a   _____   People can't make enough money fishing.
    b   _____   People can't make enough money from fishing.
3   a   _____   People destroy the beauty of the island through littering.
    b   _____   People destroy the beauty of the island littering.

We now have another detail for figuring out the pattern for *a-* prefix use related to prepositions. But there is still another part to the pattern for *a-* prefix use. This time, however, it is related to pronunciation. For the following *-ing* words, try to figure out what it is about the pronunciation that makes one sentence sound better than the other. To help you figure out the pronunciation trait that is critical for this pattern, the stressed or accented syllable of each word is marked with the symbol ´. Follow the same procedure that you did in choosing the sentence in each sentence pair that sounds better.

List C: Figuring out a pronunciation pattern for the a- prefix
1   a   _____   She was discóvering a trail.
    b   _____   She was fóllowing a trail.
2   a   _____   She was repéating the chant.
    b   _____   She was hóllering the chant.
3   a   _____   They were fíguring the change.
    b   _____   They were forgétting the change.

4   a   _____   The baby was recognizing the mother.
     b   _____   The baby was wrecking everything.
5   a   _____   They were decorating the room.
     b   _____   They were demanding more time off.

Say exactly how the pattern for attaching the *a-* prefix works. Be sure to include the three different details from your examination of the examples in **Lists A, B,** and **C.**
    In **List D,** say which of the sentences may take an *a-* prefix. Use your understanding of the rule to explain why the *-ing* form may or may not take the *a-* prefix.

List D: Applying the a- prefix rule
1   She kept handing me more work.
2   The team was remembering the game.
3   The team won by playing great defense.
4   The team was playing real hard.
5   The coach was charming.

At various points during the last half century, there have been heated debates in American society about the linguistic integrity of socially disfavored language varieties. For example, during the late 1960s and 1970s, there were many debates in educational circles over the so-called "DIFFERENCE–DEFICIT" CONTROVERSY, with language scholars arguing passionately that dialect variation was simply a matter of *difference*, not *deficit*, and some educators arguing that this variation constituted a deficiency. Three decades later, in the mid-1990s, the debate flared up again, this time centered on the status of the ethnic variety African American Vernacular English, or Ebonics, as it was referred to in this debate. This time, the controversy even spread as far as a Senate subcommittee hearing on the topic and state legislation about the legitimacy of this variety in a school setting.
    When dialect differences involve groups unequal in their power relations, it is quite common for dialect myths to involve the LINGUISTIC INFERIORITY PRINCIPLE. According to this principle, the speech of a socially subordinate group will be interpreted as inadequate by comparison with that of the socially dominant group. Linguists, who study the intricate patterning of language apart from its social evaluation, stand united against any definition of dialect as a corrupt version of the standard variety. Thus, a resolution adopted unanimously by the Linguistic Society of America at its annual meeting in 1997 asserted that "all human language systems – spoken, signed, and written – are fundamentally regular" and that characterizations of socially disfavored varieties as "slang, mutant, defective, ungrammatical, or broken English are incorrect and demeaning."

When the term "dialect" is used to refer to a kind of corrupt English, it obviously carries very strong negative connotations, as many of the popular uses of dialect do. A clause such as "but it's a very colorful way of speaking" in Quote 2 may soften the negative associations, but such statements must be made explicit to mitigate the commonly held assumption that dialects aren't "as good as" some other way of speaking. Without qualification, the popular use of the term dialect carries negative connotations ranging from mildly to strongly negative.

Finally, the term dialect often serves as a kind of vague label for a particular socially disfavored variety of English. A person speaking some recognized, socially stigmatized variety of English may be said to speak "the dialect" (Quote 4). Such designations have, for example, been used to refer to the speech of low-income African Americans, as a kind of euphemistic label for this variety. In this sense, with the definite article, "*the* dialect" behaves more like a proper noun. Notice that people would not refer to a socially acceptable variety as *the* dialect.

1.3　Dialect Myths and Reality

What do these popular uses of the term dialect say about the general public's perception of dialect, especially as it differs from the neutral technical definition presented initially? As the preceding discussion points out, we have seen a popular mythology about language differences develop in our society which is at odds with the linguistic facts about language diversity. Following are some of these myths, as they contrast with linguistic reality:

MYTH:　A dialect is something that SOMEONE ELSE speaks.

REALITY:　Everyone who speaks a language speaks some dialect of the language; it is not possible to speak a language without speaking a dialect of the language.

MYTH:　Dialects always have highly noticeable features that set them apart.

REALITY:　Some dialects get much more attention than others; the status of a dialect, however, is unrelated to public commentary about its special characteristics.

MYTH:　Only varieties of a language spoken by socially disfavored groups are dialects.

REALITY:　The notion of dialect exists apart from the social status of the language variety; there are socially favored as well as socially disfavored dialects.

MYTH:　Dialects result from unsuccessful attempts to speak the "correct" form of a language.

REALITY: Dialect speakers acquire their language by adopting the speech features of those around them, not by failing in their attempts to adopt standard language features.

MYTH: Dialects have no linguistic patterning in their own right; they are deviations from standard speech.

REALITY: Dialects, like all language systems, are systematic and regular; furthermore, socially disfavored dialects can be described with the same kind of precision as standard language varieties.

MYTH: Dialects inherently carry negative social connotations.

REALITY: Dialects are not necessarily positively or negatively valued; their social values are derived strictly from the social position of their community of speakers.

As we see, the popular uses of the term dialect strongly reflect the attitudes about dialect differences which have developed in the United States over the centuries. For this reason, some groups of educators and language scientists prefer to avoid the use of the term dialect, using terms such as LANGUAGE DIFFERENCE, LANGUAGE VARIETY, or LANGUAGE VARIATION instead. Whether we prefer to use a euphemism for dialect or use it in the technical, neutral sense, we still have to confront the significant discrepancy between the public perception of linguistic diversity and the linguistic reality. In fact, given popular attitudes about dialect diversity, there is a good chance that whatever euphemism we use for the term dialect will eventually just take on the kinds of pejorative connotations that are associated with the current popular uses of the term dialect. We will use the term dialect in its linguistically neutral sense throughout this book and confront the issue of public education about language diversity as a separate matter. Educating the public about language variation constitutes an enormous challenge, and we will return to this matter in our final chapter. For the time being, it is sufficient to set forth the technical and popular uses of the dialect label and see how its popular uses have come to reflect some predominant attitudes about dialect diversity in American society.

1.4   Standards and Vernaculars

In the preceding discussion, it was difficult to avoid some reference to the dialect of English often referred to as STANDARD AMERICAN ENGLISH. The notion of a so-called standard dialect is an important one but one that is not always easy to define in a precise way for English. In some countries, such as France and Spain, language academies have been established and these institutions are responsible for determining what forms are considered acceptable for the normative "standard." They determine, for example, what new words are allowed to be included in official dictionaries and what grammatical forms and pronunciations are standard. However, in the United States we do not have such an institution, and the attempts that have been made to establish this type of agency have all failed (Heath 1976). Thus, labels such as standard English and popular terms such as "correct English" or "proper English" are commonly used but not without some ambiguity. At best, we can discuss how the notion of standard English is used and then offer a reasonable definition of the term standard English based on how it seems to function as a norm in our society.

Exercise 2

Common popular labels for what we call standard English are "correct English," "proper English," and "good English." What do these labels tell us about the public perception of standard dialects in terms of the myths about dialects we discussed above? What do they say about the ideology that informs the interpretation of dialects in our society? By "ideology" here, we mean ingrained, unquestioned beliefs about the way the world is, the way it should be, and the way it has to be with respect to language. What implications do these terms have for those dialects that are considered "corrupt" versions of the standard?

Before we get too far into this discussion, we should note that whether or not there are specific institutions set up to guide the establishment of a standard variety, language standardization of some type seems inevitable. Ultimately, we can attribute this to underlying principles of human behavior in which certain ways of behaving (dressing, speaking, treating elders, and so forth) are established as normative for the society.

As a starting point, it is helpful to distinguish between the operation of standard English on a formal and informal level. In formal standardization, the norms are prescribed for language by recognized sources of authority, such as grammar and usage books, dictionaries, and institutions like language academies. In the United States, we don't have a language academy, but we have many grammar and usage books that people turn to for the determination of standard forms. The key words in this definition are "prescribed" and "authority" so that the responsibility for the determination of standard forms rests largely outside the common users of the language. Whenever there is a question as to whether or not a form is considered standard English, we can turn to authoritarian guides of usage. Thus, if we have a question as to where to use *will* and *shall*, we simply look it up in our usage guide, which tells us that *shall* is used for first person questions (*Shall I go?*) and *will* is used in other contexts (*He will go*). At that point, the issue of a particular usage is often settled.

FORMAL STANDARD ENGLISH, or PRESCRIPTIVE STANDARD ENGLISH, tends to be based on the written language of established writers and is typically codified in English grammar texts. It is perpetuated to a large extent in formal institutions such as schools, by those responsible for English language education. It also is very conservative – that is, it is very resistant to changes taking place within the language. For some features, the usage will border on obsolescence. For example, the subjunctive use of *be* in sentences such as *If this be treason, I am a traitor* is a structure which is largely obsolete, yet this use will still be found in some prescriptive grammar books. Similarly, the maintenance of the singular form of *data* as *datum*, or even the *shall/will* distinction, has largely disappeared from spoken language, but it is still prescribed in many usage guides and maintained in written language. Without an official agency responsible for the maintenance of a uniform formal standard English in the United States, there will be some disagreement among prescriptive grammarians, but in most cases, there is fairly strong agreement among authorities. As set forth, formal standard English is most likely to be exemplified in impersonal written language and the most formal kinds of spoken language occasions, especially where spoken language has been written first.

If we took a sample of everyday conversational speech, we would find that there are virtually no speakers who consistently speak formal standard English as prescribed in the grammar books. In fact, it is not unusual for the same person who prescribes a formal standard English form to violate standard usage. For example, one of the prescribed formal standard English rules prohibits the use of a pronoun following a subject noun, as in *My mother, she took me to the show*, and many teachers will correct children who use this form. Yet we have documented these same teachers uttering a sentence such as *The students who returned late from recess yesterday and today, **they** will have to remain after school today* within a few minutes of correcting the child. The point of such illustrations is not to expose as hypocrites those who assume responsibility for perpetuating standard English norms, but to show that the prescribed formal variety is, in reality, not maintained in natural spoken language. Does this mean that standard English does not exist in our society, and that we should stop talking about this variety as if it were a real entity? On the contrary, we have evidence that people in our society do make judgments of standardness based on everyday, natural speech samples, but their judgments are apparently based on a more informal version of a standard variety used by real speakers.

INFORMAL STANDARD ENGLISH, without recourse to prescriptive authority, is much more difficult to define than formal standard English, and a realistic definition will have to take into account the actual kinds of assessments that members of American society make as they judge other speakers' standardness. As a starting point, we must acknowledge that this notion exists on a continuum, with speakers ranging along the continuum between the standard and

```
           A      B    C       D      E
Standard ------|----------|----- |----------|-------|------ Nonstandard
```

Figure 1.1 A continuum of standardness.

nonstandard poles. For example, on such a continuum, speakers may be placed at the following points, with Speaker A using few, if any, nonstandard forms, and Speaker E using many.

Ratings of standardness not only exist on a continuum; they can be fairly subjective as well. Based on different sociopsychological experiences and dialect backgrounds in American society, one listener may rate a particular speaker as standard while another listener rates the same speaker as nonstandard. This is particularly true when the regional and ethnic backgrounds of listeners are taken into account. For example, a Northern-born middle-class African American might rate a Southern white as nonstandard, while a native of the region might rate the same speaker as a standard speaker.

At the same time that we admit a subjective dimension to the notion of standardness, we find that there is a consensus in rating speakers at the more extreme ranges of the continuum. Thus, virtually all listeners will rate Speaker A in figure 1.1 as a standard English speaker and Speaker E as a nonstandard English speaker. On the other hand, there might be considerable difference in the ratings which Speakers B and C receive in terms of a simple classification into standard or nonstandard categories. Furthermore, we have found that the classification of speakers at the extreme poles of the continuum (such as Speakers A and E) tends to be consistent regardless of the socioeconomic class background of the person making the judgment.

Classifications of standardness will also be somewhat flexible with respect to the regional variety being judged. Thus, the *r*-less pronunciations which characterize Eastern New England or Southeastern American pronunciation (as in *cah* for *car* or *beah* for *bear*) may be judged as standard English, as will the *r*-ful pronunciations that characterize certain other dialects. And people may be judged as standard English speakers whether they *go to the beach*, *go to the shore*, or *go to the ocean* for a summer vacation. On this informal level, standard English is a pluralistic notion, at least with respect to pronunciation and vocabulary differences. That is, there are regional standards which are recognized within the broad and informal notion of standard American English.

What is it about a speaker's dialect that is critical in determining whether the speaker will be judged as a standard or nonstandard? There is no simple answer to this question, and people tend to give overall impressions, such as "quality of voice," "tone of expression," or "correct grammar," when they are asked to explain their judgments of standardness and nonstandardness. Despite the vagueness of such responses, there do seem to be a few relatively specific criteria that people use in judging a person's speech as standard. For one, standard American English seems to be determined more by what it is *not* than by what it is. To a large extent, American English speech samples rated as standard English by a cross-section of listeners exhibit a range of regional variation in pronunciation and vocabulary items, but they do *not* contain grammatical structures that are socially stigmatized. If native speakers from Michigan, New England, and Arkansas avoid the use of socially stigmatized grammatical structures such as "double negatives" (e.g. *They didn't do nothing*), different verb agreement patterns (e.g. *They's okay*), and different irregular verb forms (e.g. *She done it*), there is a good chance they will be considered standard English speakers even though they may have distinct regional pronunciations. In this way, informal standard English is defined negatively. In other words, if a person's speech is free of structures that can be identified as nonstandard, then it is considered standard.

The definition of informal standard English tends to be supported by an additional observation about Americans' attitudes toward dialects. For the most part, Americans do not assign strong positive, or prestige, value to any particular native American English dialect. The basic contrast in North America exists between negatively valued dialects and those without negative value, not between those with prestige value and those without. Interestingly, Americans do assign positive value to British dialects, which are not even viable options for wide-scale use in the United States and Canada. North Americans, in commenting on different dialects of American English, are much more likely to make comments about nonstandardness ("That person doesn't talk correct English") than they are to comment on standardness (e.g. "That person really speaks correct English"). Informal standard English is an operative notion that is quite real in American society, but it differs considerably from the formal standard English norm that is often taught as THE standard. For the purposes of our discussion throughout this book, we will refer to this more informal definition of the standard language rather than the formal one, since it is the informal version that plays a predominant role in our everyday lives.

Exercise 3

There are a couple of levels of standards that seem to be noticeable to people when they listen to speech. We don't usually comment on informal standard English, but we may comment on a person's speech if it is nonstandard. By the same token, however, just as it is possible to call attention to speech because it contains nonstandard forms, it is possible to call attention to speech because it sounds too formal or "proper." Forms which are too standard for everyday conversation are sometimes referred to as SUPERSTANDARD ENGLISH. In the following sets of sentences, identify which sentences characterize (1) nonstandard English, (2) informal standard English, and (3) superstandard English. What forms in the sentences are responsible for your assessment? Are there any sentences you're not sure about? Why?

1 a He's not as smart as I.
   b He's not so smart as I.
   c He ain't as smart as me.
   d He not as smart as me.
2 a He's not to do that.
   b He not supposed to do that.
   c He don't supposed to do that.
   d He's not supposed to do that.
3 a I'm right, ain't I?
   b I'm right, aren't I?
   c I'm right, am I not?
   d I'm right, isn't I?
4 a If I was going to do that, I would start right now.
   b If I were going to do that, I would start right now.
   c Were I to do that, I would start right now.
   d I would start right now, if I was going to that.
5 a A person should not change her speech.
   b One should not change one's speech.
   c A person should not change their speech.
   d A person should not change his or her speech.

Why do people sometimes comment about other people's speech because it sounds too proper?

1.5 Vernacular Dialects

At the other end of the continuum of standardness is nonstandardness. Varieties which seem to be typified by the use of nonstandard forms are often referred to as VERNACULAR DIALECTS. The term vernacular is used here simply to refer to varieties of a language which are not classified as standard dialects. The term is used in much the same way that the term *vernacular language* is used to refer to local or native languages of common communication which contrast with the official standard language of a multilingual country. Other researchers may refer to these vernacular varieties as NONSTANDARD or NONMAINSTREAM DIALECTS, but the labels are not nearly as important as understanding exactly what we mean by the label we choose.

Exercise 4

Although the choice of a label for a vernacular dialect may not seem important on one level, it can become a very important consideration when the
broader sociopolitical context of naming is taken into consideration. This is
particularly true when we consider the emotive connotations of various labels.
For example, in the past three decades, one vernacular dialect has endured
the following labels, given here in approximate chronological sequence:
Negro Dialect, *Substandard Negro English*, *Nonstandard Negro English*, *Black
English*, *Afro-American English*, *Ebonics*, *Vernacular Black English*, and *African
American Vernacular English*. And believe it or not, this is not a complete
list! Speculate about the factors that led to some of these labels and why so
many changes have taken place in the short modern history of naming this
vernacular variety. Why is there continuing controversy over the labeling of
this variety? What kinds of considerations should go into the naming of a
language variety? For example, *Ebonics*, a label originally introduced in the
early 1970s which gained great notoriety in the mid-1990s in connection
with a highly publicized resolution by the Oakland Unified School District
Board of Education, has evoked many negative comments and derogatory
parodies. In contrast, the synonymous term typically used by linguists,
African American Vernacular English, does not typically evoke such parodies. Should the public reaction to a term be a consideration in determining
dialect labels?

As with standard dialects of English, there are a number of different social
and regional factors that go into the labeling of a vernacular, and any attempt
to define a vernacular dialect on a single dimension will be problematic. Invariably, it is a complex array of factors that ultimately accounts for the delimitation
of the dialect, including dimensions of social class, region, ethnicity, situation,
and so forth. Furthermore, vernacularity, like standardness, exists on a continuum so that particular speakers may exhibit speech which is more or less
vernacular. This continuum of standardness affects the classification of vernacular speakers, just as it affects standard speakers. Thus, Speaker **D** in figure 1.1 may or may not be classified as a vernacular dialect speaker, but we can
expect a consensus of people (from the same and different dialects) to recognize
Speaker **E** as a representative of some vernacular variety. Nonetheless, it is
possible for both vernacular and non-vernacular speakers of English to identify
paradigmatic speakers of the vernacular variety in a way that is analogous to
the way that we can identify representatives of standard dialects.

Unlike standard dialects, which are largely defined by the *absence* of socially
disfavored structures of English, vernacular varieties seem to be characterized

by the *presence* of socially conspicuous structures – at least to informal standard English speakers who do not use them. In other words, vernacular varieties are the converse of standard dialects in that an assortment of marked nonstandard English structures sets them apart as being vernacular. Although each vernacular dialect seems to have a core of nonstandard structures, we have to be careful about saying that all of these speakers of a given variety will exhibit this common set of structures. Not all of these speakers necessarily use the entire set of structures described for the dialect, and there may be differing patterns of usage among speakers of the variety. In fact, attempts to isolate *the* common core of structures for a particular vernacular often lead to heavily qualified, imprecise descriptions. Such qualification is typified in the attempt of Wolfram and Christian to delimit "Appalachian English."

> There may be some question as to whether it is justifiable to differentiate an entity such as AE [Appalachian English] from other (equally difficult to define precisely) varieties of American English, particularly some of those spoken in the South. Quite obviously, there are many features we have described which are not peculiar to speakers within the Appalachian range. On the other hand, there also appears to be a small set of features which may not be found in other areas. Even if this is not the case, we may justify our distinction of AE on the basis of the combination of features. . . . Fully cognizant of the pitfalls found in any attempt to attach terminological labels to the varieties of English, we shall proceed to use the designation AE as a convenient, if loosely-defined notion. (Wolfram and Christian 1976:29–30)

Language scholars may sometimes have difficulty defining a set of features uniquely distinguishing a given vernacular variety, but it is easy to demonstrate that both professionals and non-professionals identify and classify quite accurately speakers representing the vernacular pole on the continuum of standardness. Vernacular dialects are very real and identifiable entities in American society, despite our inability to come up with a precise set of structures characterizing them. And this real-world recognition underlies the readiness of members of society to identify particular vernaculars even though linguists may encounter difficulty defining the dialects precisely. As we make our way through our description of the dimensions of American English dialects, we will discuss a number of the specific factors that go into a more precise definition of these dialects.

We can summarize the features that set apart standard dialects and vernacular dialects as follows:

FORMAL STANDARD: applied primarily to written language and the most formal spoken language situations; objective standards prescribed by language "authorities"; standards codified in usage books, dictionaries, and other written texts; a single norm for acceptable usage, conservative outlook on language forms.

INFORMAL STANDARD: applied to spoken language; determined by actual
   usage patterns of speakers; listener judgment essential in determining
   socially acceptable norms; multiple norms of acceptability, incorporating
   regional and social considerations; defined negatively by the avoidance
   of socially stigmatized linguistic structures.
VERNACULAR: applied to spoken language; determined by actual usage
   patterns of speakers; listener judgment essential in determining social
   unacceptability; stereotyping of speakers based upon linguistic forms;
   defined by the presence of socially stigmatized linguistic structures.

Since both formal and informal standard varieties are associated with middle-
class and upper-class, mainstream groups, they are socially respected, but since
vernacular varieties are associated with socially disfavored groups, they are not
considered socially respectable. This association, of course, simply reflects
underlying values about different social groups in our society and is hardly
dependent on language differences alone.

1.6   Why Study Dialects?

There are a number of reasons why the study of dialects is an attractive field of
inquiry. First, there is a natural curiosity that is piqued when we hear speakers
of different dialects. If we are the least bit interested in different manifestations
of human behavior, then we are likely to be intrigued by the facets of behavior
revealed in language. The authors have become accustomed if somewhat wary
of the responses of people at casual social gatherings when people find out that
we study dialects. Such responses range from challenges to identify where
people originally come from (guaranteeing instant credibility) to the question
of why particular groups of speakers talk as they do (usually a forewarning
of an opinionated explanation to follow). It is not uncommon to encounter
individuals from varied walks of life who profess an interest in dialects as a
"hobby" simply because dialects are so fascinating. The positive side to this
curiosity is that the study of dialects can often sell itself; the negative side, as
discussed earlier, is that the attendant set of attitudes and opinions about
American dialects makes it difficult to deal with information about them in a
neutral way. In one form or another, most professional students of dialects
have simply cultivated the natural interest that resides within us all.

As a manifestation of human behavioral differences, dialects may be studied
because they provide the opportunity to extend social science inquiry into
language, a quite natural application for fields such as history, anthropology,
sociology, psychology, and geography. Thus, one of the most extensive series of
studies ever conducted on the dialects of American English, the *Linguistic Atlas
of the United States and Canada*, carefully charted the geographical distribution

of various forms in American English as a kind of dialect geography; in fact, studies of this type are often referred to as LINGUISTIC GEOGRAPHY. At the same time, these studies attempted to trace the English settlement patterns of America through language differences, as a kind of history. And these studies noted the distribution of forms in different social categories of speakers as a kind of sociology. It is easy to see how dialect differences can be seen as a natural extension of a number of different fields within the social sciences since these differences are so integrally related to all aspects of human behavior.

Other studies have shown how the cultural and historical heritage of particular cultural groups have been maintained through their dialects, such as the cultural detachment historically linked with regions such as Appalachia and the island communities along the Eastern seaboard of the United States – for example, Tangier Island off the coast of Virginia, the Outer Banks off the coast of North Carolina, or the Sea Islands along the South Carolina and Georgia coast. From this perspective, interest in dialects may derive from a basic concern with the humanities found in fields such as folklore, history, and English. It is interesting to note that the US Government agency the National Endowment for the Humanities has been a primary source of financial support for traditional dialect surveys over the years.

Motivation for studying dialects may naturally go beyond "objective" social science inquiry and the more "up close and personal" investigation of different social and ethnic heritages. In some cases, dialect differences may be studied in connection with a growing self- or group awareness. Thus, members of a particular social group may seize upon language differences as part of consciousness raising. It is no accident that language and gender issues have become an important topic in the last 25 years, as attention has been drawn to gender-differentiated social roles and asymmetrical power relations based on sex in our society. Similarly, the rise of interest in African American Vernacular English coincided with the general development of cultural consciousness in other spheres of life in the late 1960s and early 1970s. The emphasis on the identificational issues surrounding English dialect variation might strike members of majority or "mainstream" cultural groups as somewhat overstated, until we realize how central language is to the identification of self and group. Issues of nationalism and identity often come to a head over language, as demonstrated by the attention paid to the issue of French versus English in Canada. In a similar way, the status of the Dutch-based language Afrikaans in South Africa is hardly a simple language issue; it reflects deeper issues related to political and ethnic self-determination.

The historical consideration of the English language in the United States shows that the very notion of American English itself was strongly tied to nationalism. Noah Webster, the parent of generations of English dictionaries, issued the declaration that "as an independent nation, our honor requires us to have a system of our own, in language as well as government" and that "a national language is a bond of national union." In this context, studying American English as compared with British English might be motivated by a feeling of patriotism and loyalty to the United States. It is easy to compile an extensive list of cases in which nationalism and group consciousness movements were motivating factors for studying about languages and dialects.

At the other end of the spectrum, the study of dialect differences might be justified on a linguistic theoretical basis. That is, scholars may examine language variation in an effort to understand the basic nature of language as a cognitive and human phenomenon. This theoretical concern may range from the investigation of how language changes over time and space to the representation of the cognitive capabilities of a speaker of a language. In this context, the examination of dialects may provide an essential and unique data base. William Labov, one of the pioneers in modern sociolinguistics, set forth this motivation in the published version of his doctoral dissertation, *The Social Stratification of English in New York City*, when he stated that "my own intention was to solve linguistic problems, bearing in mind that these are ultimately problems in the analysis of social behavior" (Labov 1966:v–vi). Empirical data from the study of dialects thus may contribute to our understanding of some central issues concerning the nature of language variation. For example, data from the study of variation within language increase our understanding of the kinds and amount of variation which may be contained within a single language and those which may not.

Finally, there is the applied motivation for studying dialects. Many students in education and the health professions have become interested in dialects because of the "usefulness" of the information as it relates to another primary activity such as teaching or language assessment. Virtually all fields of education related to activities which are primarily language-oriented such as reading and language arts, as well as language service professions such as speech and language pathology, have recognized the need to understand both general principles and specific descriptive details about dialects. In fact, in one dramatic case of litigation which took place in Ann Arbor, Michigan, in 1979, the courts ordered teachers to attend workshops on dialects because of the potential impact of such information on the interpretation of reading behavior by vernacular-speaking students. Similarly, a widely publicized resolution adopted by the Oakland School Board in 1996 maintained that an understanding of the vernacular variety spoken by African Americans should be used as an important bridge for teaching proficiency in standard English.

In addition, information about dialect diversity may be applied to the legal process. Knowledge of dialects has been relevant in cases that range in focus from language-based racial discrimination to the representation of verbatim testimony in transcripts of vernacular dialect speakers. Knowledge about dialects obviously has extensive applications, and some of these will be examined in more detail later.

After reading the previous paragraphs, we might wonder if there is any justifiable reason for not studying dialects. The glib answer to this question is, "Probably not!" However, when we consider the full range of reasons for studying dialects, as well as the fact that there is a rich historical tradition underlying each motivation, it is easy to see why there are scholars who feel that knowledge about dialects should be a central component of our educational process, as fundamental as any other "routine" topic covered in our education.

Exercise 5

On a personal level, consider which of the above motivations matches your interest most closely. Is there more than one reason that appeals to you? Rank in terms of priority the major reasons given above as they relate to your interest (basic curiosity, social science inquiry, humanities study, personal and group identity, linguistic study itself, the application of knowledge about dialects to another primary field). Are there other reasons you can think of for studying dialects? Has the need to study dialects been oversold? Why or why not?

1.7   A Tradition of Study

There is a longstanding tradition of collecting and studying data on variation in English, typically guided by the kinds of motivations cited above. As we already mentioned, some of the earliest collections of American English were concerned with those aspects of American English which set it apart from British English, particularly with respect to vocabulary. Vocabulary is one of the most transparent ways in which dialects differ, and vocabulary studies are a common way in which dialect differences are profiled. Typical of relatively early works on dialect differences was Pickering's 1816 work entitled *A Vocabulary, or Collection of Words and Phrases which have been Supposed to be Peculiar to the United States of America to which is Prefixed an Essay on the Present State of the English Language in the United States*. Some of the early studies of the dialect structures of American English *vis-à-vis* British English were imprecise and based largely on vague impressions, but others represented a fairly meticulous and exhaustive approach to the cataloging of dialect differences. It is also interesting to note that politicians and statesmen often became involved in language issues. For example, Benjamin Franklin suggested an early spelling reform, and John Adams proposed an academy for establishing an American standard as differences between British and American English began to emerge and the social and political implications of this divergence were considered.

As the United States became securely independent, the focus changed from the relationship between American and British English to the diversity within American English itself. The American Dialect Society was formed in 1889 for "the investigation of English dialects in America with regard to pronunciation, grammar, phraseology, and geographical distribution" (Grandgent 1889). This concern with geographical distribution coincided with a period of fairly widespread migration and resettlement and was motivated by a strong historical rationale, as dialectologists began to fear that the original American English dialects would fade away as old boundaries to intercommunication were erased. The initial hope of the American Dialect Society was to provide a body of data from which a dialect dictionary or series of linguistic maps might be derived. A considerable amount of data towards this end was published in the Society's original journal, *Dialect Notes*, but it was not until 1928 that a large-scale systematic study of dialect geography was undertaken, titled the *Linguistic Atlas of the United States and Canada*. Along with the historical goals already mentioned, this survey aimed to correlate dialect differences with different social classifications, an incipient stage in the development of a field of study that would blossom fully several decades later. A comprehensive set of *Linguistic Atlas* surveys for different areas of the United States and Canada was proposed and the initial survey of New England undertaken. As one of the nation's initial areas of settlement by English speakers, New England was a logical starting place, given the project's focus on historical settlement patterns. Fieldworkers combed the region looking for older, lifetime residents from whom they might elicit particular items of pronunciation, grammar, and vocabulary. Quite typically, the fieldworkers ended up recording up to ten or twelve hours of elicited forms. Of course, in the early stages these recordings consisted of on-the-spot phonetic transcriptions without the aid of any mechanical recording equipment. Some of this work is still ongoing, despite some severe criticisms about the techniques for gathering data and the approach to describing language variation that was the basis for these studies.

Almost a hundred years after the establishment of the American Dialect Society, one of its major goals is finally being realized, namely, the publication of the *Dictionary of American Regional English* (Cassidy 1985, 1991, 1996). Three volumes, covering the letters A–O, have now appeared, with the completion of the five-volume work projected for the first decade of the twenty-first century. This much-heralded, comprehensive work dates its modern history to 1962, when Frederic G. Cassidy was appointed general editor. It taps a wealth of data sources, including its own extensive dialect survey of the United States, the various *Linguistic Atlas* projects, and the publications of the American Dialect Society, among others. The American Dialect Society remains a small but active organization concerned with language variation in American English. Its quarterly journal, *American Speech*, balances the traditional focus on regional variation with a more current emphasis on social, ethnic, and gender-based variation in a readable format.

Beginning in the 1960s, research on dialects in the United States focused much more specifically on social and ethnic variation in American English than on regional variation. Part of this emphasis was fueled by a concern for language-related social problems, particularly problems related to educational issues of the American underclass. Some linguistic descriptions of vernacular dialects such as African American Vernacular English and Appalachian English became the basis for programs which sought to remedy educational inequities and shortcomings. The application of sociolinguistic data to solving social problems remains a continuing issue to the present day. For some investigators, however, following the pioneering work of Labov, the fundamental nature of linguistic variation as a theoretical issue in linguistics became a rationale for sociolinguistic inquiry. Although some current investigators motivate their dialect studies exclusively on a theoretical basis, the more typical rationale combines theoretical and applied or social perspectives. The last three decades have witnessed an unprecedented proliferation of studies of vernacular varieties of English of varying quality and perspective. In fact, one comprehensive bibliography of African American Vernacular English (Brasch and Brasch 1974) listed over 2,400 entries related to this variety over two decades ago; another annotated bibliography of Southern American English (McMillan and Montgomery 1989) listed over 3,800 works, the majority of which relate to the vernacular dialects of the South. The range of vernacular dialects considered over the past several decades has been extended to include both urban and rural varieties of American English, as well as English varieties developed from contact situations with other languages. Both newly developing and older, vanishing varieties of English are included in this focus. Indeed, no vernacular dialect seems safe from descriptive scrutiny, and no social or ethnic group is assured of sociolinguistic anonymity.

Methods of data collection and the kind of data considered necessary for adequate analysis have also shifted drastically during the past several decades. Spontaneous, casual conversation became the favored kind of data for analysis, replacing the earlier emphasis on direct probes to elicit particular forms. Some fairly creative techniques were devised to enhance the possibility of recording good "naturalistic" data, aided by advancing technology in audio and video recording equipment. In addition, more careful and systematic attention was paid to an array of social factors, ranging from the social relationships and personal identities of speakers to the situations and audiences that contextualize speech. Such developments naturally were aided by perspectives from other fields in the social sciences such as psychology, anthropology, and sociology. Advances in the analysis of data now incorporate more rigorous quantitative methods, including automatic data-processing programs for handling data on language variation and graphics programs for generating dialect maps. At the same time, increasing emphasis is now being placed on developing and implementing qualitative methodologies that will yield results superior to those achieved by impressionistic observations and anecdotal evidence concerning the patterning of isolated language forms. A traditional dialectologist, frozen in the time frame of a half century ago, would hardly recognize what constitutes dialect study today. The underlying motivations for studying dialects in the present day may be well established in the historical record, but the field has undergone some fairly profound changes in its focus and methods. Finally, current dialect study is characterized by more of an "entrepreneurial" spirit than in the past. Specialists in different areas of dialect study have carved out productive and useful niches for the application of information gleaned from the study of dialects, ranging from dialect training programs for actors projecting different regional and social roles to consultation services offering the analysis of language variation for legal deliberation of various types. And the range of applications for dialect study continues to expand as we enter the twenty-first century.

1.8   Further Reading

Bauer, Laurie, and Peter Trudgill (eds) (1998) *Language Myths*. New York: Penguin. This collection of articles exposes the kinds of myths about language and language diversity that are perpetuated in popular culture. Among the myths relevant to this book (each discussed in its own chapter) are "New Yorkers can't talk properly," "Black Americans are verbally deprived," "Southern speech is slovenly," and "Shakespearean English is spoken in the mountains."

Baugh, John (1991) The politicization of changing terms of self-reference among American slave descendants. *American Speech* 66:133–46. Baugh considers the evolution of changing terms of self-reference among African Americans and the sociopolitical context of dialect labeling. It should be read along with a companion article in the same issue by Geneva Smitherman titled "What is African to me? Language and ideology, and African American?" (*American Speech* 66:115–32).

Finegan, Edward (1980) *Attitudes Toward English Words: The History of a War of Words*. New York: Teachers College Press. This work traces the concept of "good English" throughout the nation's history, showing how this notion has been used and abused.

Labov, William (1972d) The logic of nonstandard English. Chapter 5 in *Language in the Inner City: Studies in the Black English Vernacular*. Philadelphia: University of Pennsylvania Press, 201–40. This popular and influential article which appears as a chapter in Labov's *Language in the Inner City* deals with basic misconceptions about vernacular dialects. Historically, it constituted a critical argument for the linguistic integrity and conceptual adequacy of vernacular dialect. It has been reprinted in numerous anthologies, including the *Atlantic Monthly* (June 1972) under the title "Academic ignorance and Black intelligence."

Mencken, H. L. (1962) *The American Language: An Inquiry into the Development of English in the United States*, Supplement I. New York: Alfred A. Knopf. The initial chapters of Mencken's classic work, chapters 1 through 4 in particular, provide an intriguing account of the early developments of American English, with rich references to early commentary about this emerging variety by politicians and general observers of language. Although the commentary is now dated, it is still worthwhile reading from a historical vantage point.

2

Why Do Languages Have Dialects?

One of the dialects of American English that we have studied in detail is that spoken in Ocracoke, an island in the Outer Banks island chain off the coast of North Carolina. Ocracokers, who have been relatively isolated from mainland North Carolina for nearly 300 years, are well known for their distinctive language variety and are proud of their dialect heritage as well (e.g. Wolfram and Schilling-Estes 1997; Wolfram, Schilling-Estes, Hazen, and Craig 1997). In fact, once when we were discussing the unique island dialect with one of the prominent members of the Ocracoke community, he remarked, "I definitely think there's a place for all kinds of dialects. There could be nothing worse in this world [than] if we all spoke the same way."

Fortunately, this islander has nothing to worry about: Speakers of American English are far from all speaking the same way, and it doesn't look like the various regional and social dialects of the United States are in any danger of merging into a single language variety any time soon. In fact, dialectologists have evidence that some varieties of American English are actually becoming more rather than less distinctive from one another, as is commonly assumed.

As we begin our investigation of the rich dialect diversity that characterizes American English, we may want to start by asking the question, "Why are there so many dialects in the first place?" What are the factors that lead to language diversity, and why does dialect diversity persist in the face of mass communication, increased mobility, and growing cultural homogenization? In our efforts to answer these questions, we must consider both social and linguistic factors. Socially, we look to the same types of factors that account for general regional and social differences among people, whether these differences are in style of dress, in architecture, or in amount and kind of interpersonal interaction. Linguistically, we look to the way we produce and perceive language as well as how individual language features are organized into coherent systems. These linguistic and social factors may come together in a myriad of ways, resulting in a multitude of dialects. In the following sections, we examine some of the social and linguistic considerations that help explain the development of dialect variation.

2.1 Sociohistorical Explanation

One side of the explanation for dialects is found in the social and historical conditions that surround language change. At the same time that language operates as a highly structured communicative code, it also functions as a kind of cultural behavior. It is only natural, then, that social differentiation of various types should go hand-in-hand with language differences. Dialects are most likely to develop where we find both physical and social separation among groups of speakers. In the following sections, we discuss some of the chief social factors that set the stage for dialect differentiation.

2.1.1 Settlement

One of the most obvious explanations for why there are dialects is rooted in the settlement patterns of speakers in a given region. The history of American English does not begin with the initial arrival of English speakers in the "New World." As we discuss in detail in chapter 4, some of the dominant characteristics still found in varieties of American English can be traced to dialect differences that existed in the British Isles to begin with, to say nothing of the kinds of English spoken in other English-speaking regions that contributed to the dialects of the Americas (for example, the kinds of English spoken by Caribbean Blacks). The earliest English-speaking inhabitants in America came from different parts of the British Isles, where dialects were already in place, and speakers from different dialect areas tended to take up residence in different parts of America. Many emigrants from Southeastern England originally established themselves in Eastern New England and Tidewater Virginia. Others, from northern and western parts of England, situated themselves in the New Jersey and Delaware area. In addition, Scots-Irish emigrants from Ulster set up residence in Western New England, upper New York, and many parts of Appalachia. From these points, the population fanned westward in a way that is still reflected in the dialect configuration of the United States today. The major dialects of American English are focused around population centers established by emigrants from the British Isles, such as Boston, Richmond, and Charleston. Notice, for example, how the configuration of the dialects of the Eastern United States as given in chapter 4 (figure 4.2) still reflects the distribution of early British habitation in the New World.

Settlement generally takes place in several distinct phases. In the initial phase, a group of people moves to an area where there are attractive environmental qualities. The immigrants bring with them the culture of their origin. In the next phase, all currently available land is occupied, and a new cultural identity emerges, as a cohesive society develops in the region. The creation of this new culture is often accompanied by the elimination of established cultures and ways of speaking; thus, in the process of forging an "American" culture out of various European cultures, colonists in the New World overwhelmed numerous Native American cultures – and languages. Today, there exist very few Native American languages, and numbers of speakers are dwindling rapidly. This is not to say that Native American languages played no part in the development of American English dialects; but it cannot be denied that the languages and language varieties which the original European emigrants encountered when they first arrived in the New World have been almost completely supplanted by varieties of English.

In the third phase of settlement, regional populations define roles for themselves with respect to more widespread systems of transportation and communication. A response to national commerce and culture becomes an important part of the definition of the localized population, as it maintains and adjusts aspects of its dialect that reflect and help comprise its unique identity.

The forerunners of the dominant cultural group in a given region typically establish cultural and linguistic areas that persist in time, although the original features that characterize each area may change in a number of ways, and other features may take their place. Much has changed in English over the centuries of its existence in America, but the initial patterns of habitation by English speakers from various parts of the British Isles, as well as by emigrants who spoke languages other than English, are still reflected in the patterning of dialect differentiation in the United States today.

2.1.2   Migration routes

Once primary population centers are established, dialect boundaries will often follow the major migratory routes from these initial points. Thus, the lines of demarcation in the classic delineation of American English dialects (see figure 4.2) reflect both original settlement and migratory flow. It is no accident that many of the dialect boundaries show an east–west fanning pattern, since these were the major migratory routes taken from the earliest points of habitation along the east coast. For example, a major dialect boundary runs across the state of Pennsylvania, separating the so-called North from Midland dialect. North of the line, speakers distinguished between the pronunciations of *horse* and *hoarse* and *which* and *witch*; south of the line, they did not. These pronunciation patterns went along with a number of traditional vocabulary differences such as the use of *pail* versus *bucket*, *teeter-totter* versus *seesaw*, and *stoop* versus *porch*. In the trough of the northern boundary through Pennsylvania and the southern boundary running through Delaware and Maryland a major early migration route existed. This high-density east–west flow is still reflected in major highway networks that run through the area. Major population centers within this Midland region carved out their own cultural and linguistic niches rather than simply conforming to the patterns that characterize the Midland in general, but the evidence of early routes of movement is still unmistakable in the present configuration of American English dialects.

The primary east–west migratory pattern reflects the movement of speakers of European descent, but other groups show different patterns. For example, African American migratory patterns are primarily south–north, emanating from different points in the South. African American speakers from South Carolina and North Carolina migrated northward along a coastal route into Washington, DC, Philadelphia, and New York. The migratory route of inland African Americans from the Deep South, on the other hand, led into Midwestern areas such as St Louis, Chicago, and Detroit. The vernacular dialects of eastern coastal cities such as Washington versus those of Midwestern cities such as Chicago still reflect some differences attributable to these different migratory routes, cutting across the east–west routes that typified Anglo-American migration. We also have to keep in mind that future migrations may eventually erase long-established dialect lines. For example, Southern dialect areas may soon be drastically altered if non-Southerners continue pouring into the region as they have in recent years.

2.1.3 Geographical factors

Geographical factors may play a role in the development of dialects, not because of topography *per se*, but because rivers, lakes, mountains, valleys, and other features of the terrain determine the routes that people take and where they settle. Major rivers such as the Ohio and Mississippi played an important role in the development of American English dialects, as Britishers and other Europeans established inland networks of commerce and communication. It is thus not surprising that a major east–west dialect boundary runs along the course of the Ohio river. On the other hand, the Mississippi River, running a north–south route, deflected the westward migration of Midland populations northward, creating a discontinuous boundary between the Northern and Midland dialect areas which is still in place to some extent today.

Terrain which serves to isolate groups also can serve a critical role in the development of dialects. For example, African Americans living in the Sea Islands off the coast of South Carolina and Anglo-American residents of the Outer Banks islands of North Carolina historically have been isolated from mainland speakers and their language varieties. In both cases, distinctive varieties of English were fostered. However, the two varieties were and are quite different from one another, because the first non-indigenous inhabitants of each island community spoke very different varieties to begin with. The Outer Banks dialect is characterized by the retention of a number of features from earlier versions of English, including such unusual lexical items as *mommuck*, meaning 'to harass or bother', and *quamish*, meaning 'sick in the stomach'. On the Sea Islands, a historical creole language, GULLAH, was perpetuated, which set off this variety from mainland African American vernacular varieties as well as Anglo varieties. Of course, both dialects have also introduced innovative dialect features over the centuries, but these changes have not always paralleled changes taking place in mainland varieties of American English.

When we cite the significance of geographical boundaries, we are really talking about lines of communication and the fact that discontinuities in communication develop between communities due, in part, to geographical conditions. The most effective kind of communication is face-to-face, and when groups of speakers do not interact on a personal level with one another, the likelihood of dialect divergence is heightened. Combined with various other sociological conditions, natural boundaries of various types provide a firm foundation on which dialect differences may be grounded.

2.1.4   *Language contact*

Along the paths of resettlement and migration, contact with other language groups often takes place. This contact can influence both general language development and specific dialect formation as the languages borrow from each other. For example, in the seventeenth century, American English was influenced by Native American languages of such families as the Algonquian, Iroquoian, and Siouan. This influence is reflected in the lexical items from various Native American languages which have made their way into general American English, such as *moccasin*, *raccoon*, and *chipmunk*. In the eighteenth century, American English was influenced by French, which gave the language such words as *bureau*, *depot*, and *prairie*. German gave American English *delicatessen*, *kindergarten*, and *hamburger*, while early Spanish contact gave it *canyon*, *rodeo*, and *patio*. All of these items are now in such widespread use across the varieties of American English that they are no longer considered dialect-specific features.

In areas where contact with other languages has been intensive and localized, borrowings from the language may remain restricted to a given dialect. For example, in New Orleans, where French influence historically has been particularly strong, we find such dialect-specific terms as *lagniappe* 'a small gift or bonus'. Interestingly, *lagniappe* itself is a concatenation of several borrowings; originally, it comes from the Quechua (Native American) term *yapa*, which was borrowed into Spanish as *la napa* and finally into French as *lagniappe*. Other localized terms include such German terms as *stollen* 'a kind of cake' in Southern Pennsylvania and the Spanish term *arroyo* 'a kind of gully' in the Southwest. In many cases, lexical borrowings reflect cultural borrowings; thus,

English speakers in New Orleans have borrowed a number of terms from Cajun French which pertain to Cajun cooking, while Southwestern varieties of English now incorporate a number of lexical items from Spanish which relate to particular ranching practices.

Exercise 1

Following are some words which are borrowed from French, Spanish, and German. For the most part, these words are regionally restricted to areas where extensive contact with native speakers of one of these languages took place. Identify the language that each of the words comes from, as well as the region where you would expect to find the item.

> coulee, arapajo grass, serape, foosnocks, cuartel, pumpernickel, zwieback, levee, rathskeller, pirogue

Do you know the meanings of all of the above words? Which ones give you the most difficulty?

Dialect influence from language contact is not limited to vocabulary items, although this is the most obvious kind of influence to the casual observer. Certain suffixes have been borrowed from other languages as well, such as German *-fest* in *songfest*, *slugfest*, and *gabfest* and the French suffix *-ee* in items like *draftee*, *enlistee*, and *trainee*. (Note that *-ee* is simply a feminine ending in French, as is *-ette* in both English and French.) In Southeastern Pennsylvania, with its heavy influx of German settlers, the use of the syntactic structure *Are you going with?* for *Are you going with me/us?* is most reasonably accounted for by tracing it to the German construction *Gehst du mit?*, literally 'Are you going with?'. And in the South, the absence of the *be* verb in sentences such as *They in the house* or *We going to the store* among both African Americans and Anglo Americans may be due to the influence of the language variety spoken by blacks early in the history of the United States. Thus we see that other languages have had a profound influence on the development of English dialects on a number of levels of dialect patterning. We will discuss in more detail the various contributions of different linguistic groups to the formation of American English in chapter 4.

Historical patterns of settlement, conquest, migration, and language contact are important factors in the development of dialect differences, but they are not the sole considerations. Groups of speakers who share a common background in terms of these factors still manage to differentiate themselves along dialect lines.

This is because there are sociological and psychological bases for talking differently that have to be recognized along with historical and geographical factors.

2.1.5   Economic ecology

How people earn their living often goes hand-in-hand with how populations are distributed geographically and culturally. In the United States, there is a full complement of ecologically based occupations, including fishing in coastal areas, coal mining in the mountains, and farming in the plains. Different economic bases not only bring about the development of specialized vocabulary items associated with different occupations; they also may affect the direction and rate of language change in grammar and pronunciation. The distinction between the rural, agriculturally based lifestyle which historically has characterized much of the United States and the urban, industrialized focus of the nation's major population centers is reflected in dialect differences on all levels of language organization.

In American society, metropolitan regions typically have been centers of change, while rural locales have been slower to change. This difference in the speed with which cultural innovations are adopted encompasses linguistic innovations as well. Many older language features, such as the *a-* prefix in *She was a-hunting and a-fishing* or the *h* in *Hit's nice out today*, are today retained only in rural areas. If dialectologists want to observe whether an older form of English is still in use in a particular area, they will typically seek out older, lifetime residents of rural areas; and if they want to see if a recent language change has been adopted, they will seek out younger speakers from metropolitan or suburban areas. Originally, urban–rural distinctions in this country had a strong economic base. Today, however, these distinctions carry a host of social and cultural meanings besides particular ways of making a living, all of which may be conveyed by the different language varieties spoken in these different types of regions. Sometimes, language changes may originate in rural areas if the social meanings attached to rural forms become important to people in urban and suburban areas. Rural language features are often associated with long-established heritage in a given area; such associations may become important if a formerly insular dialect area is suddenly faced with an influx of outsiders. For example, as we shall see in chapters 4 and 5, the rural Southern form *fixin' to*, as in *She's fixin' to go to church now*, has recently spread from rural to urban areas in Oklahoma in the face of mass migrations into the state by non-Southerners (Bailey, Wikle, Tillery, and Sand 1993). Further, as more and more of the American population becomes concentrated in the suburbs rather than the city, we are finding that the center of language change in the US is moving outward from the heart of the city as well. We discuss the suburbanization of America and its effects on American dialects in chapter 4.

2.1.6 Social stratification

Social stratification is a fact of life in American society. We may debate the number of distinct classes or the basis for their delineation, but in reality social status differences cut across virtually all regional varieties of American English. Members of different social classes distinguish themselves from one another in a whole range of social behaviors, including the type of language they use, whether they reside in a Southern community like Anniston, Alabama, or a large Northern metropolitan area like New York City. In fact, it is difficult to talk about regional dialect differences in American English without qualifying our discussion in terms of social status considerations. For example, when we talk about Appalachian English features such as *hit* for *it* or *a-hunting and a-fishing*, we have to be careful to note that these features are used at different rates among different social groups in Appalachia and may not even be used at all by those of higher social or cultural status or those who seek to be "upwardly mobile." It is also important to note that there are a number of features of English language variation, such as the use of "double negatives" (for example, *She ain't been nowhere*), different irregular verb forms (for example, *She done it*), and doubly marked comparative forms (for example, *more bigger*), whose distribution among various populations is best explained by starting with considerations of social status difference. In other words, these features tend to be found among lower-status speakers in all dialect regions rather than being confined to speakers in particular areas.

Social class differences play a role not only in language variation across space but also in language change over time. It is sometimes assumed that language change begins in the upper classes, perhaps because speakers in this social stratum feel a need to distance themselves as far as possible from the lower classes who continually strive to emulate them. One linguist even went so far as to say that language change is reducible to the "protracted pursuit of the elite by an envious mass, and consequent 'flight' of the elite" (Fischer 1958:2). However, numerous sociolinguistic studies have shown that there is a range of social and psychological factors that bring about language change besides social class differences. In addition, as we will see in chapter 6, most language changes in progress which have been studied in detail actually originate in social classes that are far from "elite," namely, the upper working class and lower middle class. Thus, even though the picture is not quite as clear as some early sociolinguists painted it, social class differences do play a major role in the patterning of language variation and change and must be taken into account in our exploration of American English dialect variation.

Sometimes, it is believed that extremely small communities which are isolated from the mainstream population are free of social class differences. While this may be true to an extent, our in-depth study of such communities on the Outer Banks islands of North Carolina has shown that, despite a lack of obvious differences in social status, such as type of home or dress, islanders nonetheless distinguish themselves socially in a number of ways, including how much property they own on the island, how much they travel, and how they use language. Thus, it seems that no matter how small and seemingly homogeneous the community, social status differences play an essential role in shaping dialect differences and can never be entirely discounted.

2.1.7   Communication networks

Who people talk to on a regular basis can sometimes be an important factor in the development of dialect differences. The interactional patterns that typify people's conversational contact exist on a couple of levels. As we have already mentioned in our discussion of migration routes and language contact, the dialects of entire communities or regions may be affected by patterns of transportational flow and population movement. A city like Washington, DC, is very different from a city like Charleston, West Virginia, in terms of population movement and, hence, conversational contact. In fact, in Washington, DC, there is so much movement into, out of, and through the region that it is common to assume that "everybody is from someplace else," an assumption that makes defining the local norm rather difficult. People in the area are unsure of what a "native Washingtonian" is supposed to sound like, and the area has adopted a "standard"-sounding, non-Southern dialect norm, even though the areas surrounding Washington, DC, are quite Southern. On the other hand, people in Charleston, West Virginia, where population movement is comparatively minimal, do not have difficulty distinguishing a native from a non-native; and the dialect norm is clearly based on Southern mountain, or Upper Southern, speech. We see, then, that sweeping patterns of cross-communication among speakers of various dialects have played and continue to play a major role in the development of American regional dialects.

On another level, we can talk about communication networks in terms of individual patterns of intercommunication, or SOCIAL NETWORKS. At this level, we are concerned with such issues as what kinds of speakers residents of a given community tend to interact with most often on a daily basis: Do they communicate most regularly with family, neighborhood friends, and friends of friends; or are there patterns of sustained contact with people outside the immediate community? We are also concerned with the DENSITY and MULTIPLEXITY of speakers' social networks. In a HIGH-DENSITY network, speakers all tend to interact with one another; in other words, "everybody knows everybody" in such networks. Those in MULTIPLEX NETWORKS tend to interact with the same people in a number of different social arenas; for example, they may work with family members or socialize and live in the same neighborhood as their co-workers. In contrast, speakers in LOW-DENSITY networks all know a particular individual but don't necessarily interact with each other, while those in UNIPLEX NETWORKS interact with different sets of people in different social spheres. Researchers have shown that social network density and multiplexity can have a significant impact on dialect maintenance and change. In particular, speakers in high-density, multiplex networks tend to cling to localized, vernacular language varieties far more tenaciously than speakers in uniplex, low-density networks, who are quicker to adopt language features from outside their local communities.

2.1.8 Group reference

Often, people want to be considered as a part of a particular social group as opposed to other groups, and so they project their identity with this group in a number of ways, including "talking like" other members of the group. Sometimes, group membership is voluntary and sometimes it is rooted in consignment to a particular social group without choice. In either case, though, group membership may end up carrying connotations of pride and loyalty. The linguistic means for conveying this pride may range from the relatively superficial adoption or heightened use of a couple of language features to the use of entire language systems, including pronunciation and grammatical features. For example, teenagers may adopt several "slang" lexical items in order to distinguish themselves from adult speakers, while members of a particular ethnic group, perhaps African Americans or Native Americans, may project their group membership via a complex array of grammatical, phonological, and lexical structures. In a groundbreaking study of language variation and change in Martha's Vineyard, a historically isolated island community off the coast of Massachusetts, William Labov demonstrated how members of established island families heightened their usage of certain unusual vowel sounds in order to distinguish themselves from the increasing numbers of tourists on the island. We have found similar patterns of selective heightening in the use of traditional dialect features in our investigations of Ocracoke Island, North Carolina, which is also witnessing an influx of tourists and new residents after generations of isolation from speakers of outside language varieties. Whether speakers project their in-group identity through the use of one or two language features or through the use of an entire language variety does not necessarily have any bearing on the depth of the significance of this symbolic projection of identity. A teenager who does not adopt some of the slang terms of a peer group, or an islander who does not use a particular distinctive vowel pronunciation, may be making a superficial language choice, but the choice may hold formidable consequences in terms of group acceptance.

In American English, the various social meanings associated with ethnic and regional varieties may force speakers to have to choose between "fitting in" and "talking correctly." Thus, some features of African American Vernacular English may be associated with ethnic solidarity at the same time they are socially stigmatized by the mainstream culture. Similarly, Appalachian English is associated with a rural, stigmatized vernacular at the same time it is associated with people's native roots. Faced with the dilemma of choosing between group solidarity and evaluation of social and educational status by external groups of speakers, it is not uncommon for speakers of vernacular dialects to attempt a sort of dialect balancing act. For example, native speakers of a vernacular dialect in East Tennessee who have moved away may feel constrained to shift to some degree back to the native dialect when visiting with family back home. If they fail to do so, not only will they fail to fit in with family members but their relatively standard speech patterns may even be interpreted as a kind of symbolic rejection of family ties. An individual's dialectal range is often related to flexibility in terms of balancing considerations of status and solidarity. Some speakers of American English dialects are amazingly adroit at balancing two dialects in order to live in two different worlds – the world of in-group identity and the world of mainstream social status. Others are not as successful in balancing their dialects and pay the social consequences of rejection by a local in-group or the condemnation of wider society.

2.1.9   Personal identity

Not only do dialects and dialect features carry connotations of membership in particular regional or social groups, but they also carry a host of other symbolic meanings, many of which pertain to character attributes and personal identity. For example, when listeners hear a Southern accent, not only do they identify the speaker as being from a Southern dialect region, but they may also automatically assign (perhaps unconsciously) a set a character traits to the speaker. These traits may range from such positive qualities as warmth and hospitality to such negative attributes as poverty and lack of intelligence. Similarly, speakers, particularly males, of varieties associated with lower classes or with certain minority ethnic groups are often considered to be tough and street-smart at the same time they are held to be poor and uneducated. Because of the association of dialect features with certain character traits, speakers may use language to project personal qualities in addition to group membership status. For example, an Anglo teenager who wants to be "cool" may adopt features of African American Vernacular English, while used car salespeople may intensify their usage of Southern vernacular speech when talking with customers or making a television commercial in order to convey warmth and honesty.

Conversely, speakers may avoid features associated with characteristics which they do not wish to project. Thus, speakers may refrain from using vernacular features such as double negatives because they do not wish to be considered "uneducated." In place of these vernacular features, speakers will adopt features of standard varieties of English, not necessarily because they wish to project membership in the middle and upper classes who usually use more standard English but because they wish to project the character traits associated with standard English in American society, such as competence, intelligence, and achievement. In American society, it is possible to be dumb but "talk smart" and, conversely, to be smart but "talk dumb." When the first author of this book gives class lectures using some nonstandard features of English, some students consider him to be unintelligent because of his speech patterns. In fact, he has had students confide to him that they initially had trouble believing that he could be a competent teacher and still "talk like that." Of course, we realize that there may be other factors which cause students to doubt this professor's intellectual abilities, but certainly language plays a major part in students' assessments of his character traits.

It is important to bear in mind that an individual speaker does not always project the exact same set of personal characteristics through language. Rather, a speaker may project different traits at different moments during the course of daily conversational interaction. For example, we may normally use standard language forms while at work to project an air of authority and competence, but we may switch into more vernacular speech when talking with a co-worker who is also a friend about an upcoming social event. Thus, through language, speakers are able to convey information about their personal identity on a number of different levels, ranging from their relatively permanent membership in certain well-established social groups, including social class and ethnic groups, to their more short-lived association with particular character types, such as the street-smart youth or the warm-hearted friend. Because language and identity are inextricably intertwined, we expect as much variation in language as we find in its speakers; and we even expect variation within the speech of individual speakers, since we all regularly shape our identity, sometimes in very subtle ways, to suit the communicative situations in which we find ourselves at any given time. (See LePage and Tabouret-Keller 1985 for more on identificational considerations in language variation.)

2.2 Linguistic Explanation

The other side of explaining dialects is rooted in the structure of language as opposed to the structure of society and the make-up of individual speakers. It is sometimes assumed that the dialects of a language may differ in multifarious, random ways. This is not true. Instead, the evidence from actual dialect divergence indicates that there are underlying principles of language structure that guide the ways in which the dialects of a language will differ from each other. Different kinds of social pressures may lead to the acceptance or rejection of the potential changes that lead to dialect divergence, but the language changes themselves will be systematic and follow certain orderly principles of language development.

As a starting point, we need to understand that all languages are dynamic systems which are constantly in the process of changing. Certainly, the language Shakespeare used in his plays is different from today's English, as was the English of the Elizabethan period compared to a period several centuries earlier. In fact, the English language has changed so much in the course of history that scholars have divided it into four separate types of English: Old English, which was spoken from about 600 to 1100, Middle English, spoken from 1100 to 1500, Early Modern English, spoken from 1500 to about 1800, and Modern English, which is what we speak today. To illustrate the dramatic changes that have taken place in the language over time, consider the following excerpt from the Lord's Prayer, as it appeared at four different time periods:

> Old English (about 950 AD):
> Fader urer ðu bist in heofnas, sie gehalgad noma ðin.
>
> Middle English (about 1350 AD):
> Oure fadir þat art in heuenes, halwid be þi name.
>
> Early Modern English (about 1550 AD):
> O oure father which arte in heven, hallowed be thy name.
>
> Modern English (about 1985 AD):
> Our father who is in heaven, may your name be sacred.

The English language today is also undergoing change, and people several centuries from now will look back on the English of this period as "archaic," just as we look at the English of several centuries ago. In fact, the only languages not undergoing change are *dead languages* – that is, languages with no native speakers, such as classical Latin or Greek.

Under constant pressure to change the way they speak, some groups of speakers adopt certain changes while others hold out against these changes but adopt different ones. If a new language feature continues to be used by a certain group but not by others, then a dialect difference is born. Eventually, the adoption of different language changes by different groups of speakers may lead to the splitting of two dialects into entirely separate languages, particularly if contact between the groups is severed. However, this radical differentiation has not yet affected the myriad varieties of English which exist throughout the world, although sometimes we may find it very difficult to understand speakers of varieties which are quite different from our own.

Sometimes, the pressure for a particular language or language variety to undergo change comes from within the language itself. Languages are highly intricate systems. The patterns which underlie any given language are constantly being adjusted and readjusted on the basis of how the particular language system is organized, and so language changes occur. These kinds of innovations are called CHANGES FROM WITHIN, because they take place apart from the influence of other languages. Changes may also originate from contact with other languages or dialects. Structures may be borrowed from other varieties, or pre-existing structures may be altered by their contact with the structures of a neighboring language variety. Features may also be entirely subsumed by those of competing language varieties. For example, one of the best-known features of the dialect of Ocracoke, North Carolina, is the pronunciation of the *i* vowel in words like *high* and *tide* as more of an *oy*, so that a phrase such as *high tide* sounds like "hoi toide." In fact, Ocracokers and other residents of the North Carolina Outer Banks are so well known for this pronunciation that they are often called "hoi toiders" for 'high tiders'. However, this distinctive pronunciation is being rapidly supplanted by mainland *i* and is destined to fade into obscurity if current language change processes continue unchecked. When changes take place due to language contact, they are referred to as CHANGES FROM OUTSIDE. Although we distinguish the two sources of change, they often work hand-in-hand, since the internal structure of a language system may dictate what items from outside will be adopted and how.

Interestingly, some of the same language changes that lead to dialect differentiation look very similar to the types of alterations which speakers make when they are in the process of acquiring a language – whether their native tongue or another language. For example, in some vernacular dialects, including New York City English, it is common for speakers to pronounce *th* sounds as *d* or *t*, so that words like *this* and *with* are pronounced as something like *dis* and *wit*. This process of changing *th*'s into some other sound is also common in the speech of people who are learning English as a second language; for example, a non-native speaker may say *tink* or *sink* for *think*. In addition, we find that children who are learning how to talk often figure out how to produce the *th* sound only after they have mastered a number of other language sounds.

Unfortunately, the similarities which people have noticed among dialect variants and some features of first and second language acquisition have often led to the erroneous conclusion that vernacular dialects are nothing more than imperfectly learned versions of the standard variety. In reality, the features which characterize both language acquisition and the language changes that lead to dialect differentiation are simply the result of natural processes which have to do with how language is articulated, how it is organized, and how it is processed in the human mind. Standard language varieties sometimes resist the natural pull of these processes, because language standards are based on permanence and consistency of linguistic form.

The fact that dialect differences often have to do with the underlying principles of human language systems also helps explain why we sometimes find that dialects which have no apparent contact with each other share similar features. For example, the use of *was* with all types of subjects (as in *we was* or *they was*), the formation of plurals such as *oxes* and *deers*, and the dropping of final consonants in words like *test* and *desk* (*tes'* and *des'*) are common to Hispanic English vernacular varieties in California, Native American English vernacular varieties spoken on reservations in the Southwestern United States, and the African American Vernacular English spoken in Northern urban areas, despite the absence of significant contact between these groups. Why is it that these structures are so far-reaching in their adoption? As we said above, the answer lies in the way language structures are organized into systems and in the processes of physical production and perception. At this point, let us look at some of the underlying principles that help us account for the systematic ways in which the dialects of America differ from each other.

2.2.1   Rule extension

As we discussed in chapter 1, every language and dialect is governed by an intricate set of unconscious "rules" which dictate when we use certain forms and when we don't. Sometimes these rules correspond to standard English rules and sometimes they don't. For example, when we produce a simple phrase such as *the blue house*, we are conforming to a rule of English which states that adjectives such as *blue* must precede nouns like *house*. We know that this is a language *rule* and not simply "common sense," because there are a number of languages in which a different rule is in operation – namely, one which states that we must place adjectives after nouns, as in the Spanish phrase *la casa azul*, which translates word-for-word as 'the house blue'. One of the principles underlying language organization that leads to language change and to dialect differentiation is that speakers seem to prefer language rules that are as general as possible. Thus, over time, a language rule of limited application may come to apply in more and more situations and to affect broader sets of items. This process is known as RULE EXTENSION. For example, a longstanding rule of English states that speakers should use one form of the personal pronoun for subjects (for example, *I walk, we walk, she walks*) and a different form when the pronoun serves as the object of a verb or preposition (as in *Pat saw me* or *Terry gave the book to her*). Over the centuries, English speakers have extended this rule, so that pronouns may now appear in object case even when they are not acting as objects. Thus, we frequently hear sentences such as *It's me* for 'It is I' and *Me and Charlie went to the store* for 'Charlie and I went to the store', even though grammar books caution us against such linguistic uses. In fact, this rule extension has become so much a part of our unconscious language knowledge that many of us feel like we are speaking very unnaturally indeed when we try to abide by the "grammar rules" by saying things like *It is I* or *This is she*.

Rule extension also affects pronunciation patterns. For example, we have mentioned that some dialects, such as British English and traditional Eastern New England English, are characterized by the loss of *r* in certain positions in words and sentences, as in *pahk* for 'park' or *cah* for 'car'. Unexpectedly, speakers of such "*r*-less" dialects often insert "extra" *r*'s, called INTRUSIVE R, in places where speakers of most English varieties would not have *r*, as in a phrase such as *the idear of it* for 'the idea of it'. In British English and some *r*-less varieties of American English, these extra *r*'s are actually the result of rule extension. *R*-dropping is governed by a rule which states that *r*'s at the ends of words are dropped only when the next word begins with a consonant but are retained when the next word begins with a vowel. Thus, in a sentence such as *Park the car by the house*, the final *r* in *car* would be dropped, because the next word begins with a consonant (*cah by*). However, in a sentence such as *Park the car over there*, the final *r* in *car* would be added in, because the following word begins with a vowel (*car over*). This rule has been extended to apply to words which never really ended in *r* but which seem like they did because they end in a vowel sound, just like *r*-less *car* (*cah*) or *far* (*fah*). Thus, a word like *idea* is now pronounced as *idear* when it comes before a vowel-initial word, as in *the idear of it*, just as *cah* is pronounced as *car* when it comes before a vowel (*car over there*). And just as *cah* is pronounced as *cah* when it comes before a consonant (*Park the cah by the house*), *idea* is pronounced simply as *idea* when it occurs in a similar environment (*the idea behind it*). (In some varieties, *r* may even be added to vowel-final words at the end of sentences, as in *I got the idear*, in a further extension of the *r*-insertion pattern.)

The rule which states "add *r* onto vowel-final words (including *r*-less words like *cah*) when they come before vowel-initial words" operates in a subtle way and often goes unnoticed by outside observers, who may mistakenly assume that speakers of *r*-less dialects *always* drop word-final *r*'s and *always* add *r*'s to the ends of vowel-final words like *idea*. However, close examination reveals that *r*-lessness and *r*-insertion are actually intricately patterned – and that these two seemingly opposing pronunciations are the result of a single language rule whose operation has been gradually extended over time.

Rule extension is just one of the natural linguistic tendencies that leads to language change and dialect differentiation. For one reason or another, some rule extensions are accepted by some groups of speakers but rejected by others. Dialects will inevitably share many rules, but these rules may be more or less general in different varieties, and so the dialects will seem quite different. No inherent linguistic value can be attached to how general or restricted a particular rule is, and all language varieties, including the standard variety, contain both general and highly specific rules.

2.2.2   Analogy

The tendency for languages to become as systematic as possible is also evidenced in another common mechanism of language change, ANALOGY. In general terms, analogy refers to a similarity between two essentially unlike things upon which a comparison may be based. In language science, analogy refers specifically to the process of taking language forms which are similar in some way, either in meaning, in function, or in sound or appearance, and making them more similar in form. For example, in English, most plural nouns are of the form *noun* + *s*, with the exception of a couple of nouns such as *oxen* and *deer*. It is common for speakers of vernacular dialects to regularize these irregular plurals, producing forms such as *oxes* and *deers*. This regularization takes place via analogy: Because the plural meaning is almost always indicated by *-s* or *-es*, speakers alter the form of irregular plural words so that the plural meaning corresponds with the *-(e)s* ending in these cases as well.

There are two types of linguistic analogy. The first type, which we have just illustrated, is called FOUR-PART or PROPORTIONAL ANALOGY. This type of analogy involves changing the form of words which derive a certain meaning in an irregular way so that they conform to the shape of words which derive this meaning in a more regular way. This change process can be expressed as a four-part relationship:

$$x \text{ is to } x' \text{ as } y \text{ is to } y' \quad \text{OR} \quad x : x' :: y : y'$$

Plugging the language forms into the "formula," we get such expressions as:

cow : cows :: ox : oxes
cow : cows :: sheep : sheeps

Four-part analogy also underlies the regularization of irregular past and participle verb forms which we often find in vernacular dialects. For example, we may hear speakers who say *knowed* for *knew* or *growed* for *grew*. The analogical formula would look something like this:

walk : walked :: grow : growed

The other type of linguistic analogy is called LEVELING. Leveling involves taking a group of words which have different forms for different subject persons and numbers and making them more similar or identical. For example, consider the subject person and number "set," or PARADIGM, for the verb *to be* in standard English. Two paradigms are given below, those for present and past tense:

Present		*Past*	
I am	we are	I was	we were
you are	you (pl.) are	you were	you were
she/he/it is	they are	she was	they were

Clearly, the person-number sets for present and past *to be* are both highly irregular. Speakers of vernacular dialects tend to regularize or "level" these irregular paradigms, producing sets such as the following:

I was	we was	I was	we was
you was	you (pl.) was	you was	you was
she/he/it was	they was	she was	they was

Sometimes, the forms on which speakers base their leveling may vary, and so differences among vernacular dialects result. For example, in the Outer Banks of North Carolina, it is common for speakers to regularize past tense *to be* based on *were* rather than *was* – but only in negative sentences. In positive sentences, past tense *to be* is sometimes based on *was*, but it usually patterns as in standard English. Thus we find the following paradigms in Outer Banks English (Schilling-Estes and Wolfram 1994):

Positive		*Negative*	
I was	we were (was)	I weren't	we weren't
you were (was)	you were (was)	you weren't	you weren't
she was	they were (was)	she weren't	they weren't

Exercise 2

For each of the following examples, state whether the regularization is due to four-part analogy or leveling.

1 This class is even badder than the last one.
2 Joe helped hisself to more mashed potatoes.
3 He just don't understand me.
4 Kate brung me a present.
5 That's the beautifulest cat I've ever seen.

Sometimes, four-part analogy may be based on patterns which are not as commonplace as the *-(e)s* plural ending or the *-ed* past tense. For example, speakers of vernacular dialects may regularize a form like *bring* to *brang* or *brung* rather than *bringed*, by analogy to forms such as *sing/sang/sung* and *ring/ rang/rung*. This type of change is known as MINORITY PATTERN ANALOGY, since it involves reshaping irregular forms on the model of a minor pattern rather than a major pattern such as the predominant *-ed* past tense. Although it may seem like speakers are not really regularizing anything but merely substituting one irregular form for another when they say *brung* for *brought*, in reality, this change is a regularization of sorts, since the *sing/sang/sung* past tense pattern is more common in English than the very limited *bring/brought/brought* pattern.

Occasionally, minority pattern analogy does result in what we might call "irregularization." For example, the past tense of *dive* historically is the regular form *dived*. However, in many American English varieties, it is being replaced with *dove*, by analogy to forms like *drive/drove* and *ride/rode*. Similarly, we occasionally find "irregularization" of plural forms. For example, the form *dwarves* is newer than *dwarfs* and was most likely created via minority pattern analogy with forms such as *elf/elves* and *wolf/wolves*, words with which *dwarf* commonly co-occurs in fairy tales.

For the most part, though, the predominant movement is toward regularization rather than irregularization, and whenever new words enter the language – or old words take on new meanings – they are almost always given regular plural and past tense forms. Thus, we do not hear *netwrought* for *networked*, *flew out* for *flied out* (in baseball), or *kang* for *kinged*, as in *She kinged me in checkers*.

It is important to realize that, just as with rule extension, analogical change does not represent imperfect learning or language decay. If it did, then we would have to admit that the English language has fallen into grave disrepair since its Old and Middle English days. For example, in Middle English, there were just as many plurals which ended in *-n* or *-en* as with *-(e)s*. In fact, the *-(e)n* ending was so commonplace that some plurals were regularized to *-(e)n* from *-s*; for example, the plural of *shoe*, which originally ended in *-s*, became *shoon*. Gradually, however, almost all Middle English *-(e)n* plurals were regularized to *-(e)s*. Thus, although *oxen* remained *oxen*, *kine* became *cows* and *shoon* reverted back to *shoes*. This regularization took place through the same process of analogy which gives us such "incorrect" or "uneducated" forms as *oxes* and *deers* today; it just so happens, however, that most of the plural forms which were regularized during the transformation from Middle English to Modern English gained social acceptance, while forms like *oxes* and *deers* have yet to do so. Interestingly, the social acceptability of forms has nothing to do with the forms *per se*. Rather, forms are selected (usually unconsciously) for "acceptability" in an arbitrary way. For example, if a Modern English speaker were to regularize the plural of the rodent known as a *mouse* as *mouses*, the form would be considered unacceptable (unless the speaker is a young child, in which case the form is "wrong" but "cute"). At the same time, if a speaker pluralizes a computer *mouse* as *mouses*, the regularized form is perfectly acceptable. In fact, if the speaker were to use *mice* for *mouses* in a sentence such as *Everyone in our office got new mice for their computers*, the form would sound quite odd indeed.

Similarly, a large number of formerly irregular verb forms have found their way into standard English as regular verbs. For example, *help* once had such irregular past tense forms as *healp* and *hulpon*, while the past tense of *work* was *wrought*. In addition, although verbs used to show person–number distinctions in the past tense, these distinctions have been completely leveled out in all English verbs except *to be*. Even verbs with irregular past tense forms, such as *thought* or *sang*, show the same form for all persons and numbers in the past tense and so can be considered to be "regular" in at least one way. And even changes resulting from minority pattern analogy sometimes make their way into standard English. For example, the past tense of *ring* was originally *ringed* but was later changed to *rang* on the basis of analogy to *sing/sang/sung*.

Again, the only thing separating verb forms like *helped* and *rang* from forms like *knowed* and *brang* is social acceptability; all of these regularized verbs are bona fide language forms resulting from the application of very natural processes of language change. From a strictly linguistic standpoint, which regularized forms become standard and which are consigned to nonstandard status is purely accidental. From a sociological perspective, of course, it is no accident that the forms associated with socially favored groups become established as standard forms while those associated with low-status groups remain nonstandard.

2.2.3 The transparency principle

At first glance, it seems as if rule extension and analogy will cause the English language to just keep getting simpler and simpler over time and that eventually we won't have to worry about such matters as different pronoun forms for use in different places in sentences, irregular verb forms, or subject–verb agreement. However, the tendency for speakers to make things as easy as possible on themselves by reducing dissimilar forms with similar meanings (e.g. *I was, you were*) to similar forms (e.g. *I was, you was*) is counterbalanced by the need to ensure that meaning distinctions are as clear as possible to listeners. This need to make meanings as obvious as possible is sometimes referred to as the TRANSPARENCY PRINCIPLE. It ensures that, while speakers of many varieties feel free to eliminate markers which convey certain meaning distinctions, they nonetheless preserve a host of other distinctions and even introduce a few which we don't find in standard English. For example, the same speakers who eliminate subject–verb agreement marking on past tense *be* would never eliminate positive–negative marking (e.g. *I was/I wasn't*) and in fact may enhance the marking of negativity in a couple of different ways. For example, instead of using different verb roots for different subjects (*I am/you are*; *I was/you were*), they may use different roots for positive and negative forms in addition to an -*n't* negative ending, as in Southern American *can* vs. *cain't* (with a different root vowel sound) or the general vernacular use of *am/is/are* for positive sentences and *ain't* for negatives. In addition, speakers may use so-called "double negatives" to ensure that listeners pick up the negative meaning of their utterances, as in *I didn't do nothing* for 'I didn't do anything'. In fact, speakers of vernacular dialects often attach a negative marker to every element in negative sentences to which such markers can be added, as in a sentence such as *I ain't never learned nothing from nobody*. For this reason, linguists prefer the term MULTIPLE NEGATION or NEGATIVE CONCORD (that is, negative agreement) to "double negatives," since we often find more than two negative markers per sentence.

Again, here is a case in which an underlying principle of language organization, the transparency principle, has resulted in language forms which are judged as nonstandard, "uneducated," or even "illogical" (as we see, for example, in the old grammatical adage, "two negatives make a positive"). And, once again, it is easy to demonstrate that these negative judgments are strictly social rather than linguistic. For example, it was once considered quite standard to use multiple negatives in English; in fact, the writings of even renowned literary figures such as Chaucer are replete with multiple negation. In addition, the standard versions of a number of modern languages call for multiple rather than single negation. Thus, if you wish to say "I don't know anything" in modern Spanish, you have to say "No sé **nada**," which translates literally as "I don't know **nothing**," rather than "No sé **algo**," literally "I don't know **anything**." The only difference between structures such as Spanish *No sé nada* and Old English *ic ne wāt nāwiht* 'I don't know nothing', on the one hand, and Modern English *I don't know nothing*, on the other, is a difference in the social value ascribed to multiple negation at a given time or in a given place. Furthermore, the prestige accorded to multiple negation could very well change if the socially privileged people in American society begin to use it and to uphold its usage as "proper" and "educated."

2.2.4   Grammaticalization

Not only may meaning distinctions be doubly marked, but they may also be added. It is fairly common for speakers of some vernacular varieties of English to rearrange the language resources they already have on hand in order to create a clear marker of a certain meaning which is important to them but which is not very clearly marked in the standard variety. Linguists refer to the process whereby a new meaning becomes linked to a particular grammatical structure as GRAMMATICALIZATION. For example, in some varieties of Southern

American English, speakers may string together two or more standard English helping verbs, such as *might* and *could*, in order to convey a meaning which is slightly different from that of either *might* or *could*. Thus, a sentence such as *I might could go with you* doesn't mean either *I might go* or *I could go* but instead means something like *I may be able to go with you but I'm not really sure*. In other words, the use of these double helping verbs, technically called DOUBLE MODALS, conveys a meaning of lessened intensity which cannot be indicated in standard English except through substantially rewording the original sentence.

Another Southern American helping verb form which serves to convey a meaning which is not readily indicated in standard English is the word *liketa*, as in *It was so cold out there, I liketa died*. Historically, *liketa* comes from *like to have* and seems simply to have been equivalent in meaning to *almost*. However, in some American dialects which use this form today, the meaning has been altered in a subtle way, so that *liketa* cannot be used to refer to things which almost took place in real life but only to things which almost happened in a figurative sense. Thus, when a speaker utters the sentence, *It was so cold, I liketa froze*, she is not conveying that she was in any real danger of freezing but only that she was very, very cold. Because of the non-factual way in which *liketa* is now sometimes used, dialectologists refer to this construction as COUNTERFACTUAL *liketa*.

A final example of a meaning difference conveyed through different verb forms is the use of *be* by speakers of African American Vernacular English where speakers of other varieties would use *am*, *is*, or *are* (e.g. *He always be coming to school late*). It is a common misperception among speakers of other varieties to assume that speakers of African American Vernacular English always use *be* instead of *am*, *is*, or *are*. In reality, *be* is used only in certain types of sentences, namely, those which indicate habitual or ongoing actions or states, as in *He always be coming to school late*. In other types of sentences, speakers of African American Vernacular English use *am*, *is*, or *are* (*He is coming to school right now*) or no form of *be* at all (*He coming to school right now*). Thus, *be* in African American Vernacular English serves to convey a meaning distinction which can only be conveyed through words other than verbs in standard English, just as *might could* and *liketa* add subtle nuances of meaning to the verbs they modify in Southern American English.

Because tendencies such as adding new meaning distinctions and doubly marking existing meanings are in competition with principles that seek to eliminate "extra" linguistic markers of meaning, language change may follow very different paths in different areas, depending on which type of principle wins out in a given instance. Thus, we see that the seeds of dialect differentiation are planted deep within the language system itself. And when we superimpose onto this system the myriad of social factors which influence whether a certain language change will be adopted or not, the potential for the wide divergence of dialects over time becomes very great indeed.

2.2.5   *Pronunciation phenomena*

The language-internal processes we have so far discussed tend to affect the formation of words and the structure of sentences. There are also a number of natural processes which lead to pronunciation changes and subsequent dialect differentiation. These processes have to do with several different factors, especially with how language sounds are produced and perceived and how they are organized into systems. These processes tend to be commonplace and to operate in neat, regular ways. There are a couple of other pronunciation-related processes which are not as common and which operate more sporadically. We will talk about these latter processes once we have discussed the more regular processes.

Articulation-related changes
It is a linguistic and physiological fact that some language sounds are more difficult to articulate than others because they involve more complex movements of the tongue or other organs of speech or more intricate coordination among the various articulators such as the tongue, teeth, and vocal cords. For example, the slightly different but related sounds which occur at the beginning of the words *think* and *these* happen to be quite difficult for humans to produce and therefore are relatively rare in the languages of the world. This is why, as we mentioned earlier, native speakers of English acquire these sounds late in their language development and adult second language learners or vernacular dialect speakers often use other sounds in place of these sounds. For example, second language learners may use *t* or *s* for *th* (as in *tink* or *sink* for 'think'), while native speakers of vernacular varieties may use *t* or *f*, as in *wit* or *wiff* for 'with'. Thus, some dialect differences in pronunciation are the result of using more "natural" language sounds than those which are difficult and relatively "unnatural" to pronounce.

Other articulation-related pronunciation changes involve altering sounds when they occur in certain sequences, following certain natural principles of human language production. One very common change is for neighboring sounds to become more similar to one another, a process known as ASSIMILA-TION. Pronunciations which derive from assimilation are so commonplace that they are often considered simply to be part of standard English. For example, the prefixes meaning "not" which we find on the words *impossible*, *illogical*, and *irregular* all derive from the same *in-* prefix (as in *inexcusable*). In each case, however, the pronunciation (and spelling) of the *n* has been altered to make it more like the first sound in the word to which it attaches: In the first case, *n* becomes *m* because both *m* and *p* are produced by putting both lips together; in the second and third cases, the *n* has become completely assimilated to the following *l* and *r* by "turning into" the exact same language sound.

Other pronunciations which result from assimilation are confined to certain regional or social dialects. For example, it is common for speakers of Southern

American English to pronounce words such as *wasn't* and *business* as *wadn't* and *bidness* (Schilling-Estes 1995). The reason that the *z* sounds in the middle of these words are changed to *d*'s is that they occur next to *n*'s. Both *n* and *d* are language sounds which are produced by fully blocking the airflow in the mouth (although air escapes through the nose with *n*). The *z* sound, however, is unlike these sounds, because it is produced with only partial air blockage (as evidenced in the buzzing we hear when *z*'s are produced). When we change *z* to *d*, we are changing it to a sound in which airflow is completely blocked in the mouth, just like *n*. Thus, even though at first glance *d* doesn't seem any more similar to *n* than *z*, a close examination of articulatory processes reveals that changing *z* to *d* before *n* really is a process of assimilation. In this case, however, the pronunciations which result from this assimilation have not been accepted as part of standard English; in fact, a number of speakers in this country do not even produce them.

Another process affecting sounds in sequence is WEAKENING. Weakening involves producing sounds which involve less blockage of airflow in the mouth and is especially likely to occur when sounds occur next to sounds which involve little or no obstruction of the airflow, particularly vowels. It is important to remember that when linguists refer to the process of "weakening," they are not making a value judgment about the worth of a particular sound or sound system but are simply referring to how strongly the airflow is blocked in the mouth when a given sound is produced. The sound systems of all languages and dialects contain both strong and weak sounds; in fact, all vowels are inherently "weak" sounds, since they involve no blockage of airflow in the mouth whatsoever. Furthermore, all sound systems are subject to weakening processes regardless of their social valuation.

A given consonant may weaken in various ways, leading to differentiation among dialects. For example, when speakers of American English produce the *t* that occurs in the middle of words like *butter* and *better*, they almost always weaken it to a *d*-like sound. This sound is actually a quick tap, called a FLAP, of the tip of the tongue to the roof of the mouth rather than a full-fledged *d* sound. Speakers of some varieties of British English may also weaken *t*'s in the middle of words; however, they do so in a different way. Instead of pronouncing *t* as a flap, they pronounce it as a slight "catch" in the throat, which sounds almost like they are leaving out the *t* entirely, as in *bo'l* for *bottle*. This "catch," called a GLOTTAL STOP, is actually a quick closing and re-opening of the vocal cords. It is found in some varieties of American English, particularly some types which are spoken in New York City, and also happens to be found in the middle of the phrase *uh oh*. It is not an easy sound to describe on paper, however, because English has no letter for it, although a number of languages do. Phonetically, the sound is indicated as [ʔ], a question mark without a period.

Not only may sounds be weakened, but they may be completely lost when they occur in certain sequences. It is common, for example, for speakers to omit consonants when several of them cluster together in a row, since such clusters are "unnatural," in the sense that there is a natural principle of human language organization which holds that consonants should alternate with vowels rather than cluster together. Most English speakers tend to drop at least one consonant from the clusters which occur at the ends of plural words like *sixths*, *tempts*, and *tests*; and they also sometimes leave off the final consonant in non-plurals such as *test*, *friend*, or *desk*. This is particularly likely to occur in informal speech and when the word following the cluster begins with a con-sonant, as in *des' by the window* for 'desk by the window'. Speakers of some vernacular varieties have extended this process of word-final consonant loss so that they may drop final consonants before vowels as well as consonants, as in *des' over there* for 'desk over there'. Consonant loss is so commonplace that it has even made its way into formal standard English. For example, the "silent" *k* at the beginning of *knight* and *knee* used to be pronounced, as did the *gh* at the end of *knight* (with *gh* being pronounced as something like the final *ch* in German *Bach* or Scottish English *loch*).

Another way to eliminate consonant clusters is to break them up by inserting vowels. Thus, speakers of some vernacular varieties say *deskes* or *desses* for *desks* as well as *athelete* for *athlete*. Consonants are sometimes inserted into words as well, though this process does not have to do with cluster simplification but with the overlap of articulatory gestures which occur in quick succession. For example, it is very common for speakers to insert *d*'s between *n*'s and *r*'s, which is why the Old English word for *thunder*, *þunrian*, gradually became *thunder* (and why children often refer to Donner and Blitzen as **Donder** and Blitzen). Occasionally, the "extra" consonants which we sometimes find in ver-nacular dialects are the result of such insertion, as for example when speakers of some varieties pronounce *chimney* as *chimbley*. Most often, however, the additional consonants we sometimes find in vernacular dialects represent reten-tions of sounds which were lost in other English varieties, including standard English. For example, when older rural Southern speakers say *hit* for *it*, they are not inserting *h*'s but rather preserving a pronunciation which goes all the way back to the Old English period.

Some pronunciation changes have more to do with how sounds are per-ceived by listeners than how they are pronounced. For example, people often pronounce *et cetera* as *eksetera*, not necessarily because the latter is any easier to say but because *et cetera* sounds like *eksetera* (or even *extra*) in fast speech. Similarly, we may hear people say *aestetic* for *aesthetic*, once again due to perception rather than pronunciation-related factors. As with articulation-based language change, perception-based changes sometimes make their way into standard English. For example, the reason why some words ending in *augh* and *ough*, as in *laugh* and *rough*, are today pronounced with a final *f* is that the sound originally indicated by the final *gh* (which we have already described as similar to the *ch* in Scottish English *loch*) is readily misperceived as *f*.

Sound systems

One very important class of pronunciation changes relates to how sounds are organized into systems rather than how individual sounds or strings of sounds are produced or perceived. As we have already hinted at, some sounds which seem to us to be quite different (e.g. *z* and *d* as in *wasn't* vs. *wadn't*) are actually very similar in terms of how they are produced in the mouth. If we examine our language closely, we also find that some sounds which we consider to be the "same" are actually produced somewhat differently. For example, the *p* that occurs in words like *pit* and *pot* is produced with a distinct puff of air, called ASPIRATION, following the sound, while the *p* in *spit* and *spot* is not. We can test this for ourselves by holding a thin piece of paper close to our lips and uttering the words *pit* and *spit* in succession. Notice how much the paper moves for *pit*, while it barely moves at all for *spit*. Thus, the two types of *p*'s, which we consider to be the same, are actually not the same at all. In fact, there are languages, such as Thai or Hindi, in which the two *p*'s are considered to be two different language sounds; and there is even a separate phonetic symbol for each type of *p*: [pʰ] represents aspirated *p* (as in *pit*), while [p] stands for unaspirated *p* (as in *spit*).

In essence, the main thing separating sounds which are considered to be the "same" from those which are held to be "different" is whether or not the sounds can be used to make a meaning difference in the language. Thus, in English, *d* and *z* are different language sounds because they can be used to distinguish a word like *dip* from a word like *zip*. Conversely, [p] and [pʰ] are not two different sounds, because there is no word [pɪt] (as opposed to [pʰɪt]) which has a meaning different from 'pit'. In Thai, however, word pairs with [p] and [pʰ] abound. For example, *paa* means 'forest' while *pʰaa* means 'to split'.

When two sounds can be used to make meaning differences, they are called PHONEMES. Linguists indicate that a given sound is considered to be phonemic in a particular language by enclosing it in slashes (e.g. /p/, /b/); if they are concerned merely with the physical sound itself rather than its meaningful status in a sound system, they enclose the sound in square brackets (e.g. [p], [pʰ]). Even though sounds which are considered to be different phonemes, or different meaningful sounds, may sometimes be produced rather similarly (as with [z] and [d] in English), it is very important for languages to keep different phonemes different enough so that listeners can recognize them as different. Sometimes, when a sound takes on a new pronunciation, it becomes very similar to another sound and so the latter sound is changed as well, in order to ensure that the two sounds remain distinct enough to convey meaning differences. This process of CHAIN SHIFTING is most likely to affect vowels, since vowels are differentiated from one another chiefly by very subtle differences in the height of the tongue and how far forward in the mouth the tongue is when the vowel is produced. Consonants, on the other hand, are differentiated by where the tongue hits the mouth (or at least comes very close), how completely the tongue blocks airflow, whether or not air comes out of the nose during the production of the sound, and whether or not the vocal cords vibrate when the sound is produced.

Because vowels are not as clearly distinct as consonants, if one vowel is even slightly altered in pronunciation, then it begins to sound like vowels which are produced with similar tongue positioning. If speakers still hope to preserve a meaning distinction between this altered vowel and "neighboring" vowels, then the neighboring vowels will have to be altered in pronunciation as well. In turn, these alterations lead to further alterations, and a sort of "domino effect" may result. We will discuss chain shifts in more detail in chapters 3 and 5. For now, all we need to know is that such shifts are commonplace and once led to a sweeping change in the pronunciation of all long vowels in English. For example, words with the vowel sound of *name* used to be pronounced with the vowel of *father*, words with the vowel of *beet* were pronounced with the vowel of *bait*, while those with the vowel of *time* were pronounced with the vowel of *team*. Chain shifts are also underway currently in American English dialects; in fact, they are proceeding quite differently in different areas of the country, leading to increased dialect differentiation rather than the decreased differentiation we might expect in the face of mass communication and improved methods of transportation. We will discuss these current chain shifts in chapter 5.

Sporadic sound changes
Finally, we should mention sound changes which do not necessarily operate in neat, systematic ways but which are more sporadic in nature. Among these are changes involving making sounds more unlike each other rather than more like each other and changes involving the re-ordering of sounds within a word. The first type of change, called DISSIMILATION, often affects sounds which are not immediately adjacent and seems to affect mostly *r* and *l* sounds: It is rather difficult to pronounce words when they contain a number of *r*'s or *l*'s, and so speakers may leave out some of these sounds or even change *r*'s to *l*'s and vice versa, in order to create a more "balanced" word. The pronunciation of *corner* as *co'ner* in some Eastern US dialects, in which the first *r* has been deleted, is a case of dissimilation, as is the pronunciation of *colonel* as *kernel*, where the first *l* has been changed to an *r*. These pronunciations are general and widespread, but sometimes dissimilation is confined to certain regional or social varieties. For example, the pronunciation of *library* as *lib'ary* is a case of dissimilation which is largely confined to speakers of lower social classes. This pronunciation is widely regarded as "uneducated," even though it results from the same process that gives us such socially acceptable forms as *co'ner* for *corner*. Despite how common dissimilation is, it does not operate in any sort of regular way; it affects some words but leaves other very similar words untouched. Thus, while

many speakers say *lib'ary*, nobody ever says *cont'ary* for 'contrary', even though the structures of the two words are very much alike.

Another process that affects words sporadically is the rearrangement of sounds, or METATHESIS. Again, this process has led to a number of pronunciation changes which are fully accepted as part of mainstream or standard English and, again, it often involves *l*'s and *r*'s, particularly *r*'s. For example, words such as *bird*, *first*, and *third* used to be *bryde*, *frist*, and *thridde*, respectively, in Old English. Nowadays, metathesis is responsible for a couple of dialect differences, including the highly stigmatized pronunciation of *ask* as *aks* by speakers of African American Vernacular English and some other vernacular dialects. Interestingly, the *ask/aks* alternation goes all the way back to Old English, when it represented a regional rather than ethnic dialect variation.

Syllable structure considerations
Often, sounds are added, deleted, or moved around in order to create syllables that conform to a natural language principle which states that, as far as possible, consonants and vowels should alternate with one another. In other words, consonants should occur next to vowels and vice versa, but speakers should avoid putting consonants next to one another or producing a number of vowel sounds in a row. The most natural syllable (and the one which is produced earliest by babies) is one consisting of a single consonant plus a single vowel, as in *me* or *ma*. Syllables which end in a consonant, as in *man* or *bad*, are not too difficult to pronounce either; but, as we have already mentioned, once consonants begin clustering at the ends of syllables (or at the beginning), speakers begin omitting consonants – or inserting vowels – in order to restore the natural order of consonant–vowel alternation. Thus, a word such as *test* becomes *tes'*, while *athlete* becomes *athelete*. Similarly, speakers sometimes move sounds around so that words consist of simple syllables of the form consonant + vowel (CV). For example, the stigmatized pronunciation of *nuclear* as *nukular* is the result of moving the *l* to break up a consonant cluster and to give us three CV syllables in a row.

It is important to keep in mind that, just as with the word formation and sentence structure change processes we discussed above, the pronunciation changes which lead to dialect differentiation do not always represent simplifications. In other words, it is not the case that vernacular varieties have "simpler" sound systems than standard varieties. Thus, although such processes as consonant cluster reduction and the pronunciation of *th* as *d* or *t* may technically be described as simplifications, other processes, such as the chain shifting of vowels or certain cases of metathesis, do not produce structures which are simpler in any way. In addition, we must bear in mind that even seemingly straightforward simplification may take many forms. For example, speakers who seek to reduce the consonant cluster in *tests* may say *tesses* or *tess*, with the double *s* in the latter word representing a single *s* which is lengthened in duration. Similarly, speakers who are simplifying a word like *wasn't* may say *wadn't*, as discussed above; but they may very well pronounce *wasn't* as something like *won't* instead, as in *He won't at supper last night*. This latter pronunciation, found in a number of rural Southern varieties, is the result of the complete assimilation of the *z* sound to the following *n*. In addition, the *a* has been rounded into *o* through assimilation to the preceding *w*, which is produced with rounded lips. Because the natural principles which guide pronunciation change do not always produce simpler forms and because natural changes may proceed in very different directions in different areas or among speakers of different social and ethnic groups, the potential for the development of dialect differences in pronunciation is very great indeed. In fact, pronunciation differences are often the first features people notice when they encounter a dialect which is different from their own.

2.2.6   Words and word meanings

So far, in our discussion of the principles underlying language change and dialect differentiation, we have not yet mentioned lexical and semantic differences – that is, differences in words and word meanings. One of the most noticeable differences among dialects are the different vocabulary words we find in different language varieties. Most likely, we are all familiar with the fact that speakers in different parts of the country use different words to refer to various foods and drinks; for example, we may have heard both *soda* and *pop* being used to refer to a particular kind of carbonated beverage, as well as such terms as *sub*, *hoagie*, *grinder*, and *hero* to refer to a submarine sandwich. One of the main reasons why we find such wide differentiation in dialect words has to do with one of the most basic facts which underlies human language: The relationship between the sounds that make up a given word and the meaning or meanings associated with this word is essentially arbitrary. That is, there is no one "true" name for a given object or idea. Thus, even a common, everyday substance like bread is associated with quite different words in different languages; for example, *bread* is *pain* in French and *chleb* in Russian. Similarly, different dialects of a single language may use quite different words, such as *soda* vs. *pop*, to refer to one and the same item.

In addition to being arbitrary, word meanings also happen to be rather vague: A given word tends to have not only a central, core meaning but also a host of peripheral meanings and associations which make it difficult to pin down the meaning of the word with precision. Sometimes, two dialect areas may share a word, but speakers in each area may have chosen a different sub-meaning as the word's central meaning. For example, we have encountered the unusual word *mommuck* in several of the dialect areas we have investigated in North Carolina. In the Outer Banks of North Carolina, the word means 'to harass or bother', as in "Don't mommuck me; I've had a hard day." However, in Robeson County, North Carolina, located in the Southeastern mainland portion of the state, near the South Carolina border, *mommuck* has a slightly different meaning, 'to make a mess of', as in "He mommucked up his homework." Clearly, the two meanings are related; speakers in each dialect area have simply seized on a different facet of the word's overall meaning as the word's principal meaning. Interestingly, *mommuck* can be traced back at least as far as Shakespeare's day, when it had yet another meaning: 'to tear or shred', as in "He mommucked his shirt in a fit of rage." Thus, we see that word meanings can shift, sometimes rather drastically, over time as well as over space. We will discuss various ways in which MEANING SHIFT can occur in chapter 3.

Another reason why we have different words in different language varieties has to do with factors which lie outside the linguistic system itself. Sometimes, speakers need different words because they have to – or want to – talk about different things in different dialect areas or in different cultural groups. Thus, it is not surprising that there is a host of terms for marine-related items and activities in coastal areas such as the Outer Banks islands of North Carolina that are not shared with speakers in Ohio or Montana or even in inland regions of North Carolina. For example, Outer Banks residents may make reference to a *nor'easter* for 'a storm from the north and east' or to a *peeler crab* for 'a crab that is shedding its shell in preparation for growing a new and larger one'. On the other hand, people who live in non-coastal areas of North Carolina have no occasion to talk about such maritime-related matters. Similarly, we may find quite different food-related terms in different areas simply because the foods people eat vary greatly from region to region. Even within a single dialect area, we find lots of variation in what people talk about. For example, working-class New Yorkers may use a whole set of vocabulary words which are not used by members of upper classes, and vice versa. Some of these terms will be related to occupation, but others will pertain to cultural activities and general lifestyle differences.

When speakers moving into a region or taking up a particular trade encounter items or concepts for which their language or language variety currently has no term, they may come up with a term in several different ways. First, they may simply make up, or COIN, the word, as, for example, with the Ocracoke term *meehonkey*, which refers to a special type of hide-and-seek which used to be played on the island. Second, they may create a word out of existing language resources. There are a number of different ways of doing this, which we will discuss in detail in chapter 3. One of the most common processes is COMPOUNDING, or putting two existing words together to get a new term whose meaning may be completely unrelated to the meanings of the original words. The Southern American term *hushpuppies*, which refers to bite-sized pieces of deep-fried cornmeal batter, is an example of a compound word, as in the Eastern coastal term *breakwater*, which refers to a barrier which prevents water from eroding coastal land or to the process of erecting such barriers. Finally, as we discussed earlier in this chapter, terms for regionally or culturally specific items or concepts may be borrowed from other languages. Early in the history of American English, borrowings came from Native American, European, and African languages; nowadays, borrowings may come from just about any language in the world.

As with new pronunciations, word-formation processes, and sentence structures, it is difficult to predict which new lexical items will be widely adopted and which will remain restricted to particular groups of speakers. However, we do know that many of today's common English words started out as dialect-specific items and then spread across dialects to the point where they have become identified as common English vocabulary items. For example, the words *bisque* 'a cream soup', *cruller* 'a type of doughnut', and *ranch* all began as regionally restricted terms but are now part of the general word stock of English.

By the same token, there are also present-day items which were once in widespread usage but have since retracted to regional usage only. For example, the use of *garret* for 'attic', or *yonder* for 'over there' in rural Southern dialects are local retentions of older items which were once in much wider use in the English language. When a particular group of speakers does not participate in a change taking place elsewhere in the language, the result may be the retraction of a general English vocabulary word to dialect-specific status.

2.3   The Final Product

As we come to the end of our examination of some of the important linguistic and sociohistorical factors underlying the language changes which lead to dialect differences, we must bear in mind that none of these factors works in isolation. The role of each linguistic and sociolinguistic factor in the development of a given dialect, whether in the past, present, or future, is often difficult to specify with great precision. This uncertainty, however, does not detract from the highly structured nature of the resultant variety or from the important roles which dialect differences fulfill in society.

Perhaps the creation of a gourmet dish by a master chef is the best analogy we can draw for how various linguistic and sociolinguistic factors are brought together in the formation of a new dialect. Starting with a number of separate ingredients and working mostly by "feel" or "instinct" rather than with measuring cups, the chef combines differing amounts of various items using several different techniques. While the cooking process is still underway, the chef may alter the basic composition of the dish by adding "just a' pinch" of this or "a touch" of that. The resultant dish turns out to be a delicious concoction when prepared by the chef, but it is extremely difficult to replicate. Similarly, dialects are formed when sociohistorical and linguistic factors come together in proportions that are sometimes difficult to measure precisely. The resultant language variety, however, turns out to be a unique dialect whose distinctive flavor would be lost if it were mechanistically constructed of precise portions of readily identifiable linguistic and sociolinguistic ingredients.

2.4 Further Reading

Hock, Hans Henrich, and Brian D. Joseph (1996) *Language History, Language Change, and Language Relationship: An Introduction to Historical and Comparative Linguistics*. Berlin/New York: Mouton de Gruyter. This book provides a comprehensive introduction to the linguistic principles which guide language change. Of particular interest are chapters 4 through 9, in which the principles of phonological, morphosyntactic, lexical, and semantic change are discussed. Unlike some other historical linguistics texts, this book provides plenty of examples from English at various stages in its historical development rather than primarily using examples from ancient languages.

Kurath, Hans (1971) The origins of the dialectal differences in spoken American English. In Juanita V. Williamson and Virginia M. Burke (eds), *A Various Language: Perspectives on American Dialects*. New York: Holt, Rinehart and Winston, 12–21. This reprint of an article originally published in 1928 offers a brief overview of the original British influences on American English and discusses some of the migratory patterns that account for the geographical dispersion of dialect forms. As a summary of the state of dialect knowledge prior to the launching of the *Linguistic Atlas of the United States and Canada*, it is an important historical document.

Labov, William (1972b) *Sociolinguistic Patterns*. Philadelphia: University of Pennsylvania Press. Several chapters in this collection, particularly chapters 1, 4, 5, and 7, reveal how the processes of linguistic change interact with social forces in the development and continued delimitation of the varieties of English.

Milroy, Lesley (1987) *Language and Social Networks*, 2nd edn. *Language in Society 2*. Oxford/Cambridge, MA: Blackwell. In this book, Milroy outlines her highly influential social network model for the spread of linguistic innovations. She traces the diffusion of several language changes through various social networks of differing types in the Ballymacarrett, Hammer, and Clonard communities of Belfast.

3

Levels of Dialect

When we casually observe that a group of English speakers uses a different word for what some of us call a *submarine* sandwich, that some speakers pronounce the word *chocolate* differently from the way we do, that some people say *The house needs painted* while others say *The house needs painting*, or that speakers greet each other with *What's up?* or *Hey!* instead of *Hi!*, we are actually noting different forms of language variation. In the first case, we notice a vocabulary difference, in the second, we note a pronunciation difference, where speakers use the same word but produce it differently, and in the third instance, we are noticing a grammatical difference, where different speakers form certain sentences in different ways. Finally, *What's up?*, *Hey!*, and *Hi!* represent different ways of accomplishing the function of greeting.

Languages are structured on several different levels, and each of these levels is subject to dialectal variation. These levels include PHONOLOGY, the sound system of a language; GRAMMAR, the formation of words and how words are combined into sentences; SEMANTICS, the meanings of words; and PRAGMATICS, the use of language forms to carry out particular communicative functions. We are not surprised to find dialect differences on all these levels; what is of greater interest are the specific differences that arise, the general principles that can account for these differences, and the various social meanings these differences are assigned in our society. In this chapter, we examine some dialect differences on each of these different levels and consider how these differences are viewed in American society.

3.1 Lexical Differences

As we discussed in the previous chapter, one of the most transparent levels of dialect variation is the lexicon, or vocabulary, of a language. Most of us can remember times when our failure to recognize a word used by some regional or social group resulted in confusion, if not outright communication breakdown.

We may have been surprised when we traveled through the United States and ordered *sodas*, only to find that we received different drinks under this label in different regions. Or we may have been surprised to discover that different people were referring to the same kind of animal when they talked about *mountain lions, cougars*, and sometimes even *panthers*. And many parents have shaken their heads in dismay when their teenagers issued a compliment using the latest descriptive adjective such as *bad, killer*, or *fresh*. Just about everyone has a collection of favorite anecdotes about lexical differences among the dialects of English, and dialect words from different regions or social groups are a common topic for conversation.

As we mentioned in chapter 2, there are a number of different ways in which lexical differences can manifest themselves. Because the relationship between a real-world object and the word used to describe it is essentially arbitrary, we often find that different labels are used to describe the same object (or idea) in different dialect areas. For example, *green beans* and *string beans* are simply different labels for the same vegetable, while *quilt* and *comforter*, as used by some speakers, refer to the same type of bed covering. We also find different words in different dialect areas because we find different objects and activities in different regions. Thus, people who live in coastal areas routinely use a host of marine-related terms (e.g. *nor'easter* and *peeler crab*) that those who live in inland areas may never have heard. The multitude of terms that arise in different dialect areas may spring from any of a number of word-formation processes. We have already mentioned in chapter 2 that new words may be completely made up, or COINED; in addition, they may be borrowed from other languages or created out of already existing words. Following in table 3.1 is a list of some of the ways in which new words can be created. These words may be associated with social groups or regional groups of various types, including groups who share a particular interest. A new word typically starts out with a restricted range of usage, and if it persists only among a regional or social subset of speakers, it becomes established as a dialect form. If it spreads across a wide range of English dialects, then it may become part of the English language as a whole. The examples in table 3.1 illustrate both broad-based and dialectally restricted items as developed through the different processes available for new word creation.

Not only do different dialects use different words, but they may use the same words with different meanings. Because meanings are usually rather vague, meanings may change over time in a number of ways. Dialect differences in word meaning result when a meaning changes in one way in a given dialect but some other way (or not at all) in other dialect areas. One common type of meaning change is for a word to BROADEN or NARROW in meaning. For example, when the word *barn* was brought from Britain to America, it was used to refer to a building that was used only for storing grain. Its meaning was gradually broadened so that it could be used to refer to a building for storing all sorts of

Table 3.1   Some of the ways in which new words can be created

Process	Definition	Examples
compounding	two or more existing words are combined to form a new word	*in-group*, *honeysuckle*, *breakwater*, *fatback*
acronyms	new words are formed by taking the initial sounds or letters from existing words	*radar* (radio detecting and range) *WASP* (White Anglo Saxon Protestant) *UN* (United Nations)
blending	parts of two words are combined to form a new word	*smog* (smoke/fog) *brunch* (breakfast/lunch) *sitcom* (situation/comedy) *broasted* (broiled/roasted)
clipping	words are formed by shortening existing words	*gas* (gasoline) *dorm* (dormitory) *'za* (pizza)
conversion	words are shifted from one part of speech to another without any change in their form	*run* (as a noun in "They scored a run") *tree* (as a verb in "They treed a cat") *breakwater* (as a verb in "Everything around the island is breakwatered.")
proper names	proper nouns, which refer to a specific person, place, or thing, are changed into common nouns, which refer to a general class of items	*sandwich*, *frigidaire*, *xerox*
borrowing	words from other languages are incorporated into the language or dialect	*chipmunk* (Ojibwa) *delicatessen* (German) *arroyo* (Spanish)
folk etymology	words are altered to make their meanings more transparent	*cold slaw* (from *cole slaw*), *old timers' disease* (from Alzheimer's disease)
back formation	shorter words are created from longer words based on the removal of what appears to be an affix but is in reality part of the original word	*burgle* from *burglar*, *orientate* from *orientation*
recutting	words are reanalyzed into component parts which differ from the original parts	*an apron* (from *a napron*), *-aholic*, as in *workaholic* (from *alcohol* + *ic*), *a whole nother* (from *an* + *other*)
derivation	words are created through the addition of a derivational affix	*bewitched* from *bewitch* + *ed*

farm-related items, including animals and even machinery. However, this broadening took place only in America, resulting in a dialect lexical difference between America and Britain; in Britain, *barn* still means a storage place for grain alone. Other broadenings which have occurred in the history of English affected such familiar words as *holiday* (originally 'holy day', a day of religious significance), *butcher* (originally, 'slaughterer of goats'), *companion* ('someone with whom you share bread'), *bird* ('young bird'), and *drive* ('to drive an animal'). And broadening still occurs today. One prominent case is the broadening of brand names, which originate as labels for products manufactured by one particular company but may develop into more general terms for certain types of products. Americans throughout the country use *kleenex* to refer to facial tissues of any type and *xerox* to refer to photocopying in general, no matter what brand of machine they use. On a more dialectally restricted level, speakers in the American South may refer to refrigerators as *frigidaires* or to all brands of dark-colored carbonated beverages as *Co-Colas*.

Narrowings are also commonplace, both historically and currently and on both a regional and national level. For example, the word *meat* once referred to food in general but now refers only to one type of food. Similarly, the word *deer* referred to any type of animal, and the word *girl* could once be used to refer to a child of either sex. As with broadenings, some narrowings affected American English but left British English untouched. For example, the word *corn* in Britain is still used to refer to any type of grain, while its meaning has narrowed to refer only to one specific type in America. In our studies of the dialect spoken in the Outer Banks islands of North Carolina, we have encountered some interesting narrowings which are highly regionally specific. On the island of Ocracoke, common nouns such as *creek* and *ditch* have narrowed into proper nouns. Thus, on Ocracoke, *The Creek* refers only to one specific body of water, while *The Ditch* refers only to the inlet which allows boats to enter *The Creek*.

Innumerable English words have narrowed or broadened in meaning over time, and this is an ongoing process. Some of these shifts end up correlating with specific regional and/or social groups and hence become dialect items. Others simply become part of the common stock of English words as their changing meanings spread among dialects.

Another type of change is MEANING SHIFT, or a change in the primary meaning of a word, often in the direction of one of the word's sub-meanings. One of the most noteworthy historical examples of meaning shift involves the word *bead*. Originally, this word meant 'prayer', but it came to refer to a particular type of jewelry because rosary beads were often worn in the Middle Ages while saying prayers. Other shifts include *knight* (originally, 'young person'), *nice* (originally, 'ignorant'), and even *pen* (from the Latin *penna* 'feather'). Some meaning shifts involve what is referred to as METAPHORICAL EXTENSION, or extending the use of a word so that it can refer to items which are very different from those originally referred to, based on a common meaning feature shared by the two classes of items. Thus, the term *submarine*, which literally refers to an underwater boat, has been metaphorically extended to apply to a type of sandwich which is similar in shape to the seagoing vessel. Similarly, the word *offshore*, which literally means 'located off the coast', can be used on Ocracoke Island to refer to people who are crazy or silly – that is, *outlandish* (another metaphorical extension of a similar nature). There are many instances of "new meanings for old words" across the dialects of English, although in many cases speakers may be completely unaware of the fact that the words they use in daily conversation originally had quite different meanings from what they do today.

Exercise 1

Following are some sets of lexical items which reflect the cross-dialectal vocabulary differences we find in the regional dialects of American English. For each set of words, first attempt to determine whether the different terms are the result of the broadening or narrowing of a general English word or of lexical innovation. If the word represents an innovation, which of the processes discussed above (e.g. compounding, borrowing, etc.) were used to create the word? Are there cases which seem to involve metaphorical extension?

1 baby's breath/chalkweed/mist 'a type of plant, gypsophila'
2 pail/bucket 'a container holding water'
3 baby buggy/baby carriage/baby coach 'a vehicle for transporting a baby'
4 earthworm/angleworm/fishing worm/night crawler 'a type of worm used in fishing'
5 faucet/spigot/tap 'a device with a valve for regulating the flow of a liquid'
6 creep/crawl 'what babies do before walking'
7 kerosene/coal oil/lamp oil 'a petroleum derivative'
8 lowland/low ground/bottom land/savannah 'land that usually has some standing water with trees or bushes growing on it'
9 armload/armful 'as much as can be carried with two hands together'
10 snap beans/string beans/green beans 'a type of vegetable with a stringy fiber on the pods'

The inventory of lexical differences among the dialects of American English covers a wide range of categories, and the number of dialectally sensitive words runs well into the thousands. In the questionnaire for eliciting items in the *Dictionary of American Regional English*, 41 different categories of lexical difference are outlined. Topography, food, furniture, animals, and equipment related to rural occupations lead the list, but the range of possible differences is virtually unlimited and encompasses many terms for physical and emotional states as well as those for concrete items.

In the preceding discussion, we focused on lexical differences in so-called CONTENT WORDS – words that refer to objects, ideas, events, or states in the real (or imagined) world. There are also differences pertaining to FUNCTION WORDS such as prepositions (e.g. *in, on, under*) and articles (e.g. *the, a/an*), items more likely to indicate grammatical information than semantic content. In many cases, differences in function words are confined to particular phrases. For example, different prepositions may be used in the phrase *sick to/at/in/on one's stomach* and *of/in the morning* (as in *We drink coffee of the morning*), while different articles may appear in a phrase such as *have a/the toothache*. In other cases, the difference involves the use or non-use of a function word in a particular type of construction. Thus, speakers in some dialect areas will say *She lives in Coal City* while others say *She lives __ Coal City*. Since content words far outnumber function words, dialect differences involving function words are not as common as those involving content words. However, some of the function word differences can be quite diagnostic in setting apart varieties.

In most instances, the kinds of lexical differences we have discussed above are considered to be regional curiosities, and little significance in terms of social status or personal worth is attached to them. Lexical differences do carry social associations on other dimensions, such as urban–rural or "modern"–"old-fashioned," but people are not usually socially stigmatized purely on the basis of saying *soda* versus *pop* or *garret* versus *attic*. An exception to this observation are TABOO WORDS, which are popularly known by such labels as "four-letter words," "swear words," or "curse words." These items certainly stigmatize their users in particular social situations, but in American society, these items are viewed more in terms of socially appropriate behavior than social group differentiation. Speakers of any social class or ethnic group may be considered ill-mannered if they use these terms in inappropriate circumstances, while the use of these terms by females traditionally has been considered inappropriate under *any* circumstances. All dialect groups recognize taboo terms, although the conventions for usage may differ to some extent from group to group, as may the classification of particular terms as taboo items. For example, the use of *bloody* as an intensifier (e.g. *Where's the bloody car?*) is considered acceptable if odd in American English but is quite offensive to British English ears, while the word *tits* to refer to female breasts is not nearly as unacceptable in some rural American dialects as it is in non-rural dialects.

Some sets of vocabulary items are associated with groups who share a particular interest rather than with regional or sociocultural groups of speakers.

These interests may range from technical or academic fields such as computer programming or linguistics to recreational activities like football or popular music. Any novice computer user who is looking for *user-friendly documentation* on how to *surf the net* using the latest *web-browser* is well aware of the specialized vocabulary that has grown up around computer technology. It is not unusual for a beginning computer user to confront so many technical terms in a single sentence as to make it practically incomprehensible. By the same token, a casual observer of a Sunday afternoon football game may be told that "The Giants' *nickel defense sacked* the Cowboys' *quarterback* in the *shotgun formation* with an all-out *blitz*." Such specialized vocabularies, or JARGONS, cut across all types of social groups and arise via the same processes of word formation and meaning change that give rise to regional, social class, ethnic, and gender-based lexical differences. In popular culture, the term "jargon" is sometimes used by confused or annoyed observers to refer to vocabulary which seems to be purposely obscure. However, what may be incomprehensible "mumbo-jumbo" to outsiders may simply be a necessity for precise, detailed communications among those who are heavily involved in a specific field.

A more deliberately secretive jargon, such as a special vocabulary used by criminals, is referred to as an ARGOT. Some dialectologists and lexicologists have become outstanding specialists in the vocabulary of various "underworld" groups, although there are certainly special fieldwork problems associated with the investigation of such speech communities.

3.2   Slang

SLANG is one of those labels that gives dialectologists fits. In popular culture, the label is used freely to refer to everything from the general use of a ver-nacular dialect (e.g. "They don't speak Standard English; they speak slang") to specialized vocabulary words that are technically considered jargon (e.g. "Computer people use a lot of slang") to individual words that are socially stigmatized (e.g. "*Ain't* is a slang word"). The rather loose, imprecise way the term *slang* is often popularly used has caused many dialectologists to shy away from using this label at all. As one dialectologist put it, "Until slang can be objectively identified and segregated or until more precise subcategories re-place the catchall label SLANG, little can be done to analyze this kind of lexis" (McMillan 1978:146). The *Dictionary of American Regional English* explicitly rejects the use of this label because it is "imprecise" and "too indefinite" (Cassidy 1985:xvii). At the same time, some dictionary-makers, or LEXICOGRAPHERS, do employ the term to mark dictionary entries, with varying degrees of reliability among them. In addition, there exist special dictionaries devoted to slang, such as the *Historical Dictionary of American Slang* (Lighter 1994).

From a strictly linguistic standpoint, words are words, and those that are labeled as slang are not unique in terms of the processes by which they are formed or the ways in which their meanings come about. From the perspective of language as a kind of social behavior, however, there is a group of words labeled "slang" that have a special status in American culture, even though we can't come up with *the* definitive list or with a single linguistic criterion for distinguishing these items from non-slang terms. What distinguishes items classified as "slang" is their sociopsychological role rather than their linguistic composition. The notion of relegating some words to this special status has been around a long time (over 2,000 years, according to some records). Sociolinguists and psycholinguists can hardly afford to continue dismissing this category of items on the basis of a lack of precision in its characterization. In recent years, several dialectologists have devoted themselves to the careful examination of slang, and our discussion here follows closely the contributions of Bethany K. Dumas and Jonathan Lighter (1976) and Connie Eble (1989, 1996).

Part of the problem with defining slang comes from the fact that terms appear to be classified as slang based on a *set* of characteristics rather than a single attribute. Furthermore, slang terms appear to be arranged along a "slang scale," so that some items are considered to be more "slangy" than others. Just about everybody would agree that a term like *clueless* for 'ignorant, oblivious' is a slang item and that *unaware* is not, but a term like *dense* seems to fall between the extremes. A realistic definition of slang should take into account the gradient nature of "slanginess," along with the understanding that some terms are firmly situated at one end of the slang scale or the other – that is, they are unquestionably considered to be true slang terms or genuine non-slang items by all listeners and users.

One of the prerequisite features of slang items is their connotation of informality. Granted that formality and informality are not always easy to define in themselves, there are some social situations that are fairly readily identified as formal or informal. In situations that we intuitively feel are informal, we find that formal words simply sound "wrong" or incongruous, while the opposite is true in situations we consider to be formal. Slang items are always found at the informal end of the continuum. A person who is rather slow-witted or comparatively oblivious to his or her surroundings might be described variously as *incognizant, unenlightened, unaware, blind, dense, clueless,* or *spacey,* but the conversational occasions considered appropriate for these different items differ drastically. Imagine how a student would feel if he or she walked out of a meeting with an academic advisor who had just accused him or her of "spacing" on a major exam – or how a teenager would feel if her or his best friend referred to a rather obtuse acquaintance as "incognizant" or "unwitting" during a lunchtime conversation. In each case, the terms used would be considered inappropriate because slang terms such as *spacing* are reserved for informal occasions while formal terms such as *incognizant* are more appropriate for use on formal, serious occasions than in casual conversation among peers. To begin with, then, words classified as slang carry strong informal overtones.

Another attribute of slang items is their potential for indicating a special familiarity with a group outside of the mainstream adult population. An item like *clueless* is not only marked as informal, it is also associated with speakers who fall within a relatively narrow age range and who are considered to be "less responsible" than the adult members of society. Similarly, terms associated with minority ethnic groups might be labeled slang, such as the term *brother* or *sister* as used by African Americans with a special in-group meaning to refer to other African Americans (e.g. *He's a brother*). Words associated with social groups outside of the mainstream have a high likelihood of being labeled slang, and items that are associated with localized peer-group identity are almost always considered slang. Slang items are often cultivated in the context of close-knit peer groups, and the idea that the particular use of a term might be mysterious or secretive may make it even more appealing as a symbol of in-group membership. This is one reason why teenagers and college students, with their emphasis on peer-group relationships, are often the primary source of new slang terms. That adults and people in other locales are totally unfamiliar with these terms is hardly a problem – in fact, a group of teenagers may revel in the restricted sphere of usage of their terms. Not all items classified as slang have strong group identity associations, but many of the more extreme cases on the "slang continuum" do.

Another attribute of slang relates to its role as a special kind of synonym. Slang terms typically have well-known, neutral, conventional synonyms. English speakers who use *kick the bucket* for 'die', *toasted* for 'drunk', or *bumpin'* for 'good' know that in each case there is a ready alternate term but choose not to use it. Psychologically, or, more properly, psycholinguistically, the slang term is thus viewed as an intentional replacement, or a "flouting," of the conventional, more neutral term. Listeners presume that a person who uses *clueless* is deliberately choosing not to use a neutral, conventional term such as *unaware* and that a speaker who uses *barf, puke, ralph, yak*, or *worship the porcelain goddess* instead of *regurgitate, vomit*, or *throw up* is making a deliberate choice as well. It is not necessarily the case that every single item which is considered to be slang is associated with a synonymous item of more neutral connotations, but most items with the slang label are considered to be intentional replacements of more ordinary terms.

Finally, we should observe that slang items are often perceived as having a short life span. Certainly, some slang items are short-lived, particularly those associated with local peer groups. But many items have considerable staying power. For example, *dough* for 'money', *cram* for 'study intensely for a short period of time', *smooth* for 'excellent', and *flunk* for 'fail' have been around since at least the turn of the twentieth century – longer than some terms which have been incorporated as conventional words of English. Nonetheless, in popular culture, slang items tend to be viewed as ephemeral, and the (mis)perception that a given term is brand new and destined to be short-lived may actually contribute to its being classified as slang in the first place. Of course, many slang terms lose their connotations of "slanginess" once they have been in use for some time, while many others vanish from use altogether. However, some items have persisted as slang terms for quite a long time and show no signs of fading out of use or becoming part of mainstream English. It is impossible to predict which of today's slang words will become part of the lexical stock of mainstream English, which will die, and which will remain "slangy" for years to come. Only time will tell if an item like *clueless* will catch on and become a stable part of the language or whether it will fall by the wayside along with other short-lived slang items.

The definition of slang which we have presented may seem somewhat imprecise, particularly if we are looking for a single criterion for definitively separating slang from non-slang items. However, we have to keep in mind that slang tends to exist on a continuum and that, to some extent, one person's slang may be another person's conventional lexical item. Some items, characterized by extremes in terms of the attributes mentioned above, are considered slang by virtually all English speakers, while others, which possess some but not all of these attributes, are of more indeterminate status. So far, we have yet to find a native speaker of American English who does not consider items like *rad* ('excellent') or *bumpin'* slang, but there is much more latitude in the classification of other items, such as *rip off* for 'steal' or *buck* for 'money'. The items *rad* and *bumpin'* are closely associated with teenage peer-group usage in informal settings, and no one expects them to be around very long. On the other hand, a term like *rip off* for 'steal' is relatively informal but not as informal as an item like *barf*, and *rip off* is now used in some relatively neutral contexts. Furthermore, *rip off* has been around for quite a while, and any connotations of in-group identity which it might have had are rapidly fading. Situated between slang and conventional lexical items on the "slang scale" are items that are sometimes referred to as COLLOQUIAL – that is, items that share the attribute of informality with slang but are not closely associated with in-group identity or with flouted synonymy.

Exercise 2

Part One

Rate the following items in terms of how strongly you feel that each constitutes a "slang" item. Use a three-point scale, where 3 is the highest (you have a strong feeling that the item is slang) and 1 is the lowest (you don't believe that the item is slang). For example, an item like *rad* for 'excellent' might be given a rating of 3 while *great* would be given a 1.

1   chicken 'afraid'
2   zilch 'nothing'
3   buck 'dollar'
4   get it 'understand'
5   frisk 'search'
6   jerk 'undesirable person'
7   awesome 'good'
8   neat 'good'
9   bumpin' 'good'
10   cool 'good'

Part Two

With your ratings of the above words in hand, now rate each item in terms of the four attributes given below. Rate items for each attribute, using a scale of 1 to 3, with 3 indicating that an item possesses an attribute to a high degree and 1 indicating the possession of the attribute to a low degree or the complete absence of the attribute. For example, a rating of 1 for informality would indicate that an item is not informal, a rating of 2 indicates that it is somewhat informal, and a rating of 3 indicates that it is quite informal. In this rating scheme, *clueless* would receive a 3 for informality, 2 or 3 for group identity, 3 for its association with neutral synonyms, and 2 or 3 for anticipated life span.

Attributes	*Score*		
Informality	1	2	3
	(neutral)	(informal)	(very informal)
Group identity	1	2	3
	(none)	(limited)	(strong)
Association with neutral	1	2	3
synonyms	(weak)	(moderate)	(strong)
Anticipated life span	1	2	3
	(long)	(medium)	(short)

Add the scores from the attribute scale for each item, so that all items have a cumulative rating between 4 and 12. At this point, you have two scores, one for the overall rating of each item and one based on cumulative attributes. Now compare the two scores with each other. Do you see a correlation between the ratings? Do the words you rated as 3 in Part One have high ratings for each individual attribute? If not, are there any attributes that seem to contribute less to the overall identification of an item as slang than others? Which ones seem less critical in defining slang?

3.3 Phonological Differences

Like lexical differences, phonological variation among the dialects of English can be highly noticeable. When most people use the word *accent*, they are focusing mostly on pronunciation differences; and listeners are quick to hone in on the distinctive vowel sounds associated with "the Southern drawl," the "broad *a*" and "dropped *r*" of Boston speech, or the "dropped *g*" of vernacular dialects across the country. At the same time, some differences in phonology may be quite subtle and may not be noticeable to casual observers – or even to the speakers who use them – although they still serve to set apart different dialects. Phonological patterns can be diagnostic of regional and social differences, and a person who has a good ear for dialects can often pinpoint a speaker's general regional and social affiliation with considerable accuracy based solely on phonology. Certainly, the use of a few critical pronunciation cues can narrow down a person's place of origin to at least a general region of the United States, if not to the precise county of origin.

There are several ways in which phonological differences may be manifested in the dialects of American English. One of the most striking differences involves the pronunciation of various vowel sounds. As discussed in chapter 2, it is quite possible for a sound to be pronounced in a number of different ways but still be considered a single meaningful sound or phoneme. Thus, *p* may be produced as [p] or [pʰ] in English, but both versions, or VARIANTS, are considered to represent the phoneme /p/. Even more variation is possible within vowel phonemes. For example, most varieties of English have a vowel phoneme represented as /ɔ/, as in *bought*, *cough*, and *raw*, but the way this phoneme is produced varies widely. In some regions, it may sound similar to the vowel in *book* and *look* (phonetically [ʊ]), while in others it sounds like the vowel in *father* or *cot* (phonetically [a]). Similarly, the phoneme /æ/, as in *bag* and *bad*, may sound somewhat similar to the vowel in *bit* or *rip* or, once again, like the vowel of *father* or *cot*.

As we discussed in chapter 2, a pronunciation difference in one vowel often sets off a whole string of pronunciation changes in related vowel sounds, resulting in a wholesale vowel shift or CHAIN SHIFT. In order to investigate vowel shifts in more detail, we need to understand how various vowels are produced in the mouth. Vowels are differentiated from one another along several dimensions: the height of the tongue in the mouth when the vowel is produced, how far forward or backward the tongue is, how much muscle tension is involved, and whether or not the lips are rounded during the production of the vowel. We can obtain a convenient picture of where the tongue is positioned during the production of various vowels by drawing a chart in which the roof of the mouth is located along the top, the front of the mouth on the lefthand side, and the back of the mouth on the right. The result is a chart such as that in

High vowels

---

[i] (*beet*)   [u] (*boot*)

    [ɪ] (*bit*)   [ʊ] (*put*)

      [e] (*bait*)   [ə] (*about*)   [o] (*boat*)

Front vowels   [ɛ] (*bet*)   [ʌ] (*but*)   **Back vowels**

      [æ] (*bat*)   [ɔ] (*bought*)

        [a] (*father*)

Low vowels

Figure 3.1   A chart of American English vowels according to tongue position.

figure 3.1. Note that the chart is not drawn as a square because the space in our mouths is more trapezoidal in nature.

Figure 3.1 indicates that each vowel has its own "space," referred to as PHONETIC SPACE, within the vowel trapezoid. The notion of phonetic space is important because the shift of one vowel in phonetic space often has an effect on adjacent vowels. As one vowel moves phonetically closer to a nearby vowel (e.g. [æ] may move forward and upward, into the "territory" of [ɛ]), the latter vowel may shift its phonetic value to ensure that the two vowels remain phonetically distinct enough to make meaningful distinctions in words – that is, to ensure that the two vowels remain distinct phonemes. This second movement may trigger the movement of a third vowel, and thus a whole sequence of movements may be set in motion. For example, there are currently some dialects of American English in which the lowering and fronting of [ɔ], as in *caught*, to [a] (so that *caught* sounds like *cot*) has triggered the fronting of [a] to near [æ], so that *lock* sounds almost like *lack*. This shift in turn is causing /æ/-words to sound more like /ɛ/- or even /e/-words, so that words such as *bag* and *bad* may sound something like *beg* and *bed* (or even *bade*). This vowel movement or ROTATION, illustrated in figure 3.2 below, is part of a vowel shift pattern currently taking place in the Northern US, particularly in large cities such as Chicago, Detroit, and Buffalo. We will discuss this shift in more detail in chapter 5, as well as a couple of other important vowel shifts which are currently taking place in American English dialects.

Chain shifting has also played a large part in the historical development of English. In fact, if it weren't for a major chain shift which took place from around 1450 to 1650, today's English would sound more like the English of

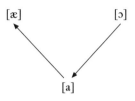

Figure 3.2 An illustration of chain shifting in the low vowels of American English.

Chaucer's time than the English we are used to hearing today. For example, words with "i" vowels (as in *time*) would be pronounced with "ee" sounds (phonetically [i]), as they were in Middle English (and as they still are in a number of continental European languages); words with "ee" spellings would be pronounced with [e] rather than [i] (thus, *meet* would sound like *mate*); while words with "ou" (as in *house*) would be pronounced with [u] (as in *hoos* for *house*). In fact, we can still hear some of these old pronunciations in some dialect areas in the British Isles; for example, some Scots English speakers may say *hoos* for *house* or *neet* for *night*.

There are several English vowel sounds which we haven't included in the chart in figure 3.1: /ay/ as in *time*, /aw/ as in *down*, and /ɔy/ as in *boy*. These sounds, called DIPHTHONGS, are each made up of two different vowel sounds and are pronounced by gliding from one sound into the other. The /ay/ diphthong is produced by gliding from [a] as in *father* to [i] or [ɪ], as in *beet* or *bit*; /aw/ is produced by gliding from [a] to [u] or [ʊ], as in *boot* or *put*; and /ɔy/ is produced by gliding from [ɔ] as in *bought* to [i] or [ɪ]. In each case, the first element of the diphthong is called the NUCLEUS, since it is the primary part of the vowel, and the second element is called the GLIDE, since speakers glide up to this vowel in producing the diphthong. Not all speakers of American English pronounce these three diphthongs exactly as we have just described; in fact, differences in diphthongs can be highly salient in terms of delimiting the different dialects of the US.

Of particular importance in this regard is the /ay/ vowel. Regional pronunciations of the /ay/ vowel are often highly noticeable to speakers from outside the region as well as to speakers who use the pronunciations themselves. For example, Southern Americans are perhaps more well known for their pronunciation of /ay/ as [a], as in *tahm* for 'time', than for any other dialect feature, while residents of the Outer Banks islands off the coast of North Carolina are so well known for their production of /ay/ as something like an [ɔɪ], as in *toid* for 'tide', that they are often called – and call themselves –"hoi toiders" for "high tiders." The pronunciation change affecting /ay/ in Southern speech is referred to as MONOPHTHONGIZATION, since speakers who say [ta:m] for [taɪm] have taken the /ay/ diphthong – a two-part vowel – and turned it into a monophthong, or one-part vowel, by leaving off the [i] glide. The /ɔy/

diphthong may also be monophthongized in Southern varieties, as in [bɔːl] for 'boil', and /aw/ may be subjected to the same fate as well. In the Outer Banks, the distinctive /ay/ sound is not due to monophthongization but rather to using a vowel other than [a] as the nucleus of the diphthong – in this case a vowel which is closer to the [ɔ] of *caught* (but not quite this vowel) than the [a] of *father*.

Outer Bankers are also known for an unusual /aw/ sound, which is characterized by a nucleus which may be more like [æ] or [ɛ] than [a] and a glide which may sound like [ɪ] rather than [ʊ]. Thus, we may hear pronunciations such as *hace* [hɛɪs] or *hice* [haɪs] for 'house' as well as *dane* [dɛɪn] or *dine* [daɪn] for 'down'. In other dialect areas, such as Philadelphia, /aw/ may be pronounced with an [æ] nucleus rather than an [a] (e.g. [dæʊn] 'down'), while in an area such as Tidewater Virginia (and in many parts of Canada), /aw/ is pronounced with an "uh" ([ʌ]) nucleus, so that a phrase such as "out and about" may come out sounding more like "oat and a-boat," at least to the casual observer.

Sometimes, when a vowel moves into the phonetic space of another vowel, the tendency to preserve distinctiveness does not come into play and the two vowels simply share the same phonetic space. When this happens, the distinctiveness between the two vowels is lost, and we say that a MERGER has occurred. Such mergers may take place in certain regions or among certain social groups but not in others and so may lead to dialect differences. One of the most noticeable and most widespread mergers currently taking place in American English dialects is the merger of /ɔ/ and /a/, so that the vowels in word pairs such as *caught/cot*, *hawk/hock*, and *Dawn/Don* now sound alike. As we will discuss in chapter 5, the area affected by this merger is quite large and is growing rapidly, spreading from centers such as western Pennsylvania to encompass a vast portion of the American west. This merger is so commonplace that it may soon be considered part of mainstream or "standard" English rather than a mere regional variation. In fact, the second author of this book was surprised to find that a group of college students she was teaching refused to believe that [ɔ] and [a] are two different vowels in English. Apparently, these students had never even heard the vowels pronounced differently, let alone produced them that way themselves.

In many instances, a merger only takes place in restricted phonetic contexts. Sounds are highly sensitive to their phonetic context, including the sounds they occur next to, the positions they occupy in words, and whether or not they occur in accented, or stressed, syllables. It is quite common for a merger to take place in one phonetic context but not in another. In one well-known case (which happens to be highly socially stigmatized), the vowels of *bit* [ɪ] and *bet* [ɛ] are merged, but only when the following segment is a nasal sound such as [n]. Thus, in many Southern American dialects, there is no contrast between items such as *pin* and *pen* (both are usually pronounced as [pɪn]) or *tinder* and *tender.* In these same dialects, the vowels of *pit* [pɪt] and *pet* [pɛt] actually remain distinct, even though caricatures of Southern speech by outsiders may erroneously depict all [ɪ]'s and [ɛ]'s as sounding the same. Similarly, speakers of many Northern dialects do not distinguish between *morning* and *mourning*, and others do not distinguish between *sure* and *shore*. In these cases the critical phonetic environment for the merger, or neutralization of contrast, is the following [r]. Other mergers are not confined solely to one particular phonetic context but are nonetheless more likely to occur in one environment than in other places. For example, the merger, or near-merger, of the [ɪ] of *pill* with the [i] of *peel* in Southern American English is more likely to take place before [l] than in most other contexts. Similarly, the merger of the [u] in *fool* with the [ʊ] of *full* which is affecting some Northern and Southwestern varieties is also more likely before [l] than other sounds. In American English, vowels that are followed by nasal sounds such as [m] and [n] and liquid sounds such as [r] and [l] are more likely to undergo changes and be subjected to mergers than vowels in other phonetic environments. Following is a list of some mergers which currently characterize several varieties of American English:

Mergers in American English dialects
- /ɔ/ and /a/, as in *Dawn* and *Don* (Western Pennsylvania, gradually fanning out to encompass much of the Western US)
- /i/ and /ɪ/, as in *field* and *filled* (Texas and the South)
- /e/ and /ɛ/ before /l/, as in *sale* and *sell* (Texas and the South)
- /u/ and /ʊ/, as in *pool* and *pull* (Texas and the South)
- /e/, /ɛ/, /æ/, /ʌ/ before /r/, as in *Mary, merry, marry, Murray*
- /ɪ/ and /ɛ/ before nasals, as in *pin* and *pen* (South)

Exercise 3

One of the interesting cases of vowel merger before [r] involves the vowels of the words *merry, Mary, marry,* and *Murray,* or *berry, beary* (acting like a bear), *Barry,* and *bury.* Ask several people who come from different regions of the country to pronounce these items and observe which items are pronounced the same and which are pronounced differently. What patterns of merger and distinction do you observe? What other sets of items fall into this general pattern? Can you identify any correlation between dialect region and the patterns of merger and non-merger in the speech of those you question?

There are also cases in which differences between consonants may be eliminated, or NEUTRALIZED. One classic case of neutralization is so-called "*g*-dropping." When the nasal segment represented phonetically as [ŋ] (often spelled "ng") occurs at the end of a word in an unstressed syllable (as in *fighting*) it can be produced as the sound [n] (*fightin'*). This process makes the final nasal segment of *taken* [tekɪn] and *takin'* [tekin] or *waken* [wekɪn] and *wakin'* [wekɪn] phonetically the same. Unfortunately, the popular term "*g*-dropping" to describe this process is somewhat misleading, since the process really involves the substitution of one nasal sound for another rather than the loss of a sound.

In many Southern dialects, the [z] and [ð] sounds in words such as *wasn't* and *heathen* become [d] before nasal sounds, resulting in pronunciations such as *wadn't* and *headn*. Thus, we can say that the contrast between [z] and [ð] is neutralized before nasals in these varieties. And, of course, there is the stereotypical *dese*, *dem*, and *dose* for *these*, *them*, and *those*, in which [d] and [ð] are neutralized word-initially, as well as the neutralization in some vernacular dialects of [f] and [θ] in word-final position, as in *roof* for 'Ruth'. While there are a number of cases of neutralization across dialects, the phonetic contexts in which these processes occur are usually highly restricted. The limited nature of most cases of neutralization is due to the fact that neutralization is often the result of how sounds are pronounced when they occur next to each other rather than to how sounds are organized into systems. Thus, as we discussed in chapter 2, the neutralization of [z] and [ð] before [n] in Southern American English has nothing to do with a "shift" in which [z] and [ð] move into the phonetic territory occupied by [d]. Rather, it has to do with the fact that it is more natural to pronounce two "stop" consonants in sequence – that is, two consonants in which airflow is completely stopped in the mouth for a split second – than to pronounce a sound in which air is not completely stopped before a stop consonant. Both [d] and [n] are stop consonants in that airflow through the mouth is cut off in the production of these sounds. However, [z] and [ð] are what we refer to as FRICATIVES – that is, consonants in which air is not completely blocked in the mouth during the production of the sound.

The kinds of differences illustrated so far all concern instances in which a sound in one dialect corresponds to a different sound in another variety. As we discussed in chapter 2, there are also instances where sounds are added or deleted, affecting the basic sequencing of sound segments. As with most cases of neutralization, the addition and deletion of sounds has to do with how sounds are pronounced when they occur in a particular sequence or with the arrangement of sounds into syllables rather than with overall changes in the organization of sound systems. Thus, addition and deletion processes tend to be restricted to certain phonetic contexts as well. For example, there are a number of dialects in which [r] and [l] may be deleted, as in *ca'd* [kad] for 'card' or *he'p* [hɛp] for 'help'. However, this deletion occurs only when the [r] or [l] follows a vowel; further, [l] is fully deleted only when it follows a vowel and precedes a LABIAL consonant – that is, one which is articulated using the lips, such as [p] or [f], as in *he'p* (hɛp) for 'help' or *woof* [wʊf] for 'wolf'. In other pre-vocalic environments (e.g. *cold*), [l] is likely to be weakened, or pronounced in a more vowel-like way, but it will not be completely absent. Deletion may also be contingent upon where a particular sound occurs in a word or whether the sound occurs in a stressed or unstressed syllable. For example, the deletion of the [w] sound of the word *one* in a phrase such as *young 'uns* 'young ones' or *second 'un* 'second one' is contingent upon the [w] being in word-initial, unstressed position.

Other cases of deletion have to do with how sounds are arranged into syllables. As discussed in chapter 2, it is not very "natural" for syllables to contain groups or clusters of consonants, and so these clusters tend to get reduced. Thus, speakers of practically all varieties of American English tend to reduce the final consonant clusters in words such as *west* [st], *find* [nd], *act* [kt], or *cold* [ld] to a single consonant, as in *wes'* [s], *fin'* [n], *ac'* [k], and *col'* [l] – particularly when speaking in informal style. Speakers of relatively standard varieties tend to restrict this process to instances in which the word following the cluster begins with a consonant (e.g. *Wes' Point, col' cuts*). On the other hand, speakers of some vernacular dialects may reduce the cluster regardless of the following segment (e.g. *Wes' End, col' outside*).

In another process relating to the sequencing of syllables, unstressed syllables at the beginning of words may be deleted, resulting in such pronunciations as *'lectricity* for 'electricity' or *'member* for 'remember'. There are also cases in which the number of syllables in words differs across dialects because of the deletion or insertion of vowels within the word. *Tire* and *fire* are two-syllable sequences in some dialects (i.e. [taɪ.ɚ], [faɪ.ɚ]) but single syllables in others. For example, in a number of Southern varieties, these words may be pronounced as *tar* and *far*. Similarly, an item like *baloney* consists of three syllables for most English speakers (*ba-lo-ney*) but only two syllables for some other speakers (*blo-ney*).

As mentioned above, one of the most important differences between Southern and non-Southern dialects involves the absence of the [i] glide on the /ay/ diphthong, so that words like *ride* and *time* are pronounced as *rahd* [ra:d] and *tahm* [ta:m] in Southern American varieties. Conversely, Southern American English is also distinguished from other varieties by the addition of a glide to some vowels which are not typically glided in non-Southern varieties. In some cases, the addition of this glide actually leads to changes in syllable structure. In most non-Southern varieties, words such as *bed* and *Bill* are clearly monosyllabic. However, in some Southern dialects, the vowels in these words are given such a prominent glide that the words sound almost like two-syllable sequences, as in *beyud* [bɛyəd] for 'bed' and *Biyul* [biyʊl] for 'Bill'. According to some researchers, the diphthongization, or BREAKING, of monophthongal vowels is actually becoming more prominent in Southern varieties at the same time it continues to be absent from non-Southern dialects (e.g. Feagin 1987).

Thus, despite the popular belief that American dialects are becoming increasingly alike due to mass media and other forms of intercommunication, we see that Southern varieties are actually becoming more distinct from other dialects in their production of various vowel sounds.

Finally, we should mention the potential for pronunciation differences that have to do with such matters as the intonational contours of sentences, the stress patterns of words, and the timing of syllables. These differences are referred to as SUPRASEGMENTAL or PROSODIC differences, since they involve overarching "melodic" considerations rather than individual sound segments and their arrangement into syllables. Although prosodic differences have been studied in far less detail than segmental differences, they have been shown to occur across the dialects of American English. For example, a study of intonational contours conducted a couple of decades ago (Tarone 1973) indicated that speakers of African American Vernacular English use a wider range of intonation than speakers of other US varieties. Similarly, it has been noted that some women tend to exhibit a wider pitch range than men and that women have an extra-high pitch range not typically found among men (Brend 1975).

Variations in the stress patterns of words, mostly related to individual lexical items, also serve to separate the dialects of American English. For example, depending on what regional dialect they speak, speakers may stress either the first or second syllable in items such as *júly/ julý*, *hótel/ hotél*, and *théater/ theáter*. Speakers may also give different rhythmic patterns to syllables and phrases according to what dialect they speak. For example, Spanish-influenced varieties of American English are often characterized by what is referred to as "syllable-timed rhythm," where each syllable in a phrase such as *in the garden* is pronounced with equal length. On the other hand, speakers of most other American English dialects tend to have "phrase-timed rhythm," in which syllables which are more strongly stressed (e.g. the first syllable of *gárden*) are held longer than other syllables in the phrase.

There are also varieties which exhibit a generalized lengthening of syllables. For example, evidence indicates that speakers of Southern American varieties tend to prolong vowel sounds for a slightly longer time than speakers of other varieties. This difference in vowel duration may be partly responsible for the popular perception that Southerners speak "slower" than most non-Southerners. However, we have to keep in mind that not all Southerners speak slower than all non-Southerners; in fact, there are some Southerners who speak faster than non-Southerners. Further, the subtle speech-rate differences that do exist between Southern and non-Southern varieties are often exaggerated in popular characterizations of Southern speech, most likely because speakers of Southern American English are often stigmatized as "dumb" and "uneducated" and thus "slower" than speakers of non-Southern varieties. Although speech-rate features are often assigned great importance among casual observers of language variation, dialectologists have found that such differences do not appear to be nearly as major as they are made out to be and so do not tend to focus much attention on this type of dialect variation.

Although there may be some social stigma attached to certain pronunciation differences, phonological dialect differences, particularly vowel differences, are usually considered to be matters of curiosity rather than grounds for condemnation. Speakers may comment on the *o* of Wisconsin speech or the "broad *a*" of Boston as regional peculiarities without attaching particular social stigma or prestige to them. Consonantal differences are more apt to be socially diagnostic than vowel differences and may even lead to the stigmatization of speakers as "stupid" or "uneducated," as in the case of *dese*, *dem*, and *dose* for 'these', 'them', and 'those'; *baf* for 'bath'; and *takin'* for 'taking'. While phonological differences may be of relatively little importance in terms of social prestige, they do play a central role in terms of regional identity. Thus, Southerners are more readily identified as Southerners by their /ay/ vowels than by any other single dialect feature, and Southerners themselves have come to take pride in their distinctive pronunciations as a badge of their unique regional identity and cultural heritage.

In terms of the principles governing the organization of language systems, it is difficult to explain why certain pronunciation changes take place in some regions or among some social groups and why other changes take place elsewhere. For example, it is hard to explain why speakers on the North Carolina mainland say *tahd* for 'tide' while those on the Outer Banks say *toid*. However, once a given pronunciation takes hold, it may persist for quite a long time as a symbolic marker of regional or social group identity.

3.4 Grammatical Differences

Grammatical variation may be discussed in terms of two basic levels of organization. One level, called MORPHOLOGY, relates to the way in which words are formed from their meaningful parts, or MORPHEMES. A word such as *girls* consists of two morphemes, the noun *girl* and the plural suffix -*s*; a word such as *buyers* consists of three morphemes, the verb *buy*, the agentive suffix -*er*, which changes a verb into a noun, and the plural suffix -*s*. Suffixes such as -*er*, which change the part of speech, or grammatical class, of the word to which it attaches, are referred to as DERIVATIONAL suffixes. Endings such as the plural -*s* which do not alter the basic grammatical class and which serve to augment rather than change meaning are referred to as INFLECTIONAL suffixes. English has a relatively small set of inflectional suffixes, consisting solely of plural -*s*, (e.g. *girls*, *houses*), possessive -*s* (e.g. *John's hat*, *the girl's hat*), third person present tense -*s* (e.g. *She runs*), past tense -*ed* (e.g. *John guessed*), participle -*ed* (e.g. *He has helped*), progressive -*ing* (e.g. *He is running*), and the comparative and superlative endings -*er* and -*est* (e.g. *smaller*, *smallest*).

Inflectional morphemes in English are susceptible to language variation in two ways, both of which make perfect sense in terms of the principles of language organization discussed in chapter 2, particularly the principle which states that language patterns should be as regular and straightforward as possible. In some cases, this principle leads to the loss of inflectional morphemes, whereas in other cases, it leads to the creation of different inflectional morphemes. For example, some vernacular varieties, such as African American Vernacular English, are characterized by the loss of the third person singular -*s* suffix (e.g. *She run* vs. *She runs*). This loss is the result of regularization: The third person singular verb form is the only one which takes any suffix at all in the present tense; if we eliminate this -*s* ending, then all present tense verbs now have exactly the same form, no matter what subject we use them with (except *to be*, which is more irregular than other verbs). This regularization is illustrated below:

Standard English		*Vernacular variety*	
I run	we run	I run	we run
you run	you (pl.) run	you run	you (pl.) run
he/she/it runs	they run	he run	they run

African American Vernacular English also exhibits the absence of the -*s* possessive ending, as in *John hat* vs. *John's hat*. In this case, the ending has been lost because, in essence, it is a redundant marker which is not really needed. The positioning of *John* and *hat* is sufficient to indicate that *John* stands in a possessive relationship to *hat*. Similarly, in some Anglo-American Southern varieties, the plural -*s* ending may be absent from nouns indicating weights and measures (e.g. *Go about four mile up the road*) but only when the plural noun is preceded by a specific number, since this number serves as a clear marker that the following noun is plural, thus making the -*s* ending superfluous.

Making language forms as regular and straightforward as possible also sometimes leads to the addition of inflectional endings. For example, in order to regularize the irregular person-number set, or paradigm, of possessive pronouns (*mine, yours, hers/his/its, ours, yours, theirs*), speakers of vernacular dialects may add various sorts of inflectional endings to some of the pronoun forms, as illustrated below:

Standard English		*Vernacular variety I*		*Vernacular variety II*	
mine	ours	mines	ours	mine	ourn
yours	yours (pl.)	yours	yours	yourn	yourn
hers/his/its	theirs	hers/his	theirs	hern/hisn	theirn

Finally, regularization may lead to the use of different inflectional markers in different dialects rather than to the differential presence or absence of such markers. For example, the irregular plural ending -*en* on *oxen* may be regularized to -*es* in vernacular varieties, while irregular past tense verbs may be marked with the regular *-ed* suffix (e.g. *throwed* vs. *threw*) rather than by a vowel difference as in standard varieties.

Morphological differences which are due to regularization are among the most socially diagnostic structures in American English, and listeners draw sharp distinctions between vernacular and standard speaking groups on the basis of the use or non-use of regularized morphological forms. In part, the prominence of regularized morphological forms may be attributed to the fact that all speakers have a strong tendency to regularize irregular forms. This tendency can be resisted only by paying special attention to the irregular forms, which must be learned by rote since they are not as linguistically "natural" as regularized forms. This focused attention on learning these forms subsequently makes them sensitive to social marking. In other words, because speakers of standard varieties may have struggled to learn irregular forms such as *oxen* and *thought* during their school years, they will be quick to notice when regularized forms are used and just as quick to stigmatize speakers who use them. However, as we have mentioned a number of times, regularized morphological forms are the result of highly natural linguistic processes and actually lead to language patterns which are more neatly structured, from a strictly linguistic viewpoint, than their standard, irregular counterparts.

Furthermore, we have to keep in mind that not all vernacular word-formation processes are the result of regularization or simplification. As we will recall from chapter 2, there is a tendency to mark forms as clearly as possible so that listeners will pick up on all intended meanings, and this tendency "competes" with the tendency toward regularity and simplicity of language form. Thus, vernacular word-formation processes may involve complications as well as simplifications, and vernacular speakers may sometimes use inflectional endings where they are not strictly "needed," just to ensure that meanings are clear. For example, speakers of some vernacular varieties may "double mark" comparative and superlative adjectives, as in *more farther* or *most fastest*, and highly vernacular speakers may even double mark plurals, as in *feets* or *woodses*. We also have to keep in mind that speakers of vernacular varieties may sometimes retain morphological markings which have been lost in standard varieties through processes of regularization and simplification. For example, speakers of some historically isolated Southern varieties such as Appalachian English may retain an *a-* prefix on *-ing* verbs (*She was a-huntin' and a-fishin'*) even though this prefix, which used to indicate ongoing action, has long since vanished from standard varieties of English.

The other major level of grammatical organization, SYNTAX, refers to the structuring of words into larger units such as phrases or sentences. As with morphology, we find that the tendency toward making meaning differences as distinct as possible may lead to dialect differentiation in syntax. For example, as discussed in chapter 2, it is common for speakers of vernacular varieties to use auxiliary, or helping, verbs to give verbs special meanings which can only be indicated in standard varieties through adding a good bit of additional material to the sentence, if the meaning can be conveyed at all. For example, vernacular varieties may be characterized by special auxiliaries such as COMPLETIVE *done*, as in *He done washed the clothes*, HABITUAL *be*, as in *Sometimes my ears be itching*, and COUNTERFACTUAL *liketa*, as in *It was so cold, I liketa froze*. If speakers of standard varieties wish to convey the meanings indicated by these special auxiliaries, they must resort to complex constructions such as *He washed the clothes and has now completely finished washing them*, *Sometimes my ears itch and sometimes they don't*, and *It was below freezing outside, so I could have frozen in theory, but I was in no real danger*. Auxiliaries may also cluster together in different ways to convey special meanings. Thus, DOUBLE MODALS (e.g. *might could*) are commonplace in Southern varieties and serve to convey a meaning of lessened intensity. For example, a sentence such as *I might could go* indicates that the speaker may be able to go but isn't quite sure.

Other verb-related differences in syntactic structure do not have to do with how verbs are used to convey special meanings but rather with the types of structures that can co-occur with particular verbs. For example, some verbs take a particular kind of object in one dialect and a different kind of object, or no object at all, in another dialect. Thus, some vernacular dialects of English use the verb *beat* without an object (e.g. *The Cowboys beat*), whereas other varieties only use it with a direct object – that is, as a TRANSITIVE VERB (e.g. *The Cowboys beat the Giants*). In a similar vein, the verb *learn* in some dialects may co-occur with a subject indicating the person who is conveying knowledge to someone else, as in *The teacher learned me my lesson*. In other dialects, including standard varieties, *learn* can take as its subject only the person or people who are the recipients of the knowledge, as in *The students learned the lesson*; otherwise, the verb *teach* must be used. Although the reduction of the *teach/learn* pair to *learn* alone is highly stigmatized, there are other verbs indicating similar relationships of converseness which have been reduced to a single verb with little or no negative social repercussions. For example, the verb *rent*, as in *The landlord rented an apartment to me* and *I rented an apartment from the landlord*, was originally used only with subjects indicating the recipient of the item of property, as in the latter example above. The reciprocal verb *let* was used when the subject indicated who was bestowing the item, as in *The landlord let the apartment to me*. Interestingly, speakers of British English still use the *let/rent* distinction, even though *rent* alone is quite "proper" according to the rules of standard American English.

In another case of dialect differentiation based on the types of structures that can co-occur with particular verbs, we find that the verb *need* may co-occur with either *-ing* or *-ed* verbs, depending on the dialect area. In most of the US, *need* takes an *-ing* complement, as in *The car needs washing*. However, in some areas, most notably Western Pennsylvania and Eastern Ohio, *need* takes an *-ed* verb, as in *The car needs washed*. The *need* + verb + *-ed* pattern is also found in some areas of the British Isles, particularly Scotland. Although using an *-ed* verb with *need* may sound awkward or even "wrong" to speakers who use *-ing* with *need*, there is nothing intrinsically more "correct" or more logical about using the *-ing* form. This is evidenced in the fact that there is a verb which is very similar to *need* – namely, *want* – which takes an *-ed* rather than *-ing* complement in all US dialect areas (e.g. *I want the car washed*). Interestingly, though, there are parts of England, including parts of the Midlands and North, where *want* takes *-ing* (*I want the car washing*), thus demonstrating that *-ed* with *want* is no more "correct" than *-ing* with *need*.

Another type of syntactic variation involves patterns of AGREEMENT among different elements in a sentence. Agreement relations can be seen as either co-occurrence relations or as the "double marking" of meaning. For example, in standard varieties of English, we say that third person singular present tense verbs must "agree" with their subjects (e.g. *She runs five miles every day*) because whenever a third person singular subject occurs, it must co-occur with the *-s* form of a verb. However, the *-s* marker also represents a "double marking," in the sense that we can clearly tell that a sentence has a third person singular subject without the *-s* marker on the end of the verb simply by looking at the subject itself.

Agreement patterns between subjects and verbs in English have changed substantially during the course of the history of the language. In particular, there has been a longstanding movement toward reducing the extent of agreement. In standard varieties of English today, the only agreement marking with almost all present tense verbs is the third person singular *-s* (or *-es*, as in *goes*) which we have just been discussing. In the past tense, of course, there is no agreement marking at all, since we use the same verb ending (*-ed*) no matter what subject the verb occurs with (e.g. *I/you/she/we/they walked*). In Old and Middle English, however, there were agreement endings for use with first, second, and third person subjects, as well as for use with both singulars and plurals and for both past and present tense verbs. This complex agreement system eventually developed into today's simpler system. Today, there are only a couple of verbs that still show slightly more complicated patterning in the present tense – namely, *be*, which is clearly highly irregular, and *do*, whose third person singular form, *does*, has a different vowel sound in addition to an *-es* ending. In the past tense, only *be* remains irregular, since it has two forms, *was* and *were*.

Among speakers of vernacular dialects, there is a strong tendency to continue the tradition of eliminating complications and irregularities in the English subject–verb agreement system. This tendency may be manifested in several different ways, including the frequent use of *don't* with third person singular subjects in vernacular dialects throughout the US (e.g. *He don't like me anymore*), the regularization of *be* (e.g. *We was going to the store*), and the absence of the third singular *-s* form, as discussed above (e.g. *She walk a mile every day*).

Other vernacular subject–verb agreement patterns have to do with the retention of historical agreement patterns. For example, in varieties such as Appalachian English and Outer Banks English, speakers often use *-s* endings with third person plural subjects (e.g. *People goes, The boys works in the store*) as well as with third person singular subjects. Although a structure such as *people goes* is highly stigmatized, it is not the result of ignorance of the standard English subject–verb agreement pattern; nor does it represent a lack of subject–verb agreement. Rather, it is a retention of a pattern that was commonplace and, indeed, perfectly acceptable, a couple of centuries ago in such varieties as Scots-Irish English, spoken in the province of Ulster in what is now Northern Ireland.

As with a number of other language structures we have looked at thus far, we find that the use of the *-s* verb ending with third person plural subjects shows a rather intricate patterning that may not be evident at first glance. Speakers who use *-s* in the third person plural do not use it with all third person plural subjects to an equal extent. Rather, the *-s* ending is used more frequently with certain types of subjects, including so-called collectives. Collectives are nouns that identify some sort of group or collection. They may be fairly specific, as in *government, family*, or *team*; or they may refer to more general collections of people or objects, as in *people, some of them*, or *a lot of them*. Because each of these words and phrases refers to one group composed of a number of members, there has always been a certain amount of uncertainty as to whether collective nouns should be treated as singular or plural. Some varieties, including standard American English varieties, classify them as plural and so use them with plural verbs, as in *people go*. Others classify them as singular and thus use them with verbs ending in *-s*, as in *people goes*. Neither agreement system can really claim to be the definitive, "correct" form, however. This is evidenced in the fact that, although general collectives such as *people* are considered to be plural in standard American English (e.g. *People are visiting*), there are some specific collectives which are held to be singular (e.g. *The government was debating the issue*; *The team was winning*). Interestingly, these specific collectives are considered to be plural in standard British English (*The government were debating*; *The team were winning*), a variety which is certainly highly regarded for its "correctness." Thus, we see that subject–verb agreement patterns, which we often consider to be based on rigid, inflexible rules, are not even consistent across current standard varieties of English, let alone in vernacular varieties or in a single variety over the course of time. This is an important realization indeed, considering that many speakers of American English believe that "standard" subject–verb agreement patterns are inflexible and permanent.

Syntactic agreement relations may affect other elements of a sentence besides subjects and verbs. In particular, the "double negatives" we discussed in chapter 2 (e.g. *I didn't do nothing*) may be viewed as "negative agreement" as well as double marking, since double negation, or, more properly, multiple negation, involves using indefinite forms (e.g. *nothing* rather than *anything*) which agree with the negative form of the verb. Many distinctive dialect differences in syntax involve agreement patterns between words or morphemes, and they are among the most evident social markers within American English.

Finally, syntactic differences may involve the basic linear arrangement of words in phrases or sentences. Although there is considerable variation across languages with respect to the sequencing of different types of phrases within sentences, there is relatively little variation of this type within English itself. Nonetheless, there are a few occasions where the ordering of elements within sentences varies across regional or social dialects. For example, the ordering of words in questions may vary, as in *What that was?* vs. *What was that?* Similarly, the placement of adverbs may differ slightly in different dialects, as in *We'd all the time get into trouble* vs. *We'd get into trouble all the time*. Given the possibilities for sequencing differences in sentences, however, these differences play a relatively minor role in the differentiation of American English dialects.

Exercise 4

The following sentence pairs represent different kinds of syntactic variation as discussed above. These types include the following: (1) the use of auxiliaries or verbal markers to give verbs special meanings (e.g. the use of double modals or counterfactual *liketa*), (2) co-occurrence relations among sentence elements (e.g. whether or not a verb needs an object), (3) agreement patterns (e.g. agreement between subjects and verbs), and (4) variation in the linear order of structures (e.g. *He's all the time talking*). Identify the type of syntactic variation in the following sentence pairs or sets of sentences according to the categories set forth above. For example, a sentence pair such as *The Rams beat/The Rams beat the Cowboys* would be classified as type 2 in this classification, since the variation relates to whether or not the verb *beat* takes an object. In your description of each difference, be as specific as possible about the variation you observe.

1   *Did ever a stray animal come to your house?/Did a stray animal ever come to your house?*
2   *Some people makes soap from pig fat/Some people make soap from pig fat.*
3   *They started to running/They started a-running/They started running.*
4   *There's six people in our family/There're six people in our family.*
5   *They made him out the liar/They made him out to be the liar.*
6   *We once in a while will have a party/We will have a party once in a while/ Once in a while we will have a party.*
7   *The dog ugly/The dog's ugly.*
8   *The man béen met him/The man met him a long time ago.*

3.5   Language Use and Pragmatics

Knowing a language involves considerably more than knowing the meanings of the words and the phonological and grammatical structures of the language. In every language and dialect, there are a variety of ways to convey the same information or accomplish the same function, and the choice of *how* to say something may depend upon *who* is talking to *whom* under *what* social circumstances. The term PRAGMATICS is used to refer to how language is used in its social setting to carry out particular functions. One important concept in the study of pragmatics is the SPEECH ACT, which refers to an utterance which accomplishes a social action, such as getting someone to perform an activity, making a promise, or apologizing.

Speakers of all languages and dialects are quite capable of performing the same basic kinds of speech acts – directing, requesting, apologizing, and so forth – but how these speech acts are carried out and the conditions under which they are considered to be appropriate may vary considerably across cultural groups. Statements may be strong and direct or they may be softer and less direct. For example, consider the range of sentences that might be used to direct a person to take out the garbage.

> *Take out the garbage!*
> *Can you take out the garbage?*
> *Would you mind taking out the garbage?*
> *Let's take out the garbage.*
> *The garbage sure is piling up.*
> *Garbage day is tomorrow.*

Each of these sentences may be used to accomplish the same goal of getting the person to take out the garbage. However, the sentences show varying degrees of directness, ranging from the direct command at the top of the list to the indirect statement regarding the reason the activity needs to be undertaken at the bottom of the list. The sentences also differ in terms of relative politeness and situational appropriateness. For example, a person of superior status (e.g. parent, supervisor) could use the most direct form when speaking with a subordinate, whereas a person of subordinate status might not have the option of using a direct command. Knowledge of when and how to use certain forms is just as important for communication as the knowledge of particular forms, and the failure to abide by cultural conventions for language use can have important implications for how people are perceived within and across social groups.

Different cultural groups often have contrasting expectations about the appropriate use of direct or indirect expressions. Working-class African American parents have sometimes been observed to be more direct than Anglo Americans in speaking to children, especially in correcting them. For example, a working-class African American parent or teacher might use a direct order in directing a child who has strayed: "Get back here, Melvin!" In a similar situation, however, an Anglo American teacher might attempt to accomplish the function of getting the child to return to the group by saying, "Melvin, you need to stay with the group" or "Melvin, would you like to stay with the group?" Indirectness has come to be valued in some settings, such as the school or workplace. Thus, teachers have been taught that "I like the way Jeffrey is keeping his eyes on the blackboard" is better than "Look at what I'm writing on the blackboard, Stephanie." Contrasting expectations about directness may lead to misunderstandings across different groups. Children who are accustomed to a more direct style of adult communication may, for example, misconstrue indirect commands as less sincere than their more direct counterparts and thus consider compliance with the directive optional rather than obligatory. On the other hand, children who are used to more indirectness may feel threatened or intimidated by the directness of some adults who accept directness as the norm.

It has been shown that women in positions of authority in the workplace are often more indirect in their instructions to workers than male authorities and that conflict arises when women do not meet expectations of indirectness. Thus, women who use direct commands may be given such negative labels as "pushy" or even "bitchy," whereas men who are direct in their instructions to workers may be labeled simply as "aggressive," a word which is far less negative than "pushy" and may even be considered positive. In matters of directness vs. indirectness, gender differences may play a more important role than factors such as ethnicity, social class, or region, although all these factors tend to intersect, often in quite complex ways, in the determination of the "appropriate" degree of directness or indirectness for any given speech act.

Related to the issue of cultural differences in directness is the distinction between literal and non-literal language use. For example, a statement such as "What are you doing?" can have both a literal and a non-literal interpretation. It may be interpreted literally as a request for explanation among workers who are performing a task together. However, if a teacher or parent utters this sentence upon entering a classroom full of misbehaving children, it is not intended to be a literal request for information but an indirect directive to get the children to stop misbehaving. In fact, if the children were to respond to the question as if it were a literal request (e.g. by answering "We're playing tag"), this might evoke a more direct reprimand, perhaps about the inappropriateness of the response itself (e.g. "Don't act smart!").

Conventions for interpreting statements as literal or non-literal vary considerably among different cultural groups, as does the value accorded to literal vs. non-literal language use. For example, Shirley Brice Heath (1983) found that Anglo Americans in one particular working-class community valued perfectly factual children's stories more highly than African Americans in the same community, who placed higher value on stories which were embellished by non-literal language use, including invented quotations. This contrast contributed to the negative valuation of African American children by schoolteachers, since storytelling conventions in the classroom setting were largely reflective of Anglo rather than African American values regarding literalness. Conventions regarding literal meaning can also vary within ethnic groups, based on such factors as gender. For example, Marjorie Harness Goodwin (1990) noticed that whereas pre-adolescent African American boys frequently referred to their abilities and actions in exaggerated terms, African American girls of the same age criticized each other for bragging. In some cultural groups, not only is exaggerating one's abilities considered inappropriate, but even making literal statements about one's personal qualities is considered to be "bad manners," since it is expected that personal strengths will be downplayed, in keeping with a value on personal humility. Thus, we see that underlying cultural values often enter into the determination of situational appropriateness concerning literal and non-literal meaning, as they do for directness and indirectness.

Unfortunately, we have a tendency to become so accustomed to our own community's linguistic strategies for carrying out speech acts that we fail to notice when contrasting conventions within another group might be interfering with communication. Our initial reaction is to interpret differences in language use based on our own group's conventions for communicating. For example, we interpret more directness than we are accustomed to as rudeness and less literalness as lying. Conversely, we interpret more indirectness than we are used to as weakness and more literalness as a lack of tact.

Although there are many types of language-use differences, a couple of areas are particularly sensitive to variation. One involves ADDRESS FORMS – that is, the titles and names speakers use when referring to the people they are talking to, such as the use of *Mr* or *Ms* with a last name or the use of a first name only. Considerations of social status, age, gender, familiarity, and group identity all come into play when determining the form of address which is appropriate for a particular person in a given situation, but in most instances, these diverse social factors can be reduced to the dimensions of power and solidarity. Loosely defined, "power" refers to how much control conversational participants have over each other, while "solidarity" refers to how much intimacy there is between addressors and addressees. Different regional and social groups weigh power and solidarity differently in determining appropriate address forms, and thus speakers in these groups may use quite different address forms to address a single individual in a given social setting. For example, many middle-class Anglo Americans treat social status as more important than age in their choice of address forms, so that an older person working as a laborer may be addressed by his or her first name by a younger person. Conversely, speakers in many other ethnic communities in America consider age to take precedence over social status, and so they will address the same laborer by title and last name if they are younger than he or she.

There are various combinations of titles and names that may be used in addressing people, including some that are unique to specific regions. In the South, a wide range of adults are addressed with the respect labels *Sir* and *Ma'am*, including parents, whereas in the North only a few adults with special status are addressed by these forms. Similarly, although non-Southerners tend to think of titles such as *Mr*, *Mrs*, and *Ms* as indicative of unequal power relations, Southern speakers may use *Mr* or *Miss* with a first name to indicate special closeness. For example, young children or subordinate workers may address Marge and Walt Wolfram as *Miss Marge and Mr Walt*. In some situations, such address forms suggest a sort of extended kinship relationship, so that children of Marge and Walt's close friends might address the couple as *Miss Marge and Mr Walt* but only until the children reach adolescence. Such terms have also been used traditionally in the South by long-term domestic help in addressing their bosses in the home. In the North, the terms *aunt* and *uncle* may be used to indicate extended kinship with close friends of parents, including godparents.

Dialect differences in address forms are frequently judged as "rude" or "polite" by speakers from outside a particular regional or social group, and those who use inappropriately "familiar" forms are held to be "rude," while those who use inappropriately "formal" terms are considered to be insincerely deferential, or overly "polite." In reality, of course, different address forms are simply reflective of different conventions for "appropriate" language use. (See Brown and Levinson 1987 for more on matters of what constitutes "politeness.")

Related to address forms are conventions for greeting and leave-taking, which involve ritualized forms that are not to be interpreted literally. In most cases, greeting routines simply involve rote memorization of a limited set of formulaic exchanges and an understanding of the appropriate circumstances for their use. Thus, the appropriate response to "What's happening?" when used as a greeting among African American speakers is simply a rote response such as "Nothing to me" rather than a literal or spontaneous response such as, "A number of students are currently on their way to class, and you and I are talking." Similarly, speakers learn to respond to the greeting "What's up?" with "Not much," even if they are undergoing dramatic, life-changing experiences, while they learn to reply to "How ya doing?" with "Fine," even if they are currently feeling miserable. Of course, greeting routines may vary across different settings. For example, telephone greetings are different from face-to-face encounters, and those accompanying service exchanges (e.g. between customer and employee) are different from greetings between friends. For our purposes, however, it is most important to recognize that greeting routines are sensitive to regional, ethnic, gender, and status differences in American society. Although greetings are highly ritualized and are not meant to be taken literally, their social significance in establishing conversational relationships cannot be minimized.

Similarly, conversational closings carry great social weight at the same time that their informational content may be limited. Speakers do not simply turn away from each other abruptly and without explanation when ending a cooperative conversation. First of all, a participant "passes" a potential turn in the conversation by saying something like "OK," "Well," or "So." This signals a desire to end the conversation, which may be accepted or rejected by the other participants. Then a speaker engages in one of several leave-taking routines, including offering a compliment (e.g. "It was nice to talk to you"), providing a "reasonable" excuse for terminating the conversation (e.g. "I'll let you get back to your work now," "I've got a meeting in five minutes"), or making reference to a future meeting ("See you later"). We cannot say things such as "This conversation is boring, so I'm leaving" or "I'd rather be talking to Yancey than you," even if such a feeling represents the real reason for closing a conversation. As with other areas of language use, conventions for "appropriate" leave-taking may vary from group to group. Thus, it is not surprising that an older speaker expecting a conventionalized and relatively formal parting statement such as "I enjoyed talking with you" may interpret a younger speaker's innovative and informal closing, "I'm outta here," as rude and inappropriate.

Failing to recognize conventional cues for closing a conversation can lead to some awkward situations, and someone who is talking with speakers from a different cultural group may not be able to figure out the appropriate moment for leave-taking or how to allow the other speakers to exit the conversation gracefully. Even within a single culture, there are vast differences in how conversations are closed. For example, many of us have come across speakers who do not seem to be able to pick up on any of our cues that we wish to terminate a conversation, even though they share a common cultural background with us. Knowing how to close off a conversation is just as important as knowing how to start one, and those who fail to do so "appropriately" may be subject to the same sort of social censure as those who use the "wrong" address forms or give commands which are unexpectedly direct or indirect.

Topics of conversation also may differ according to the social or regional group of the participants involved. The determination of "safe" topics of discussion may vary according to situational context and social relationships among speakers. A middle-class Anglo American might consider a question like "What do you do for a living?" as an appropriate conversational opener at a casual social gathering, but the same question might be considered inappropriate by some minority groups in the same situation. The appropriateness of direct questions about income and cost (e.g. house, car, etc.) may also vary from group to group. Regional and social groups may also differ in the amount of "small talk" that is appropriate before getting to the heart of the interaction. For example, "small talk" may be an important preliminary to getting down to business in some Southern areas but is not considered to be necessary by speakers in some other regions. Conventions for raising new topics and continuing with old ones also vary across groups. Some groups expect speakers to respond to all new topics raised in a conversation, while in other groups conversational participants may simply pass over a new topic without comment and without giving offense.

As with differences in other areas of language use, cross-cultural differences concerning conversational topics may lead to misunderstandings and negative evaluations of speakers from cultural groups other than one's own. However, we must bear in mind that a difference such as the use of more "small talk" than we are accustomed to does not mean that a speaker is "beating around the bush." Nor does less small talk mean that speakers are overly cold and businesslike. Rather, such differences are simply reflective of differences in cultural conventions for the appropriate use of language in its social setting.

Once a topic is chosen and a conversation initiated, then matters of conversational "turn-taking" arise. Knowing when it is acceptable or obligatory to take a turn in a conversation is essential to the cooperative development of discourse. This knowledge involves such factors as knowing how to recognize appropriate turn-exchange points and knowing how long the pauses between turns should be. It is also important to know how (and if) one may talk while someone else is talking – that is, if conversational *overlap* is allowed. Since not all conversations follow all the "rules" for turn-taking, it is also necessary to know how to "repair" a conversation that has been thrown off course by undesired overlap or a misunderstood comment.

Cultural differences in matters of turn-taking can lead to conversational breakdown, misinterpretation of intentions, and conflict. For example, people from cultural groups who are accustomed to relatively long pauses between turns (e.g. Native American Vernacular English speakers in the Southwest) may feel that they have been denied their fair share of the conversational "floor" when they are talking with people who are used to shorter pauses, because the short-pause speakers always step in and speak before the long-pause people. To further complicate matters, another feature of long-pause conversational style is a prohibition against overlapping talk. Those who do not allow overlapping conversation may feel interrupted by speakers from groups who are used to conversational overlap, such as Jewish speakers in New York City. Conversely, those who are accustomed to their listeners' interjecting comments while they are speaking may feel that those who fail to do so are not showing enough involvement in the conversation and are unenthusiastic about the subject matter.

One particular type of overlapping talk which is found among a wide range of social and regional groups is BACKCHANNELING. Backchanneling involves interjecting small utterances such as *Mmmhmm, Uh-huh, Yeah,* and *Right* – or even just nodding the head – into the conversation in order to let the current speaker know that he or she may continue speaking. Different groups naturally vary in terms of the kinds of reinforcement offered to speakers by their listeners, and sometimes these differences may lead speakers to feel that their conversational contribution is not being appreciated (when there is too little backchanneling) or that their listeners are displaying insincere interest in what they have to say (when there is too much or the wrong kind of backchanneling). It has even been shown that if listeners do not display appropriate variation in the backchanneling signals they use (e.g. alternating between *Right*, *Yeah*, and *Mmmhmm*), then the message conveyed by the signals will be one of lack of support for the current speaker rather than increased support. Thus, if we are talking with someone who simply keeps repeating *Mmmhmm* with the same basic intonation, we will most likely come to the conclusion that this person is bored by what we are saying.

In the past couple of decades, gender differences in turn-taking and overlapping talk have been studied in detail. The results of these studies clearly defy the widespread stereotype in American culture that women talk more than men (e.g. James and Drakich 1993). Research shows that in mixed-sex conversation, men tend to take more speaking turns than women; they also "hold the floor" longer than women. It is not as clear whether men interrupt more than women, partly because it is not easy to define what constitutes an interruption. As we have just discussed, many cases of conversational overlap are supportive rather than disruptive (e.g. James and Clarke 1993). There are a number of language-use differences besides matters of turn-taking that correlate with gender differences. We will discuss these in more detail in chapter 7. For now, it is sufficient to understand that such differences exist and lead to misunderstandings every bit as much as differences which are correlated with region, ethnicity, or age. In fact, one can argue that gender differences in language use lead to greater misunderstanding than these other differences, since women and men interact with one another on a daily basis, while those from different regions or ethnic groups may not always come into frequent contact with one another.

Exercise 5

Think of some types of behaviors you have observed among members of a social group other than your own that you have traditionally thought of as offensive. Classic cases might involve talking with the opposite sex, service encounters at stores, cross-ethnic encounters, and so forth. What kinds of language use tend to go along with this behavior? In what ways might language-use conventions contribute to your impression? What is different about the conventions of your cultural/dialectal group compared to the other group? Are there aspects of your perception that, upon further reflection, might simply be related to how you interpret the language routines of other cultural groups rather than the intentions of the speakers?

As we have seen, there are a number of different rules or conventions that govern our conversational format and interactional style. Furthermore, there are a variety of factors that have to be considered, ranging from broad-based cultural values about who can talk to whom about what to minute details concerning how certain subtle intentions may be expressed in a given community. Given the number and significance of the factors that enter into the selection of strategies for carrying out conversation, the likelihood of misinterpretation is almost staggering. Certainly, there are many shared language-use conventions across the varieties of American English, but there are also important differences among groups that can lead to significant misunderstandings across regional and social dialects.

The acknowledgment of language-use differences as a legitimate domain of dialect studies is relatively recent compared to the traditional focus of dialect studies on language form (i.e. lexical items, pronunciations, grammatical structures), but the social significance of language-use differences should not be understated. In fact, some of the major areas of social dissonance and conflict among different social and ethnic groups in American society are directly tied to people's failure to understand that different groups have different language-use conventions which may have nothing to do with the intentions that underlie particular language uses.

3.6   Further Reading

American Speech. A publication of the American Dialect Society. University: University of Alabama Press. This quarterly journal contains articles on all levels of dialect differences in American English dialects, balancing more technical treatments of dialect forms with shorter, non-technical observations. A regular section entitled "Among the New Words" contains lists of lexical items that have been innovated in the different ways discussed above.

Cassidy, Frederic G. (general editor) *Dictionary of American Regional English, Volume 1: Introduction and A–C* (1985), *Volume 2: D–H* (1991), *Volume 3: I–O* (1996). Cambridge, MA: Harvard University Press, Belknap. This dictionary of regional vocabulary words is fascinating and extremely comprehensive. The introductory articles in Volume 1, by Frederic Cassidy and James Hartman, set forth some of the major phonological and grammatical processes which have led to differences in American English dialects.

Eble, Connie (1996) *Slang and Sociability: In-Group Language Among College Students.* Chapel Hill/London: University of North Carolina Press. This book provides thorough discussions of the nature, origins, and social functions of slang among college students. Numerous example words are given.

Goodwin, Marjorie Harness (1990) *He-Said-She-Said: Talk as Social Organization among Black Children.* Bloomington: Indiana University Press. This description of adolescent African American speech combines an in-depth conversational analysis of speech with more broadly based ethnographic studies of the speech community.

Labov, William (1991) The three dialects of English. In Penelope Eckert (ed.), *New Ways of Analyzing Sound Change*. New York: Academic Press, 1–44. Labov views dialect differences from the perspective of entire vowel systems rather than from the traditional viewpoint, in which each vowel is considered as a separate entity. This is a critical article which forces a reconsideration of the basis for delimiting dialects. Up-to-date information on Labov and his colleagues' continuing research on the vowel systems of American English can be obtained by consulting the following web address:

http://www.ling.upenn.edu/phono_atlas/home.html

Lighter, Jonathan E. (1994) *Historical Dictionary of American Slang, Volume 1: A–G*. New York: Random House. This book provides a list of slang terms, with historical derivations, in dictionary format.

Williams, Joseph M. (1975) *The Origins of the English Language: A Social and Linguistic History*. New York/London: The Free Press. This book offers a relatively readable overview of the history of the English language and includes discussions of lexical, semantic, grammatical, and phonological changes which have taken place in the language over the course of history.

Wolfram, Walt, and Natalie Schilling-Estes (1997) *Hoi Toide on the Outer Banks: The Story of the Ocracoke Brogue*. Chapel Hill/London: University of North Carolina Press. This book, designed for non-experts, provides an in-depth description of the lexical, phonological, and grammatical features of one American English dialect, with numerous examples and discussions of the processes that led to the formation of these features.

4

Dialects in the United States:
Past, Present, and Future

When people ask us what we do for a living, and we reply that we study American English dialects, one of the next questions inevitably is, "How many dialects are there?" This question is surprisingly difficult to answer, despite the fact that researchers have been investigating language variation in America for at least a century. Discrete boundaries between dialects are often difficult to determine, since dialects share many features with one another. In addition, even the smallest dialect areas are characterized by incredible heterogeneity. Speakers use different language forms – or identical forms at different percentage rates or in different ways – based not only on where they live but also on such factors as their social class, their ethnicity, their gender, and even whether or not they view their home region as a good place to live. Further, different dialect boundaries may emerge depending on which level of language we choose to focus on. Early dialectologists in America relied chiefly on regional lexical items in their delimitation of dialect areas, while a number of today's researchers place more emphasis on phonology. The dialect areas that are emerging as a result of this new focus on pronunciation correspond roughly with dialect areas as determined by vocabulary words; however, some new lines have been drawn based on this newer type of dialectology. Finally, we have to consider the fact that languages and dialects are constantly changing. In the United States, the natural tendency toward language change is compounded by the tendency of the US population toward ever-increasing mobility. When speakers relocate, particularly in large numbers, they carry with them the seeds of dialect change; these seeds are nurtured by language itself, since language seems to be pre-programmed for continual change.

An appeal to speakers' subjective classifications does not help us out much in delimiting the dialects of American English. Studies of PERCEPTUAL DIALECTO-LOGY, that is, the study of how speakers themselves outline dialect boundaries, show considerable variation in these boundaries from speaker to speaker, and especially from region to region (Preston 1986). For example, a speaker from Southern Indiana will typically draw the boundary for the Southern dialect area differently from a speaker from Detroit or Buffalo. But even within the same region, there may be different assessments of dialect boundaries. Thus, we have heard classifications of Appalachian dialects that range from "everybody in Appalachia talks the same way" to "every hollow has its own dialect" – and these assessments were given by speakers in the same community. So we have to conclude that determining clear-cut regional dialects is considerably more elusive and complex than it appears at first glance, whether we appeal to objective or subjective criteria.

Exercise 1

Think about your own perceptions regarding the regional dialects of American English. What major regional dialects come immediately to mind? How about the dialect(s) where you live? Are there major and minor regional dialects where you live? What kind of features do you associate with these different dialects? Ask several other people about their perceptions of the area, including both natives and non-natives of the region. Ask them what characteristics they associate with the speech of the area and how it is distinguished from that of other areas.

Despite the difficulty of delimiting dialect areas, it is nonetheless useful to be able to consult a "dialect map" as we explore regional, social, ethnic, gender, and stylistic variation in American English. In this chapter, we will sketch out a rough picture of the American dialect landscape, beginning with the dim outlines which arose when the first English-speaking colonists arrived in the New World and gradually filling in our picture as the inhabitation of America by immigrant groups was completed. Finally, we will discuss how our dialect map might look in the future, addressing such questions as whether or not American dialects are fading as a result of such factors as improved methods of transportation and widening channels of communication, including cable TV and the Internet. Our discussion in this chapter is based largely on the work of traditional dialectologists and on the work of linguistic and cultural historians, although results from some newer approaches to dialect study are incorporated as well. Here, we focus chiefly on the cumulative results of these dialect studies, reserving our discussion of the studies themselves, as well as theoretical considerations underlying the investigation of regional dialects, for chapter 5 and subsequent chapters.

4.1   The First English(es) in America

When the first successful English settlement was founded in Jamestown, Virginia, in 1607, British English was quite different from what it is today.

American English, of course, was non-existent. As we mentioned in chapter 2, scholars refer to the language of this time period – the language of Shakespeare and the Elizabethan era – as Early Modern English, to distinguish it from today's English (Modern English or Present-Day English) as well as from the English of Chaucer's day (Middle English, spoken from about 1100 to 1500) and from even earlier varieties of the language (Old English, *c*.600–1100). Not only was Early Modern English in general quite different from today's language, but there was also quite a bit of variation within the language at that time. Since the beginnings of English, there have existed a number of distinct dialects within the British Isles, dialects which arose and were continually enhanced by longstanding lack of communication between speakers of different dialect areas, as well as by the fact that the notion of a unified "standard" language was not firmly established until around the mid-1700s. Dialect differences in earlier varieties of British English had a profound effect on the development of the dialects of the United States, since people from different speech regions tended to establish residence in different regions of America. In fact, some of today's most noticeable dialect differences can be traced directly back to the British English dialects of the seventeenth and eighteenth centuries.

Contrary to popular perceptions, the speech of the Jamestown colonists more closely resembled today's American English than today's standard British speech, since British English has undergone a number of innovations which did not spread to once-remote America. For example, even though Shakespearean actors, speaking in "proper" British style, pronounce words such as *cart* and *work* as *caht* and *wohk* (that is, without the *r* sounds), in reality many of Shakespeare's contemporaries would have pronounced their *r*'s, just as do most Americans today. Similarly, the early colonists would have pronounced the /æ/ vowel in words like *path*, *dance*, and *can't* as the low front vowel [æ] (as in *cat*), just as Americans do today, even though British standards now demand a sound similar to the [a] of *father*. This vowel, which is located between [a] and [æ], is most closely approximated in American English by the Chicago pronunciation of the vowel in *pop* and *lock*, as well as the second vowel in *Chicago*.

In addition to pronunciations, there are certain words and word meanings that have been handed down to today's Americans by the first colonists, despite the fact that British speakers have long since abandoned them. For example, Americans can use the word *mad* with its early meaning of 'angry', while British speakers can only use it to mean mentally unbalanced. Americans can also use the word *fall* to refer to the season which follows summer, but British speakers only use the term *autumn*, even though both terms coexisted for centuries in Britain. There are also a few syntactic structures that have been preserved in American English which were lost from British English. The American use of *gotten*, as in *Has he gotten the mail yet?*, is a relic form, supplanted in Britain by *got* (*Has he got the mail?*); further, the British use of *done* in a question–answer pair such as *Did you leave your wallet in the car?/I might have done* arose after English had sunk its roots in American soil. Thus, Americans reply to questions such as the above with *I might have* or *I might have done so* but never with *I might have done*, a distinct British-ism.

Most of the early colonists in the Jamestown area – that is, Tidewater Virginia – came from Southeastern England, the home of Britain's cultural center, London. Thus, these speakers would have spoken varieties of English which were quite close to the emerging London standard rather than the more "rustic" varieties spoken in outlying areas such as Northern and Southwestern England. The fact that Tidewater Virginia was long associated with "proper" British speech led to one of its chief defining characteristics, the loss of *r* after vowels and before consonants in words such as *cart* and *work*. Even though, as we mentioned above, English was largely *r*-pronouncing, or *r*-ful, in the early 1600s, the loss of *r*, or *r*-lessness, was not uncommon in Southeastern England at this time. It gradually gained prestige in this region and finally became a marker of standard British speech, a development which most likely had occurred by the mid-eighteenth century or so. As *r*-lessness was gaining in prestige in England, colonists in Tidewater Virginia were building a prosperous society based on plantation agriculture. The aristocrats of this region, descended from fairly *r*-less Southeastern English speakers, maintained strong ties with the London area and its standard speakers, and so *r*-lessness was established in lowland Virginia. This is in sharp contrast to the piedmont and mountain regions to the west of the Tidewater, and indeed to most varieties of American English today, which are *r*-ful rather than *r*-less. Most of the English speakers who established residence in the uplands of Virginia, more than a hundred years after the founding of Jamestown, were vernacular speakers from Britain's *r*-pronouncing regions or were descended from these speakers. In particular, the *r*-pronouncing Scots-Irish from Ulster were to have an enormous impact on the speech of the Virginia colony and on American English in general. We will discuss the contribution of the Scots-Irish to American English momentarily.

Another reason for the *r*-ful character of upland Virginia speech is that this region was subject to more dialect mixing than the Tidewater area, which remained relatively homogeneous for a number of generations. When a number of different dialects come into contact with one another, differences among the varieties may be ironed out. For some reason, most likely the preponderance of Scots-Irish settlers in the American colonies, the reduction of dialect differences in early America tended to produce *r*-ful rather than *r*-less speech, even if a number of settlers in "mixed" areas initially brought *r*-less speech with them. Finally, speakers in upland Virginia (as well as other *r*-pronouncing regions, which we will discuss below) were *r*-ful because they did not maintain as much contact with Britain as their neighbors to the east. Settlers in the piedmont and mountain regions tended to establish small farms rather than large plantations and to lean toward democracy rather than aristocracy. In addition, they were less wealthy than plantation owners and were not able to afford luxuries such as travel or schooling in London.

As in Tidewater Virginia, speakers of "proper" southeastern speech were prevalent in Eastern New England, beginning with the founding of the Massachusetts Bay Colony in 1620. Thus, Eastern New England was established as an *r*-less dialect area, in contrast with neighboring dialect areas such as Western New England (west of the Connecticut River Valley) and New York State, which became *r*-pronouncing regions for the same reasons that upland Virginia did: (1) settlement by *r*-pronouncing speakers, (2) the reduction of dialect differences in the face of dialect contact and language contact, and (3) relative lack of contact with London as compared with speakers in Eastern New England. To this day, Eastern New England survives as an *r*-less island in the midst of a sea of *r*-fulness. The strongly *r*-less character of New England speech is evidenced in the fact that it is often caricaturized through phrases such as "Pahk the cah in Hahvahd Yahd" for "Park the car in Harvard Yard." Interestingly, one of the most stereotypically *r*-less regions in this country, New York City (as evidenced in phrases such as "toity-toid street" for "thirty-third street"), began life as an *r*-ful speech area. In fact, it wasn't until at least the mid-1800s that *r*-lessness, which spread into the city from New England, was fully established there. Today, *r*-lessness is receding sharply in New York City English, as well as in Eastern New England and Tidewater Virginia. Regions traditionally characterized by *r*-less speech are depicted in figure 4.1.

Exercise 2

In the decades following World War II, *r*-lessness has been receding sharply in the US. What do you think the reason for this decline might be? Consider caricatures of New York City and Boston speech (e.g. *toity-toid street* 'thirty-third street', *pahk the cah* 'park the car') as you shape your answer. Compare the decline of *r* in the US with its historical rise and continued maintenance in British speech. What do the changing patterns of *r*-fulness and *r*-lessness in America and Britain tell us about the inherent value (linguistic and/or social) of particular dialect features?

Following the establishment of the Massachusetts Bay Colony, a number of other important settlements were founded in the mid- to late 1600s. These include several settlements in the Connecticut River Valley area beginning in 1635, as well as settlements in the Hudson River Valley, including what was later to become New York City, beginning in the 1640s. In addition, Providence, Rhode Island, was established in 1638 by several families from the Massachusetts Bay Colony who were dissatisfied with the severity of religious

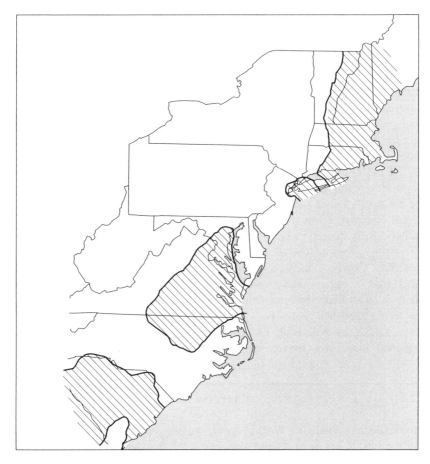

Figure 4.1   Traditional regions of *r*-lessness and *r*-fulness in American English (adapted from Kurath and McDavid 1961: map 32; copyright © The University of Michigan Press).

and social practices in Salem and Boston. While Boston was to become the cultural and linguistic center of Eastern New England, influencing speech patterns throughout Massachusetts and up into lower Maine, Western New England would develop its own characteristic speech patterns, which radiated outward from the initial settlements in the lower Connecticut Valley. Further, Rhode Island would persist as a dialectal subregion for centuries, evidence for the strong and enduring character of dialect boundaries established in an era of minimal intercommunication between speakers of different areas, including even neighboring regions.

Some of the chief differences between traditional Eastern New England and Western New England speech derive from cultural differences which have distinguished the two areas since their initial settlement by English speakers. Many early residents of Eastern New England made their living from the sea, and so the traditional dialect is rich with nautical terminology, including such words as *nor'easter*, which refers to a storm from the north and east, and *lulling down* and *breezing up*, used, respectively, to refer to decreasing and increasing winds. A number of these nautical terms have their origins in the speech of the western counties of England rather than the southeast, since people from the seagoing west were frequent settlers along the coastal areas of early America.

Far to the south of New England, the Tidewater Virginia speech area also shares important connections with Western England, particularly the southwestern counties. Even today, there are portions of the Tidewater, chiefly along its easternmost edge, whose speech is quite different from general Tidewater English. For example, there are strong pockets of *r*-fulness in the midst of an otherwise *r*-less speech community. Most likely, the easternmost portion of the Tidewater derives its character from relatively heavy settlement by speakers from Southwestern England, a region characterized by strong *r*-fulness, among other features. In addition, the highly distinctive speech of the Delmarva Peninsula, the Chesapeake Bay Islands (including Tangier Island, Virginia, and Smith Island, Maryland), and the Outer Banks islands of North Carolina is to this day far more reminiscent of the speech of Southwest England than of the Southeastern English from which Tidewater English proper is descended.

As we move inland, traditional regional dialects tend to be characterized by a preponderance of farming terms rather than nautical words. Thus, the traditional Western New England dialect is replete with terms pertaining to an agricultural lifestyle, in contrast with neighboring Eastern New England speech. Of special interest are terms which relate to localized farming practices. For example, a *stone drag* refers to a piece of equipment used for extricating stones from the rocky New England soil, while the term *rock maple* refers to the sugar maple, an important source of income for early farmers in Western New England.

The traditional speech of rural New York State is also replete with localized farming terms. However, its overall character is rather different from the speech of neighboring Western New England, due in part to the influence of Dutch and German on speakers. The Dutch had control of the Hudson Valley area until 1644, when the British took over; in addition, a huge influx of Germans, chiefly from the Palatinate, began pouring into New York and Pennsylvania in the early 1700s. The Dutch and German influence on traditional New York speech is evidenced in terms such as *olicook* 'doughnut' (from Dutch *oliekoek* 'oil cake') and *thick milk* 'clabber' (from German *dickemilch* 'thick milk'), which remained current in the region through the early years of the twentieth century. In recent years, most of these words have faded out of use or have spread far beyond the region (e.g. *cruller* 'doughnut', from Dutch *krulle* 'curly cake') and so no longer serve as markers of New York speech. In fact, the only Dutch and German terms that truly remain intact in the region are place names such as *Brooklyn* and *Harlem* (from Dutch *Breukelyn* and *Haarlem*, respectively).

Another of the nation's earliest cultural and linguistic centers was Philadelphia, established in the 1680s by Quakers under the leadership of William Penn. The Quaker movement was organized in North England and the northern Midlands, and so Philadelphia was, from the first, far less like Southern England in its speech habits than New England. Also prevalent in Philadelphia from its earliest days were emigrants from Wales and Germany. Almost immediately, the Germans, many of whom were of the Moravian, Mennonite, and Amish sects, began moving westward into Pennsylvania and began developing their own distinctive culture and language, Pennsylvania Dutch. Pennsylvania Dutch is not really Dutch but rather a unique variety of German which developed in the New World, partly in response to speakers' contact with English and partly as a result of longstanding isolation from European German varieties. One of the most important groups to settle in early Philadelphia was the Scots-Irish. In 1724, thousands of Scots-Irish arrived in Delaware and then proceeded northward into Pennsylvania, New York, and New England. The initial wave of immigration was followed by numerous others throughout the course of the eighteenth century, with immigration reaching its peak in 1772–3 but persisting well into the twentieth century.

The Scots-Irish were descendants of Scots who had emigrated to Ulster in the north of Ireland at the beginning of the seventeenth century in order to seek economic gain and to escape discrimination and persecution at the hands of the English. At the time of the initial migrations to Ulster, Scots English was more distinct from London speech than today's highly distinctive Scots English is from standard British English, or RP (Received Pronunciation) English. The English spoken in Scotland in the early 1600s tended to become less distinctive as the centuries passed; however, the old, highly distinctive speech tended to be preserved in Ulster, since the Scots-Irish did not maintain much contact with Scotland, or with England. Thus, the variety of English which the Scots-Irish brought to America in the early 1700s was a rather archaic form of Scots English. It was little influenced by Irish English, since most Irish people in the Ulster area spoke Gaelic rather than English. Among its other characteristics, Scots-Irish was strongly *r*-ful, and as it established itself in America, it successfully resisted the incursion of *r*-lessness via such cultural centers as Boston and Richmond. At the time of the American Revolution, the Scots-Irish speech variety was already having an enormous impact on the development of American English: It is estimated that around 250,000 Scots-Irish had migrated to America by 1776 and that fully one in seven colonists was Scots-Irish at this time. The impact of the Scots-Irish would only strengthen over time. From their initial settlement areas, particularly Pennsylvania, the Scots-Irish and their descendants would spread throughout the Mid-Atlantic states and the highlands of the American South; and their influence can even be felt throughout the Northern and Western US, where *r*-ful speech predominates to this day, despite the fact that *r*-lessness dominates in Great Britain today. Eventually, some two million immigrants of Scots-Irish descent made their way to America during the 1700s, 1800s, and 1900s.

As early as the 1730s, the Scots-Irish began moving westward into the heart of Pennsylvania, where they encountered the Pennsylvania Dutch. From these colonists the Scots-Irish picked up such German terms as *sauerkraut* and *hex*; in addition, they borrowed the musical instrument known as the dulcimer, which would later become a trademark of Scots-Irish culture in the Southern highlands, as well as the German-style log cabin, a hallmark of American pioneer culture throughout the frontier period. Because the Germans had already claimed much of the prime farming land in Pennsylvania, the Scots-Irish quickly turned toward the hill country. As early as the 1730s, they began traveling southward down the Shenandoah Valley. From there they fanned out into the Carolinas, Kentucky, and Tennessee, bringing with them such enduring features of Southern American English as the use of *you all* for plural *you* and special subject–verb agreement patterns, such as the use of -*s* with certain types of plural subjects (e.g. *The people likes the food*; *A lot of them likes to eat*). By 1776, there were already several thousand Scots-Irish living in Eastern Kentucky and the Tennessee Valley, and they continued to pour into the area throughout the Revolutionary War.

The importance of the Scots-Irish in the early settlement of America and the early development of American English should not obscure the importance of the Highland Scots, who began arriving in America as early as 1739, settling in heavy concentrations in such areas as the Cape Fear River Valley in North Carolina, or the Irish, who were among the first Europeans to emigrate to America and among the largest immigrant groups in the nineteenth century. Features of today's American English which may come from Irish English include the use of *you'uns* for plural *you* by speakers in areas ranging from Pittsburgh and the Smoky Mountains of Western North Carolina, as well as the vernacular construction *I seen* for *I saw*.

As the Scots-Irish established their yeoman farming culture in the highland South, they remained relatively isolated from the plantation culture which was flourishing in the lowland South. We have already mentioned one major center of plantation culture, the lower Virginia area, especially Richmond. The most important center, however, was Charleston, South Carolina, established in 1670. From the beginning, Charleston was a far more heterogeneous speech area than Richmond. Its original settlers were English, Irish, and Welsh; these were quickly followed by such widely varied groups as Huguenots from France, Dutch people from Holland and New Amsterdam, Baptists from Massachusetts, Quakers from Louisiana, and a number of Irish Catholics. Another vitally important group were Africans, imported from the west coast of the continent to serve as slaves in South Carolina's booming rice plantations. Among the most important planters were a group of Barbadians, who established plantations to the north of Charleston and initiated an active trade with the West Indies that was to play a vital role in the formation of the language and culture of Charleston. Very quickly, Charleston's booming rice-based economy led to its establishment as the largest mainland importer of African slaves. As early as 1708, its population was comprised of as many blacks as whites, and by 1724, there were three times as many blacks as whites.

The early development of black English in the American South (today called African American Vernacular English, or AAVE) has been intently studied and hotly debated by linguists for decades. Many believe that it began as a PIDGIN, a trade language created in order to facilitate communication among speakers who speak mutually unintelligible languages. The slaves who were brought to the New World spoke a number of different African languages. As often happens when speakers of different languages are brought together, it is likely that the New World slaves developed a modified language, based on English, in order to communicate with one another and with their white owners. This pidgin language, developed for maximally efficient communication in a relatively limited number of contexts, eventually developed into a CREOLE, a language which can be used in all communicative contexts. Gradually, the creole spoken by blacks in America became more and more similar to the white English varieties surrounding it, so that today, African American Vernacular English is far more like general American English than the creole languages of the West Indies, with which AAVE may share historical roots.

Among the features of present-day AAVE which have led scholars to posit that it has creole origins is the use of aspectual markers such as habitual *be* (*Sometimes my ears be itching*) and remote time *béen* (*We béen ate homemade biscuits when I was a child* 'We ate homemade biscuits a long time ago, when I was a child'), since it is common for creole languages to develop aspectual markers not found in the superordinate, or SUPERSTRATE, languages on which they are based (in this case, English). Other features that suggest African roots include word-final consonant cluster reduction, as in *wes'* for *west*, and the use of stops for certain fricative sounds, as in *bidness* for 'business'. It is likely that these two phonological processes are common in AAVE because neither consonant clusters nor certain types of fricatives are common features in West African languages, and so when early blacks in America encountered these features in English, they would have altered them to make English more like their native languages.

Another argument for the creole origins of AAVE is the existence of an English-based creole called GULLAH which is spoken by black speakers on the Sea Islands, off the coast of South Carolina and Georgia. Gullah is the only English-based creole still alive in the US, and it is closely related to the creoles of the Caribbean. Further, it seems to bear relation to such West African creoles as Krio, spoken in Sierra Leone. It is believed by some that Gullah is a remnant of a once-widespread black creole which eventually became African American Vernacular English, preserved through the longstanding isolation of its speakers. We discuss the origins of African American Vernacular English in more detail in chapter 6, when we introduce some opposing viewpoints, particularly the Anglicist Hypothesis, which holds that AAVE has strictly English origins.

It is important to note that not only did English have a strong influence on the language of black slaves but also that the West African languages of the slaves had an impact on English. For example, from West Africa, English has acquired such words as *okra, yam, gumbo,* and *tote.* In addition, it is possible that such Southern white speech features as the absence of *be* in sentences such as *They gonna go* for 'They **are** gonna go' and the use of fricative sounds for one another (as in *birfday* for 'birthday') derive from features of early black English as well.

Exercise 3

Recent study of the speech of African Americans in a historically isolated community in rural North Carolina (Wolfram, Thomas, and Green 1997) indicates that older AAVE speakers in this community exhibit a number of pronunciation features which are more characteristic of neighboring Anglo varieties than of "classic" AAVE. Younger speakers, on the other hand, exhibit typical AAVE pronunciations. What does this pattern suggest about the creole vs. English origins of AAVE? How would you modify your response given the fact that AAVE speakers of all ages in this community have been shown to exhibit such classic AAVE features as the absence of the *be* form with third person singular subjects (e.g. *She nice*) and third person singular absence (e.g. *She go there all the time*)?

The influence of Charleston speech, both white and black, quickly spread throughout the lowlands of South Carolina and into Georgia, where settlement was halted for a number of decades at the Ogeechee River, the borderline between white and Native American territory. Florida was not as heavily influenced by the Charleston hub in the colonial years as the rest of the Lower South, since it was under Spanish rule until the early 1800s and was not subject to extensive settlement by English speakers until relatively late. For the most part, the English which radiated outward from Charleston was *r*-less, just like the plantation speech centered around the Tidewater Virginia settlement hearth.

One final center of early settlement in America which played a role in shaping the dialect landscape was New Orleans. The construction of New

Orleans by the French began in 1717, but it was some years before significant numbers of settlers could be persuaded to live in this swampy, oppressively humid area. The earliest settlers were, of course, French, with an admixture of German. Slaves from Africa and the West Indies were also among the earliest inhabitants, although New Orleans plantations were never as prosperous as those of the Atlantic colonies. Blacks in the New Orleans area developed their own creole language, based on French rather than English, which is the ancestor of today's Louisiana Creole. The year 1765 marks the arrival of another very important cultural group in Louisiana, the Acadians, or 'Cajuns. The Acadians were a people of French descent who had been deported from the Canadian settlement of Acadia (now Nova Scotia and New Brunswick). They brought with them a variety of French which was quite different from and more archaic than the Parisian French of the mid-1700s; today the speech variety of the Acadians in Louisiana survives as Cajun. Very few settlers from Britain or of British descent came to New Orleans in its earliest years, although their numbers began to increase after 1763, when Britain defeated the French. Spain took over control of New Orleans in 1763, but the impact of the Spanish language on this speech region has always been very slight, with the French influence far outweighing that of any other linguistic group, as evidenced in such regional terms as *lagniappe* 'a small gift', as well as terms of French origin which originated in this region but later spread throughout the US, such as *bisque* 'a cream soup' and *brioche* 'a kind of coffee cake'. In 1803, New Orleans passed into American hands, and settlers of British descent finally began inhabiting the region in significant numbers. This strong English presence in New Orleans, however, came far too late to erase the heavy French influence, which only now is beginning to fade from New Orleans speech.

4.2   The Pre-Revolutionary Dialect Landscape

Let us take a moment to review the American English dialect landscape that had emerged by the time of the Revolutionary War. It is noteworthy that all of today's most distinctive dialects had already been established at this early date. In the North, we find the New England dialect area, centered on Boston. This area can be subdivided into Eastern New England and Western New England (with Southwestern New England speech being more distinctive than Northwestern). New York forms a separate dialect area, and the state itself can be further divided into Upstate New York (including the heavily Dutch-influenced Hudson Valley area) and Metropolitan New York (New York City being a dialect region in its own right). There is a clear boundary marking off lowland Southern speech from the rest of the nation; this area can be subdivided into the Atlantic South, the speech region which draws its character from Tidewater Virginia in the North and Charleston in the South, and the distinctive New Orleans region, or Delta South. Some current dialectologists (e.g. Carver 1987) place the Southern highlands within the Southern dialect area; however, traditional dialect maps consider the heavily Scots-Irish-influenced Upper South to be part of a Midland dialect region which fans out from the Philadelphia hub to encompass significant portions of Pennsylvania, New Jersey, Maryland, Ohio, Indiana, and Illinois in addition to the Southern highland region, which consists of Western Virginia and North Carolina, West Virginia, Kentucky, Tennessee, and Northern Arkansas. Kentucky, Tennessee, and Northern Arkansas are included in the Upper South dialect region even though portions of these states are not mountainous but rather are extensions of the coastal plain area to the south. Portions of Western Oklahoma, too, now fall within the Upper South speech region as well, although English had not been established in this area at the time of the Revolutionary War.

We will discuss the rather complex settlement history of the mid-section, or Midland area, of the Eastern states below; for now, it is sufficient to understand that there was far more dialect mixing in the Midland area than in the North or South, since speakers from three regions, the Upper South, New England/New York, and the Mid-Atlantic (itself a dialectally mixed region) came together in this dialect area. It is partly the dialectally mixed nature of the Midland region that has led some dialectologists in recent decades to revise the traditional American dialect map in favor of a map in which the Midland is split into two dialect regions: the Lower North and Upper South. A traditional map which depicts three major dialect divisions, the North, Midland, and South, is given in figure 4.2. A map which does away with the traditional "Midland" label is given in figure 4.3. Note that, no matter what the mid-section of the Eastern States is called, the dialect boundaries separating this portion of the country from the extreme northern and southern portions of the US remain intact.

It is also worthy of note that the traditional dialect map of figure 4.2 is based on data which were gathered in the 1930s and 1940s, testament to the persistence of the dialect boundaries which were laid down during the formative years of the nation. Only in the latter half of the twentieth century are we beginning to see evidence for the breakdown of some of these longstanding dialect areas. For example, New England speech appears to be becoming less distinctive from that of surrounding areas, and a number of traditional New Orleans speech varieties are fading as well. However, sometimes even when traditional dialect features are lost, they may be supplanted by new features whose distribution follows the same lines as the old features, thus preserving the dialect boundary. For example, whereas many terms associated with old-fashioned methods of farming have understandably passed out of the New England lexicon, some newer terms pertaining to newer lifestyles, such as the

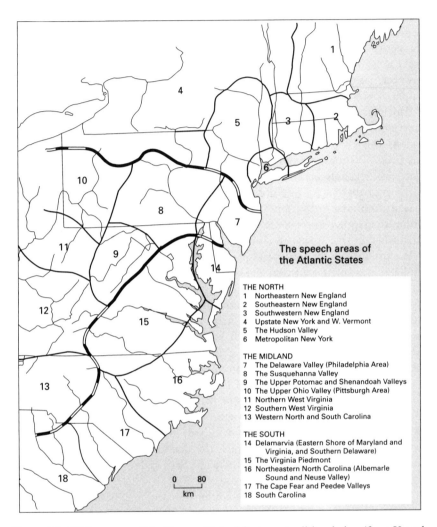

Figure 4.2   Dialect areas of the Eastern United States: a traditional view (from Kurath 1949: figure 3; copyright © The University of Michigan Press).

use of *rotary* for 'traffic circle' or *parkway* for a divided highway with extensive plantings, are largely confined to the traditional New England dialect region. Such regionally confined terms, according to Craig Carver, offer "proof that dialect expressions inevitably spread or die out, but that dialect boundaries remain relatively stable and alive" (1987:32). We will discuss the fate of traditional dialect regions in the US in more detail in the final section of this chapter.

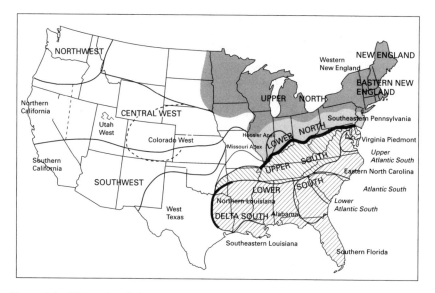

Figure 4.3 The major dialect areas of the United States: a revised perspective (from Carver 1987:248).

4.3   The Rise of an American English

When the Thirteen Colonies became the United States, there were already indications that American English was becoming a separate entity from British English. We have already hinted at the changes which took place in American English due to contact with various foreign languages. For example, English was influenced by French in the New Orleans area, Spanish in Florida, German in Pennsylvania and New York, and by West African languages such as Mande, Mandingo, and Wolof throughout the Lower South. Another source of influence were the numerous Native American languages spoken by the indigenous inhabitants of the Americas. As we discussed in chapter 2, American English acquired such terms as *raccoon, hominy*, and *bayou* (from Choctaw *bayuk* 'a small, slow-moving stream', through New Orleans French) from various Native American languages, including languages of the Algonquian, Muskoghian, Iroquoian, Siouian, and Penutian families. In addition, the development of English in America was affected by contact between speakers of English varieties which originated in different parts of the British Isles, including such varieties as Southeastern English, Southwestern English, the Midland English of the Quakers, Scots English, Scots-Irish, and even Gaelic. For example, such words as *shenanigan* 'trickery, mischief', *smithereens*, and *shanty* most likely come from Irish Gaelic, although their etymology is not completely certain.

In addition, general American usages such as *He's in the hospital* (compare the British *He's in hospital*) and Appalachian English *He's got the earache* 'He has an earache' may be the result of transfer from Irish Gaelic to English, since early Irish English speakers in America tended to use definite articles in a number of constructions where speakers of other English varieties would omit them.

Language and dialect contact were not the only factors responsible for the creation of a uniquely American brand of English. When early emigrants arrived in America, they encountered many new objects, plants, animals, and natural phenomena for which they had no names. Some names they borrowed from other languages, particularly Native American languages such as those of the Algonquian family, but other labels were innovated using the resources of the English language. For example, *seaboard*, *underbrush*, and *backwoods* are all compounds which were created in America; in addition, some existing words were given new meanings to better suit the American landscape. Thus, *creek*, which originally meant 'small saltwater inlet' (still a current meaning in Great Britain and parts of the Southeastern US coast), came to be used in America to refer to any sort of small stream, in particular a freshwater stream. Proof that English in America very quickly became distinct from British English is found in the fact that, as early as 1735, Britishers were complaining about American words and word usages, such as the use of *bluff* to refer to a bank or cliff. In addition, the term "American English" actually appeared in print in 1782.

A number of innovations which distinguish American from British English were undertaken quite self-consciously by early Americans, who wanted to indicate their political separation from Britain through their language. For example, Thomas Jefferson was a frequent coiner of new words (for example, *belittle* is an invention of his), while Benjamin Franklin was a staunch advocate of spelling reform for American English. The greatest champion of this cause, however, was the early American lexicographer Noah Webster, who gave Americans such spellings as *color* for *colour*, *wagon* for *waggon*, *fiber* for *fibre*, and *tire* for *tyre*.

Despite resistance to British English in early America, there is no doubt that British English standards continued to exert considerable influence on Americans for quite some time. The spread of *r*-lessness throughout the South and in New England may be due to emulation of British standards. In addition, other sweeping changes in British English which took place during the Early Modern English period occurred in America as well. For example, *thee* and *thou* were replaced by *you* in both Britain and America at this time (though they still persist in some English dialects), and third person singular *-eth* (e.g. *He maketh me to lie down in green pastures*) was replaced by *-s* on both sides of the Atlantic as well. Pronunciation changes, too, affected both British and American English varieties. For example, when the earliest emigrants from Britain arrived in America, they pronounced the diphthongs /ay/ (as in *high* and *tide*) and /aw/ (*down*, *loud*) with mid central nuclei (that is, [ʌɪ] and [ʌʊ]) rather than with the low central nuclei which characterize standard British and American English today ([aɪ] and [aʊ]). The change from mid central to low central nuclei took place during the course of the Early Modern English period, after initial British settlement in America. Although some dialectologists maintain that the [ʌɪ] and [ʌʊ] sounds we find in such American dialect regions as Tidewater Virginia are relics of older English, a number of scholars now believe that [ʌɪ] and [ʌʊ] were changed to [aɪ] and [aʊ] throughout America as well as Britain and that today's Tidewater sounds are actually innovations which took place subsequent to the development of [aɪ] and [aʊ] on both sides of the Atlantic Ocean (Chambers 1973).

Although American English shared innovations with British English and instituted its own language changes, the traditional dialects of American English are rather conservative, or RELIC, in character when compared with standard British English. Interestingly, this is particularly true of the two dialect areas which once kept pace with changes in British English more so than the rest of the country, New England and the South. For example, these two dialect areas are replete with lexical items from Elizabethan and even earlier English. Thus, in New England we may still hear terms such as the fourteenth-century word *rowan* ('a second crop grown in a hayfield which has been harvested'), while in the South we may hear such fifteenth-century terms as *foxfire* (a phosphorescent light caused by fungi on decaying wood), *kinfolk* (family, relatives), and *liketa* 'almost' (*He liketa broke his neck*). The Midland dialect area has long been more innovative than its neighbors to the north and south, chiefly because immigrants from the British Isles, Europe, and points beyond continued to pour into this area long after New England and the South were effectively settled. The fact that New England and the South are partners in linguistic conservatism is evidenced in the fact that the two regions traditionally have shared a number of dialect features, despite their geographic distance from one another. For example, the two regions share such older lexical items as *piazza* 'porch' (an early borrowing from Italian) and such pronunciation features as *r*-lessness. As we have mentioned above, *r*-lessness was at one time an innovative feature in American English, but it is now receding sharply. Ironically, the *r*-fulness that characterizes Midland American English and which is spreading throughout New England and the South at a remarkable rate came to America as something of a relic feature, used chiefly by speakers from regions far from the London cultural center which gave birth to *r*-less speech.

4.4   American English Extended

Just as initial British and Continental European settlement patterns along the Eastern Seaboard dictated the dialects of the East Coast, so too did these initial dialect boundaries play a large role in determining the dialect landscape of the interior of the US. For the most part, settlers tended to move directly westward as America expanded, so that Northern states in the interior tended to be inhabited by speakers from New England and New York, the middle states to be inhabited by Midland speakers, and the Southern states by Southerners. The dialect areas which resulted from this settlement pattern are shown back in figure 4.3. In the latter half of the eighteenth century, Anglos in New England and New York began pushing westward beyond New York into Ohio, driven by overcrowding, high land prices, steep taxes, and extreme religious and social conservatism. The northeastern corner of Ohio, called the Western Reserve, became an important region of New England speech and was to remain for many years a sort of dialect island in a state largely dominated by Southern and Midland dialects. The opening of the Erie Canal in 1825 deflected migrations from New York and New England from the Ohio River Valley to the Great Lakes, reinforcing the linguistic insularity of the Western Reserve and populating Michigan. After 1833, thousands of people came to Detroit by regular steamer service, fanning out from there into Michigan and Northern Illinois. By 1850, most of lower Michigan had been settled by New England farmers.

For the most part, Indiana was bypassed by New England settlers, who were swayed by reports of high land prices and undesirable living conditions. Some of the earliest Anglo settlers in neighboring Illinois were miners, who flocked to the northwestern portion of the state beginning in 1822. Chicago began to be transformed from a small settlement to one of the nation's greatest cities in the 1840s, when steamboats began bringing settlers on a regular basis. By 1850, Anglo settlement in Illinois was firmly established. Anglos also pushed into Wisconsin in the early years of the nineteenth century; most came to this state from New England, but there was also an important contingent of settlers from Western Europe, including Norway, Ireland, and especially Germany.

In general, then, the northern US is largely a region of New England expansion. It forms a large dialect area which is extremely unified through the easternmost portion of the Dakotas and is referred to simply as the North by traditional dialectologists but as the Upper North by Carver (1987). Classic items characterizing the North are phonological features such as the different pronunciation of the vowels in *horse* and *hoarse*, the use of [s] rather than [z] in *greasy*, and the pronunciation of *root* with the same vowel as that used in *put* rather than the vowel of *boot* – that is, the pronunciation of *root* as [rʊt] rather than [rut]. Traditional lexical items which typify Northern speech include the use of *pail* (vs. *bucket*) and *eaves(trough)* for *gutter*. Grammatical features include items like *dove* as the past tense of *dive* and phrases such as *sick* **to/at** *the stomach* (vs. *sick* **in/on** *the stomach*).

There are several important subregions in the North. The largest of these is the Inland North, comprised of the entire North minus New England, which has tended to remain more linguistically conservative than the rest of the

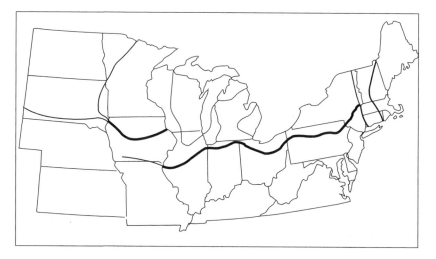

Figure 4.4   The Upper Midwest dialect region (from Carver 1987:90).

Northern speech region. Another important subregion is the Upper Midwest, centered on Minnesota and encompassing all of the Dakotas, most of Nebraska, Northern Iowa, Northern Illinois, all of Wisconsin, and Western Michigan. This region draws its dialectal distinctiveness, in part, from the numerous non-English-speaking Europeans who were among its earliest non-native inhabitants, particularly in the northernmost section of the region, where speech was once distinctive enough to render this area a subregion of the Upper Midwest subregion. In fact, the 1860 census (the first to record origin of birth) shows that 30 percent of those living in Minnesota, Wisconsin, and Northern Michigan were born outside the US, a higher percentage than almost anywhere else in the US at this time. The extent of the Upper Midwest dialect boundary is depicted in figure 4.4.

It is interesting to note that a discontinuity in the primary boundary separating the North from the Midland occurs at the Mississippi River, along the Illinois–Iowa border. This is because the Mississippi facilitated South-to-North migration into Iowa, creating a sort of "dialect fault line." Beyond the Mississippi, the cohesiveness of the North weakens significantly, due to the ever-widening sphere of influence of Midland speech varieties as one proceeds westward.

The westward expansion of the American Midland was accomplished chiefly by three groups of speakers: those from the Upper South, the Mid-Atlantic states, and the New England/New York dialect area. For the most part, the three streams remained separate, at least up to the Mississippi, giving rise to a three-tiered settlement and dialectal pattern, most notable in Ohio, Indiana, and Illinois. Settlers from the Upper South had pushed into the heart of

Tennessee and Kentucky by the latter part of the eighteenth century and from there continued into Southern Missouri and Northern Arkansas. In some places, heavy concentrations of Southern settlement extend beyond the boundaries of the Southern Midland (or the Upper South, in Carver's terms), forming anomalous dialect pockets called APEXES. The best known of these is the HOOSIER APEX, a pocket of Southern speech in lower Indiana and Illinois; in addition, the encroachment of Upper Southern speech into Missouri is considered to constitute a dialectal apex as well.

Also pushing westward along with Upper Southerners were settlers from the Mid-Atlantic, chiefly Pennsylvania and Maryland, who traveled along the Ohio River and the National Road (a road which extended from Cumberland, Maryland, to Southern Illinois, the precursor of today's US 70), settling in Ohio, Indiana, and Central Illinois. Subsequently, they pushed on into Iowa, Missouri, and other points west of the Mississippi, where they fanned out broadly, to encompass portions of states as far north as North Dakota and as far south as Oklahoma. Besides Upper Southern and Midland speakers, there were also a limited number of speakers from New York and New England who settled in the Midland. However, they tended to confine themselves to the northern portions of this dialect area, in effect pushing the bounds of the Northern dialect area southward rather than contributing substantially to the character of the Midland dialect. Because speakers from the Mid-Atlantic and Upper South also tended to remain separate in their settlement of the Midlands, Carver maintains that a dialect boundary should be drawn in the middle of the Midland region, to separate an Upper South region from the Lower North, the area of primary settlement by Mid-Atlantic speakers.

At the same time that the Upper North and Midland dialect boundaries were being extended westward, the South was expanding as well. Several dialect lines were laid in Georgia, since settlement was halted at the Ogeechee River for a number of decades until 1805 and at the Chattahoochee for a number of years beginning in the 1830s. Alabama also forms a separate subdialectal area, since it was settled rather late in comparison with the majority of the South and since its settlers tended to be from both Lower Southern and Upper Southern dialect regions. However, Mississippi is Lower Southern in character, as are portions of Eastern Texas and the extreme southeastern portion of Oklahoma. As we noted above, most of Florida forms a separate subregion, as does the delta area in Southern Louisiana.

As the English language was transported westward in America, dialect mixing intensified, and American English became more and more different from British English, where mixing did not occur on as grand a scale in the British Isles as in the US. At the same time, the leveling out of dialect differences within the US increased, as speakers from different dialect areas came into increasing contact with one another, particularly speakers in the ever-expanding Midland dialect region. Another factor which had some impact on the development of American English in the 1800s and beyond were the numerous foreign immigrations which took place during the nineteenth and early twentieth centuries. Millions of Irish people poured into America, mostly via New York, in the 1830s and 1840s. The Germans came in even greater numbers in the 1840s and 1860s, along with more than five million Italians, who came to America between 1865 and 1920. In addition, there were several other groups who immigrated in significant numbers, including about three million Jews from Eastern and Central Europe who came to the US between 1880 and 1910, and nearly two million Scandinavians, who arrived in the 1870s. By and large, the impact of non-English languages on American English was relatively limited and usually involved a handful of lexical items (e.g. Italian terms for various foods, such as *spaghetti* and *manicotti*; Yiddish words such as *kosher* and *schmooz*), since most immigrants quickly adopted English rather than maintain their native tongue. German is something of an exception, since Germans were one of the largest immigrant groups to come to America (with more than seven million having arrived since 1776). The influence of German thus can be felt not only in vocabulary (e.g. *delicatessen*; *check*, from German *Zeiche* 'bill for drinks') but also in syntax (e.g. *Are you going with?* in Southeastern Pennsylvania) and morphology (e.g. the *-fest* ending of *gabfest*, *slugfest*, etc.).

A large majority of the non-English immigrants who came to the US in the nineteenth century settled in the North and Midland portions of the country rather than in the South, which further intensified dialect differences between Southern and non-Southern speakers. However, Southern American English had already been heavily influenced by such languages as French in the New Orleans area, Spanish in Florida and Texas, and Native American and West African languages throughout the entire region. In addition, there were several important German settlements in the South, including in the western parts of Virginia and neighboring West Virginia, as well as in the San Antonio–Austin–Houston area of Texas.

4.5 English Reaches the West Coast

While immigrants were pouring into the US in the 1800s, all sorts of Americans were pushing westward toward the Pacific Coast, particularly after the California Gold Rush of 1849. Although dialect boundaries break down in the Western US, several dialect areas nonetheless can be recognized. The most coherent of these is Northwest, which encompasses the entire state of Washington as well as most of Oregon and Western Idaho; and the Southwest, which spans more than a thousand miles, from West Texas to Southern California. Again, the dialect areas of the West can be viewed in figure 4.3. The Southwest can be broken down into two subdialects, one centered in Southern California and the other in Texas. Both areas had long been dominated by Spanish speakers, first under Spanish and Mexican rule and then under the US government. The influence of Colonial Spanish on the speech of the Southwest is pervasive to this day, chiefly in the lexicon, which is replete with such terms as *corral*, *canyon*, and *fiesta*, all three of which, of course, are now part of general American English.

Southern Texas remains largely Spanish-speaking to this day, particularly south of the San Antonio River, while East Central Texas (which we will call simply Central Texas) was heavily populated by English-speaking settlers after 1836, when Texas became an independent republic. The southern portion of Central Texas was populated mostly by speakers from the Gulf States (Alabama, Georgia, Mississippi, and Louisiana), while the northern portion was settled by speakers from the Upper South, particularly Tennessee, Kentucky, Missouri, and Arkansas. Settlement by English-speaking peoples in West Texas took place somewhat later than in East Texas, essentially as an extension of settlement in the north central part of the state, Upper Southern in its speech character.

English-speaking settlers did not begin arriving in Southern California until the 1850s, but by the 1880s, Los Angeles had become a thriving population center whose cultural and linguistic influence eventually would spread northward to Oregon and Central Washington and eastward into Western Idaho, most of Nevada, and Southern Arizona. Northern California received its first major influx of English speakers in 1849, with the advent of gold fever, and migrations to the famed mining region became even heavier after 1869, when the Transcontinental Railroad was completed. However, the cultural and linguistic influence of San Francisco and its environs would be eclipsed by that of Los Angeles within a matter of decades. In turn, the linguistic influence which Southern California would exert throughout the West would be obscured by that of Texas, whose speech patterns eventually spread throughout most of the Great Plain and Rocky Mountain states.

The Pacific Northwest forms a relatively coherent dialect area (at least by Western US standards) and is centered on the Portland area. The earliest English speakers in the Northwest were the British, who had settled the Puget Sound area of Washington by 1828. Following closely on their heels were trappers and traders from New England. These people were so prevalent on the Oregon coast, even as early as the latter years of the eighteenth century, that Native Americans in the area once referred to all white people as "Bostons." Following the establishment of a successful American settlement in Northwestern Oregon in 1843, English-speaking settlers began arriving in the Northwest in large numbers, at first from the Ohio Valley states and Tennessee, and later from Missouri, Illinois, and Iowa. In addition, there was a significant Scandinavian presence in the region from the end of the nineteenth century.

The New Englanders who populated the Pacific Northwest during its earliest decades of English-speaking settlement brought with them a number of Northern dialect features which persisted into the early twentieth century, including lexical items such as *gunny sack* for 'burlap bag' and pronunciation features such as the use of a British-like *a* vowel in words such as *path* and *grass*. This latter feature is now a relic feature in the US and is largely confined to portions of Eastern New England and certain highly localized relic areas of the Pacific Northwest. In contrast, the Southwest has few Northernisms, particularly in the immense area dominated by the Texas hub. The persistence of New England speech features as far west as Washington and Oregon is testament to the enduring character of the dialect boundaries established in the earliest decades of English in the New World. At the same time, however, the sharp boundaries which were established in the seventeenth and eighteenth centuries and documented in the early twentieth become increasingly blurred as we move farther from the original centers of settlement in both space and time.

4.6 American English Dialects in the Twentieth Century and Beyond

Finally, let us examine the dialect contours of the US in the twentieth century and consider the dialect profile which is likely to arise in the twenty-first. As we have already mentioned, the traditional dialect boundaries of the US, particularly those in the Eastern US, were drawn based on information from linguistic surveys which were conducted in the 1930s and 1940s. This does not mean, however, that the dialect contours of the traditional dialect map (Kurath 1949: Figure 3) reflect the speech patterns of this time period. Rather, since most of the speakers surveyed were older, the patterns more closely reflect dialect divisions in the late nineteenth and very early twentieth centuries, when these speakers' speech patterns were actually established. Thus, it is by no means certain that the dialect boundaries depicted in figure 4.2 were still firmly in place in the 1940s and beyond. The boundaries depicted in figure 4.3, very similar to those in figure 4.2, are based on data gathered between 1965 and 1970 in addition to the earlier data (Carver 1987), which suggests that dialect divisions may not have changed greatly in the first half of the twentieth century. However, the data from the latter half of the twentieth century do provide evidence that some dialect areas are losing the distinctiveness they still possessed in the early part of the twentieth century, among them Eastern New England.

As we consider the extent to which the traditional dialect landscape has been altered in the twentieth century, we must bear in mind that a number of important sociocultural changes have taken place since the first widescale linguistic surveys were conducted in the US. There are four types of changes that are of prime concern: (1) changing relations among cultural contact groups, (2) new patterns of migration within the US, (3) the redefinition of cultural centers, and (4) improved means of transportation and increased access to formerly remote areas.

During the course of the twentieth century, immigrants have continued to pour into America. Many are members of the same cultural groups who came in large numbers in the nineteenth century (e.g. Germans, Italians, Irish), while others are new to the US or are now arriving in significant numbers for the first time. The languages brought by these new immigrant groups may affect general American English, as did the languages of previous generations of immigrants (most likely through lexical borrowing). In addition, these languages may also serve as substrates for the creation of new ethnic varieties of English. Thus, Vietnamese English, with roots in the extensive migration of Vietnamese into the US following the fall of Saigon in the mid-1970s, has become a recognized variety, characterized by features such as the use of unmarked past tense forms (e.g. *When we were children, we go to the market with our mothers*). Similarly, Hispanic English is now so widespread in such states as Florida, Texas, and New Mexico, as well as a number of major cities throughout the country, that it is a recognized variety as well. Although Spanish influence on English is longstanding, this influence was not pervasive enough to lead to the formation of a distinctive dialect of English until recent decades, when new influxes of Spanish-speaking peoples began immigrating in large numbers. For example, Mexican Americans now form the biggest minority group in Texas, and they are the majority ethnic group in two of Texas's five biggest cities: San Antonio and El Paso. In Florida, most Hispanics are of Cuban ancestry, although a number of Puerto Ricans and Central Americans have also settled in the state. Many of Hispanic origin who settle in the US continue to speak Spanish, whether as their sole language or in addition to English or other languages. Others speak primarily English. Often, they speak a variety of English which has been influenced by a Spanish substrate; such Hispanic-English dialects may even serve as native dialects for speakers who do not learn Spanish as their first language. Characteristics of Hispanic-English varieties include such features as the use of a monophthongal /e/ vowel in words like *lake* and *late* rather than the diphthongal pronunciation which characterizes Anglo American English ([leɪk], [leɪt]), as well as the merger of such phonemes as *ch* /č/ and *sh* /š/ (e.g. *shoe* as *chew* [ču], *chain* as *Shane* [šen]), /i/ and /ɪ/ (e.g. *pit* as *peat* [pit], *rip* as *reap* [rip]), and /ɔ/ and /ʌ/ before /l/ (e.g. *hall* as *hull*) (Santa Ana 1993; Thomas 1993).

In addition to the changing patterns of cultural contact which result from new patterns of immigration, we also find changing cultural relations among members of different ethnic groups who have long resided in America. The desegregation of ethnic communities is an ongoing process in American society which continually brings speakers of different ethnicities into closer contact with one another. The expected result of this interethnic contact is the erosion of ethnic dialect boundaries; however, research indicates that ethnolinguistic boundaries can be remarkably persistent, even in face of sustained daily inter-ethnic contact, most likely because ethnic dialects are an important component of cultural and individual identity. Furthermore, our own research on inter-ethnic dialect contact has shown that even when speakers do cross ethnic dialect lines by adopting features from other ethnic groups, they may subtly alter the adopted features in order to convert them into markers of their own ethnolinguistic identity. For example, the Lumbee Native Americans who reside in a tri-ethnic community in Southeastern North Carolina appear to be adopting some features of African American Vernacular English as they come into increasing contact with neighboring speakers of AAVE. However, they do not necessarily use the adopted features at the same rate or in the same way as AAVE speakers. Thus, although both Lumbee Native Americans and African Americans may now use constructions such as *Sometimes my ears be itchin'* to indicate a habitual action or an ongoing state, only Lumbees can use *be* in other types of constructions, as in *Those girls in the picture be my sisters*. The Lumbee may appear to be conforming to neighboring African Americans through their use of *be*, but close examination of the patterning of this form in each ethnic community indicates that simple accommodation does not adequately charac-terize the emerging language contact situation.

Not only are speakers coming into contact with different cultural and lin-guistic groups through immigration and desegregation, but we also find that cross-cultural and cross-dialectal mixing results when large populations of speakers migrate from one region of the country to another. Historically, the significant migrations of English-speaking people in the US have run along east–west lines. However, in the twentieth century several large migrations along north–south lines have taken place as well. For example, beginning in the post-World War I years, large numbers of rural southern African Amer-icans began migrating northward into such major cities as Chicago, Detroit, and New York. As we mentioned in chapter 2, there were two streams of northerly migration: African Americans from such states as North and South Carolina tended to migrate along a coastal route to Washington, DC, Philadel-phia, and New York, while those from the Deep South tended to migrate via a Midwestern route into St Louis, Chicago, and Detroit. There are some subtle dialect lines that seem to mark these routes of migration. For example, AAVE speakers in Midwestern cities are less likely to use [v] for [ð] in items such as *bruvver* 'brother' and *smoov* 'smooth' than their counterparts in Eastern Seaboard locales such as Philadelphia and New York.

For the most part, it seems that the descendants of the African Amer-icans who migrated northward following World War I, particularly those of the working class, have remained relatively isolated from surrounding white speakers, and so there has been little cross-assimilation between black and white speech varieties in America's large northern cities. Only in certain cul-tural areas has African American Vernacular English made a large impact on Anglo American English. For example, because popular music has been heavily influenced by African Americans, so too has its lexicon, as evidenced in the widespread usage of such AAVE-derived terms as *jazz*, *riff*, and *jam*. In addition, youth culture in America relies heavily upon African American music, fashion, and ways of speaking. Linguists debate whether non-native speakers of AAVE can really "pick up" the dialect, using all of its (unconscious) rules correctly; however, there is no denying that adolescents all over the nation can be heard to use certain AAVE lexical items, set phrases, and pronunciations, whether or not they have managed to integrate these various features into a coherent dialect whole.

In recent decades, the American South has witnessed a large influx of speakers from Midland and Northern dialect areas, who are settling in the area in increasing numbers due to such factors as economic opportunity and desirable climate. It is unclear at this point exactly how great an impact the speech of these non-Southerners has had or will have on the traditional Southern dialect. At first glance, the effect seems enormous indeed, especially in areas such as Miami, Florida; Houston, Texas; and the Research Triangle Park area of North Carolina, where Southerners are overwhelmed by non-Southerners to such a degree that it is becoming increasingly rare in these areas to locate young people with genuine "Southern accents." However, there are factors which work to counter the dialect inundation that may result from such linguistic SWAMPING. For example, Southerners have long viewed their dialect as a strong marker of regional identity and often even as a source of cultural pride, and such feelings about a speech variety may certainly help preserve it, even in the face of massive linguistic pressure from outside groups. Thus, for example, Guy Bailey and his colleagues (Bailey, Wikle, Tillery, and Sand 1993) have found that some Southern dialect features in Oklahoma, including the use of *fixin' to* (as in *She's fixin' to go the races*), have persisted and even spread in the face of increasing settlement within the state by non-Southerners. Bailey and his colleagues also noticed that heavy use of the *fixin' to* form correlates with regional pride, as measured in people's responses to the survey question, "Is Oklahoma a good place to live?" Thus, it seems that *fixin' to* carries strong symbolic meaning as a marker of regional identity; this symbolic meaning may play a key role in the form's ability to stay afloat in the face of linguistic swamping.

But what of the fate of forms which do not carry important symbolic meaning? In our investigations of Ocracoke, North Carolina, a formerly isolated island community which is now being inundated by tourists, we have found that language features which do not carry heavy symbolic meaning are receding more rapidly than those which are culturally meaningful. For example, the traditional Ocracoke pronunciation of the /ay/ vowel as more of an [ɔɪ] (as in "hoi toide" for 'high tide') is a widely known marker of regional identity, while the traditional pronunciation of the /aw/ diphthong as [æɪ] or [ɛɪ] (as in *dane* for *down*) is little noticed, even though it is prevalent in the speech of older islanders. As the traditional dialect fades away, [æɪ] for /aw/ is fading rapidly along with it. However, [ɔɪ] is receding more slowly, and some speakers even heighten its usage. The fact that [ɔɪ] and [æɪ] are receding in quite different ways in Ocracoke suggests that forms which are not highly valued as social markers may be more prone to replacement by outside language features than those which carry significance as markers of regional or social identity.

If indeed only those dialect forms which carry special social significance are likely to be retained in the face of pressure from outside dialects, perhaps the true result of linguistic swamping in the American South will be neither the complete loss of Southern speech varieties nor their preservation in "pure form." Rather, the result may be a sort of linguistic FOCUSING, in which a few highly noticeable dialect features are retained while other, less "important" features are readily relinquished. Such linguistic focusing may give the appearance that a particular dialect is becoming more rather than less distinctive from surrounding varieties as it struggles against competing varieties. In reality, though, only a few of its features are distinctive; it just so happens that these features are extremely conspicuous and readily serve to make listeners "sit up and take notice."

A third type of sociocultural change which has affected America in the twentieth century is the shifting of cultural centers. Early in the century, Americans began leaving the rural countryside in large numbers for the economic opportunities offered by the nation's large cities. One of the linguistic effects of this shift in population is that some dialects, or dialect features, which were formerly markers of regional speech have been transformed into markers of social class or ethnic or cultural identity. Thus, some of the Southern regional features which form part of African American Vernacular English (e.g. *r*-lessness, the pronunciation of /ay/ as [a]) became markers of ethnic rather than regional identity in the large northern cities to which AAVE was transplanted. Similarly, it has been shown that as Anglos in the Midwestern cornbelt leave their farms for the economic opportunities of the city, they are bringing with them certain linguistic innovations which characterize rural speech (e.g. the pronunciation of /aw/ as [æʊ] instead of [aʊ]). They then use these rural language features as a symbolic means of asserting their belief in rural values and a rural lifestyle even though they are surrounded by urban culture and dialect forms in the midst of the big-city atmosphere. Further, the English varieties developed by the immigrant groups who poured into America in the nineteenth century came to serve as markers of intra-city ethnic identity rather than as indicators of European (or other) nationality *per se*; in addition, these speech varieties also came to serve as indicators of lower-class status, as did African American Vernacular English and other varieties whose roots are in rural dialects.

Another change in the linguistic landscape brought about by increasing urbanization is the loss of much of the traditional vocabulary, largely rural in nature, whose distributional patterns underlie the traditional dialect map. However, as we discussed above, the loss of traditional dialect terms does not necessarily entail the erasure of dialect boundaries. Thus, although many traditional rural terms have disappeared from the New England dialect area, a number of new terms have come into the dialect which follow the same dialect boundaries as the older words.

In the latter years of the twentieth century, the major stream of population movement is no longer toward the heart of the city but toward the periphery, or the suburbs. As the cultural centers of the nation, large cities have long served as the focal point for linguistic innovations. As the center moves outward, so too should the locus of linguistic change. For example, Penelope Eckert (1989) demonstrated that suburban Detroit serves as a center of language change among adolescent teenagers in the greater Detroit area. However, more work is needed to assess the full effect of the suburbanization of America on the configuration of its dialects. For example, even if we accept the fact that language change now begins in the suburbs rather than the heart of the city, we need to determine if the actual process of language change has changed as well. In other words, does language change still proceed in the same manner, via the same steps, in the suburbs as in the city, even though the two types of areas are characterized by quite different interactional patterns among residents?

The final type of sociocultural change we must bear in mind as we consider the current and future development of American English dialects is the ever-widening network of transportation and intercommunication which has spread across the US landscape throughout the twentieth century, providing access to even the remotest of speech communities. The twentieth century has seen the development of major interstate highways, as well as the paving of roads in outlying areas throughout the country. Bridges and ferry services now connect islands to the mainland, air travel has broken down a number of formidable geographic barriers, and formerly isolated regions have become havens for tourists and other outside visitors. Furthermore, telephones, cable television, and, in recent years, Internet communications are bringing Americans from across the country into closer communicative contact than ever before.

One of the most important linguistic consequences of this increasing contact has been the emergence of a phenomenon we call DIALECT ENDANGERMENT. As some of the more remote areas of the nation are opened to intercommunication with the outside world, their distinctive language varieties, fostered in isolation and spoken by relatively small numbers of people, may be overwhelmed by encroaching dialects. Such a fate is currently befalling a number of islands on the Eastern Seaboard which have become increasingly accessible to tourists and new residents during the latter half of the twentieth century. For example, our in-depth studies of Outer Banks English off the coast of North Carolina indicate that the dialect indeed is in a MORIBUND, or dying, state (Schilling-Estes 1996;

Wolfram and Schilling-Estes 1995); there are also indications that the distinctive varieties spoken in the Chesapeake Bay islands to the north of Ocracoke and on the Sea Islands to the south (home to the Gullah speech community) are endangered as well.

In our studies of Ocracoke Island on the North Carolina Outer Banks, we have found an appreciable decline in the use of traditional dialect features over the course of just three generations. This decline corresponds with a decline in the traditional marine-based economy and a huge increase in the tourism trade on the island. For example, the best-known feature of Ocracoke English, the pronunciation of the /ay/ vowel as something like [ɔɪ], is fading rapidly, as are the use of such grammatical features as *a*-prefixing (*She went a-fishin'*) and the incidence of lexical items like *meehonkey* 'an island game of hide-and-seek'. As the traditional features of the Ocracoke dialect recede, they are being supplanted by dialect features from mainland areas, including a surprising number of features from non-Southern dialect areas.

Despite the seemingly imminent demise of dialects such as Ocracoke English, it may be possible for speakers of POST-ISOLATED, or POST-INSULAR, dialects to successfully resist the encroachment of outside varieties. They may have to alter their dialect in order to do so, perhaps through focusing, perhaps through using features from surrounding varieties in their own way, or through introducing new features but restricting their sphere of usage to the local in-group. Even though the resultant dialect may be somewhat different (or very different) from the dialect as it existed in its traditional form, dialect boundaries may be preserved in some form; and the speech of the formerly isolated, or post-insular, community remains distinctive from that of surrounding varieties. Thus, our studies of Smith Island, Maryland, located in the Chesapeake Bay, to the north of Ocracoke, show that the dialect spoken in this island community is actually becoming more rather than less distinctive as it dies (Schilling-Estes 1997; Schilling-Estes and Wolfram 1996). For example, islanders are heightening rather than lessening their use of certain unusual vowel sounds, as well as increasing their usage levels of distinctive grammatical features such as *We'd go hunting of a morning* for 'We'd go hunting in the mornings'. Despite the increasing distinctiveness of the Smith Island variety, the dialect is dying out, not necessarily because it is being focused on fewer and fewer highly noticeable features but simply because it is rapidly losing speakers. As the maritime industry in this community declines, more and more islanders are moving to the mainland, since the island does not host a large tourism industry. Only the hardiest islanders remain behind to eke out a living from the water as best they can. Most likely, the dialect intensification that characterizes the speech of these islanders is due to an increasing sense of solidarity as fewer and fewer islanders manage to cling to the traditional Smith Island way of life. Or it may be due to a kind of sociolinguistic selectivity, a "survival of the dialect fittest" of sorts: Islanders who value their lifestyle strongly enough to remain on the island despite the obstacles will most likely be those who possess heightened island features to begin with.

A comparison of the dialect death process in Smith Island with that of Ocracoke reveals that dialect death may proceed in quite different directions in different areas. It is nearly impossible to predict the direction which dialect recession will take in any given community, since a number of factors intersect in quite complex ways in such situations, ranging from the linguistic attributes of the features which are in danger of being lost to the type of population shift affecting speakers of the dying variety.

Given the sociocultural forces which work toward the dissipation of long-standing dialect boundaries in the US and the sociolinguistic forces which work toward their preservation, what will be the fate of American English dialects in the twenty-first century? Dialect surveys based largely on phonological systems, in particular, vowel systems, rather than isolated lexical items and scattered pronunciation details, are currently underway, and preliminary results are encouraging, at least to those, like us, who lament the demise of distinctive varieties of American speech. The key figure in current pronunciation-based dialectology is William Labov. In agreement with traditional dialect geographers (e.g. Kurath 1949), Labov (1991) initially determined that there were three major dialect divisions in the US. Although the exact path followed by Labov's dialect lines differs slightly from Kurath's, the basic separations are still between a Southern dialect area, a Midland region (characterized by the merger of the [ɔ] and [a] vowels in word pairs such as *hawk* and *hock*), and a Northern area, which Labov calls the Northern Cities area, since the pronunciations which characterize this region are most prominent in the region's large cities. A map which outlines these three areas through indicating the extent of the Midland [ɔ]/[a] region is given in figure 4.5.

Labov further indicates that the three basic dialect divisions may actually be intensifying rather than weakening. As we will discuss in more detail in chapter 5, it appears that the vowel systems which characterize the Northern Cities and the South are becoming more distinct from one another, as well as from the intervening Midland area.

Exercise 4

Given the fact that television and other forms of mass media now expose speakers to all sorts of dialects, particularly the American standard, why do the basic dialect divisions in the US appear to be holding steady and perhaps even strengthening? Why do you think television has little effect on dialect differences, despite the popular perception that it serves as the primary culprit in the erosion of longstanding dialect boundaries?

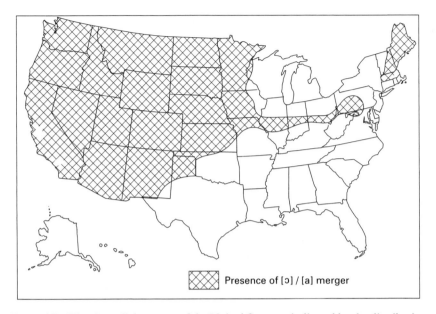

Figure 4.5   The three dialect areas of the United States as indicated by the distribution of the [ɔ]/[a] merger.

In more recent years, Labov has uncovered further evidence for the persistence of dialect boundaries, even in the face of increased intercommunication among members of different speech communities. Data from an ongoing telephone survey of dialects throughout the US indicate that there may actually be four rather than three major dialect areas: the North, Midland, South, and West. Areas within the North, South, and West sections tend to show more uniformity than the Midland area. The Midland shares the /ɔ/–/a/ merger with the West, but other dimensions of this dialect are too diverse to be classified with the West. A map indicating dialect boundaries based on Labov's telephone survey (TELSUR) is given in figure 4.6. Lines indicate major dialect boundaries; symbols indicate certain vowel pronunciations which serve to delimit dialect boundaries. We will discuss the vowel systems of the major US dialect areas in more detail in chapter 5.

It is difficult to say whether the new dialect divisions which Labov is uncovering in his most recent work represent longstanding boundaries which previous methods of dialectology failed to reveal or whether the divisions have actually arisen during the course of the twentieth century. At any rate, dialect difference in America is by no means a thing of the past, and there is every indication that the boundaries whose foundations were laid when the first English colonists arrived in Jamestown in 1607 will continue to exist in some form long into the twenty-first century.

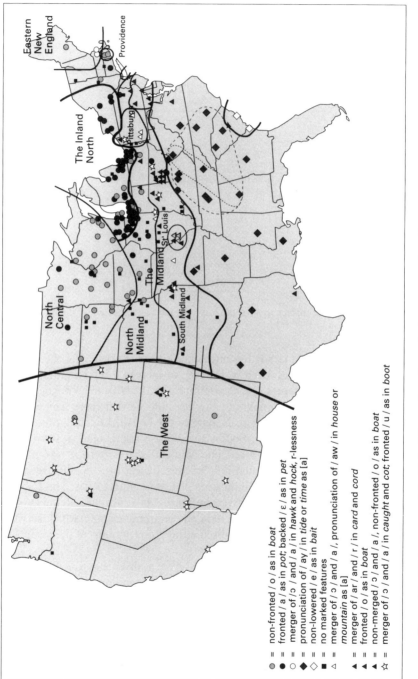

Eastern
New
England

Providence

The Inland
North

Pittsburgh

St. Louis

The
Midland

North
Central

North
Midland

South Midland

The West

⬤ = non-fronted / o / as in *boat*
⬤ = fronted / a / as in *pot*; backed / ε / as in *pet*
○ = merger of / ɔ / and / a / in *hawk* and *hock*, r-lessness
◆ = pronunciation of / ay / in *tide* or *time* as [a]
◇ = non-lowered / e / as in *bait*
■ = no marked features
◁ = merger of / ɔ / and / a /, pronunciation of / aw / in *house* or *mountain* as [a]
▲ = merger of / ar / and / r / in *card* and *cord*
◀ = fronted / o / as in *boat*
◀ = non-merged / ɔ / and / a /, non-fronted / o / as in *boat*
☆ = merger of / ɔ / and / a / in *caught* and *cot*; fronted / u / as in *boot*

Figure 4.6   Dialect areas of the United States, based on telephone survey data (from Labov, Ash, and Boberg 1997).

4.7 Further Reading

Carver, Craig M. (1987) *American Regional Dialects: A Word Geography*. Ann Arbor: University of Michigan Press. Based on data from linguistic surveys conducted under the aegis of the *Linguistic Atlas of the United States and Canada* in the 1930s and 1940s and the *Dictionary of American Regional English* in 1965–70, Carver carefully delineates the dialects of American English, eliminating the "Midland" area established by traditional dialect geographers. His discussions of dialect areas and dialect features are interwoven with a detailed account of the dialect history of the US. A number of illustrative maps are provided.

Downes, William (1984) Rhoticity. In *Language and Society*. London: Fontana, 112–51. This chapter provides a detailed discussion of the history and current status of *r* in British and American English dialects. Of particular interest is Downes's discussion of the viewpoints of several researchers regarding the disputed history of *r*-lessness.

Kurath, Hans (1949) *Handbook of the Linguistic Geography of New England*. Ann Arbor: University of Michigan Press. In this work, Kurath presents what has come to be regarded as the traditional dialect map of the United States. Subsequent dialectologists have made slight revisions to this map, but Kurath's original lines, for the most part, remain intact.

Kurath, Hans, and Raven I. McDavid, Jr (1961) *The Pronunciation of English in the Atlantic States*. Ann Arbor: University of Michigan Press. Although the detailed phonetic description presented in this work may be somewhat daunting to the novice linguist, the introductory sections provide useful information on the dialects of the Eastern Seaboard. Also of great interest is a series of maps which outline the regional distribution of dialect pronunciations on a feature-by-feature basis.

McCrum, Robert, William Cran, and Robert MacNeil (1986) *The Story of English*. (A Companion to the PBS Television Series.) New York: Elisabeth Sifton Books/Viking. This companion volume to the Public Broadcasting Service Series "The Story of English" provides a readable, non-technical account of the history of the English language. Chapter 7, "Pioneers! O Pioneers!," is devoted to a discussion of the development of American English, and several other chapters contain interesting information on the subject as well. Some of the linguistic details presented in this book are inaccurate, but the general discussion of the history of American English is reliable enough and far more entertaining than most historical linguistic works.

Montgomery, Michael (ed.) (1989) Language. In Charles Reagan, Wilson, and William Ferris (eds), *Encyclopedia of Southern Culture*. Chapel Hill/London: University of North Carolina Press, 757–92. This chapter provides an excellent and highly readable overview of the past, present, and future of Southern American English. Included are sub-sections on such varieties as African American Vernacular English, Gullah, Appalachian English, and New Orleans English.

Preston, Dennis R. (1986) Five visions of America. *Language in Society* 15:221–40. Preston's research on perceptual dialectology focuses on how people in various regions view dialect divisions, as opposed to the typical "objective" linguistic criteria typically used by dialectologists in outlining dialect boundaries. Preston's work shows that perceptions regarding dialect boundaries are generated by linguistic differences, caricatures in popular culture, and considerations of local identity. The perspective presented in this article provides a useful complement to traditional dialect survey-based approaches to the demarcation of regional dialects.

5

Regional Dialects

As we have seen in previous chapters, the investigation of the regional dialects of American English has been a major concern for dialectologists and sociolinguists since at least the early part of the twentieth century, when the *Linguistic Atlas of the United States and Canada* was launched and dialectologists began conducting large-scale surveys of regional dialect forms. Although the traditional focus on regional variation took a back seat to concerns for social and ethnic dialect diversity for a couple of decades, there has been resurgent interest in the regional dimension of American dialects in more recent years. This revitalization was buoyed by the publication of the first several volumes of the five-volume *Dictionary of American Regional English* (Cassidy 1985, 1991, 1996), as well as some new cartographic software programs for plotting the regional distribution of dialect forms.

Linguists have long debated the precise place of regional dialect studies in the overall investigation of language variation, given the fact that traditional regionally based studies have concentrated on the geographical distribution of individual words as opposed to overall patterns of language organization. The focus on cartographic plotting in such studies has led some to the conclusion that regional dialect study is really a branch of geography rather than a kind of linguistic study. Certainly, studies of regional variation may be informed by models and methods from the fields of cultural and historical geography, but there is no inherent reason why the study of regional variation cannot mesh models from geography with the rigorous study of linguistic variation proper. In fact, linguists have historically turned to dialect diversity in search of answers to fundamental questions about language patterning and language change. By the same token, the study of regional distribution always profits from the precise structural description of forms that detailed linguistic study provides. Some recent studies of language variation have neatly integrated models from these distinct vantage points in insightful and informative ways (Labov 1994).

Because of the importance of the investigation of regional variation in the overall examination of language variation in American English, we delve further

into this subject in this chapter. At this point, we investigate various methodologies for studying regional variation, as well as the underlying principles
which may govern the spread of linguistic forms over time and space.

5.1 Eliciting Regional Dialect Forms

The traditional approach to charting regional dialect patterns starts with the
elicitation of diagnostic dialect forms from speakers representing local communities within a broader geographical area. In most major projects conducted
under the aegis of the *Linguistic Atlas of the United States and Canada*, targeted
areas constituted major regions of the United States, such as New England, the
Upper Midwest, the Gulf States, and so forth, but studies run the full gamut
of regional size, including state surveys or even subdivisions within states.

Traditional questionnaires can be quite exhaustive and may take hours to
administer as each possible dialect form is probed. For example, the questionnaire used for the *Dictionary of American Regional English* (*DARE*) contains
over 1,800 questions in all. The actual questions used to elicit forms may vary,
depending on the item. Typical elicitation frames include the following:

    (1)   Labeling Based upon a Description of an Item
          e.g. *What do you call a small amount of food that's eaten between meals?*
               What do you call the heavy metal pan that's used to fry foods?
    (2)   Labeling an Item Present at the Scene
          e.g. *What do you call that piece of furniture you're sitting on?*
               What time is it in this picture?
    (3)   Completing Incomplete Phrases or Sentences
          e.g. *When your skin and eyeballs turn yellow, you're getting _____.*
               When a pond or lake becomes entirely covered with ice, you say it's
         _____.
    (4)   Listing Topical Inventories of Items
          e.g. *What kinds of wild flowers do you have around here?*
               What kinds of snakes do you have around here?

The aim of elicitation is simply to get subjects to offer the appropriate
dialect variant without biasing their choice by suggesting a variant of the item
in the elicitation frame.

A fieldworker's notes may include the variant offered by the subject in
response to a particular question frame, appropriate notes about reactions to
forms, familiarity with alternative forms, and any other relevant observations.
In figure 5.1, we have excerpts from the fieldnotes of a leading American
dialectologist, Raven McDavid. The interview was conducted in 1946 in

Pronunciation

What are the two parts of an egg? One is the white; the other is _____.
Variants: *yok, yelk, yulk, yilk, yoke*
Response: *yulk;* "*heard*": *yelk*
What color would you say the yolk of the egg is?
Variants: *yellow, yallow, yillow, yollow, yeller*
Response: *yellow*; heard from grandmother, "old-fashioned": *yillow, yollow*: "new way": *yallow*
When your skin and eyeballs turn yellow, you're getting _____.
Variants: *yellow jaundice, janders, yellow janders, jaundice*
Response: *jaundice, jandice* "I say either"

Grammar

I wanted to hang something out in the barn, so I just took a nail and _____.
Variants: *drive, druv, driv, drove, droove*
Response: *drove a nail*
The nail didn't get in far enough; you'd say, "It's got to be _____."
Variants: *driv, drove, droven, driven*
Response: *driven*
A schoolboy might say of a scolding teacher, "Why is she blaming me, I _____ wrong."
Variants: *ain't done nothing wrong, haven't done anything wrong.*
Response: *I haven't done anything wrong.* [Fieldworker noted subject never used double negatives except quotatively, e.g. "I never had no head for machinery."]

Vocabulary

Where did you keep your hogs and pigs? Did you have a shelter or was it open?
Variants: *hog pen, pig pen, hog lot, hog crawl, cattle crawl*
Response: *hog pen, pig pen*; "old-fashioned or obsolete": *crawl, hog crawl, cattle crawl*
harmonica (with reeds and blown, as distinct from a "Jews' harp")
The thing you put in your mouth and work back and forth and blow on it.
Do you remember any other names for it?
Variants: *harp, breath harp, French harp, mouth organ, mouth harp, harmonica*
Response: *mouth organ*

(Data provided by the editorial staff of the *Linguistic Atlas of the Middle and South Atlantic States,* University of South Carolina)

Figure 5.1   Samples from a *Linguistic Atlas* worksheet.

Charleston, South Carolina, with a white female, age 69, who was an artist and author as well as a member of the highest social class in the community.

The excerpt (from Wolfram 1981:47–8) includes sample questions designed to elicit pronunciation, grammar, and lexical forms as contained in the fieldwork manual used by each fieldworker in the survey. The existence of an established dialect survey questionnaire format also provides a convenient basis for comparing dialect surveys in different communities and in the same community at different points in time. For example, in *American Regional Dialects: A Word Geography* (1987), Carver compares a set of common items elicited in the *DARE* surveys of the 1960s with items elicited in surveys conducted in connection with the *Linguistic Atlas of the United States and Canada* project, launched in 1929. He concludes that "despite enormous changes in the distribution and currency of the regional vocabulary during the middle third of the twentieth century, these subregions [of New England] and their particular dimensions have remained intact" (1987:51). Similarly, Ellen Johnson, in *Lexical Change and Variation in the Southeastern United States* (1996), compares items in similar populations across a 55-year time span to show how the dialect vocabulary of the Southeastern United States has shifted over time. She shows further that various cultural and social variables such as education level, rurality, and age have remained fairly constant in their effect on the lexicon as it has changed during this period.

Exercise 1

Following are some dialect variants, including pronunciation, grammar, and vocabulary items. For each of the items, construct reasonable question frames that would enable a fieldworker to elicit the items without using the item itself in the question. Try your questions on some speakers and evaluate the relative success of your frames. What kinds of items seem the easiest to elicit, and what items the most difficult?

Pronunciation

1   The production of the vowel in *ten* and *tin*.
2   The production of the the first vowel in *ferry*, *fairy*, and *furry*.
3   The production of the vowel in *caught* and *cot*.

Grammar

1   The plural form of *deer*.
2   The past tense and participle form (e.g. *has_____*) of *creep*.
3   The use of indefinite forms in a negative sentence (e.g. *He didn't go anywhere/nowhere*).

Lexical

1   The use of the term *frying pan, skillet, spider*, etc.
2   The use of *dresser, chest of drawers, bureau*.
3   Distinctions between different shades of purple in the color spectrum.

5.2 Mapping Regional Variants

Once the data have been collected from community representatives, the variants are plotted on a map in some fashion. In the typical plotting, distinct symbols are used to indicate different variants of the diagnostic item given by subjects. In a classic example of this cartographic method, from Hans Kurath's *A Word Geography of the Eastern United States* (1949: Figure 66), the distribution of *pail* and *bucket* is charted for subjects interviewed in the 1930s and 1940s as a part of the initial phase of the *Linguistic Atlas* project. In the map in figure 5.2, the larger symbols indicate that four or more communities in the area used the variant in question.

Charting the variants for each item and community on a map was originally done completely by hand, a time-consuming task that required careful attention to cartographic detail. In more recent years, this process has been aided immeasurably through the use of computer-generated cartographic plots. Plotting programs allow researchers not only to plot their data more quickly but to display their data in a variety of formats. In figure 5.3, we provide a computer-generated map of the same data captured in figure 5.2. The plotting includes four degrees of probability shading for the elicitation of the *pail* variant, with the darkest squares showing the highest probability that speakers will use the term *pail* (75–100 percent) and the white squares showing the lowest probability (0–25 percent) that this term will be elicited. In current dialect mapping, probabilities are preferred over depictions of the simple use or non-use of forms, because they more accurately reflect the tendencies when variable data are involved.

Plotting programs such as the one used to produce figure 5.3 are now readily available to researchers. For example, a cartographic plotting program for Macintosh users is distributed free from the *Linguistic Atlas of the Middle and South Atlantic States* at the University of Georgia at http://hyde.park.uga.edu.

Computerized cartographic methods were first used in connection with the *DARE* surveys beginning in the early 1960s. In figure 5.4 is a comparison of a conventional, hand-drawn map and a computer-generated map from *DARE*. An extra demographic wrinkle in the *DARE* map is its proportional representation of states on the basis of population density, rather than geographical area. Accordingly, a state such as Texas is not nearly as large as New York, even though it is much more expansive geographically, since New York accommodates a higher proportion of the population of the United States than Texas. The proportional map seems distorted compared to traditional maps based solely upon geographical space, but it adds the important dimension of population distribution to the consideration of regional variation. As we shall see when we discuss dialect diffusion later in this chapter, population density can be an important factor in the geographic spread of dialect variants.

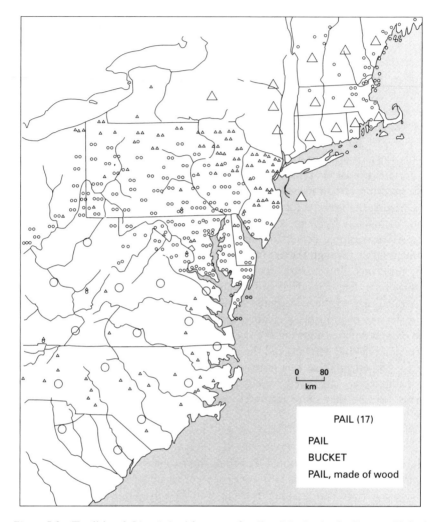

Figure 5.2 Traditional *Linguistic Atlas* map of *pail* and *bucket* in the Eastern United States (from Kurath 1949: figure 66; copyright © The University of Michigan Press).

The development of computerized cartographic techniques certainly has gone a long way toward eliminating the time-consuming and painstaking work that was once involved in mapping patterns of geographical distribution by hand and has made cartographic plotting accessible to a wider audience of researchers and students.

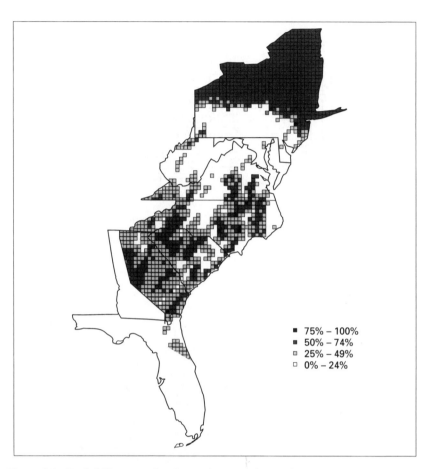

Figure 5.3 Probability map for the occurrence of *pail* (from Kretzschmar 1996:32, figure 14. Reprinted with the permission of Cambridge University Press).

5.3 The Distribution of Dialect Forms

For some regionally diagnostic items, the distribution of dialect forms shows a "group-exclusive" pattern in which communities in one area use one variant while those in another region use a different one. For example, the map of *pail* and *bucket* displayed in figure 5.3 shows a line of demarcation that sets apart southern and northern regions of Pennsylvania: South of the line *bucket* is used and north of the line *pail* is used. When the distribution shows a fairly clear-cut demarcation, a line indicating the limits of the different variants, or ISOGLOSS, may be drawn.

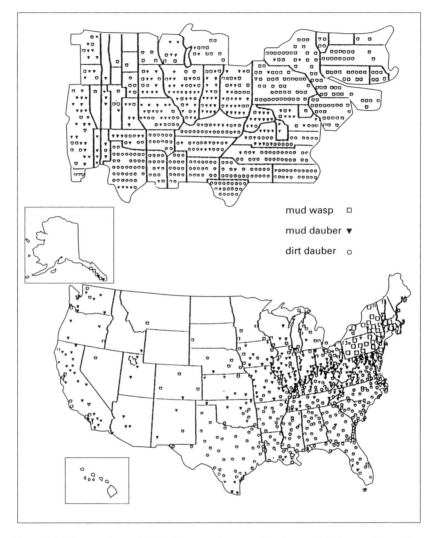

mud wasp □

mud dauber ▼

dirt dauber ○

Figure 5.4 Comparison of *DARE* map and conventional map of dialect variants (from Cassidy 1985:xxix, figure 7. Reprinted by permission of Harvard University Press, Copyright © 1985 by the President and Fellows of Harvard College).

Isoglosses set apart zones of usage in a very discrete way, but not all patterns of usage are as clear as that delimited for the use of *pail* and *bucket* in Pennsylvania in the 1930s and 1940s. In many cases, variants are more interspersed, making it difficult to draw a meaningful isogloss. Thus, in the South, there are pockets of usage for *pail* in Virginia, North Carolina, and Georgia. Furthermore, there are often TRANSITIONAL ZONES, where the variants coexist, so that an individual speaker might use both *pail* and *bucket*. In fact, transitional zones are more typical than the abrupt pattern of distribution implied by isoglosses, especially in more densely populated areas. Isoglosses are certainly useful in indicating the outer boundaries of regional usage patterns, but they must be used with important qualifications. In fact, in most cases, isoglosses represent ideal rather than real patterns of delimitation, a "convenient fiction existing in an abstract moment in time" (Carver 1987:13).

In a microscopic view of regional variation, each isogloss indicates a different dialect area, but this reduces the definition of regional dialect to a trivial one. When the overall responses to dialect questionnaires are considered, different isoglosses may show similar, if not identical, patterns of delimitation. These clusters, or BUNDLES OF ISOGLOSSES, are usually considered significant in determining regional dialect areas. For example, when the isogloss for *pail* and *bucket* is considered along with those for *darning needle* vs. *dragonfly* and *whiffletree* vs. *swingletree*, the isoglosses tend to coincide, as shown in figure 5.5.

Predictably, major regional areas are typically determined by having larger bundles of isoglosses than minor dialect areas. Using this approach, the initial phase of the *Linguistic Atlas* survey of the Eastern United States ended up proposing several major regional dialects and some minor dialect areas. For example, Kurath, in his *Word Geography of the Eastern United States* (1949), presented a map of major and minor areas which became the standard representation of regional dialects along the Eastern Seaboard for almost a half century. As we discussed in chapter 4, this map delimits three major regional areas, the North, the Midland, and the South, with a number of subregional dialects for each major area. This map is reprinted in figure 5.6.

A number of direct quantitative measures have been proposed for determining the relative significance of isogloss bundles. One of the more systematic and comprehensive analyses of regional dialects using isogloss patterning is found in Carver's *American Regional Dialects: A Word Geography* (1987), which is based primarily upon lexical data (800 diagnostic lexical items) taken from the files of *DARE*. This analysis uses the notion of ISOGLOSSAL LAYERING to determine major and minor regional varieties. The term LAYER, taken from physical geography, is used to refer to a unique set of areal features, but the importance of this concept lies in the fact that it is used to capture overlap and divergence in regional dialects by examining levels of layering rather than independent sets of isogloss bundles. The most concentrated regional dialect area, where the most dialect features are shared, is the PRIMARY DIALECT area. In SECONDARY and TERTIARY areas, there is progressively less sharing of dialect variants. For example, the core of the Northeast American English dialect shares 20 to 24 isoglosses from the inventory of diagnostic lexical dialect items, whereas secondary layers share 15 to 19 isoglosses, and so forth. While this approach does not eliminate some of the basic problems with isoglosses already pointed out, it captures the hierarchical nature of overlap and divergence in regional

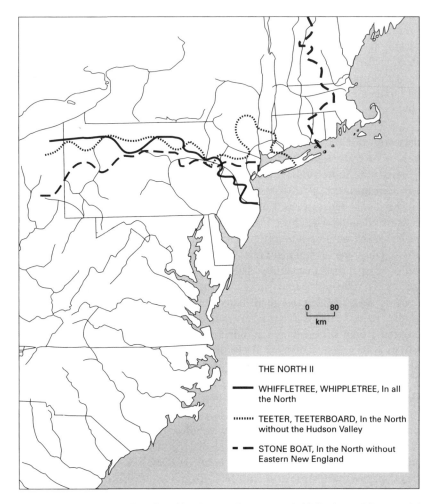

Figure 5.5   Sample of a bundle of isoglosses (from Kurath 1949: figure 5A; copyright © The University of Michigan Press).

varieties. As an example of layering, Carver's (1987) analysis of the extension of the Northern dialect area into the Western United States is given in figure 5.7. The areas labeled as primary represent the core areas of the westward extension of Northern and Inland Northern dialect features, whereas the secondary and tertiary areas represent less concentrated layers of these extensions.

Layering can also be represented hierarchically. For example, Carver's Western dialect layers can be presented in the form of a hierarchical tree, as in figure 5.8.

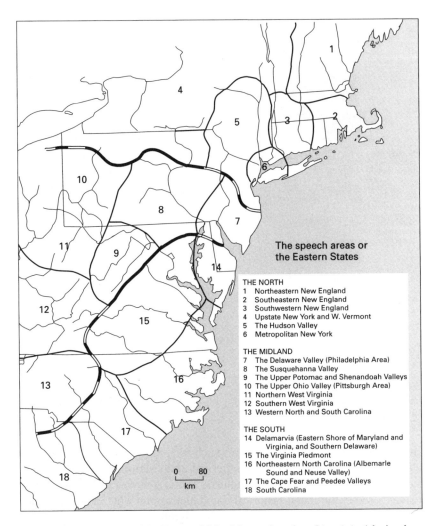

Figure 5.6 Dialect areas of the Eastern United States, based on *Linguistic Atlas* isoglosses (from Kurath 1949: figure 3; copyright © The University of Michigan Press).

The fact that lexical variation is so often used as a primary basis for regional dialects has been a major source of contention among students of language variation. For example, Carver's regional analysis is based exclusively on lexical differences. Some linguists have maintained that lexical differences are among the most superficial types of linguistic structure, and therefore among the least reliable indicators of dialect areas. However, it is interesting to note that Carver's lexical boundaries correlate well with boundaries arrived at independently in

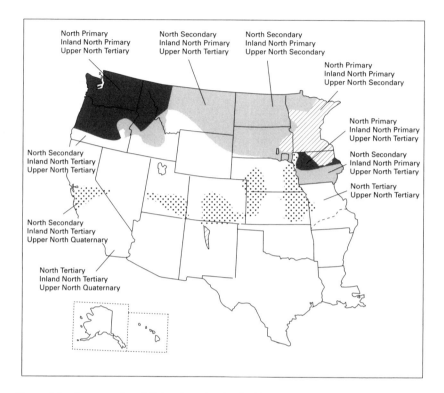

North Primary
Inland North Primary
Upper North Tertiary

North Secondary
Inland North Primary
Upper North Tertiary

North Secondary
Inland North Primary
Upper North Secondary

North Primary
Inland North Primary
Upper North Secondary

North Primary
Inland North Primary
Upper North Tertiary

North Secondary
Inland North Primary
Upper North Tertiary

North Tertiary
Upper North Tertiary

North Secondary
Inland North Tertiary
Upper North Tertiary

North Secondary
Inland North Tertiary
Upper North Quaternary

North Tertiary
Inland North Tertiary
Upper North Quaternary

Figure 5.7   An example of dialect layering in the Western United States (from Carver 1987:214).

cultural geography, including features such as architectural practice, religion, political ideology, and a number of other culturally significant variables. Thus, lexical items, regardless of their linguistic status, serve as indicators of more broadly based cultural and historical foundations upon which regional dialects rest, and they should not be dismissed as insignificant.

Many phonological variables naturally show regional variation in a way that parallels with, or, in some cases, departs from the patterns shown for lexical items. Figure 5.9 shows the regional distribution of *r*-lessness, taken from James W. Hartman (1985). The areas marked **1** represent regions where the postvocalic *r* of *course* or *car* is frequently absent, whereas the areas marked **2** have a "weakened" *r* or "less retroflexion" of the tongue according to Hartman (1985:lxi).

As with lexical variables, we may expect a kind of regional isogloss layering for phonological variables. For example, we expect to find a core Southern or core Northern area, where the highest concentration of shared phonological features is found, and secondary and tertiary zones surrounding these primary areas.

Layer
West

Regions

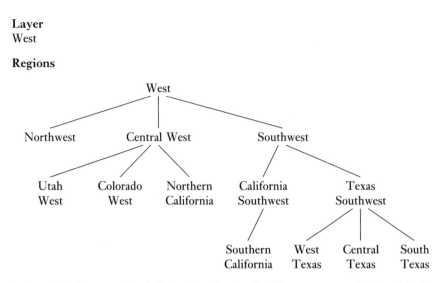

Figure 5.8 An example of dialect layering in the West, represented hierarchically (from Carver 1987:243).

Figure 5.9 The regional distribution of *r*-lessness (from Hartman 1985:lix).

Some of the diagnostic dialect items in phonology involve single items or particular sound units, such as the pronunciation of *greasy* as [grisi] in the North and [grizi] in the South or the pronunciation of *aunt* and *ant* as distinct vs. homophonous items. Ultimately, though, regional pronunciations are best

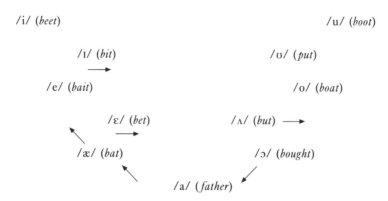

Figure 5.10   The Northern Cities Vowel Shift (adapted from Labov 1991).

viewed in terms of entire sound systems, or sets and subsets of sounds that work together, particularly sets of vowel sounds. As we mentioned in chapters 3 and 4, investigations of vowel systems conducted in the past couple of decades (Labov 1991) have revealed that there are three major systematic changes currently underway in the US, each one of which serves to delimit a major dialect area.

One pattern of change is called the NORTHERN CITIES VOWEL SHIFT. In this change pattern, or vowel ROTATION pattern, the low long vowels are moving forward and upward and the short vowels are moving downward and backward. For example, a vowel like the /ɔ/ in *coffee* is moving forward toward the /a/ of *father*. The low vowel in a word like *pop* or *lock*, in turn, moves toward the [æ] of *bat*, which, in turn, moves upward toward the vowel [ε] of *bet*. At the same time, another rotation moves the short vowel [ɪ] of *bit* toward the [ε] of *bet*. The [ε], in turn, moves backward toward the [ʌ] vowel of *but*, which is then pushed backward. Diagrammatically, the shift may be represented as in figure 5.10. Recall that the vowels are arranged so that vowels produced with greater tongue height appear at the top of the chart, and those produced with greater fronting of the tongue appear on the left. For convenience, "key words" in terms of idealized standard American English phonemes are given. The arrows indicate the direction in which the vowels are moving.

Regionally, the vowel rotation pattern depicted in figure 5.10 starts in Western New England and proceeds westward into the northern tier of Pennsylvania, Northern Ohio, Indiana, Illinois, Michigan, and Wisconsin. It is more concentrated in the larger metropolitan areas. More advanced stages of this change can be found in younger speakers in the largest metropolitan areas in this Northern region, such as Buffalo, Cleveland, Detroit, and Chicago.

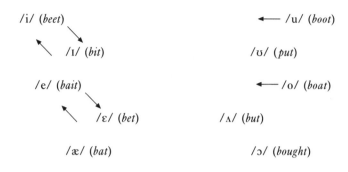

Figure 5.11 The Southern Vowel Shift (adapted from Labov 1991).

Exercise 2

Identify in the following list of words those items that would be involved in the Northern Cities Vowel Shift. Is the vowel of the word involved in the low long vowel rotation (e.g. *coffee*, *bat*) or the short vowel shift (e.g. *bit*, *but*)? Three answers are possible: (1) the vowel is *not* involved in the Northern Cities Vowel Shift, (2) the vowel is involved in the *low long* vowel rotation, (3) the vowel is involved in the *short* vowel rotation.

1	*beet*	6	*stack*
2	*step*	7	*loft*
3	*pat*	8	*top*
4	*look*	9	*cut*
5	*tip*	10	*rope*

The second major vowel rotation pattern, the SOUTHERN VOWEL SHIFT, is quite different from the Northern Cities Vowel Shift. In this change pattern, the short front vowels (the vowels of words like *bed* and *bid*) are moving upward and taking on the gliding character of long vowels. In standard American English, a vowel like the long *e* of *bait* actually consists of a vowel nucleus [e] and an upward glide into an [i], whereas a vowel like the short *e* [ɛ] of *bet* does not have this gliding character, at least not in the idealized standard variety. In the Southern Vowel Shift, the vowel of *bed* takes on a glide, becoming more like *beyd* [bɛɪd]. Meanwhile, the front long vowels (the vowels of *beet* and *late*) are moving somewhat backward and downward, and the back vowels are moving forward. The rotational patterns that characterize the Southern Vowel Shift are indicated in figure 5.11.

Exercise 3

Identify in the following list of words those vowels that would be involved in the Southern Vowel Shift. Is the vowel of the word involved in (1) the short vowel shift (e.g. *bid*, *bed*), (2) the long vowel shift (e.g. *beet*, *late*), or (3) the back vowel shift (e.g. *boat*, *boot*)?

1	*lid*	6	*loop*
2	*rate*	7	*wrote*
3	*leap*	8	*bought*
4	*red*	9	*shed*
5	*keep*	10	*rid*

Because the Southern Vowel Shift and Northern Cities Vowel Shift are characterized by very different rotation patterns, the two varieties are becoming increasingly different from each other. From a regional standpoint, the distribution of the Southern Vowel Shift is largely confined to the traditionally defined South, with differing stages of progression defined in terms of core and secondary areas of the South not unlike that shown for lexical items by Carver. Also, it appears that the Southern Vowel Shift is more advanced in rural areas of the South than metropolitan areas. This is because Southern speakers in metropolitan areas are influenced by the speech of non-Southerners to a greater degree than are Southerners in rural locales. Thus, the focal area of change for the Southern vowel system is the converse of that observed for the Northern system, in which changes radiate outward from and are most advanced in urban areas rather than rural locations.

Exercise 4

Identify whether the vowels in the following words are involved in the Northern Cities Shift or the Southern Vowel Shift. In some cases, the same vowel may be involved in either the Northern Cities Shift or the Southern Vowel Shift, but the rotation will be in quite different directions. There are three types of answer: (1) Northern Cities Shift, (2) Southern Shift, and (3) both the Northern Cities and the Southern Shift, but rotating in different directions. In cases where the same vowel is subject to both the Northern and Southern Shift, identify the direction of the rotation that differentiates the shift. You might try producing some of these vowel differences, especially if you know someone who is a good model for the particular shift.

1	*bed*	6	*lost*
2	*cap*	7	*give*
3	*pop*	8	*leap*
4	*lock*	9	*kid*
5	*loop*	10	*said*

The third major dialect region is defined chiefly by its lack of participation in the sweeping rotations of either the Northern Cities or Southern Vowel Shift. In this region, the vowel /æ/, a pivotal vowel in the Northern Cities Shift, is relatively stable, and there is a merger of the low back vowels [ɔ] and [a], in items such as *cot* and *caught* or *hawk* and *hock*. The approximate area encompassed by this LOW BACK MERGER has already been set forth in chapter 4, figure 4.5. It appears that this merger radiates from two centers, one centered in Eastern New England, near the Boston area, which extends well to the north but not very far to the south, and the other centered in Western Pennsylvania which extends to the northern boundary of the traditional Midland area east of the Mississippi River. The western extension of this dialect region covers most of the American West, with a transitional area running through Wisconsin, Minnesota, Iowa, Kansas, Arkansas, and then southward to the southernmost portions of New Mexico and Arizona. In the West, the low back vowel merger is not a metropolitan phenomenon, as indicated by the fact that speakers in Los Angeles and San Francisco do not typically participate in this merger.

As we demonstrated in chapter 4, the three major dialect regions which emerge based on systematic vowel changes actually approximate the traditional Northern, Southern, and Midland regions as defined chiefly in terms of lexical variation. Further, the three phonologically based dialect areas encompass areas which are "exceptional" in terms of their vowel shift patterns, just as the traditional North, South, and Midland contain pockets of lexical nonconformity. Thus, whether or not we view the dialect areas of the US in terms of vocabulary or phonology, major metropolitan areas such as New York City and Philadelphia constitute exceptions to the dialect rule; in fact, large cities such as these may be said to comprise their own dialect areas, since the interactional patterns which affect language in major cities are usually quite different from the communicative interactions which take place in neighboring, less heavily urbanized areas.

Exercise 5

Can you think of other examples in which a particular regional pronunciation only seems to affect one word, as with *aunt/ant* and *greasy/greazy*? (Hint: Consider the way natives of a particular city or state may pronounce its name). There are some linguists who would say that pronunciation differences in *greasy/greazy* and *aunt/ant* are actually lexical rather than phonological differences, since they affect only one item and are not the result of general phonological processes. Do you agree?

Regional grammatical variations can also be represented in ways similar to the phonological and lexical distributions displayed above, although these kinds of isoglosses are less commonly found in the dialect literature. In most cases, geographical studies of grammatical variables have been limited to morphological variants, such as past tense forms of irregular verbs like *dive* (*dove* or *dived*) or different prepositional uses such as *sick to/at/on my stomach*. Most of these cases surveyed in regional dialect studies focus on single forms in grammar rather than general rules. This is not to say that there is no geographical distribution of syntactic patterns, but simply to note that most surveys focus on individual items rather than overarching grammatical patterns.

As an example of regional distribution in syntax, consider the use of *anymore* in affirmative sentences such as *They watch a lot of videos **anymore***. In contexts such as this one, *anymore* means something like "nowadays." This regionally-based pattern departs from the general English pattern in which *anymore* can only be used with negative sentences such as *They don't watch movies **anymore*** or in questions such as *Do they watch movies **anymore**?* The regional distribution of positive *anymore* runs a distinct Midland course though Central Pennsylvania, Ohio, and Indiana and westward into Missouri, Utah, and a number of other Western states. It is also found in mountainous regions of the South (which form part of the Midland dialect area, according to the traditional dialect divisions of Kurath 1949). It does not appear that Northern and Southern dialect areas use the form at all, unless they have been particularly influenced by Scots-Irish, as seems to be the case, for example, with the North Carolina Outer Banks.

As we saw in chapter 3, dialect analysis may focus on lexicon, phonology, grammar, or language use. While lexical and phonological levels have been investigated from a regional perspective, language use has not. Since the consideration of language-use differences such as politeness conventions or apologies is a more recent addition to the investigation of language variation, there is no tradition at all for mapping regionally differentiated dialect variants on the level of language use, although there is no reason why this dimension could not be surveyed in a way parallel to the other levels of language organization.

5.4   Dialect Diffusion

How do dialect features spread from region to region? What mechanisms promote or inhibit the spread of dialect forms? Is there a general model of

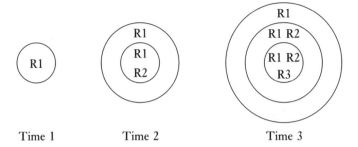

Time 1   Time 2   Time 3

Figure 5.12   Wave model of language change in time and space.

dialect DIFFUSION that accounts for the spread of dialect variants? These are the
kinds of questions that often occupy dialectologists as they attempt to explain
the spread of dialect features.

From one perspective, the distribution of regional language features may be
viewed as the result of language change through geographical space over time.
A change is initiated at one locale at a given point in time and spreads outward
from that point in progressive stages so that earlier changes reach the outlying
areas later. This model of language change is referred to as the WAVE MODEL, in
which a change originating at a given locale at a particular point in time spreads
from that point in successive layers just as waves in water radiate out from a
central point of contact when a pebble is dropped into a pool of water.

As a hypothetical example of how the language-change process proceeds
across space and time, let us assume that there are three linguistic innovations,
or rule changes, within a language: R1, R2, and R3. We assume further that all
three changes originate at the same geographical location, the FOCAL AREA
for the language change. Each one starts later temporally than the other, so R1
is the earliest innovation, R2 the next, and R3 the third. This relation is given
in figure 5.12.

At Time 1, R1 is present at the location where the change originated but not
in outlying areas. At Time 2, R1 may have spread to an outlying area while
another innovation, R2, may have been initiated in the focal area. At this point,
both R1 and R2 are present at the focal site, R1 alone is present in the
immediately outlying area, and neither R1 nor R2 may have spread to an area
further removed from the focal area. At Time 3, the first change, R1, has
spread to the more distant area, but not the later changes, R2 and R3. In this
hypothetical pattern of diffusion, we see that the successive dialect areas marked
by isoglosses reflect successive stages of language change over time. The spread
of dialect forms that follows such a straightforward time and distance relation
is sometimes referred to as CONTAGIOUS DIFFUSION.

Although dialect diffusion is usually associated with linguistic innovations
among populations in geographical space, a horizontal dimension, it is essential

to recognize that diffusion may take place on the vertical dimension of social space as well. In fact, in most cases of diffusion, the vertical and horizontal dimensions operate in tandem. Within a stratified population, a change will typically be initiated in a particular social class and spread to other classes in the population from that point, even as the change spreads in geographical space. For example, sociolinguistic researchers such as Labov (1966; 1972b) have shown that much change in American English is initiated in the upper working class and lower middle class and spreads from these groups to other classes.

In the spread of regional dialects, it is quite possible for an innovative form to skip an area which is isolated for physical or social reasons. Most often such areas are geographically distant from focal areas, but sometimes, physical barriers to communication, such as mountainous terrain or a body of water, may block the spread of a change from a relatively nearby focal point. Prime examples of such insular areas include the relatively isolated southern mountain ranges of Appalachia and some of the islands along the Atlantic coast, such as Tangier Island, Virginia, Smith Island, Maryland, and the Sea Islands off the coast of South Carolina and Georgia. It is, however, wrong to equate the retention of some older, RELIC FORMS with dialects frozen in time, as in the popular mythology that people on the Eastern Shore of Maryland, the Outer Banks of North Carolina, or in the mountains of Appalachia speak "pure Elizabethan English." While such varieties certainly are insulated from some of the changes that characterize surrounding dialects, changes take place in these varieties. However, the changes may be of a different type or occur at a different rate. Social and demographic factors such as social and ethnic isolation among neighboring groups may similarly play a significant role in delegating areas to relic status. Thus, African American working-class groups in Northern metropolitan areas within the United States may maintain some older Southern rural dialect forms such as the production of *ask* as *aks* or the use of completive *done*, as in *Kim done took out the trash*, despite the fact that they are one or two generations removed from their Southern roots. Patterns of ethnic and social segregation have, in fact, inhibited significant changes such as the Northern Cities Vowel Shift from greatly affecting inner-city African American communities, which may remain immune to such changes while maintaining a Southern-based vernacular dialect.

As noted above, a number of qualifications need to be made with respect to the simple wave model of dialect diffusion captured in figure 5.12. In fact, this model rarely works out neatly or symmetrically. Because of various physical, social, and psychological factors, the direction of spread can take a variety of configurations. According to Everett Rogers (1983), who researches the general diffusion of cultural innovation, at least five factors influence the diffusion of customs, ideas, and practices: (1) the phenomenon itself, (2) communication networks, (3) distance, (4) time, and (5) social structure. Although linguistic structures present a unique type of phenomenon for the examination of diffu-

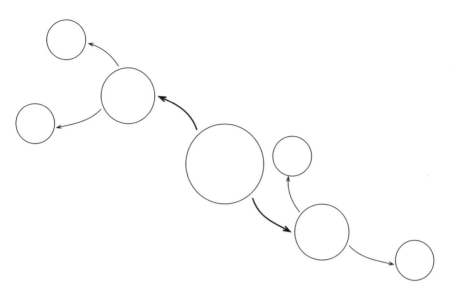

Figure 5.13   Hierarchical model of dialect diffusion.

sion, the other factors influencing diffusion, such as communications networks, distance, and social structure, are hardly unique to the dispersion of linguistic innovations. As we shall see, a full set of sociocultural and physical factors affects dialect diffusion just as it does other types of cultural innovation. Thus, a wave model of dialect diffusion which considers only distance and time in accounting for dialect diffusion is often too simplistic in accounting for the facts of dialect spread.

A GRAVITY MODEL or HIERARCHICAL MODEL (Trudgill 1974) often provides a better picture of dialect diffusion than a simple wave model. According to this model, which is borrowed from the physical sciences, the diffusion of innovations is a function, not only of the distance from one point to another, as with the wave model, but of the population density of areas which stand to be affected by a nearby change. Changes are most likely to begin in large, heavily populated cities which have historically been cultural centers. From there, they radiate outward, but not in a simple wave pattern. Rather, innovations first reach moderately sized cities which fall under the area of influence of some large, focal city, leaving nearby sparsely populated areas unaffected. Gradually, innovations filter down from more populous areas to those of lesser population, affecting rural areas last, even if such areas are quite close to the original focal area of the change. The spread of change thus can be likened, not so much to the effect of dropping a stone into a pond, as with the wave model, but to skipping a stone across a pond. Figure 5.13 illustrates such a model. Note that larger circle sizes indicate higher population density.

The reason linguistic and other innovations often spread in a hierarchical pattern is due to the fact that greater interpersonal contact is maintained among places with larger populations, and heavy contact strongly promotes the diffusion of innovations. However, even as the amount of interaction between two areas is directly proportional to the population density of these areas, so it varies inversely with the distance between the two locales – that is, interaction diminishes as the distance between two population centers increases. This interplay between the population density of two areas and the distance which separates them thus parallels the effects of density and distance on gravitational pull – the amount of influence two physical bodies exert upon one another – according to the physical scientific gravity model.

A number of American dialect studies reveal patterning whereby linguistic innovations "skip" from one population center to another, leaving rural areas unaffected until the final stages of the change. For example, Robert Callary (1975) showed that [æ] raising in words like *tag* and *bad* (so that these words sound similar to *teg* and *bed*) and [a] fronting in words like *lock* and *pop* spread from Chicago to downstate Illinois in a hierarchical pattern; in fact, his study showed that [æ] raising correlated with the size of the speaker's community, so that the larger the community, the greater the incidence of raising. Population density, in itself, does not cause vowel raising, but it is symbolic of the current role that metropolitan centers play as focal points for cultural change, as well as the kinds of communication networks in which change may be facilitated. The vowel-raising phenomenon presented above, part of the Northern Cities Vowel Shift, is now centered in large Northern metropolitan areas. Intervening rural areas are not affected, and some inner-city ethnic groups are also unaffected by these changes. In most cases of hierarchical diffusion, the spread of innovation is from relatively large regional centers to smaller, more localized towns. When changes actually do proceed strictly from larger cities to smaller, we have so-called CASCADE DIFFUSION.

The gravity model takes into account the factors of distance and communication networks as a function of population density, but it still doesn't recognize the role of other social structures and physical factors in the spread of dialect forms. For example, a change may reach a smaller city before a slightly larger area, perhaps for geographic reasons, such as difficult terrain, or for social and demographic reasons, such as a high concentration of a certain social class in a given city. The social and demographic characteristics of a region may serve as even stronger barriers to or promoters of change than its geographic features. Changes do not spread evenly across all segments of a population, since some demographic groups are simply more resistant to or accepting of change in general, or to certain specific changes, than others. Labov's research (1966; 1972b) indicates that members of "upwardly mobile" social classes, such as the upper working class and lower middle class, as defined in traditional socioeconomic terms, are quicker to adopt innovations than members of other classes.

Further studies show that women are often among the leaders in linguistic change and that younger speakers are generally quicker to adopt new speech forms than older members of a given speech community. Thus, it is essential, in tracking the spread of a change, to investigate the usage of a form, not only across different regions, but across different age groups, gender groups, and socioeconomic classes.

In examining diffusion, it is also necessary to include a closer look at local communication networks than that provided by the gravity model, which simply holds that, in general, denser populations communicate more with one another than do residents of sparsely populated areas. A focus on more local-ized communication networks is found in the work of Lesley Milroy (Milroy 1987) and James Milroy (Milroy 1992), who have done a number of studies on the effects of the social networks of individual speakers and small groups of speakers on the diffusion of linguistic innovations. The results of the Milroys' social network studies show that, in general, populations whose social networks involve frequent, prolonged contact with the same small peer group in a number of social contexts are more resistant to linguistic innovations than are populations whose social ties are looser. In other words, speakers with dense and multiplex networks are not as quick to adopt new language features as those whose com-munications are spread out among many people of different social groups.

In examining the effect of local social networks on the spread of linguistic innovations, we find that the first people to adopt changes are those with loose ties to many social groups but strong ties to none, since strong ties inhibit the spread of change. In order for the changes adopted by these people, called innovators, to make their way into more close-knit groups, they need to be picked up by so-called early adopters – people who are central figures in tightly knit groups but who are risky enough to adopt change anyway, perhaps for reasons of prestige. Because these early adopters are well regarded in their social groups, the changes they adopt are likely to be picked up by other members of these groups, thereby diffusing through a large segment of a population.

Given that urban populations are generally considered to be bound by looser ties than rural societies, one can easily see how the Milroys' model for linguistic diffusion parallels the gravity model; both models maintain that innovations begin in urban populations. The chief difference in the two models is that, under the gravity model, increased interaction of any type leads to increased diffusion of innovations; the Milroys maintain, however, that the interaction must be of a certain type in order for innovation to spread. Further, the Milroys' model affirms Labov's conclusions that "upwardly mobile" social classes are the quickest to spread innovations. The individuals who comprise these classes are most likely to maintain loose social ties with a number of people from outside their immediate peer groups, as they strive to move out of their current social class. Similarly, it is not surprising under this model that women often lead linguistic change, since, in close-knit communities, it is usually women who hold jobs that bring them into contact with members of social groups other than their own. Thus, the consideration of local social networks doesn't necessarily provide us with further description of how linguistic innovations diffuse through a given population; rather, it gives us a potential explanation for the diffusion patterns that dialectologists and sociolinguists have already observed.

Language change is not, however, simply a by-product of interaction and demographic attributes. As we saw in chapter 4, the social meanings attached to dialect features may have a profound effect on the spread of language change. Thus, Bailey, Wikle, Tillery, and Sand (1993) have shown that, although some linguistic innovations in Oklahoma (e.g. the merger of [ɔ] and [a] in word pairs such as *hawk* and *hock*) have spread throughout Oklahoma in the expected hierarchical pattern, other features, most notably the use of the special modal *fixin' to*, as in *They're fixin' to go now*, displayed exactly the opposite diffusion pattern. That is, *fixin' to* initially was most heavily concentrated in the rural areas of the state. After World War II, it began to spread to larger population centers and has now reached the state's most urban areas. Bailey, Wikle, Tillery, and Sand explain this CONTRAHIERARCHICAL pattern of diffusion by pointing to the fact that *fixin' to* is regarded as a marker of traditional Southern speech. In the face of large influxes of non-Southerners into the state, *fixin' to* has spread from the rural areas where it traditionally has been most heavily concentrated into urban areas as speakers throughout the state seek to assert their Southern identity. Forms such as the merger of [ɔ] and [a], on the other hand, are markers of urbanization and sophistication, and so they spread outward from cities into rural areas. We see, then, that the social meanings attached to linguistic forms can drastically affect the process of linguistic diffusion. Linguistic markers of local identity may be of such importance over a widespread region that these forms actually take root and spread, effectively reversing the usual direction of linguistic diffusion.

We have noted several overall patterns of diffusion in the preceding discussion: CONTAGIOUS DIFFUSION, in which a dialect form spreads in a wave-like pattern as a primary function of distance rather than population; HIERARCHICAL or CASCADE DIFFUSION, in which the diffusion proceeds from larger populations down through smaller ones, bypassing intervening rural areas; and CONTRA-HIERARCHICAL DIFFUSION, in which dialect forms spread from more sparsely populated rural areas to larger urban areas. Interestingly, all three patterns may co-exist in a given area. Thus, the survey of Oklahoma speech conducted by Bailey, Wikle, Tillery, and Sand (1993) shows cascade diffusion for the [ɔ]–[a] merger, contrahierarchical diffusion for the spread of *fixin' to*, and contagious diffusion for the merger of [ɪ] and [ɛ] in words like *field* and *filled* or *kill* and *keel*. Quite obviously, the social meaning of different dialect forms has to be considered along with geographical, demographic, and interactional factors in explaining patterns of dialect diffusion.

5.5   How Many Dialects: The Final Analysis

Although there have been a number of different approaches to the investigation of regional variation in American English, the results of these investigations tend to show a surprising degree of agreement. Further, despite ever-increasing intercommunication among different dialect areas, the dialect lines which were laid down when the first English speakers began arriving in the US remain relatively intact. The distinction between the North and South is certainly secure and, in some respects, is actually becoming stronger rather than weaker – at least in terms of phonology. In addition, the Midland and West continue to remain less dialectally distinctive than the traditional Northern and Southern dialect areas. Returning, then, to our initial question of how many regional dialects there are in the US, we can now answer with some confidence that there are three major divisions. With respect to more detailed dialect subdivisions, however, we can provide no definitive answers. Disputes over such divisions continue; and most dialectologists still frame their response to the question of how many dialects of American English there are with considerable qualification.

5.6   Further Reading

American Speech. A publication of the American Dialect Society. University: University of Alabama Press. Articles on various dimensions of regional variation are regularly published in this quarterly journal. Readers may refer to periodically published indices for studies of particular structures and regions.

Bailey, Guy, Tom Wikle, Jan Tillery, and Lori Sand (1993) Some patterns of linguistic diffusion. *Language Variation and Change* 5:359–90. This article uses data from the Survey of Oklahoma Dialects (begun in 1991) in order to demonstrate that linguistic innovations are diffusing throughout Oklahoma in a variety of patterns, including hierarchical, contrahierarchical, and contagious. A number of illustrative maps are included.

Kretzschmar, William A., and Edgar W. Schneider (1996) *Introduction to Quantitative Analysis of Linguistic Survey Data.* Thousand Oaks: Sage. This book provides an introduction to the quantitative analysis of linguistic survey data, using data from the *Linguistic Atlas of the Middle and South Atlantic States* (*LAMSAS*) to illustrate analytical techniques. The description includes an account of how *LAMSAS* was reconceived in terms of computerized methods of dialect mapping.

Labov, William (1991) The three dialects of English. In Penelope Eckert (ed.), *New Ways of Analyzing Sound Change.* New York: Academic Press, 1–44. This work, based solely on changes in vowel systems, offers a revised perspective on the delimitation of American dialect regions. Labov's work shows that, with respect to vowel systems, the Northern and Southern dialect regions are diverging rather than converging.

Language Variation and Change. New York: Cambridge University Press. This journal publishes articles on variability and change in language, with an emphasis on the interrelatedness of the two phenomena. Articles focus on details of linguistic structure and process, as well as on the social forces which help shape the patterning of language variation and the course of language change.

Web Sites

http://www.ling.upenn.edu/phono_atlas/home.html
This site reports on the continuing progress of Labov's ongoing telephone survey of dialects in the United States, which is based primarily on phonological data.

http://hyde.park.uga.edu
This site reports on the processing of data from the *Linguistic Atlas of the Middle and South Atlantic States* via modern plotting software and provides a useful comparison of current and older methods of analysis in lexical dialect geography.

6

Social and Ethnic Dialects

In many respects, the association of language variation with social status and ethnic identity plays a much more significant role in American society than the differentiation of English along regional lines. Regional differences are often interpreted by the American public as matters of quaint curiosity and may even hold a certain amount of aesthetic charm, but the stakes are much higher when it comes to socially and ethnically related differences in American English. On the basis of status differences, speakers may be judged on capabilities ranging from innate intelligence to employability and on personal attributes ranging from sense of humor to morality.

The social class dimension of dialect has long been recognized in the study of American English, although it was typically assigned a secondary role in large-scale regional surveys. In surveys conducted under the aegis of the *Linguistic Atlas of the United States and Canada*, three social categories of subjects were distinguished, based upon the fieldworker's overall impression of the subject. Type I subjects were those the fieldworker classified as having "little formal education, little reading and restricted social contacts," Type II were those with "better formal education (usually high school) and/or wider reading and social contacts," and Type III were those with "superior education (usually college), cultured background, wide reading and/or extensive social contacts" (Kurath 1939:44). Many descriptions of regional structures are qualified by phrases such as "used primarily by Type I informant" or "found only among Type III informants," in recognition of the important role of social status in regional variation.

Over the past several decades, the concern for status-based differences in language has become a primary rather than secondary focus in many dialect studies, and SOCIAL DIALECTOLOGY, or the study of SOCIOLECTS, is now a recognized specialization within dialectology. The investigation of the social dimensions of language variation over the past several decades has redefined the scope of American dialectology in important ways.

6.1 Defining Class

Studies that correlate linguistic behavior with social stratification must be grounded in valid classifications of speakers into social strata. On an impressionistic level, such classification seems fairly straightforward. Some people in our society have social prestige, power, and money and others have little of these commodities. Few people would disagree about the social status classification of individuals who possess these attributes to an extremely high or extremely low degree. We would hardly mistake a chief executive officer of a major corporation who resides in a spacious house in a special part of town for an uneducated, unskilled laborer from the "wrong side of the tracks." The reality of social stratification seems obvious, but identifying the unique set of traits that correlate with social status differences in a reliable way is not always that simple. Ultimately, social class distinctions seem to be based upon status and power, where, roughly speaking, status refers to the amount of respect and deference accorded to a person and power refers to the social and material resources a person can command, as well as the ability to make decisions and influence events (Guy 1988:39). For the social scientist, the challenge is to reduce these abstract notions to objective, measurable units that can be correlated with linguistic variation. Different kinds of procedures have been used with varying degrees of success in an attempt to capture the construct of social class.

The traditional sociological approach to social status differences isolates a set of objectified socioeconomic characteristics which are used to rank individuals in some way. Typical variables include occupation, level of education, income, and type of residential dwelling, with ranked levels within each variable. For example, occupations may be scaled based on categories such as the following:

Rank Occupation
1   Major professionals
    Executives of large concerns
2   Lesser professionals
    Executives of medium-sized concerns
3   Semi-professionals
    Administrators of small businesses
4   Technicians
    Owners of very small businesses
5   Skilled workers
6   Semi-skilled workers
7   Unskilled workers
    (from Shuy, Wolfram and Riley 1968:12)

Similar kinds of scales are set up for other social characteristics such as education, housing, and income, and different weightings may be assigned to variables if one trait is considered more significant than another. For example, occupation may be weighted more heavily than education or residency in computing a socioeconomic status score. The overall ranking obtained from combining scores for the different variables is the SOCIOECONOMIC STATUS, usually abbreviated simply as SES. Although this kind of ranking system results in a continuous scale, it is possible to divide the distribution of scores into discrete social status groupings of some type, with attendant labels such as upper class, middle class, working class, and so forth. Groupings may be made on a fairly simple, arbitrary basis (for example, dividing the total range of scores into four equal sub-ranges and assigning class labels), or they may be based upon more sophisticated statistical analyses of the clustering of scores distributed on the scale, thus reflecting more natural divisions in the ranking scale.

In recent years, SES scales such as the above have been subject to considerable scrutiny, as social scientists begin to realize that most of these scales are subtly grounded in the values of mainstream speakers (i.e. white male) of middle and higher classes. For example, researchers investigating language and gender have pointed out that females traditionally have been grouped into socioeconomic categories based on the characteristics of husbands, fathers, or other male "heads of household," often with wildly misleading results (e.g. Eckert 1989).

Exercise 1

Most people can think of individuals who are exceptions to the rule when it comes to the expected correlation between language variation and an objective socioeconomic status index. That is, a person assigned a low SES rating may speak like one typically associated with a high SES rating, or the converse. What kinds of factors may account for such discrepancies? Do such discrepancies invalidate the general correlation of language variation with objective SES scores? Why or why not?

As an alternative to the strict objectification of social status differences assigned by an outside social scientist, it is possible to rely upon community members to make judgments about status differences. Ultimately, the real discriminators of social class are the members of the community themselves. From one perspective, social classes are constituted by the community; they have no independent status outside the attitudes and perceptions of the group. Thus, members of a community are rated by other community members in terms of certain imputed status traits. Is a person from the "upper crust" or the "wrong side of the tracks"? Typically, communities have designations for particular subgroups in terms of the social status hierarchy, and these can be tapped to determine class distinctions. As with externally assigned objective measures, however, there are problems in relying upon community members for the assignment of social status differences. Different pictures of social class may emerge from representatives of different segments of the community, both on an individual and class level. The lower classes may, for example, perceive social class structure very differently from the upper classes.

Furthermore, the view of class presented here, which is based on analyses of Western society, emphasizes social agreement on the evaluation of prestige and behavioral norms. That is, it is believed that all social groups share certain expectations for appropriate and desirable behavior and view increases in social status as positive and desirable. In this view, sometimes referred to as the *consensus model* of social class, individual competition is emphasized over conflicts between classes. But it is also possible to view class differences as conflicts between those who control resources and means of production and can live off the profits of the workers – the bourgeoisie – and the workers who earn the profits for those in power. Under such a *conflict model*, class differences are viewed as the consequences of divisions and conflicts between the classes, and, in turn, linguistic differences are seen as a reflection of the interests of different classes and conflicts between classes. Accordingly, the standard–vernacular dichotomy may be viewed as the symbolic token of a class struggle. In other words, those who speak less standardly do not value standard speech as they do under the consensus model; rather, they use vernacular speech forms as a symbolic expression of separation from the upper classes with whom they conflict.

6.2 Beyond Social Class

Ideally, a valid assessment of social class differences should combine both objective and subjective measurements of many types of behavioral roles and values, but this is often easier said than done. Even to the extent that this is possible, such a perspective does not assure a neat fit between social status or class differences and language variation. There are other social variables that intersect with social class, including region, age, gender, and so forth; there are also additional factors pertaining to community life and relationships that may set apart linguistic variation from other social status considerations. For example, one of the important correlates of linguistic differences relates to the so-called LINGUISTIC MARKETPLACE, in which a person's economic activity, broadly defined, is associated with language variation. People in certain occupations tend to use more standard varieties of the language than members of the same social class who hold other occupations. Thus, teachers or salespeople, who have to confront public expectations of standardness, may be more standard in their language than their social status peers in other occupations where they are not expected to use standard language forms. David Sankoff and Suzanne Laberge

(1978) show that a person's LINGUISTIC MARKET INDEX, a ranking assigned to speakers based upon descriptions of their socioeconomic life histories, may correlate with standardness in language more closely than traditional social status designations.

Another parameter intersecting with strict social class relates to the SOCIAL NETWORK as we introduced this notion in chapter 2. Within a given social class or status classification there may be important differences in interactional activity which correlate with language differences. For example, social networks which are characterized by repeated interactions with the same people in a number of spheres of activity (e.g. work, leisure, and church) tend to correlate with a greater concentration of vernacular dialect features. Problems in the neatness of fit between social class and language, then, are not simply problems in the definition of social class, although these problems certainly exist. Instead, many of the difficulties in the straightforward correlation of social status with language variation relate to the ways in which different social factors interact with each other in their effect on linguistic variation.

Also, in small, isolated speech communities where "everybody knows everybody," the correlation of language differences and socio-economic differences may not be nearly as significant as in large, urban communities characterized by a high degree of social distance among different groups of speakers. For example, we have found on the island of Ocracoke, North Carolina, that some of the most vernacular speakers are men who went to college off the island and later returned to Ocracoke. These men are among the most influential and powerful people on the island, owning considerable property and making considerable amounts of money from the tourism industry, yet they maintain a strong vernacular dialect. They also interact on a regular basis with outsiders, conducting business and socializing with them more than some other islanders. Their maintenance of the vernacular is due to the fact that they wish to project a "traditional islander" identity rather than to identify with the middle- or upper-class mainlanders who typically are associated with standard speech forms. Thus, we see that matters of identity and personal presentation have to be taken into account along with conventional status measures and factors pertaining to interactional networks when considering the correlation of linguistic and social differences.

6.3   The Patterning of Social Differences in Language

Not all linguistic structures correlate with social status differences in the same way. Different linguistic variables may align with given social status groupings in a variety of ways. For example, consider the ways in which two linguistic variables are distributed across four different social strata within the African

Social and Ethnic Dialects

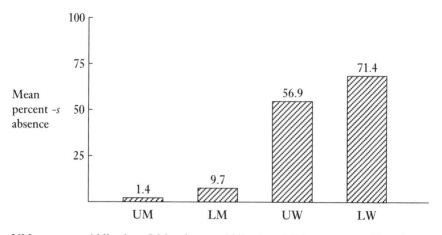

UM = upper middle class; LM = lower middle class; UW = upper working class;
LW = lower working class.

Figure 6.1   Third person singular *-s/-es* absence: an example of sharp stratification.

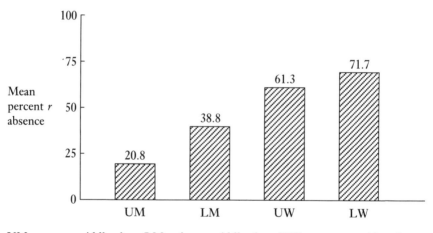

UM = upper middle class; LM = lower middle class; UW = upper working class;
LW = lower working class.

Figure 6.2   Postvocalic *r* absence: an example of gradient stratification.

American community of Detroit, Michigan. These variables are third person
singular suffix absence (e.g. *She go to the store* for *She goes to the store*) in figure 6.1 and *r*-lessness (e.g. *bea'* for *bear*) in figure 6.2.

In figure 6.1, the linguistic variation correlates with certain discrete social
layers. The middle-class groups show very little *-s/-es* absence whereas working-
class speakers show significant levels of *-s/-es* absence. The distribution of

-*s*/-*es* use shows a wide separation between middle-class and working-class groups and is therefore referred to as a case of SHARP STRATIFICATION. On the other hand, the distribution of *r*-lessness in figure 6.2 indicates a pattern of GRADIENT or FINE STRATIFICATION, in which the relative frequency of *r*-lessness changes gradually from one social class to the adjacent one.

In the examples given in figures 6.1 and 6.2, sharp stratification is illustrated by a grammatical variable and gradient stratification by a phonological one. Although there are exceptions, grammatical variables are more likely to show sharp stratification than phonological variables. This underscores the fact that grammatical features are typically more diagnostic of social differences than phonological ones with respect to the standard–nonstandard continuum of English.

Stable linguistic variables defined primarily on the standard–nonstandard continuum of English tend to be sharply stratified, whereas linguistic features undergoing change often exhibit gradient stratification. This is due, in part, to the role of social class in language change within a community. As we will discuss shortly, change tends to start in a given social class and spread from that point to adjacent social classes. The kind of correlation that exists between social status and linguistic variation may thus be a function of both social and linguistic considerations. There is no single pattern that can be applied to this co-variation.

Since there are different patterns of correlation between social stratification and linguistic variation, it is sometimes difficult to answer the question of how many social dialects there are in English. On one level, this question is best answered by examining the social stratification of particular linguistic variables. From this perspective, the answer may range from two, for a sharply stratified variable which shows a basic dichotomy between two broadly defined social groups, through six or seven varieties for finely stratified features. For linguistic variation showing a correlation with two basic social groups, the popular perception that there are two social dialects – namely a standard and a vernacular – may be matched by the reality of social stratification. However, for other variables, multi-layered social dialect differentiation is clearly indicated. It is important to understand that both continuous and discrete patterns of sociolinguistic variation may simultaneously exist within the same population.

6.4 The Social Evaluation of Linguistic Features

Although there is no inherent social valuation associated with the variants of a linguistic feature, it is not surprising that the social values assigned to certain groups in society will be attached to the linguistic forms used by the members of these groups. It is no accident that standard varieties of a language typically are associated with socially favored and dominant classes and that nonstandard dialects are associated with socially disfavored, low-status groups. The choice of particular linguistic variables for social evaluation may be arbitrary, but their social evaluation tends to correlate with the social evaluation of the groups who use them. SOCIALLY PRESTIGIOUS variants are those forms that are positively valued through their association with high-status groups as linguistic markers of status, whereas SOCIALLY STIGMATIZED variants carry negative connotations through their association with low-status groups. In grammar, most prestige forms are related to prescriptive norms of standardness or even literary norms. For example, the use of *whom* in **Whom did you see?** or the placement of *never* in *Never have I seen a more gruesome sight* might be considered prestige variants in some social contexts. Apart from these somewhat special cases, it is difficult to find clear-cut cases of prestige variants on the grammatical level of language, particularly in the grammar of ordinary informal conversation.

Examples of prestige variants are also relatively rare in phonology. The use of an "unflapped" *t* in words like *better* or *latter* (e.g. [bɛtɚ] as opposed to [bɛDɚ]) as used by a select group of "Brahmin" dialect speakers found in the Boston metropolitan area may be an example of a prestige variant, as would some other phonological characteristics of this dialect, but this is a fairly isolated, somewhat unusual situation. The pronunciations of this restricted prestige dialect are modeled more on standard British English, or Received Pronunciation, than on American English. The fact that an external norm serves as a model for prestige in this instance is actually a commentary on the relative absence of authentic prestige variants in American English dialects. In some regions, the pronunciation of *either* as [aɪðɚ] instead of [iðɚ] or the pronunciation of *vase* as [vaz] vs. [ves] may be associated with high status, but these relate to the pronunciation of single lexical items rather than phonological systems and are therefore more properly considered lexical than phonological variants.

For present-day American English, it is clear that the vast majority of socially diagnostic structures exist on the axis of stigmatization rather than the axis of prestige. Classic illustrations involving grammatical features include the familiar cases of multiple negation (e.g. *They **didn't do nothing***), regularized verb forms (e.g. *He **knowed** they were right*), and different subject–verb agreement patterns (e.g. *We **was** there*). Stigmatized phonological features include *-in'* for *-ing* (e.g. *stoppin', swimmin'*), [d] or [t] for *th* (e.g. [dey] *they*, [tɪnk] *think*). There are also lexical shibboleths such as *ain't*. It is relatively easy to come up with examples of stigmatized variants for different levels of linguistic organization as compared with prestigious variants. As we pointed out in chapter 1, this observation is part of the rationale which leads us to conclude that standard English is more adequately characterized by the absence of negatively valued, stigmatized items than by the presence of positively valued, prestige items.

It is essential to understand that stigmatized and prestigious variants do not exist on a single axis in which the alternative to a socially stigmatized variant is a socially prestigious one, or vice versa. The absence of multiple negation, for example, is not particularly prestigious; it is simply not stigmatized. Similarly, the non-prestigious variant for *either* [iðɚ] is not necessarily stigmatized; it is simply not prestigious. In fact, there are very few cases in English in which there exists a socially prestigious alternate for a socially stigmatized variant.

In discussing the social significance of linguistic variants, we must keep in mind that the popular notion that speakers who use stigmatized variants always use these variants and those who use prestige variants always use these forms is simply not true. For example, it has been shown that all speakers use the stigmatized [ɪn] pronunciation for *-ing* to some extent, with those of lower social status using more of the stigmatized variant and those of higher status showing less [ɪn] for *-ing*. We will discuss this notion more fully in chapter 9.

The discussion of the social evaluation of linguistic features up to this point has been undertaken from the vantage point of those who place high value on the widespread, institutional language norms established by higher-status groups. These norms are overtly perpetuated by the agents of standardization in our society – teachers, the media, and other authorities responsible for setting the standards of linguistic behavior. These norms are usually acknowledged across a full range of social classes on a community-wide basis. Linguistic forms that are assigned their social evaluation on the basis of this widespread recognition of social significance are said to carry OVERT PRESTIGE. At the same time, however, there may exist another set of norms which relates primarily to solidarity with more locally defined social groups, irrespective of the social status of these groups. When forms are positively valued apart from, or even in opposition to, their social significance for the wider society, they are said to carry COVERT PRESTIGE. In the case of overt prestige, the social valuation lies in a unified, widely accepted set of social norms, whereas in the case of covert prestige, the positive social significance lies in the local culture of social relations. Thus, it is possible for a socially stigmatized variant in one setting to have covert prestige in another. A local youth who adopts vernacular forms in order to maintain solidarity with a group of friends clearly indicates the covert prestige of these features on a local level even if the same features stigmatize the speaker in a wider, mainstream context such as school. The notion of covert prestige is important in understanding why vernacular speakers do not rush to become standard dialect speakers, even when these speakers may evaluate the social significance of linguistic variation in a way which superficially matches that of their high-status counterparts. Thus, widely recognized stigmatized features such as multiple negation, nonstandard subject–verb agreement, and different irregular verb paradigms may function at the same time as positive, covertly prestigious features in terms of local norms.

In recent years, the maintenance or even heightening of vernacular language features among non-mainstream speakers has been viewed in terms of power as well as prestige. For example, Scott Kiesling (1996) points out that working-class men may use vernacular variants as a means of projecting economic power rather than covert prestige, since working-class men traditionally have held occupations associated with physical toughness and manliness (and hence vernacular language features) rather than with advanced education. We discuss this alternative view in more detail in chapter 7.

As noted above, the social significance of language forms changes over time, just as linguistic structures themselves change. It may be difficult for present-day speakers of English to believe that linguistic shibboleths such as *ain't* and multiple negation were once socially insignificant, but the historical study of the English language certainly supports this conclusion. Furthermore, shifts in social significance may take place from generation to generation. As Labov (1966:342–9) has shown, for New York City, the social significance of postvocalic *r* (as in *cart* or *farm*) has shifted during the past 50 years. For the older generation, there is very little social class stratification for the use of postvocalic *r*, but younger speakers show a well-defined pattern of social stratification in which the presence of *r* (e.g. *cart*) is more highly valued than its absence (e.g. *caht*). Similarly, as we saw in chapter 4, postvocalic *r*-lessness in Southern speech was once a prestigious pronunciation, following the prestige model for British English. However, the valuation of *r*-less speech has changed over the decades, and today it is working-class rural groups in the South who are most characteristically *r*-less rather than urban upper-class speakers. Because *r*-lessness used to carry prestige, we find that older, upper-class groups in some regions of the South retain a high incidence of *r*-lessness; however, younger upper-class speakers tend to pronounce their *r*'s. At the same time, younger, rural working-class speakers may be relatively *r*-less, thus uniting older metropolitan and younger rural speakers in *r*-lessness. Quite obviously, the social valuation accorded to regional variables can shift fairly abruptly.

The social significance of linguistic variables may also vary from region to region. As a native Philadelphian, the first author grew up associating the pronunciation of *aunt* as [ant] with high-status groups. In his own working-class dialect, [ænt] was the normal pronunciation; in other words, *aunt* and *ant* were homophones in his dialect. He was quite shocked to discover in later life that the pronunciation of *aunt* he considered to be prestigious and even "uppity" was characteristic of some Southern dialects regardless of social status, including highly stigmatized vernacular varieties such as African American Vernacular English. Meanwhile (actually a couple of decades later), the second author grew up in a Southern dialect area assuming that [ant] was a highly stigmatized pronunciation associated with vernacular rather than standard dialects. In a similar vein, postvocalic *r*-lessness may be associated with the prestigious Boston Brahmin dialect or the RP (Received Pronunciation) English of the British Isles at the same time it is socially disfavored in other settings, such as present-day New York City.

Although some socially diagnostic variables have regionally restricted social significance, other variables may have general social significance for American English, in that a particular social evaluation holds across regional boundaries. Many of the grammatical variables mentioned above have this type of broad-based significance. Virtually every population in the United States which has been studied by social dialectologists shows social stratification for structures like multiple negation, irregular verb forms, and subject–verb agreement patterns. On the whole, phonological variables are more apt to show regionally restricted social significance than are grammatical variables. No doubt, this is due to the fact that grammatical variables have been ascribed the major symbolic role in differentiating standard from vernacular dialects. Phonological variables show greater flexibility, as they are more likely to be viewed as a normal manifestation of regional diversity in English. As noted earlier, this is particularly true in the case of vowel differences.

There are several different ways in which speakers within the sociolinguistic community may react to socially diagnostic variables. Speakers may treat some features as SOCIAL STEREOTYPES, where they comment overtly on their use. Items such as *ain't*, "double negatives," and "*dese, dem*, and *dose*" are classic features of this type. Stereotypes can be regionally specific or generalized and may carry either positive or negative connotations. Thus, items like *ain't* and *dese, dem* and *dose* are widely recognized as "bad grammar," while features like the pronunciation of *high tide* as something like "hoi toide," which characterizes the speech of coastal North Carolina, are strongly stereotyped but only locally. Further, the latter feature carries positive associations in that it is often associated with "British English" or "Shakespearean English." However, it still qualifies as a stereotype because it is the subject of overt commentary.

As with other kinds of behavioral stereotyping, we have to be careful to differentiate the actual sociolinguistic patterning of linguistic stereotypes from popular beliefs about their patterning. These beliefs are often linguistically naive, although they may derive from a basic sociolinguistic reality. For example, people tend to believe that working–class speakers always use the stereotypical *dese, dem*, and *dose* forms and middle-class speakers never do. This belief is not supported empirically, although there certainly is a correlation between the relative frequency of the nonstandard variant and social stratification. Similarly, the Outer Banks "hoi toide" vowel certainly is a defining dialect trait of the region, but it is in flux and its rate of usage is highly variable. Furthermore, stereotypes tend to focus on single vocabulary items or selective subsets of items rather than more general phonological and grammatical patterns. For example, speakers may focus on a single lexical item like *ain't* or the restricted pronunciation pattern involving *tomatoes* and *potatoes* in which *'maters* and *'taters* is stigmatized and *tomahtos* and *potahtos* is prestigious. Finally, we have to understand that popular explanations for sociolinguistic differences are often rooted in the same type of folk mythology that characterizes other types of behavioral stereotyping and therefore must be viewed with great caution.

Another role which a socially diagnostic feature may fill is that of a SOCIAL MARKER. In the case of social markers, variants show clear-cut social stratification, but they do not show the level of conscious awareness found for the social stereotype. Various vowel shifts, such as the Northern Cities Vowel shift discussed in chapter 5, seem to function as social markers. There is clear-cut social stratification of the linguistic variants, and participants in the community may even recognize this distribution, but the structure does not evoke the kind of overt commentary and strong value judgments that the social stereotype does. Even if participants don't talk about these features in any direct manner, there are still indications that they are aware of their existence at an unconscious level. This awareness is often indicated by shifts in the use of variants across different styles of speaking. Although we will take up the notion of speech style more fully in chapter 7, we may anticipate our discussion by noting that the incidence of prestigious variants tends to increase and the use of stigmatized variants to decrease as we use more formal speech styles. For example, a speaker who is conversing with an employer during a business meeting will use more [ɪŋ] for *-ing* but will use more [ɪn] when talking with friends over lunch.

The third possible sociolinguistic role which a socially diagnostic feature may fill is that of a SOCIAL INDICATOR. Social indicators are linguistic structures that correlate with social stratification without having an effect on listeners' judgment of the social status of speakers who use them. Whereas social stereotypes and social markers are sensitive to stylistic variation, social indicators do not show such sensitivity, as shown by the fact that levels of usage remain constant across formal and informal styles. This suggests that the correlation of socially diagnostic variables with social status differences operates on a more unconscious level than it does for social markers or stereotypes. Although social indicators have been identified for some communities of English speakers (Trudgill 1974:98), practically all of the socially diagnostic variables in American English qualify as social markers or stereotypes rather than indicators. One possible exception involves variants associated with the earliest stages of vowel shifts, such as the Northern Cities Vowel Shift. When such vowel shifts begin, the use of new vowel pronunciations tends to correlate with social class differences but does not yet show any correlation with stylistic differences. As these changes proceed, the new pronunciations will become social markers, and they may even attain the status of a stereotype.

6.5   Social Class and Language Change

One of the important contributions of the study of social dialectology has to do with the roles that different social classes play in language change. Language change does not take place simultaneously on all different social strata; instead, it originates in particular social classes and then spreads from that point, just as regional dialect change typically starts in a focal area and spreads outward from that point.

What social classes are most likely to start language change? The popular view seems to be that the upper classes originate change and that other social classes follow their lead. The model of change showing the elite leading the masses seems intuitively satisfying, but turns out to be largely mistaken. In reality, as we have mentioned in previous chapters, the lower social classes are much more responsible for language change than they have been given credit for. Furthermore, extremes in the social strata, for example, the highest and the lowest social classes, tend to be peripheral to the origin of change; it is those social classes between the extremes which bear the major responsibility for change. The middle-status groups tend to have the strongest loyalty to their local communities so they are more sensitive to local innovation. Further, those in middle-class groups also have connections to outside groups who may serve as models for language change. According to Gregory Guy (1988:58), the highest social groups are not as likely to identify with local communities, while the lowest social groups have neither strong affinity to their local community nor broader community allegiance.

In order to understand the role of social class in language change, it is essential to understand the distinction between changes that take place below the level of consciousness, so-called CHANGES FROM BELOW, and those that take place above the level of consciousness, or CHANGES FROM ABOVE. Although this distinction often happens to coincide with change in terms of social class in that the lower social classes are more likely to be active in changes from below and the upper classes in changes from above, the fundamental distinction refers to the level of consciousness, not social class. Many of the phonological changes in American English, particularly those involving vowel systems, are changes from below, or at least start out as changes from below. Changes from above tend to reflect a movement away from socially stigmatized features or toward external prestige forms that become the model to emulate. For example, the adoption of *r*-lessness in the late 1700s and early 1800s by some regional varieties in the United States based on the external, British prestige norm is an example of change from above. Conversely, and somewhat ironically, the increased use of postvocalic *r* in New York City in recent decades on the basis of dialect models outside of the area is also a change from above, but in this instance the model is other dialects of American English.

The spread of new forms through the population is only one side of language change. The other side concerns *resistance to change*. Whereas change is certainly natural and inevitable, some social groups may differentiate themselves by withstanding changes taking place in other social groups. As presented in chapter 2, many changes which take place in language involve making language systems as orderly as possible, such as the regularization of irregular grammatical paradigms. For the most part, it is the lower classes that adopt these changes initially and the upper classes that tend to resist them. The regularization of irregular plurals (e.g. *sheeps, oxes*), irregular reflexives (*hisself, theirselves*), and irregular verbs (e.g. *knowed, growed*) in the grammar – attributable to natural forces from within the grammatical system – are certainly changes in the English language which are witnessed to a greater degree in the lower classes than the upper classes. These changes, along with a number of natural phonological changes noted in chapter 2, have made some headway in the lower classes but are resisted by the upper classes in spite of their linguistic reasonableness. It is the upper classes who have the most investment in maintaining the language as it is; the lower classes have less investment in maintaining the current state of linguistic structures. Accordingly, more conscious attention by the upper classes is given to withstanding potential changes conveniently "offered" by the lower classes, even if these changes are natural adaptations of the linguistic system. Only a change in the social valuation of forms can result in the adoption of linguistically natural but socially stigmatized forms by the upper classes.

An important principle of sociolinguistic stratification thus involves the inhibition of natural linguistic changes by high-status groups. By resisting the changes that take place in the lower-status groups, the social stratification of linguistic differences is maintained and even heightened. The bottom line is that higher-status groups do not want to be mistaken for lower-status groups in language any more than they do in other kinds of behavior. Thus, high-status groups often suppress natural changes taking place in lower-status groups to keep their sociolinguistic position intact. In many respects, then, the social differentiation of language in American society is typified by the resistance to proposed changes initiated by the lower classes by a steadfast upper class rather than the initiation of change by the upper classes and subsequent emulation of these changes by the lower classes.

Exercise 2

Some of the language changes that typify lower-status groups are also found in a stage of language acquisition by the children of high-status parents because they involve such natural linguistic extensions. For example, middle-class children go through a stage of acquisition when they regularize irregular verb forms (e.g. *growed, knowed*), regularize plurals (e.g. *oxes, sheeps*), use multiple negatives (e.g. *I didn't do nothing, Nobody didn't go*), and so forth. How are these natural tendencies to regularize combatted? Do you recall being corrected about these forms? If so, who was responsible for such correction? What might happen if some of these irregular forms were not directly focused upon by parents, teachers, and other language guardians in our society responsible for socializing children into upper- and middle-class norms of linguistic behavior?

6.6 Ethnicity

Although the correlation of ethnicity with linguistic variation is indisputable, the precise contribution of ethnic group membership to the overall configuration of dialects is not always simple to isolate. Nominal classification of people into various ethnic categories in our society seems straightforward on the surface, but it is much more difficult to capture the underlying factors that ultimately define the cultural notion of ethnicity. From a sociolinguistic perspective, what is popularly identified as "ethnicity" may be difficult to separate from other social factors such as region and social class. For example, the popular notion of Jewish English has a strong regional association with New York City English; similarly, what is identified as African American Vernacular English (AAVE) is strongly linked to social status within the community as well as Southern regional English. A variety such as Chicano English in the Southwest, on the other hand, is often linked with bilingualism even though some of the features of this language variety may now be maintained by speakers who are not bilingual. Furthermore, language and dialect in and of themselves are an integral part of ethnic definition. Thus, some Native Americans in North Carolina who have lost their ancestral languages seem to distinguish themselves from surrounding contact varieties through their maintenance of a distinctive variety of English (Wolfram 1996). In fact, one of the easiest ways of recognizing members of some of these groups is by how they talk rather than by physical appearance or some other defining characteristic. Notwithstanding the qualifications that must go into the definition of ethnicity as a variable in dialect differentiation, it is safe to conclude that "in communities where the local lore acknowledges more than one ethnic group, we would expect ethnicity to be a factor in linguistic variation" (Laferriere 1979:603).

The definition of an ethnic group usually involves the following kinds of parameters (from the National Council of Social Studies, Task Force on Ethnic Studies 1976): (1) origins that precede or are external to the state (e.g. Native American, immigrant groups); (2) group membership that is involuntary; (3) ancestral tradition rooted in a shared sense of peoplehood; (4) distinctive value orientations and behavioral patterns; (5) influence of the group on the lives of its members; and (6) group membership influenced by how members define themselves and how they are defined by others. This is an expansive set of parameters, but even this definition does not always lead to clear-cut ethnic categorization. In some cases, a subjectively based self-definition turns out to be stronger in determining a person's ethnicity than any of the parameters set forth in the institutional definition.

Notwithstanding the problems involved in teasing out the ethnicity variable, there is ample evidence that ethnicity can be a key component in the definition of a dialect. The literature on American English dialects thus includes descriptions of varieties labeled Italian English, Jewish English, Irish English, German English, Puerto Rican English, Chicano English, American Indian English, Vietnamese English, and, of course, AAVE. The extent to which ethnicity *per se* contributes to the definition of dialect in these accounts, however, varies greatly, as does the amount of dialectal distinctiveness. For example, a survey of research on Jewish English concluded that this variety could be distinguished from others solely on the basis of a restricted set of lexical differences, a small inventory of phonological differences related to vowels and intonation, isolated grammatical features, and several aspects of conversational style (Gold 1981; Steinmetz 1981). By contrast, there are entire books describing the phonological and grammatical features that set AAVE apart from other dialects (e.g. Mufwene, Rickford, Bailey, and Baugh 1998; Rickford and Green 1998), as well as separate books devoted exclusively to the lexicon of African American Vernacular English (Smitherman 1994) and language-use conventions in the black community (e.g. Kochman 1981). By comparison, there are still relatively few descriptive accounts of Hispanic English in the United States despite the significance of this ethnic group.

Ethnic groups tend to form subcultures within the larger culture, and part of the distinctiveness of these subcultures may derive from linguistic differences. However, the role of linguistic distinctiveness in determining cultural distinctiveness varies greatly from subculture to subculture, depending on the social role of various ethnic groups in American society. We may hypothesize that the greater the isolation of an ethnic group from the mainstream of society, the greater its linguistic distinctiveness will be. However, there are so many other intersecting factors and sociohistorical considerations that confound the issue that this simple correlation rarely works out as neatly as we might hope for.

There are several different kinds of relationships that may exist between ethnicity and language variation. For ethnic groups which maintain a language other than English, there is the potential of language TRANSFER from the other language which is stabilized and perpetuated as a part of the English variety used by members of the ethnic group. By transfer, we mean the incorporation of language features into a non-native language based on the occurrence of similar features in the native language. For example, Marion Huffines (1984:177) notes that the English of Pennsylvania Germans in Southeast Pennsylvania is characterized by items which seem to be direct translations of German into English, such as the use of *all* ('all gone') in *He's going to have the cookies all*, *what for* ('what kind of') in *I don't know what for a car you had*, and *sneaky* ('finicky about food') in *I'm kind of sneaky when it comes to meat like that*. Similar transfer can be found in phonological features, including the devoicing of word-final stops (e.g. *bad* [bæd] → *bat* [bæt], *beg* [bɛg] → *beck* [bɛk]) and the use of falling rather than rising intonational contours at the ends of questions (Huffines 1986).

In a similar way, the use of *no* as a generalized tag question (e.g. *You go to the movies a lot, no?*) in some Hispanic communities in the Southwest may be attributable to transfer from Spanish, as can such phonological features as the merger of *ch* /č/ and *sh* /š/ (e.g. *shoe* as *chew* [ču], *chain* as *Shane* [šen]), the devoicing of /z/ to [s] (e.g. *doze* as *dose* [dos], *lazy* as *lasy* [lesi]), and the merger of /i/ and /ɪ/ (e.g. *pit* as *peat* [pit], *rip* as *reap* [rip]) (Peñalosa 1980; Santa Ana 1993). In many cases, the language features are directly traceable to transfer from Spanish. In some cases, though, it seems that the transferred feature has become fossilized and perpetuated so that speakers of Hispanic English varieties may use these features even if they are not native speakers of Spanish (Galindo 1987).

While some of the linguistic characteristics found among ethnic groups may be directly attributable to transfer from another language, others derive from more generalized strategies related to the acquisition of English as a second language rather than specific language structures carried over from another language. It is, for example, not uncommon to find the absence of marked tense forms (e.g. *Yesterday he play at the school*) among a range of English varieties with recent access to another language, including varieties of Native American English and Vietnamese English (Wolfram 1984, 1985; Leap 1993).

The tricky question regarding structures traceable to language contact is determining whether the form is simply a transitional one, which will be eliminated as soon as English becomes the native language of a generation of speakers, or whether the form will be incorporated and maintained as a distinct part of the dialect to be carried forth by subsequent generations. Hindsight seems to be the only way we can answer this question satisfactorily. In some cases, an item traceable to a language contact situation may be retained, but in a redefined form. For example, studies of Native American English in the Southwest (Wolfram 1984) indicate that tense unmarking is maintained by successive generations, but it has become tightly restricted to constructions marking habitual activity (e.g. *Before, we eat at home a lot, but now we don't*). Only the study of an ethnic English variety over subsequent generations can ultimately determine which of the characteristics derived from second-language acquisition will be integrated into the ethnic variety and which will be cast aside. For example, older speakers of Vietnamese origin living in various communities in the United States (e.g. Washington, DC, Houston, Los Angeles) exhibit extensive tense unmarking, but it is still to be determined if this feature will be maintained as part of a "Vietnamese English." To make this ultimate determination, we must look at future generations of speakers in these communities, particularly those now learning English as a first language.

All transfer from other languages is not readily transparent; the effects of an ancestral language in the determination of ethnically correlated variation may be more subtle. Labov thus observes that vowel patterns for the Jewish and Italian communities in New York City do not coincide with those of other

New Yorkers, and that this may be due to the effect of the non-English languages spoken by previous generations of Italians and Jewish people. Similarly, some speakers of Hispanic varieties show subtly different pronunciations for vowels such as the [o] of *coat* and the [u] of *boot* from surrounding Anglo speakers even when Spanish is no longer their primary language. Although the vowels of these ethnic group members ultimately may be traced to their ancestral language backgrounds, the route of influence is not nearly as direct as the kind of transfer referred to above. This, however, does not diminish the impact of ethnicity on language variation. Labov thus concludes that for the New York City vowel system "ethnic differentiation is seen to be a more powerful factor than social class differentiation, though both exist in addition to marked stylistic variation" (1966:306).

The restructuring of an item from another language may not only involve linguistic adjustment; it also may involve redefinition in terms of its social and ethnic association. Items like *chutzpah* 'impudence, guts', *schlep* 'haul, take', and the expression *I need this like a hole in the head* all can be traced to Yiddish, but their social roles and ethnic associations are different. In the case of *chutzpah*, its ethnic association is quite strong, and those who are not part of the Jewish community would only use the term as a deliberately borrowed item from that culture. The use of *schlep* is less firmly embedded in the Jewish community, although it still has an ethnic association; at the same time, it is becoming an integral part of the regional "New Yorkese" dialect. The expression *I need this like a hole in the head*, directly translated from a Yiddish expression (Gold 1981:288), is the least ethnically identifiable of these items and is not nearly as regionally restricted as an item like *schlep*. We thus see that overt ethnic association is often a relative matter and that other social variables obviously intersect with ethnicity in varying degrees.

Finally, we must recognize that ethnically correlated variation need not be traceable to previous language background at all. Some correlation simply reflects patterns of assimilation and isolation with respect to more widespread regional and social dialects. For example, Martha Laferriere (1979) shows ethnic correlations for Italian, Irish, and Jewish speakers in Boston with reference to the local pronunciation of *-or* in words like *form*, *short*, and *horse*. The usual pronunciation of the vowel in these items among non-Italians in Boston who speak fairly standard English is similar to the [ɔ] of *dog* or *law* in some other regions, but the vernacular Boston pronunciation involves lowering the tongue more toward the [a] vowel of *father* so that *short* is pronounced more like *shot* [šat] and *corn* more like *con* [kan]. (Remember that this region is largely an *r*-less dialect area to begin with.) Jews most closely follow the standard Anglo pattern (i.e. [šɔ(r)t], [kɔ(r)n]), followed by the Irish and then the Italians, who are most apt to use the lower vowel found in the vernacular pattern. These ethnic groups also reflect different stages with respect to the current change taking place in the pronunciation of the vowel. The Jewish community has virtually completed a change toward the Boston standard pronunciation (using the higher vowel [ɔ]), followed by the Irish who are in the middle of the change, and the Italians, who are just beginning a change toward the standard production.

The extent to which ethnic membership correlates with linguistic diversity varies from linguistic variable to linguistic variable. Whereas Italians and Jews do not participate in the typical New York pattern with respect to some vowels, they participate fully in the New York pattern of *r*-lessness. Similarly, the Italian, Irish, and Jewish communities in Boston participate in many of the linguistic characteristics of the regional variety in a way which is indistinguishable from other Bostonians at the same time that these ethnic communities distinguish themselves in their realization of one particular vowel.

6.7 The Case of African American Vernacular English (AAVE)

In many respects, African American Vernacular English represents the paradigmatic case for examining the role of ethnicity in dialect diversity. The sociolinguistic scrutiny of this variety dwarfs the study of other ethnic varieties by comparison. In fact, a survey of published research on American English from 1965 through 1993 (Schneider 1996:3) shows that AAVE has more than five times as many publications devoted to it than any other group; this survey includes not only other ethnic groups but regional groups as well. Furthermore, issues related to this variety have drawn widespread media attention at various intervals in the relatively brief history of social dialectology. For example, in the late 1960s, the deficit–difference language controversy discussed in chapter 1 received widespread attention in reference to AAVE, while in the late 1970s a court case over the role of dialect in reading known as the Ann Arbor case received national attention. In the 1990s, the Oakland Unified School District Board of Education passed a resolution affirming the legitimacy of AAVE as a language system and supporting its use as a bridge to learn standard English. This resolution received extensive media coverage; it even resulted in a US Senate subcommittee hearing on the status of this variety and its role in education. The so-called Ebonics controversy incited by the Oakland resolution once again highlighted the persistent controversy surrounding this variety.

There are three major issues related to the consideration of AAVE: (1) the relation of AAVE to comparable Anglo American vernacular varieties; (2) the historical roots and development of AAVE; and (3) the nature of language change presently taking place in this variety. These are, in effect, the kinds of issues that are involved in any sociolinguistic discussion of ethnic

varieties to a greater or lesser extent, although there are also unique contro-
versies associated with AAVE because of its particular history and the social
role traditionally assigned to African Americans in American society. Certainly,
no ethnic variety has been surrounded by more heated debate in American
society over the past three decades, and the controversy does not appear to be
subsiding.

In the case of AAVE, it is still often necessary to start with a disclaimer
about language and race. There is no foundation for maintaining that there is a
genetic basis for the kind of language differentiation evidenced by some black
Americans. Dialectologists can point to a number of cases in which African
Americans raised in Anglo American families talk no differently than their Anglo
peers. Conversely, Anglo Americans raised by AAVE speakers in the black
community speak AAVE – not Anglo English. Yet myths about the physical
basis of AAVE persist, so that there is a continuing need to confront and
debunk these claims. In the following sections, we consider Anglo American
and African American to be labels for culturally constructed ethnicities rather
than genetically determined racial groups.

6.8   Anglo and African American Vernaculars:
Same or Different?

In its simplest form, the issue of African American and Anglo American
dialect relations can be reduced to a question of whether the same or different
language structures are exhibited in comparable dialects spoken by Anglo
American and African American speakers. Are there features which are uniquely
used in AAVE when compared with Anglo American vernacular varieties?
To answer this question, it is necessary initially to establish what constitutes
a "comparable" Anglo American vernacular variety for comparison. Region and
class must be controlled in the comparison. The question can only be answered
satisfactorily by examining the speech of low-status Anglo American and African
American groups in the South because of the sociohistorical roots of AAVE
as a Southern-based variety spoken by lower-class speakers. All dialectologists
agree that there are many features of AAVE that set this dialect apart from
surrounding Anglo varieties in a Northern urban context, but the ethnic uniqueness of these features in Southern contexts in which there are Anglo speakers
of comparable socioeconomic status is much more debatable. Some dialectologists also maintain that social factors other than region and class have to be
considered in the comparison of speech relations, such as age, rurality, and
particular region of the South (Bailey and Maynor 1987).

The issue of African American and Anglo American speech relations is still
not totally resolved after several decades of heated debate, but some cautious

agreement on points of similarity and difference is emerging. At the same time, however, some new points of controversy have arisen. In a useful survey of the phonological and grammatical structures of AAVE in relation to comparable Anglo American varieties, Ralph Fasold (1981) concluded that there were a limited number of features in AAVE that are not found among Anglo, lower-class Southerners. Based upon a careful review of research studies up to that point, Fasold concluded that the following structures were the best candidates as unique features of AAVE.

Unique features of African American Vernacular English

1 devoicing of voiced stops in stressed syllables
    e.g.   [bɪt] for *bid*
          [bæk] for *bag*
2 present tense, third person -*s* absence
    e.g.   *she walk* for *she walks*
          she raise for *she raises*
3 plural -*s* absence on the general class of noun plurals (as opposed to such absence found on plurals indicating weights and measures as in *four mile_*)
    e.g.   *four girl_* for *four girls*
          some dog for *some dogs*
4 the use of remote time stressed *béen* to mark an action that took place or a state that began a long time ago and is still relevant
    e.g.   *You béen paid your dues a long time ago.*
          I béen known him a long time.
5 possessive -*s* absence
    e.g.   *man_ hat* for *man's hat*
          Jack_ car for *Jack's car*
6 reduction of final consonant clusters when followed by a word beginning with a vowel or when followed by a suffix beginning with a vowel
    e.g.   *lif' up* for *lift up*
          bussing for *busting*
7 copula and auxiliary absence involving *is* forms (as opposed to more generally deleted *are* forms)
    e.g.   *she nice* for *she's nice*
          He in the kitchen for *He's in the kitchen*
8 the use of habitual *be*
    e.g.   *Sometimes my ears be itching.*
          She don't usually be there.
(adapted from Fasold 1981)

Even with this restricted list of unique features, there are important qualifications that need to be made. In some cases, it is a particular aspect of the phonological or grammatical pattern which is unique rather than the pattern in general. For example, consonant cluster reduction is a very general process in English, but in many other varieties it only applies when the item is *not* followed by a vowel (e.g. at the end of an utterance or when followed by a word beginning with a consonant, such as *bes' kind* or *lif' packages*). In other cases, the difference between the patterning of a feature in AAVE and in a comparable Anglo variety may involve a significant quantitative difference rather than qualitative one. For example, *-s* third person singular absence (e.g. *she walk*) is found in both African American and Anglo American vernaculars but occurs at substantially different percentage rates in each variety. Some African American speakers show levels of absence between 80 and 95 percent while comparable Anglo American speakers show a range of 5 to 15 percent absence.

Exercise 3

In the actual study of the absence of *be* verb forms (so-called COPULA DELETION) among lower-class Anglo Americans and African Americans in the South (Wolfram 1974a), the following conclusions were reached:

- Neither Anglo American nor African American speakers delete the copula when the form is *am* (e.g. neither group of speakers utters forms like *I nice*).
- Both Anglo Americans and African Americans delete the copula frequently when the form corresponds to *are* (e.g. *You ugly*), but African Americans have a higher frequency of absence for *are* absence.
- Both Anglo Americans and African Americans delete the copula form *is* when it is followed by the item *gonna* (e.g. *She gonna do it*).
- Anglo Americans show almost no (less than 5 percent) absence of the copula form *is* with forms other than *gonna*, and African Americans show significant frequency levels of *is* absence (for example, 50 percent).

How do these kinds of observations show the complexity of descriptive detail necessary for the resolution of the question of African American–Anglo American speech relations? How would you respond to a person who observed that "copula absence can't be unique to AAVE because I hear Anglo American speakers who say things like *They gonna do it right now?*"

Debate over some AAVE structures has continued, or, in some cases, has re-emerged, despite careful reviews of the present status of AAVE in relation to other varieties such as the one offered by Fasold. For example, research by

Guy Bailey and Marvin Bassett (1986) and Michael Montgomery and Margaret Mishoe (forthcoming) indicates that finite *be* (e.g. *I be there*; *They be doing it*) is found in both Anglo American and African American varieties. At the same time, other investigators have suggested that there are additional forms that may qualify as unique AAVE forms. For example, Labov (1987) suggests that among the constructions which were overlooked in earlier descriptions of AAVE is a feature known as resultative *be done* (e.g. *I'll be done put so many holes in it you won't know what happened*).

There are also structures in AAVE which appear on the surface to be very much like constructions in other dialects of English but turn out, upon closer inspection, to have uses or meanings that are unique to the variety. These types of structures are called CAMOUFLAGED FORMS because they bear surface similarity to constructions found in other varieties of English even though they are used differently. One of these camouflaged constructions is the form *come* in constructions with an *-ing* verb, as in *She come acting like she was real mad*. This structure looks like a common English use of the motion verb *come* in structures like *She came running*, but research indicates that it actually has a special use as a kind of verb auxiliary indicating indignation on the part of the speaker (Spears 1982). The specialized meaning of indignation is apparently unique to AAVE.

A slightly different case of camouflaging is found in constructions such as *They call themselves painting the room* or *Walt call(s) himself dancing*. The meaning of this form is quite similar to the standard English meaning of *call oneself* constructions with noun phrases or adjectives such as *He calls himself a cook* or *She calls herself nice* to indicate that someone is attributing qualities or skills to themselves which they do not really possess. Thus, a person who calls him/herself dancing is actually doing a very poor imitation of dancing. The shared counterfactual meaning of the standard English and AAVE constructions obscures the fact that the *call oneself* construction does not typically occur with a verb + *-ing* construction in most dialects of English. Anglo English speakers will, for example, say *She calls herself a painter* but not typically *She calls herself painting*, whereas African American speakers are more prone to use both kinds of constructions (Wolfram 1995, 1996).

Although the debate over African American–Anglo American speech relations will no doubt continue, it is probably fair to conclude that there is a restricted subset of structures which is unique to AAVE. At the same time, however, we have to concede that the inventory of dialect differences is probably much more limited than originally set forth by some social dialectologists studying AAVE in the 1960s. However, if we admit significant quantitative differences, such as the greater occurrence of third singular *-s* absence by AAVE speakers, to our list of qualitative differences, we have to conclude that there is indeed a considerable distinction between comparable Anglo American and African American vernaculars.

Exercise 4

Studies of vernacular dialects of English have documented the use of *ain't* in a broad range of dialects. Typically, *ain't* is used for *have/hasn't* as in *She ain't been there for a while* and forms of *isn't* and *aren't*, as in *She ain't home now*. In AAVE, we find *ain't* used for *didn't* as well, as in *She ain't do it yet*. The use of *ain't* for *didn't* is rarely included in discussions of unique features of AAVE. How does a usage like this compare with other kinds of differences cited above, such as the use of inflectional suffixes or habitual *be*? Would you consider it a "camouflaged form"?

Although it is certainly possible to compare structures used by Anglo American and African American speakers on an item-by-item basis, as we have done above, the picture that emerges from such an approach does not fully represent the true relationship between these vernacular varieties. It appears that the uniqueness of AAVE lies more in the particular array of structures that comprise the dialect than it does in the restricted set of potentially unique structures. It is the co–occurrence of grammatical structures such as the absence of various suffixes (possessive, third person singular, plural), copula absence, habitual *be*, and so forth, along with a set of phonological characteristics such as cluster reduction, final [f] for *th* (e.g. *baf* for *bath*), postvocalic *r*-lessness, and so forth that seems to define the variety rather than the subset of proposed unique features *per se*. To find that a structure previously thought to be unique to AAVE is shared by an Anglo American vernacular variety does not necessarily challenge the notion of the uniqueness of AAVE as a dialect. Studies of listener perception of ethnic identity certainly support the contention that AAVE is distinct from comparable Anglo American vernaculars, as most of these studies (Shuy and Williams 1973; Baugh 1996) show correct identification of African Americans and Anglo Americans based on speech samples alone at levels of 80 percent or higher.

Up to this point, we have discussed AAVE as if it were a unitary variety in different regions of the United States. We must, however, admit regional variation within AAVE, just as we have to admit regional variation within vernacular Anglo American varieties. Certainly, some of the Northern metropolitan versions of AAVE are distinguishable from some of the Southern rural versions, and South Atlantic coastal varieties are different from those found in the Gulf region. While admitting some of these regional variations, we hasten to point out that one of the most noteworthy aspects of AAVE is the common core of features shared across different regions. Features such as habitual *be*, copula absence, inflectional -*s* absence, among a number of other grammatical and phonological structures, are found in locations as distant as Los Angeles, California; New Haven, Connecticut; Meadville, Mississippi; Austin, Texas;

and Wilmington, North Carolina, as well as in both urban and rural settings. Thus, we recognize regional variation in AAVE while concluding, at the same time, that the regional differences do not come close to the magnitude of regional differences that exist across Anglo varieties. The basic core of AAVE speech features, regardless of where AAVE has been studied in the United States so far, underscores the strong ethnic associations of this language variety.

6.9   The Historical Issue: The Creolist and Anglicist Hypotheses

There are two major hypotheses concerning the origin of AAVE: the CREOLIST HYPOTHESIS and the ANGLICIST HYPOTHESIS. According to the creolist hypothesis, AAVE developed from a creole language, a special language developed in language contact situations in which the vocabulary from one primary language is imposed on a specially adapted, restricted grammatical structure. Those who support the creolist hypothesis maintain that the creole upon which AAVE is based was fairly widespread in the antebellum South. They observe that this creole was not unique to the mainland South but rather shows a number of similarities to well-known English-based creoles of the African diaspora such as Krio, spoken today in Sierra Leone along the coast of West Africa, as well as English-based creoles of the Caribbean such as the creoles of Barbados and Jamaica. Its vestiges in the United States are still found today in GULLAH, more popularly called "Geechee," the creole still spoken by a small number of African Americans in the Sea Islands off the coast of South Carolina and Georgia. It is maintained that this creole was fairly widespread among the descendants of Africans on Southern plantations but was not spoken to any extent by whites.

Over time, through contact with surrounding dialects, this creole language was modified to become more like other varieties of English in a process referred to as DECREOLIZATION. Since this decreolization process was a gradual one, the creole predecessor of AAVE is sometimes cited as the basis for some present-day characteristics of this variety. However, we are not aware of any serious investigators of AAVE who would maintain that AAVE still qualifies as a genuine creole language. For example, copula absence (e.g. *You ugly*) is a well-known trait of creole languages, so that one might maintain that the present version of copula absence is a vestige of the creole origins of AAVE. Similar arguments have been made for the various types of inflectional -*s* absence in this variety (e.g. *Mary go__*, *Mary__ hat*), as well as phonological characteristics such as consonant cluster reduction. Both linguistic traits and the social history of blacks in the antebellum South have been used to argue for the creole origin of AAVE. J. L. Dillard's book *Black English: Its History and Usage in* *the United States* (1972) was very influential in promoting the creolist hypothesis, although creolists have now engaged in much more detailed and careful analysis since the appearance of that work in order to offer support for this hypothesis.

The alternative to this hypothesis has been referred to as the Anglicist hypothesis, so-called because it maintains that the roots of AAVE can be traced to the same source as Anglo American dialects – the dialects of English spoken in the British Isles. Briefly put, this position maintains that the language contact situation of those of African descent in the United States was roughly comparable to that of other groups of immigrants. Under this historical scenario, slaves brought with them to North America a number of different African languages. Over the course of a couple of generations, only a few minor traces of these ancestral languages remained, as blacks learned the regional and social varieties of surrounding white speakers. From this perspective, a creole language played no significant part in the history of the vernacular dialect. According to the Anglicist hypothesis, a widely recognized creole like Gullah is considered to be an anomaly among black varieties, which arose through a special set of social and physical circumstances unique to the isolated Sea Islands.

From the perspective of the Anglicist hypothesis, differences in AAVE that cannot be explained on the basis of regional and social factors result from the preservation of British dialect features in this variety which were lost from other varieties of American English. Some of the peculiar features mentioned previously, such as habitual *be* and third person *-s* absence (Schneider 1983, 1989), have been explained on this basis. In this regard, the pursuit of historical evidence centers around the scrutiny of earlier English varieties in the British Isles for features similar to those found in AAVE today. There is, of course, an accompanying search for sociohistorical facts that might place the speakers of the potential donor dialect in a position to make their linguistic contribution to those of African descent in North America.

Although the creolist hypothesis was clearly the favored position among sociolinguists during the 1970s and 1980s, several new types of data have emerged which call this position into question. One important type of data that came to light in the 1980s was a set of written records of ex-slaves. These include an extensive set of ex-slave narratives collected under the Works Project Administration (WPA) (Schneider 1989; Bailey, Maynor, and Cukor-Avila 1991) in the 1930s, letters written by semiliterate ex-slaves in the mid-1800s (Montgomery, Fuller, and DeMarse 1993; Montgomery and Fuller 1996), and other specialized collections of texts, such as the Hyatt texts – an extensive set of interviews conducted with black hoodoo doctors in the 1930s (Hyatt 1970–8; Viereck 1988; Ewers 1996). All of these records seem to point to the conclusion that earlier AAVE was not nearly as distinct from postcolonial Anglo American English varieties as would have been predicted under the creolist hypothesis. A limited set of audio recordings of ex-slaves conducted as a part of the WPA in the 1930s (Bailey, Maynor, and Cukor-Avila 1991) also seem to support this contention.

A different type of data which raises questions about the creolist hypothesis comes from the examination of black expatriate insular varieties of English. For example, in the 1820s, a group of blacks migrated to the peninsula of Samaná in the Dominican Republic, living in relative isolation and maintaining a relic variety of English up to the present day (Poplack and Sankoff 1987; Poplack and Tagliamonte 1989). A significant population of African Americans also migrated from the United States to Canada in the early 1800s, and some have lived to this day in relative isolation in Nova Scotia. The examination of the English varieties spoken by blacks in these areas by Shana Poplack and Sali Tagliamonte (1991) indicates that these insular varieties were quite similar to earlier Anglo American varieties rather than a presumed creole predecessor, again casting doubt on the creole hypothesis.

Finally, closer scrutiny of the sociohistorical situation and demographics of the antebellum South (Mufwene 1996) has indicated that the distribution of slaves in the Plantation South was not particularly advantageous to the perpetuation of a widespread Plantation Creole as had been postulated by earlier creolists. In fact, the vast majority of slaves lived in on smaller farms with just a few slaves per household rather than in the large, sprawling plantations with large numbers of slaves that are sometimes pictured in popular portrayals of the antebellum South. Whereas large, expansive plantations with large numbers of slaves might be conducive to the development and spread of a Plantation Creole, over 80 percent of all slaves were associated with families that had fewer than four slaves per household.

Studies such as those cited above have provided the impetus for a resurgent interest in the Anglicist hypothesis, although it is hardly the consensus position. For example, some studies have offered alternative data and analyses from insular dialects (Hannah 1998; Singler 1989, 1991) suggesting that there is, in fact, evidence for the creolist hypothesis in insular dialect situations. Further, the close scrutiny of particular features such as the absence of the copula (Weldon 1996; Rickford and Blake 1990) continue to support the creole genesis and affinity of AAVE. There is no evidence for copula absence in the history of the English of the British Isles; at the same time, there is extensive documentation of copula absence in creoles which might have been related to AAVE historically (Rickford and Blake 1990).

The examination of different kinds of social situations involving African Americans and Anglo Americans has suggested that the ethnic distinctiveness of AAVE can even be perpetuated in settings where there is little contact with an extensive African American community. Thus, the investigation of the speech of several members of the sole African American family of longstanding residence (130 years) on the island of Ocracoke, North Carolina, indicates that ethnic boundaries in speech can apparently be maintained for long periods of time against overwhelming demographic odds (Wolfram, Hazen, and Tamburro 1997). This family clearly maintained some distinctive traits associated with AAVE for over a century even though their only regular interaction outside of the family was with Anglo Americans speaking the distinctive Ocracoke dialect.

Obviously, the dispute over the origin of AAVE is hardly settled. At the same time, the emergence of new types of sociolinguistic data offers the opportunity to confront some of these historical issues based on the detailed, rigorous examination of essential evidence.

The issue of the historical development of AAVE has often been linked with the question of the current-day status of African American–Anglo American speech relations, but these two issues are not necessarily related. It is, for example, possible to maintain that the creolist position is essentially correct but that decreolization has been so complete as to eliminate virtually all differences that existed at a prior point in time. Furthermore, sociolinguistic contact among whites and blacks over the generations may have resulted in speakers of both ethnicities picking up features from one another so that the two dialects are no longer as different as they once were. Certainly, linguistic assimilation has been bilateral rather than unilateral. In fact, an examination of copula absence as used by Anglo Americans and African Americans in the deep South (Wolfram 1974a) indicates that Anglo Americans apparently have picked up this trait from African Americans, even though Anglos do not indicate this feature to the extent that African Americans do. On the other hand, it is possible to maintain that the Anglicist position is the correct historical one but that patterns of sociolinguistic segregation and issues of cultural identity have led to dialectal differences which resulted in the emergence of a distinct ethnic variety. In fact, in the next section we will consider the hypothesis that current-day AAVE is actually diverging from other vernacular varieties. At this point, it is adequate to observe that a particular position on the historical development of AAVE is not intrinsically tied to a position on the status of the current relationship of Anglo American and African American vernaculars.

6.10   The Direction of Change: Divergence or Convergence

How is AAVE currently changing and how has it developed in the recent past? Questions about the present direction of change must now be added to the controversy over historical origins and the relation of this variety to other varieties of English. Although it might be assumed that AAVE has gradually been converging with other dialects of English in the century and a half since the close of the Civil War, this view has been strongly challenged. Based on research conducted by Labov and his colleagues in Philadelphia in the mid-1980s, it was concluded that AAVE is actually diverging from rather than converging with surrounding vernaculars. As Labov (1985:1) put it, "their [African American residents of Philadelphia] speech pattern is developing in its own direction and becoming more different from the speech of whites in the same communities." The sociological basis for the so-called DIVERGENCE HYPOTHESIS is found in the social and economic plight of lower-class African Americans – racial isolation brought about by increasing de facto segregation and a widening socioeconomic gap between mainstream American society and lower-class minority groups. A sociopsychological corollary would be the heightened awareness of African American cultural identity and the function of a distinctive dialect in maintaining this cohesive identity.

The argument for the linguistic divergence of AAVE and vernacular Anglo English varieties has focused on a couple of AAVE features which seem to have arisen only in recent decades. These include the use of resultative *be done* (e.g. *I'll be done put so many holes in him he'll wish he wouldn't a said it*) and a special use of *-s* with verbs to mark a lively past time narrative. This narrative *-s* use is illustrated by the fluctuation of *-s* and non *-s* in the following excerpt (Labov 1987:8):

> they was playin', next thing you know he comed – the li'l boy, *he comes* and *hit* me right? I *hits* him back now. All the time, my brother and him was hittin' each other an' everything, and he start cryin'

A third feature which is suggestive of possible linguistic divergence comes from the research on habitual *be* in the South carried out by Guy Bailey and Natalie Maynor (1987). Based upon the study of older and younger black speakers in urban and rural contexts, the researchers conclude that this form is developing a unique grammatical function of habituality with the *-ing* form of verbs (e.g. *They be messing with me*). The evolution of this use among younger, primarily urban speakers, along with other developing forms, apparently constitutes evidence that the AAVE verbal aspect system is becoming more different from those of other vernacular varieties.

Although there is evidence for maintaining that the use of habitual *be* has increased and its meaning has become increasingly restricted to habituality, thus making AAVE more distinct from Anglo varieties, evidence for divergence in other features is not nearly as clear-cut. For example, structures such as the resultative *be done* construction remain quite rare and have apparently been a part of the dialect for some time, although they had not been described in detail in earlier studies of AAVE. Other structures, such as the historical narrative form cited above, may actually represent an underlying convergence with a prevalent feature of other vernacular dialects of English – the use of the so-called HISTORICAL PRESENT in storytelling contexts (e.g. *I went to the store, I goes in, and there before my eyes, I see this guy pull out a gun*). At the same time, there may be some features of AAVE that are, in fact, becoming more robust and so serving to make this dialect more distinct from other vernacular varieties. For example, John Rickford (1991) shows that core features such as inflectional -*s* absence and habitual *be* are used at higher frequency levels than reported in some earlier studies in the 1960s. To suggest that AAVE in general is becoming a more divergent dialect does not, however, accurately reflect the current linguistic status of this variety. Naturally, AAVE will continue to change, just as any other dialect may be expected to undergo change, but the present evidence does not, in fact, suggest that a radical restructuring is taking place to make this variety significantly more distinctive from Anglo varieties than it has been in the past.

Whereas the assertion that the grammar of AAVE is moving away from that of other vernacular varieties seems to be exaggerated, there is evidence that the majority of African Americans do not participate in major dialect changes taking place among Anglo speakers in some areas of the United States. In particular, the vowel systems found in some Anglo varieties may be moving away from that of AAVE. For example, African Americans in Philadelphia are not involved to a significant extent in the evolution of the unique vowel system described for the Philadelphia Anglo American community (Graff, Labov, and Harris 1986). There is also little evidence that the Northern Cities Vowel Shift discussed in chapter 5 is spreading to AAVE speakers in significant numbers in the metropolitan areas affected by this shift. In the South, characteristic Southern vowel traits, such as the fronting of back vowels like the [u] of *boot* toward front vowels such as the [i] of *beet*, tend to be primarily found among Anglo Americans, not African Americans. And, while both African Americans and Southern Anglo Americans tend to pronounce the /ay/ vowel as [a] (as in *tahd* for *tide*), only Anglo Americans use the [a] pronunciation before voiceless consonants, as in *raht* for *right* or *whaht* for *white*. In fact, in the South, *raht* and *whaht* are thought of as Anglo American pronunciations while *tahm* and *tahd* are simply considered to be Southern.

For the immediate future, it appears that AAVE will remain a stable and distinct socioethnic dialect of English, with some change but not extreme restructuring. Patterns of social separation between Anglo Americans and African Americans in many realms of social activity are still strong enough to inhibit wide-scale diffusion across dialects. At the same time, there seems to be a growing sense of linguistic solidarity and identity among African Americans that serves to unify AAVE in different locales, suggesting that mere patterns of linguistic and social contact do not completely account for the persistence and augmentation of AAVE. For example, our research team conducted a case study of four generations of an African American family who live in an isolated coastal area of the North Carolina mainland. We found that successive generations of speakers progressively relinquish their sharply localized dialect, which is quite similar to that of surrounding Anglos, and adopt more general dialect traits of AAVE. The oldest speaker we interviewed, born in 1910, is identifiable primarily as a speaker of the distinctive regional Anglo dialect, which is quite similar to the dialect of the Outer Banks of North Carolina. However, the youngest speakers of the family are fundamentally identifiable as AAVE speakers even though the local residency of the family has not changed. Increased travel, more interaction outside of the community, and exposure to other African Americans who speak AAVE have certainly had some impact on the dialect shift that is taking place in successive generations of speakers in this community. However, older family members also had contact with AAVE speakers from outside the local community but did not adopt "classic" AAVE features to the extent which might be expected. Thus, we postulate that identification with an increasingly coherent nationwide African American culture plays a large role in the adoption of AAVE features by the younger speakers in this rural community. Such cases certainly testify to the continuing and, in some cases, expanding robustness of AAVE as an ethnic variety.

6.11 Tri-Ethnic Dialect Situations

In the previous sections, we have, for the most part, limited ourselves to the discussion of ethnic contact situations involving two primary groups. But there are a number of historical situations and some current, developing situations which involve tri-ethnic contact situations. For example, a couple of historical situations in North American society involve sustained contact among Native Americans, Anglo Americans, and African Americans. In other settings, there may be contact situations involving Spanish, Vietnamese, or other languages associated with immigrant populations, and different varieties of vernacular English. For example, in Los Angeles or New York City, the dialect mix may involve a variety of Mexican or Puerto Rican Spanish, surrounding varieties of AAVE, and the local variety of Anglo American English. Or, with some Native American groups in the Southwest, the contact situation may involve Spanish, the Native American ancestral language, and a variety of English. The resultant English variety of the Hispanic or Native American speakers may be quite indicative of the status of the group in relation to surrounding groups, as well as the kinds of models that speakers are using as a basis for shaping their unique dialect.

A study of first-generation Puerto Rican adolescents in New York City conducted more than two decades ago (Wolfram 1974b) indicated that some Puerto Rican teenagers, who had extensive contacts with African Americans, were clearly assimilating features from AAVE, such as habitual *be*, copula absence, and third person singular -*s* absence. At the same time, their speech showed some features that might be attributed to influence from Puerto Rican

Spanish, such as the reduction of final consonant clusters, as in *tes'* for *test* and *win'* for *wind*. Even those teenagers who indicated limited social interaction with African Americans indicated some indirect assimilation to AAVE, although this group did not typically use core features (e.g. habitual *be* and inflectional *-s* absence). Thus, there appeared to be a pattern of both direct and indirect assimilation to AAVE in the dialect of these Puerto Rican teenagers in New York City. On the other hand, Hispanic English communities in the Southwest (Galindo 1987; Santa Ana 1991) do not appear to exhibit a comparable type of assimilation to neighboring AAVE speakers, although individual speakers who have extensive contact with AAVE speakers and highly value black culture may exhibit features of AAVE.

A somewhat different tri-ethnic dynamic exists with respect to the Lumbee Indians of Robeson County, North Carolina. The Lumbees constitute the largest Native American group east of the Mississippi, with approximately 40,000 members living in a rural, tri-ethnic situation in Robeson County, North Carolina, located along the corridor of Route 95 near the South Carolina border. Native Americans comprise approximately 40 percent of the county population, African Americans 25 percent, and Anglo Americans the remaining 35 percent. Furthermore, the three groups have co-existed in this region since the early 1700s.

The ancestral language roots of the Lumbee are a matter of speculation, since there are no clear-cut native language remnants evident in the language. Apparently, the Lumbee were a multi-tribal aggregate, with Iroquoian (particularly Tuscarora), Siouan (particularly Cheraw) and Algonquian languages having a formative influence. However, the Lumbee have been speaking English for a couple of centuries and have been monolingual for generations, so that the English they have developed in this tri-ethnic contact situation is of considerable intrigue. The study of Lumbee Vernacular English (Wolfram 1996; Dannenberg and Wolfram forthcoming) shows a mixed dialect that sets the Lumbee apart from both the contact Anglo American and African American communities. For example, the Lumbee retain a relic use of *be* forms rather than forms of *have* in constructions such as *I'm been to the store* for *I've been to the store*. They also regularize to *were* rather than *was* in sentences such as *I weren't there* or *She weren't here*. Neither of these features is found to any significant extent in neighboring vernacular varieties. At the same time that the Lumbee exhibit unique dialect features, they also indicate ethnolinguistic distinctiveness by using features from neighboring varieties in unique ways. For example, one of the features characterizing Lumbee Vernacular English is the use of finite *be(s)* in sentences such as *I hope it bes a girl* or *They bes doing all right*. Historically, the Anglo population in the area, largely of Scots and Scots-Irish descent, used this *bes* form, but this feature is now clearly obsolescent among younger Anglo speakers. On the other hand, the surrounding African American community uses the habitual *be* form we described in our survey of

AAVE. Our analysis of the speech of Lumbees of different age groups indicates that, whereas older speakers do not restrict finite *be* to habitual contexts, younger speakers are increasingly confining their use of *be(s)* to habitual contexts, thus indicating alignment with AAVE. At the same time, however, the Lumbee continue to use inflectional *-s* on *be*, as in *She bes doing it*, even though AAVE speakers do not typically use this suffix. The peculiar mix of dialect features in Lumbee Vernacular English clearly shows how a cultural group can maintain a distinct ethnic identity by molding past and present dialect features in a way which symbolically indicates – and helps constitute – their cultural uniqueness even when the ancestral language has been lost.

6.12 Further Reading

Bailey, Guy, Natalie Maynor, and Patricia Cukor-Avila (eds) (1991) *The Emergence of Black English: Text and Commentary*. Philadelphia/Amsterdam: John Benjamins. This collection of articles is focused on the analysis of the WPA recordings with ex-slaves made during the 1930s. It is a rare and unique collection, and each author comments on a different aspect of this collection using the same data base. Transcripts of the recordings are also included.

Fasold, Ralph W. (1981) The relation between black and white speech in the South. *American Speech* 56:163–89. Fasold summarizes the major findings on the similarities and differences between white and black vernacular varieties prior to the convergence–divergence debate. The article is now somewhat dated, but it remains a useful synthesis based upon empirical research available at the time.

Kroch, Anthony (1978) Towards a theory of social dialect variation. *Language in Society* 7:17–36. Kroch's article is exceptional for its attempt to explain why particular linguistic features are subjected to social evaluation. Most sociolinguistic studies are content to describe patterns of social and linguistic co-variation as opposed to trying to explain them.

Labov, William (1972b) *Sociolinguistic Patterns*. Philadelphia: University of Pennsylvania Press. Several of the most influential articles on the interaction of social and linguistic differentiation are included in this collection of Labov's early research studies. These articles set the stage for much of the social dialect research that has taken place over the past several decades.

Leap, William L. (1993) *American Indian English*. Salt Lake City: University of Utah Press. Sections in this overview, which focuses on Native American English varieties in the Southwest, include (1) speaker and structure, (2) Indian English and ancestral language tradition, (3) history and function, and (4) Indian English in the classroom. It is the most comprehensive overview of Native American English varieties currently available.

Mufwene, Salikoko S., John R. Rickford, Guy Bailey, and John Baugh (eds) (1998) *African American Vernacular English*. London/New York: Routledge. This collection brings together a set of articles by leading researchers on the history and current state of AAVE. Authors consider both historical and descriptive issues pertaining to AAVE.

Santa Ana, Otto (1993) Chicano English and the Chicano language setting. *Hispanic Journal of Behavioral Sciences* 15:1–35. This article presents an overview of some of the traits of Chicano English as well as the social settings contextualizing this variety.

Schneider, Edgar W. (ed.) (1996) *Focus on the USA*. Philadelphia/Amsterdam: John Benjamins. This collection of articles highlights some of the regional, social, and ethnic varieties found in the United States, including articles on AAVE by John Baugh, Salikoko Mufwene, and Walter Edwards, as well as an article on Cuban exile English by Frank Maas. The article by Michael Montgomery and Janet Fuller considers a set of written documents, primarily letters produced by semiliterate African Americans in the mid-1800s, which may yield important evidence for uncovering the historical origins of AAVE. Schneider also offers a useful survey of major areas of foci in the study of American English dialects over the past several decades.

7

Gender and Language Variation

Few topics in language-variation study have witnessed an explosion of interest as dramatic as that found for language and gender. Just a few decades ago, most linguists discussing language and gender were content to point to several classic studies of languages like Japanese, in which men and women use distinctly different language forms, such as different inflectional endings. Male–female language differences in English were viewed as relatively minor and uninteresting. Today, we find a very different situation. There now exists an extensive collection of studies, anthologies, and books devoted exclusively to issues of language and gender in English, including several bestsellers such as Deborah Tannen's *You Just Don't Understand*. Furthermore, many Americans have now confronted the issue of language sexism. Concern for gender equity in American society certainly encompasses language issues along with other sociopolitical concerns. In the process of investigating gender and language differences from a number of different vantage points, we have learned much about the nature of language variation and the linguistic manifestation of social relationships.

Just as researchers must be careful to explain language differences among different ethnic groups in terms of social and cultural factors rather than in terms of biological "race," so too must sociolinguists be certain to investigate language differences between women and men in terms of social factors rather than simple biological sex. In most studies of male–female language differences, the term GENDER is used in order to capture the "complex of social, cultural, and psychological phenomena attached to sex" (McConnell-Ginet 1988:76). The term "sex," on the other hand, refers simply to female or male physiology.

Sociolinguists who study in detail the patterning of lexical, phonological, and grammatical features across different regional and social groups traditionally have left unexamined the social construct of gender and simply reported on language differences between those who are biologically "male" and those who are biologically "female." This lack of focus on the social factors surrounding "sex" is due largely to the fact that male–female language differences have not traditionally been a central concern of dialect study. Among current researchers who consider their primary focus to be the investigation of male–female language differences, we find more concern with explaining such differences in terms of gender rather than sex. We also find that researchers in the field of language and gender studies tend to focus more on language-use, or pragmatic, differences than on phonological, grammatical, and lexical differences. Such research reveals that, in many respects, a strict dichotomy between "male" and "female" ways of talking (and behaving in general) is largely artificial, as there exist many important linguistic (and other) differences within groups of women and within groups of men as well as many similarities across gender groups. Further, there are a number of gender groups – and even sex groups – to which the labels "male" and "female" cannot be neatly applied (e.g. homosexuals, hermaphrodites) (Bing and Bergvall 1996).

Despite growing dissatisfaction with the male–female dichotomy presupposed by the question, "How do men and women talk differently?", we nonetheless begin our investigation of gender and language variation with this question, since it has formed the focus of language and gender study up until quite recently. In this chapter, we will first look at the investigation of male–female language differences from the perspective of dialect study and then turn toward studies which focus on gender differences in language use. Following our discussion of *how* members of different gender groups talk, we will look at how members of these groups are talked *about*. For example, we will consider such matters as the use of GENERIC *HE* (as in *Each student should bring his book*) and the replacement of the *Miss/Mrs* title with *Ms*, as well as other cases of sex-differentiated labeling in US society.

7.1 Cross-Sex Language Differences as Reported in Dialect Surveys

One of the general findings regarding male–female language differences that has emerged in the study of regional and social dialects is that women tend to use more standard language features than men, whose speech tends to be more vernacular. For example, in one of the earliest studies of sex-based language variation, John Fischer (1958) showed that, among the group of New England children he studied, girls tended to use more word-final *-ing* (as in *swimming*) than boys, who used more of the nonstandard *-in'* variant (as in *swimmin'*). Peter Trudgill (1974) showed similar patterning for *-in'* and *-ing* across sex groups in Norwich, England, as did Barbara Horvath (1985) in her investigation of the cross-sex patterning of *-in'* and *-ing* in Sydney, Australia. Other variables as well have been shown to pattern in the same way. For example, the first author of this book demonstrated greater use of standard variants by African American females than males for four phonological and four syntactic variables in inner-city Detroit (Wolfram 1969). For example, females used more [θ] than men in items such as *with*, which men tended to produce as [wɪt] or [wɪf]. In addition, females produced more postvocalic *r*'s than men as well as less multiple negation (e.g. *I didn't tell you nothing*) and less copula deletion (e.g. *She gonna go now* vs. *She is going to go now*).

A second general finding from the field of dialect study is that women tend to adopt innovative language features much more quickly than men. In other words, women tend to lead in linguistic change. Even the earliest dialect surveys ever conducted (e.g. Gauchat 1905) showed women adopting new language variants much earlier than men, and subsequent research has confirmed this pattern time and time again (e.g. Labov 1966, 1984; Cedergren 1973); indeed, women have been shown to lead men in adopting new language variants by as much as an entire generation.

The two general patterns that have emerged from the study of male–female language differences yield an apparent contradiction: Women appear to be more conservative than men, in that they use more standard variants, which often represent older language forms. At the same time, women appear to be more progressive than men, because they adopt new variants more quickly. This contradiction has been little noticed; and most researchers who conduct dialect surveys tend to assume that the former case is the norm – that is, that women simply speak more standardly than men. In fact, women are sometimes considered to be too standard for inclusion in sociolinguistic studies which are focused on "authentic" vernacular speech. Thus, a number of early social dialect studies of adolescents focused on male speech, because it was assumed at the time that vernacular dialects were maintained and transmitted primarily by adolescent males. As we shall see, more recent studies indicate that females, including teenagers, may provide excellent data on vernacular speech as well.

As part of a large-scale survey of Philadelphia speech, Labov (1984) uncovered patterns in male–female language variation which may help explain the seeming contradiction inherent in maintaining that women are simultaneously more conservative and more innovative than men. He found that women indeed were more conservative in their use of certain language features, particularly those connected with stable sociolinguistic variables (e.g. *-in'* vs. *-ing*) and those which were involved in older language changes – that is, changes which had been in progress for quite some time. However, in their use of other features – particularly features associated with newer language changes, women were found to be more innovative than men. In other words, Labov demonstrated that women were in fact both more and less conservative than men; the degree of conservatism simply depended on the sociolinguistic variable being examined. And if we look closely at other studies which indicate that women are more linguistically conservative than men, we find that the features which were investigated are stable (or nearly stable) variables as well.

Labov also showed that the patterning of male–female language differences depends not only on the language feature in question but also on the social class of the speaker. For example, women in his Philadelphia survey were

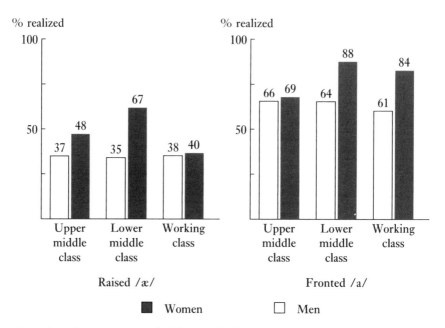

Figure 7.1 /æ/ raising and /a/ fronting in Detroit, by social class and sex (adapted from Fasold 1968).

shown to lead some vowel changes in lower social classes but to lag behind in these changes in upper classes. Similarly, Fasold (1968) showed that while Detroit females led males in all social classes in adopting certain vowel innovations, women of a particular social class – namely, the upper working class/ lower middle class – were always in advance of both women and men in all other social classes, including both lower and higher classes. Figure 7.1 illustrates this patterning for two innovative vowel pronunciations: the pronunciation of /æ/ as something like [ɛ], as in *bet* for 'bat', and the pronunciation of /a/ as something like [æ], as in *lack* for 'lock'.

7.2 Explaining Cross-Sex Language Differences: The Prestige-based Approach

Labov explained the patterns he found in his Philadelphia data by maintaining that women are more prestige-conscious than men. Thus, they display conservatism with respect to language forms which are stigmatized in the larger community (such as *-in'* for *-ing*) but are quick to adopt innovative variants, which carry local prestige and which haven't been in place long enough to acquire negative valuation in the larger community. Women in the lower middle class are most likely to avoid stigmatized features and adopt prestige features, because, according to Labov, members of this social class are more upwardly mobile than members of any other socioeconomic class, with the women in this group being particularly intent on increasing their social prestige.

Trudgill (1983) goes a step beyond Labov by attempting to outline reasons why women are more prestige-conscious than men. One factor he cites is the traditional involvement of women in the transmission of culture through childrearing, a process which might heighten the awareness of prestige norms through a desire to pass these norms along to children. Another reason Trudgill offers is the social position of women in our society, which historically has been less secure than that of men. Given a more insecure social position, women may place more emphasis on signaling social status linguistically. A final reason cited by Trudgill is the different occupational roles of men and women. Men traditionally have been rated by their occupation – by *what they do*. Women, on the other hand, have often been rated to a greater extent by *how they appear*. For example, women are much more frequently complimented on their appearance than are men, in keeping with a value on "looking good." The linguistic "cosmetic" of prestigious language may thus be more important for women than it is for men.

The tendency of males to use more stigmatized variants in their speech than females may also be seen in terms of the symbolic value of such variants in defining oneself as either masculine or feminine. For example, nonstandard forms may symbolize masculinity and toughness and so may be positively valued by men; at the same time they may be considered inappropriate for use by women, who cannot project toughness if they are to project some measure of feminine identity, at least in the traditional sense.

Despite the widespread acceptance of Labov's and Trudgill's notion that women's linguistic behavior can be explained in terms of their focus on social prestige, there are some problematic cases which seem to defy such explanation. In particular, there are a number of cases in which men have been shown to lead women in language change and in which women have been shown to use more local vernacular variants than men. For example, studies by both Trudgill (1972) and Labov (1963, 1984) indicate men leading in certain sound changes, while Patricia Nichols (1983) and Lesley Milroy (1987) show women using vernacular variants at a greater percentage rate than men in their speech communities. In addition, based on a comprehensive review of research on men, women, and prestige language forms, Deborah James (1996) concludes that usage patterns for such forms simply cannot be captured in the simplistic statement that women use more prestige forms than men. In other words, she demonstrates that, contrary to traditional sociolinguistic belief, one cannot forge a simple link between the female sex and a heightened focus on social prestige.

There are also cases in which the patterning of male–female language differences has changed over time. For example, in our studies of Ocracoke English

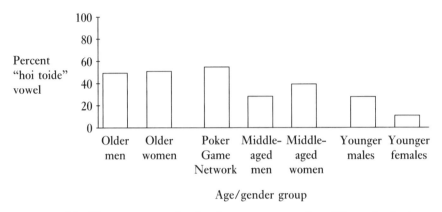

Figure 7.2   The cross-generational and cross-sex patterning of Ocracoke /ay/.

on the Outer Banks of North Carolina, we found that the cross-sex patterning
of at least one vernacular dialect feature, the well-known pronunciation of the
/ay/ vowel as more of an [ɔɪ] (as in "hoi toide" for 'high tide'), has changed
drastically over time (Schilling-Estes and Schrider 1996). Among the older
speakers we studied, we found nearly identical usage levels by women and men
for the [ɔɪ] variant, whereas we found more male–female differentiation in
middle-aged speakers and even more differentiation among the youngest speakers
in our database. Even among speakers in a single age group, we found several
different cross-sex patterns of language use. For example, among speakers in
our middle-age group, we found that women used more of the vernacular [ɔɪ]
variant than most men. However, there was one group of men who used more
[ɔɪ] than any other middle-aged speakers, male or female, as well as more [ɔɪ]
than older speakers – even though the traditional [ɔɪ] variant is, in general,
receding in the Ocracoke community. Figure 7.2 illustrates the cross-generational
and cross-sex patterning of the "hoi toide" vowel in the Ocracoke community.

Obviously, we cannot explain the patterning of the traditional Ocracoke
"hoi toide" vowel in simple terms of women's propensity to achieve social
prestige through using standard language features, because middle-aged women
speak more standardly than some of their male age cohorts but less standardly
than others. In addition, older women speak at the same level of vernacularity
as older men, which should not be the case if the former are more prestige-
oriented than the latter. In fact, it is only in the youngest age group that male–
female language differences in Ocracoke display the "typical" pattern, with
females speaking far less vernacularly than men.

Not only do prestige-based explanations fail to cover all cases of male–
female language differentiation, but they also tend to be applied only to
women's speech, even though there are cases in which men's speech patterns
could be attributed to desire for social prestige as well (Eckert 1989). For

F2 (AW)

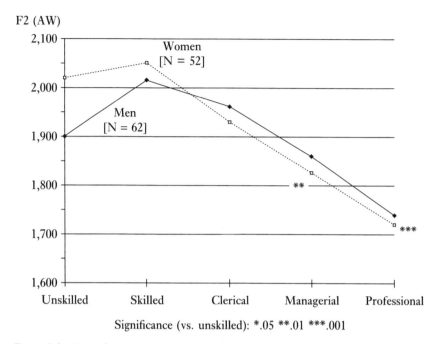

Significance (vs. unskilled): *.05 **.01 ***.001

Figure 7.3 /aw/ fronting for men and women in Philadelphia (from Labov 1984; in Eckert 1989:252, figure 1. Reprinted with the permission of Cambridge University Press).

example, sometimes the following pattern is observed: Women of increasingly prestigious social classes show progressively lower usage levels for innovative vernacular variants. Men, on the other hand, show more of a curvilinear pattern: Lower-class men show quite low levels for innovative vernacular variants, working-class men show somewhat higher levels, and middle-class men show levels which are nearly as low as those of the lower-class male speakers. This patterning has been observed for such variables as the pronunciation of /aw/ as more of an [æʊ] in Philadelphia English (Labov 1984) and the use of rising, question-like intonation on statements in Australian English (Guy, Horvath, Vonwiller, Daisley, and Rogers 1986). Figures 7.3 and 7.4 illustrate.

The patterning shown in figures 7.3 and 7.4 has been explained by maintaining that when men (unconsciously) find themselves approaching the usage levels which characterize female speech for a particular innovative language feature, they will suddenly lower their usage levels of the newer feature in order to avoid what they perceive to be a female speech pattern. However, Penelope Eckert points out that the curvilinear male pattern could just as easily be explained in terms of prestige as in terms of avoiding "sounding like a woman": Men who are situated firmly in the middle class show lower usage

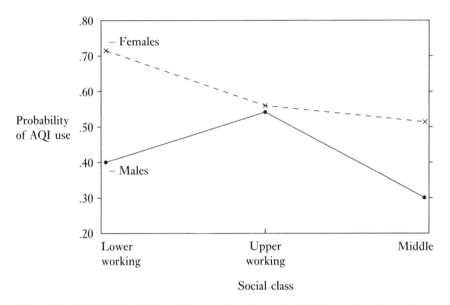

Figure 7.4 Probability of Australian question intonation (AQI) use by class and sex (from Guy, Horvath, Vonwiller, Daisley, and Rogers 1986:37, figure 2; in Eckert 1989:252. Reprinted with the permission of Cambridge University Press).

levels for innovative vernacular variants than men in the class below them simply because they are less concerned with increasing their social prestige than men in the upper working class/lower middle class.

Although we may be able to explain certain patterns of cross-sex language differentiation by maintaining that women are more concerned with social prestige than men, such explanation does not cover the wide range of male–female language differences which have been observed in speech communities across the country and throughout the world. Furthermore, the very fact that we find such a wide range of cross-sex differences indicates that these differences derive from a complex array of social factors and are not simply a by-product of biological sex.

7.3   Contact-based Explanations

A number of researchers have proposed that cross-gender language differences have more to do with patterns of contact than the value that females and males place on social prestige. Speakers who come into frequent contact with vernacular speakers will tend to adopt or maintain vernacular speech norms, while those who come into more contact with speakers whose speech represents wider language norms will adopt these more standard norms. In a number of vernacular speech communities in the United States, we find, perhaps surprisingly, that it is women rather than men who have wider social networks. This is largely because women's jobs in such communities tend to take them outside of the local community and to bring them into contact with women from other communities, while men tend to engage in locally centered occupations with men who belong to the same local community. Because this is a common pattern for male–female social contact, it is not surprising that researchers commonly find that women use more language norms from the wider community while men use more locally centered norms.

Contact-based explanations may also be used to explain cases in which women rather than men show higher levels of usage for vernacular variants. One researcher who has applied such an explanation to her findings is Nichols (1983), who investigated the use of vernacular creole language features *vis-à-vis* innovating standard forms among two groups of Gullah speakers in coastal South Carolina. One of these groups lived off the coast, in the Sea Islands, while the other lived on the mainland. Nichols focused her study on three creole features:

1 the use of *to* versus *for* (phonetically [fə]) in infinitive constructions
   e.g. I come *for* get my coat.
         I come *to* get my coat.

2 third person singular pronouns *ee* (phonetically [i]) and *em*
   e.g. And *ee* was foggy, and they couldn't see.
         And *it* was foggy, and they couldn't see.

3 static locative preposition *to* versus *at*
   e.g. Can we stay *to* the table?
         Can we stay *at* the table?

While the younger groups of speakers on both the island and the mainland showed women to be ahead of men in their use of standard forms such as infinitive *to* vs. *for* or pronominal *it* vs. *ee* or *em*, Nichols found that older women on the mainland actually used more creole features than their male counterparts. That is, the older women on the mainland were more likely to use forms like *for* for *to* or *ee*/*em* for *it* than the older males. Nichols attributed these differences to the different occupational and educational experiences of members of each gender group, particularly the different communication networks associated with these experiences. For the older mainland group, men had broader-based work experiences and traveled more than the women they lived with; consequently, they had wider communication networks. Given the differential communication networks and life experiences, women in this setting were more likely than men to preserve older vernacular forms.

We may also view the results of our study of Ocracoke English on the Outer Banks of North Carolina in light of contact-based explanations for cross-sex language patterns. When our older speakers were acquiring their dialect, there was little contact with mainland dialect areas among either men or women, and so both groups of speakers display about equal usage levels for vernacular variants. By the time our middle-aged speakers were acquiring their language variety, however, a tourism industry was blossoming on Ocracoke, and some islanders were beginning to come into contact with speakers of standard varieties. It is likely that the first speakers to do so were men, since women traditionally were confined to the domestic sphere. In addition, a number of middle-aged men joined the service and so came into extensive contact with wider language norms. Thus, the reason that most middle-aged men in our Ocracoke sample display a lower usage level for the vernacular Ocracoke [ɔɪ] vowel may be because these men, in general, had more contact than women with standard [aɪ] as they were acquiring their dialect.

The fact that one group of middle-aged men uses more of the traditional "hoi toide" vowel than anyone else in the Ocracoke community, old, young, or middle-aged, may also be accounted for by appealing to language contact. Members of this group pride themselves on their "authentic" islander identity and engage in traditional occupations and pastimes, such as fishing and crabbing, at least to the extent to which this is possible in the face of a declining maritime industry. These men spend a good bit of time working with one another and even more time socializing with each other. In fact, in a number of studies we refer to this group as the "Poker Game Network," since these men frequently get together for card games and other forms of social activity (e.g. Wolfram and Schilling-Estes 1995; Schilling-Estes 1996). It is not surprising that members of the close-knit Poker Game Network use more local vernacular forms than other members of the Ocracoke community, whose social networks extend beyond members of established island families to tourists and new residents from outside dialect areas.

However, closer examination of the Ocracoke situation has suggested to us that language contact is not the only issue at stake. Although members of the Poker Game Network may attempt to limit their occupational and social ties to established island residents, they are really not able to do so, because it is very difficult to continue to make a living on the island via traditional island occupations. Thus, the same men who fish together several times a week must supplement the income they earn this way through such means as building homes for new residents, piloting ferries which bring tourists to the island, and running hotels and restaurants. In other words, these men actually come into quite a bit of contact with outsiders, even though they may seek to portray themselves as engaging in strictly local contact.

Further, contact-based explanations for cross-sex language differences do little to explain the patterns we have observed among the youngest Ocracoke speakers in our study. The young males are considerably more vernacular than the young females; yet both these groups come into close daily contact with outsiders, since the majority of the students in the Ocracoke School now are members of families who only recently have established residence on the island.

Thus, just as with prestige-based explanations for male–female language differences, contact-based explanations can be used to account for some observed patterns of difference but not for all the multifarious patterns which we find throughout the country and even in one small section of the coastal US.

7.4 Power-based Explanations

To help account for cases in which contact-based and prestige-based explanations do not seem to apply, researchers in language variation have proposed that male–female language differences have more to do with differential power than with differential contact or desire for prestige. For example, Eckert (1990) maintains that, because women have little power in most communities when compared with men, they seek to acquire such power in symbolic ways. One of the chief ways of gaining – and projecting – symbolic power is through using standard language variants, since these variants are associated with the speech of the most powerful socioeconomic classes. Eckert's term for symbolic power is *symbolic capital*, since power of all sorts is inextricably linked to economic power in Western (and non-Western) society.

Not only can we explain women's use of standard variants in terms of the notion of symbolic capital, but we can also explain their use of innovative vernacular forms in this way. Eckert maintains that women often lead men in the adoption of new language features because such features signal symbolic membership in important local social groups. Symbolic group affiliation is more important to women than men, because women historically have been denied full membership in their surrounding communities (and in wider society as well), being relegated to a narrow social sphere and to a limited range of social roles. In support of her view, Eckert points to the results of her study of the adoption of various innovative vernacular features among adolescents in the Detroit area. She noted that usage levels for the features she studied varied greatly among the girls in her study but did not vary as much among boys. Further, there was less difference in usage levels for vernacular variants across the two sexes than within the speech of girls.

Eckert's findings indicate, first of all, that there is indeed no biological basis for male–female language differences; if there were, we would necessarily find more cross-sex than intra-sex language differentiation. More importantly, however, her findings indicate the symbolic display of group affiliation through language, since she found that the level to which girls used particular innovative variants correlated with their membership in one of several well-known social groups. Boys, on the other hand, did not display symbolic group membership through language. Most likely, this is because boys do not place as much importance on symbolic belonging as girls, since boys are brought up to become full-fledged members of local and wider society and so are not as dependent as girls on signaling membership through language.

Just as language-use patterns have nothing to do with male or female biology, so too is concern for symbolic power more closely linked with social factors than with physiology. To illustrate this, let us return to the Ocracoke case we discussed earlier. Since language contact does not fully account for the language patterns we observe among middle-aged speakers, perhaps we can turn to the notion of symbolic capital. At first glance, this seems to be of little help. Although concern for symbolic capital may account for why women speak more standardly than certain men (i.e. men in the Poker Game Network), it does not explain why women speak less standardly than the other men in our study. However, let us consider in more detail the economic situation of the Ocracoke community. As discussed above, the Ocracoke economy is being transformed from a marine-based economy to one based on tourism. As this transformation takes place, men's ability to make a living via traditional male occupations such as fishing and crabbing is diminishing rapidly. Women, on the other hand, are gaining increasing earning power as the economy changes, and they now hold most of the island's steady jobs, in stores, restaurants, and hotels. Thus, we hypothesize that it is men rather than women who are most concerned with symbolic capital on Ocracoke.

Further, we suggest that it is not only standard language variants that may carry connotations of economic power. For men in blue-collar communities such as Ocracoke, it may well be that vernacular variants are more closely associated with economic power than standard variants, since men in such communities achieve economic power through physical ability and physical strength rather than the ability to verbally negotiate the established power structures of the corporate and political arena. Thus, if a man on Ocracoke wishes to display symbolic power as his real earning power declines, he will maintain or even heighten his usage of vernacular variants rather than adopt variants of wider usage. In particular, he will heighten his usage of the Ocracoke "hoi toide" vowel, since this vowel is such a well-known feature of traditional Ocracoke speech.

Women on Ocracoke have a decreasing rather than increasing need for symbolic capital, since their real economic power has increased steadily with the increase in tourism. Thus, they have no need for the symbolic capital which the traditional language variety connotes. Furthermore, the traditional dialect does not really carry associations of increased economic power for women, since women's jobs traditionally are not centered on physical power. In addition, the traditional dialect carries crucial associations related to personal identity: It is perceived as tough and masculine and so cannot be used by women who wish to project some type of traditional feminine identity. The "macho" connotations of the traditional dialect also help explain why only certain middle-aged men show exaggerated usage of vernacular dialect features. Members of the highly vernacular Poker Game Network project a distinctly "macho" image, and they are known throughout the island as a boisterous group of "good old boys." However, other men do not rely so much on notions of toughness and "manliness" for their self-definition and so do not need to engage in heavy use of the traditional dialect.

We see, then, that differential access to power rather than differential desire for social prestige may underlie male–female language differences, at least in some communities which have been investigated by sociolinguists. Further, we see that the patterning of male–female language differences in a given community is dependent on the particular economic situation that characterizes the community and on the symbolic meaning of particular language features among community residents. Thus, in some communities we find that women strive for symbolic power to a greater degree than men and seek this power through using standard language variants. In other communities, however, men are the primary seekers of symbolic power, which they may actually attain through the use of vernacular rather than standard language forms.

Although researchers such as Eckert, Milroy and others have greatly increased our understanding of male–female language differences, it is by no means clear exactly how gender-based language variation is to be incorporated into traditional dialect study. For example, Eckert points out that relationships among different gender groups are very different from those which hold across class or ethnic groups, since the latter are characterized by social separation but the former, of course, are not. However, sociolinguists have not developed ways of capturing this difference in their examinations of the influences of social class, ethnic, and gender-based factors on the patterning of language variation. In addition, investigations of the intersection of social class and gender-based language variation are limited in that the classification of females into social class groups traditionally has been based on the socioeconomic characteristics of males with whom these females are closely associated (i.e. husbands and fathers) rather than according to the characteristics of the females themselves. And even if we do attempt to place women into socioeconomic classes based on their own characteristics, we have no way of capturing the fact that a woman's status in the occupational realm does not necessarily guarantee her equal status in other spheres, particularly the domestic arena. As Eckert states:

> Since actual power relations between men and women can be expected to lag behind . . . changes in relative positions in the marketplace, one can expect such a dynamic in language to outlive any number of economic changes. . . . Women's inequality is built into the family, and it continues in the workplace, where women are constantly confronted with a double bind, since neither stereotypic female nor stereotypic male behavior is acceptable. (1989:255)

Partly because of the difficulties associated with incorporating gender-based language differences into the study of the patterning of individual phonological, syntactic, and lexical variants, a number of researchers have chosen to focus on matters of language use instead. In addition, cross-sex differences in language use seem to be more directly reflective of male–female social differences than subtle differences in language structure and so have proven to be a highly fruitful area of study for language researchers – as well as a captivating topic of discussion for non-linguists. We turn now to an overview of approaches to language and gender which focus on language use. These approaches may be divided into three categories, based on their focus on social and linguistic *deficit*, *difference*, or *dominance* (e.g. Cameron 1996).

7.5   Language-Use-based Approaches: The "Female Deficit" Approach

The "female deficit" approach to language and gender studies can be traced at least as far back as the early 1920s, when the renowned linguist Otto Jespersen devoted a chapter of his influential book *Language: Its Nature, Development, and Origin* (1922) to "The Woman." In this chapter, Jespersen claimed that women in a number of cultures throughout the world exhibit speech patterns which differ from those of men and that these differences derive from differences in biological make-up. Among the features of "women's speech" which Jespersen noted were that women have less extensive vocabularies than men, use simpler sentence constructions, and speak with little prior thought. In other words, women's speech was held to be deficient when compared with the male "norm."

Although some early feminists reacted against the notion that men's language was "normal" language and that women's language was inferior and was to be considered a natural by-product of biological sex, Jespersen's ideas remained unchallenged within the field of linguistics for nearly half a century, even though most of the evidence for his claims comes from his examination of portrayals of women in art and literature rather than from observations of real-world behavior. It was not until Robin Lakoff published her important article, "Language and women's place" (1973), that language researchers returned to an examination of the differences between men's and women's speech, as well as to an examination of the assumption that men's language is the norm. Lakoff's work was highly influential for a number of years but has now been largely discredited, primarily because Lakoff, like Jespersen, subscribes to the female deficit theory, in that she views women's speech as weak in comparison with men's speech. In addition, she, like Jespersen, relies on literary texts and casual observation for her "data." However, unlike Jespersen, Lakoff is sympathetic to women and maintains that women's deficient speech patterns are not the result of inherent biological or mental deficiency but rather of differential experience. Further, she hints that men's greater power in society may be a factor in perpetuating women's weaker use of language. Because Lakoff's work was so influential for so many years, we list here a few of the features which she classified as "women's" speech features and offered as "proof" that women's speech indeed is weaker than that of men. Following this brief list, we discuss why Lakoff's assertions have not held up over the years.

A sampling of women's speech features, per Lakoff (1973)

(1)   Heavy use of "tag questions"
Lakoff claims that women use more structures such as, "That sounds OK, **doesn't it?**" than men. The little questions which women often "tag onto" the ends of statements have the effect, Lakoff says, of diminishing the force of the statement; in addition, they convey a lack of confidence, or even a lack of personal opinions or views, on the part of the speaker.

(2)   Question intonation on statements
Lakoff maintains that women often end statements with the rising intonation which is characteristic of questions rather than with the falling intonation which characterizes assertions. The effect of "question intonation" is similar to that of tag questions, in that it turns utterances into questionable propositions rather than definitive statements.

(3)   "Weak" directives
According to Lakoff, women tend to frame directives or commands as requests rather than direct commands. For example, women are more likely to get someone to close an open door by saying "Would you mind shutting the door?" than by saying "Shut the door!" Requests, Lakoff maintains, carry less authoritative force than directives which are framed as imperatives.

Exercise 1

In keeping with the notion that women's speech is "less powerful" than that of men, it is often asserted by researchers in language and gender that men interrupt more than women, in order to seize control of conversational interactions. Choose a mixed-sex group (e.g. a class, club meeting) and conduct a simple study of the cross-sex patternings of interruptions during the group meeting. You will need to count how many males and how many females are in the group, since the overall tabulation will have to take into account the proportion of males to females. If the group has a designated leader, do not tabulate the frequency of interruptions by the leader for this exercise (although, as a separate study, it would be interesting to observe the leader's patterns of interruptions, especially as regards the sex of the speaker being interrupted by the leader). You can set up a simple coding sheet something like the following. Be sure to be discreet in recording your tabulations at the scene of the gathering.

Setting: (e.g. discussion group, faculty meeting, etc.)
No. of males present _____ % of group _____
No. of females present _____ % of group _____
Total participants _____

	Female	Male
Interruption		

What problems did you encounter in carrying out the project? Do your findings seem to support the notion that men's language is more "powerful" than women's? Do your findings support the idea that interruptions are primarily a strategy for seizing conversational control?

Lakoff's discussion of women's speech features was highly influential and prompted an entire generation of researchers to conduct empirical work on women's language, both in attempts to find support for Lakoff's views and in attempts to prove her wrong. Results of these empirical tests have been mixed. For example, while some studies indicate that women indeed use more tag questions than men in certain contexts (e.g. Crosby and Nyquist 1977), others show that men use more tag questions (e.g. Dubois and Crouch 1975). Lakoff herself had no empirical data on this issue, other than her own introspection, a fact which she makes clear in her article. She writes: "It is my opinion, though I do not have precise statistical evidence, that this sort of tag question is more apt to be used by women than by men" (1973:55). Certainly, we have to view Lakoff's opinions with caution, since they may or may not be reflective of the language-use patterns which characterize her entire speech community; further caution is warranted if we attempt to generalize Lakoff's findings to speakers whose backgrounds are quite different from her own white, middle-class background.

Another limitation of Lakoff's work is that it is grounded in the notion that certain language features necessarily connote weakness. Researchers increasingly have come to realize that the social meanings attached to language forms are highly dependent on the social context surrounding the forms and on the interpretation conversational participants choose to give the forms. Thus, one can readily re-interpret so-called "weak" directives as "polite" directives which indicate that women are more attuned to the linguistic and social needs of fellow conversationalists than men – or even that women may possess a greater ability than men to engage in cooperative conversational exchanges. In addition, while "weak" directives may indeed be indicative of uncertainty in some situations, they may indicate mere politeness in other settings and even hostility or distance in others. For example, a speaker may suddenly start using ultra-polite language forms during a conversation with an intimate friend in order to indicate anger.

One final concern regarding Lakoff's 1973 article has to do with the broader sociopolitical implications of her perspective. Scholars in the field of language and gender have pointed out that if women consider their language to be weak and inferior, then they will feel pressure to alter their language so it is more like men's language, which is considered to be "strong," or at least free of weakness. Further, Lakoff's views place pressure on women to "decipher" or "interpret" men's language, with no corresponding pressure on men to learn to correctly understand women's use of language.

Not only have researchers cast doubt on the popular belief that women use weaker language than men, but they have also debunked several other widely held stereotypes. For example, many people believe that women talk more than men, a "fact" which is often the subject of humorous – and derogatory – commentary. Thus, husbands often jokingly state that they "can't get a word in edgewise" when their wives are around. However, studies of amount of talk by men and women actually indicate that, in general, men talk more than women. (See James and Drakich 1993 for a summary of the numerous studies that have been conducted on this topic.) And even our own research, which has not been focused on language and gender issues, supports these findings: We can't help but notice that when we go out into the field and conduct sociolinguistic interviews with men and women at the same time (for example, with a married couple), we often get very little of the woman's speech on tape, since the man does most of the talking. Of course, we have to realize that amount of talk by men and women may be drastically different in different situations, depending on such factors as the topic and setting of the conversation, as well

as who is considered to be the authority figure in a given conversational interaction. In addition, amount of talk may be measured in various ways, for example
by number of words per conversational turn or by number of minutes per
turn, and these different measures may yield quite different results. Despite
such important qualifications, however, research simply does not support the
popular opinion that women talk more than men.

Another stereotype which has been challenged is the belief, once common
among researchers in language and gender, that men interrupt more than
women. This belief stems from the notion that men hold more societal and
conversational power than women and that interruptions serve as a means of
seizing control of conversations. Numerous empirical studies have been undertaken to determine who interrupts more, and, while some of these studies
support the belief that men interrupt more than women, others indicate that
women interrupt more or, most often, that there is no significant difference in
amount of interruptions by men and women. (See James and Clarke 1993 for a
summary.)

This wide variation in research results is due to several factors. First, the
number of interruptions seems to be dependent not only on who is doing the
interrupting but who is being interrupted. For example, women tend to get
interrupted more than men by both female and male speakers. In addition, just
as with amount of talk, amount of interruption may be measured in various
ways, since it can be very difficult to determine exactly what constitutes an
interruption and what doesn't. Not all cases of overlapping speech constitute
interruption. For example, we may "talk over" someone who is offering an
opinion with phrases and responses such as "right" and "ummhmm," but
these responses are supportive, whereas true interruptions are considered to
be disruptive in some way. Further, the "rules" for what counts as an interruption may be very different in different settings. For example, during an
animated family discussion at the dinner table, children may be permitted
to engage in overlapping talk to a much greater extent than they would in a
setting such as the classroom.

Even utterances which unquestionably serve to interrupt the flow of conversation sometimes have little or nothing to do with conversational dominance. If
someone interrupts us in mid-sentence by uttering the cry of "Fire!" we are
not likely to interpret the remark as a bid for power; instead we will interpret it
as a warning issued out of concern for our safety. Similarly, if someone interrupts us in the middle of an explanation by exclaiming, "Oh! Now I get it!,"
we most likely will interpret the interruption as a positive emotional response
to sudden enlightenment rather than as a negative attempt to thwart us in our
efforts to continue our explanation. Just as so-called "weak" language features
do not always serve to convey weakness, so too do interruptions carry a number
of different connotations besides conversational dominance. Thus, there is no
clear connection between social dominance and increased interruptions.

7.6   The "Cultural Difference" Approach

As a counter to the view that women's language is deficient compared to men's, a number of researchers maintain that women's language is not inferior but simply different. The CULTURAL DIFFERENCE approach to language and gender is grounded in the belief that women's and men's speech is different because girls and boys in America grow up in essentially separate speech communities, because they typically are segregated into same-sex peer groups during the years in which they acquire many of their language-use patterns. This approach is central to the work of a number of researchers, including Deborah Tannen, a sociolinguist who is well known as the author of several best-selling books on language and gender for non-experts, including *That's Not What I Meant! How Conversational Style Makes or Breaks Relationships* (1987) and *You Just Don't Understand: Women and Men in Conversation* (1990).

Tannen seeks to explain the frequent misunderstandings that arise in cross-sex communicative encounters by claiming that women and men have very different notions of how conversations are supposed to work, as well as different expectations regarding the role of conversational interaction in building and maintaining interpersonal relationships. These differences exist because girls and boys spend most of their time in single-sex groups during the stages of their life when most of the rules for interpersonal interaction are being learned. Girls grow up in groups in which heavy emphasis is placed on cooperation, equality, and emotionally charged friendships, and so girls develop conversational styles which are cooperative and highly interactional, with each girl encouraging the speech of others and building on others' communications as she converses. In addition, girls learn to read others' emotions in quite subtle ways, because forming strong friendships is of key importance to them. On the other hand, boys grow up in groups which are hierarchical in nature and in which dominance over others is of central importance. Thus, boys develop conversational styles which are competitive rather than cooperative, and they place a heavy reliance on "proving themselves" through their words rather than on encouraging the ideas of other speakers.

The conversational differences learned in childhood carry over into adulthood, when women and men interact with one another on a frequent basis; and conversational misunderstandings result. For example, if a man dominates a cross-sex conversation, through such means as interruption and lengthy conversational turns, the woman with whom he is conversing may feel that the man doesn't care about her ideas because he doesn't allow her her fair share of talk time. According to Tannen, however, the man may not realize that he has hurt the woman's feelings, because he considers conversations to be contests rather than cooperative exchanges in which each party is to be given an equal chance to be heard. Similarly, because women are more attuned to seeking out the relational implications behind seemingly straightforward factual statements than men, women may feel that men simply "aren't trying" when they fail to understand the underlying meanings behind apparently simple statements. For example, when a woman says to her husband, "I wonder what I should do about that problem at work," she is not expecting him to respond with directives such as "Quit" or "Put up with it" but with a statement that indicates that he is sympathetic to her feelings of frustration over her job.

Tannen's books have been well received by general audiences, who seem to be glad to have discovered that there are explanations for the miscommunications that they frequently experience in their own cross-sex interactions. At the same time, her works have met with some opposition by researchers. For example, like Lakoff, Tannen has been criticized because she emphasizes that women need to learn to "read" men without placing a corresponding emphasis on men's learning to understand the conversational conventions which guide female speech. Tannen has also been criticized for overemphasizing the differences between women's and men's conversational styles and hence perpetuating the artificial dichotomy between women's and men's language. A number of proponents of the cultural difference theory, including the earliest advocates of this approach (Maltz and Borker 1982), maintain that by the time males and females reach adulthood, their conversational styles are actually quite similar. And even in childhood, it is maintained, similarities in conversational strategies far outweigh differences. For example, it has been shown that girls use the same strategies to win arguments as boys and that they are just as skillful at arguing as boys (Goodwin 1990).

Perhaps the biggest concern with cultural difference approaches such as Tannen's is that such approaches tend to downplay the power relations which underlie the different interactional styles into which boys and girls are socialized. It is not simply the case that girls are cooperative and boys are competitive because "that's the way things are." Rather, the competitiveness into which boys are socialized stems from male societal dominance – and ensures the perpetuation of such dominance. On the other hand, the cooperativeness and focus on the needs of others into which girls are socialized arises from the subordinate social position of females, who must learn to adjust their actions – and feelings – to accord with those of others because of their own lack of autonomy.

7.7   The "Dominance" Theory

The notion that male–female conversational differences are due to societal power differences between men and women has been termed the DOMINANCE THEORY. In support of this theory, researchers have pointed out that the features of so-called "male conversational style" almost always seem to be characteristic of speech which is uncooperative or disruptive in some way, a correlation we would not expect if men's conversational differences derived solely from cultural difference rather than cultural dominance (e.g. Henley and Kramarae 1994). Thus, men take up more conversational time than women, introduce new topics rather than building on old ones, and appear inattentive to the relational implications underlying factual statements, not because they come from a "separate but equal" interactional realm, but because they are clearly *not* the equals of women. Instead, they dominate women, and this dominance pervades their conversational interactions as well as their non-verbal behavior towards women.

Under the dominance theory, not only is the source of male–female miscommunication probed in greater depth than under the cultural difference theory, but the very notion of miscommunication itself is questioned. A number of researchers have suggested that men's "misunderstandings" of women's conversational style are often quite intentional. For example, Penelope Eckert and Sally McConnell-Ginet (1994) suggest that when a man making sexual advances towards a woman interprets her "no" to mean "yes," it is unlikely that he is following a conversational rule he learned in all-male peer groups which states that one accepts sexual advances by pretending to reject them. Instead, "he actively exploits his 'understanding' of the female style as different from his own – as being indirect rather than straightforward" (1994:437) in order to imbue the woman's response with the meaning that he wishes it to have. Indeed, men seem to show no difficulty in understanding and even engaging in "female-like" conversational behavior when it suits their purposes. For example, we are all familiar with "sweet talkers" who engage in highly co-operative conversational interaction with women and display great sensitivity to the emotional and relational meanings underlying women's words in order to win over or seduce the women with whom they are conversing. Thus, it seems that the communicative difficulties which we often find in cross-sex conversations do not stem solely from a genuine inability to understand; rather, they sometimes derive from unwillingness to understand.

7.8   Further Considerations in the Study of Gender-based Language Differences

Currently, a number of researchers who are investigating language and gender from the approaches of dialect study as well as language use are focusing on the unequal power relations behind male–female language differences. They are becoming increasingly careful, though, to note that, just as the use of "weak" language has nothing to do with female biology, so too is there no inherent connection between men and power. Men's dominance in society derives from the roles which have been ascribed to men by society, and the roles which men see themselves as fulfilling, rather than maleness *per se*. Indeed, as we have just mentioned, there are certain situations in which females display just as much concern for dominance as men; and we can conceive of any number of situations in which cooperation rather than competition will be uppermost in the minds of male speakers.

Current researchers are intent on investigating gender as a social construct rather than a biological given, as well as on demonstrating that gender-based language differences are not dichotomous but rather continuous. Thus, there is increasing emphasis on examining intra-sex language differences as well as cross-sex similarities, in order to determine the social and identificational correlates of language variation which are *not* tied to biological sex. For example, as we mentioned earlier in this chapter, Eckert (1990) has shown that concern for "belonging" may have a far greater effect on how fully speakers participate in sound changes than whether the speakers are male or female. In addition, researchers are placing increasing emphasis on examining the intersection of gender with other social factors, such as ethnicity, cultural background, and age. What happens, for example, when a woman, who is supposed to speak in an indirect manner, happens to be a member of an ethnic group known for its conversational directness? Similarly, how do we account for the fact that in some communities, older speakers display very different cross-sex language patterns than younger speakers – or for the fact that the male–female language differences which have been observed among middle-class Anglo American speakers do not always hold in other socioeconomic groups or in other countries?

Researchers are also placing more emphasis on investigating men's language, since it is now understood that men's language is not simply the linguistic norm but represents gendered language every bit as much as women's language. For example, Kiesling (1996) shows how men's patterns of language use in a fraternity setting are not "unmarked" but rather derive from these men's focus on achieving various forms of conversational and social power. In addition, as we discussed above, we have demonstrated how certain men on Ocracoke display linguistic patterning which is far from the community "norm," since they retain and even enhance dialect features which most members of their community are relinquishing.

Finally, current research remains focused on the fact that language forms are not inherently imbued with certain social meanings such as "strong" or "weak" or "disruptive." Rather, meanings are context-dependent, and great care must be taken to interpret the social meanings of linguistic forms in light of the conversational, social, and cultural setting surrounding the forms in question.

7.9   Talking About Men and Women

We have seen that many of the differences in how men and women talk may be grounded in power differences between men and women. It has also been claimed that men's power and women's relative lack of power are encoded – and perpetuated – in how men and women are talked to and talked about. Let us examine this claim by looking at some of the traditional differences in how men and women are referred to in American society.

7.9.1   Generic he and man

The use of the pronoun *he* and its related forms *his* or *him* to refer to a sex-indefinite antecedent (e.g. *If anybody reads this book, he will learn about dialects*) is certainly one of the most often-cited cases of sex bias found in English. It is interesting to note that alternatives to the generic male pronoun such as the use of singular *they* (e.g. *If anybody reads this book, they will learn about dialects*) were quite acceptable during earlier periods of history (Bodine 1975), but these alternatives were gradually legislated out of acceptable usage by prescriptive grammarians. For example, in 1746, the grammarian John Kirby included as one of his "Eighty-Eight Grammatical Rules" the rule that "the male gender was more comprehensive than the female" (quoted in Miller 1994). Even lawmakers spoke out against generic *they* and other alternatives to generic *he*. For example, a law passed by the British Parliament in 1850 stated that "in all acts words importing the masculine gender shall be deemed and taken to include female" (quoted in Miller 1994). It is uncertain exactly when generic *he* arose, but its usage is probably correlated with increased usage of the noun *man* to refer to "humankind," as in **Man** *shall not live by bread alone* (Smith 1985:50). Interestingly, in Old English the word *man* really was truly generic and could be used in place of both the feminine *wif* 'woman' and the masculine *wer* or *carl* 'man' (Frank and Anshen 1983).

   The prescriptive use of generic *he* in formal and written English persists despite the widespread use of generic *they* to refer to singular antecedents in informal spoken English, and attempts to use generic *they* in writing continue to meet with steadfast editorial rejection. However, in recent years, grammar books increasingly have been legislating against the use of generic *he*, and many of these books now include sections on how to avoid using generic *he* without "improperly" using generic *they*. For example, students are taught to pluralize sex-indefinite antecedents (*If people read this book, they will learn about dialects*); to use the phrase *he or she* (or *she or he*), as in *If anyone reads this book, he or she will learn about dialects*; or to alternate generic *he* with generic *she*.

(*If anyone reads this book, **he** will learn about dialects. The student will thus find that **her** knowledge of language patterning has been greatly increased.*)

Attempts to do away with generic *he* have met with resistance and ridicule for decades, with opponents arguing that the use of generic *he/man* in no way excludes women or obscures their role in society because, by longstanding convention, people readily associate these forms with the meanings 'he and she' and 'humankind'. However, experiments show that, in reality, there is a tendency for readers to associate generic *he/man* with males alone, particularly when the readers themselves are male (e.g. Harrison 1975; Martyna 1978, 1980). In addition, experiments have shown that the use of generic *he* has a significant impact on readers' comprehension of reading passages, their judgments regarding the personal relevance and worth of a given passage, and their beliefs regarding the gender of the author of the passage (MacKay 1983). For example, it has been shown that men have better comprehension than women when generic *he* is used, while women are more likely to judge that prose containing generic *he* must have been written by a man. Finally, it has been noted that unchecked usage of generic *he* can have far-reaching social implications. For example, it has been shown that women tend to avoid responding to job advertisements containing generic *he*, because they feel that they do not meet the qualifications outlined in the ads (Miller 1994:269).

7.9.2   Family names and addresses

The tradition of family names is another convention that has been cited as an example of how male–female power differences are encoded in language. The traditional adoption by women of the husband's family name may signify "that women's family names do not count and that there is one more device for making women invisible" (Spender 1980:24). It is also significant that women traditionally have had to use titles which indicate their marital status – that is, *Mrs* or *Miss* – whereas both married and unmarried men are known simply as *Mr*. There have been a number of different interpretations of the sociopolitical significance of this difference, but one of the most prominent is that this pattern indicates that women are defined according to their relationship to men, whereas men are more autonomous in terms of self-definition.

Other address forms indicate that men typically are more respected and treated with more formality than women. For example, men are more likely to be addressed with formal *sir* than women of comparable status are to be addressed as *ma'am*. Women are also more frequently addressed informally as *dear, honey,* and *sweetie* in social contexts where men of comparable status would not be addressed in this way.

7.9.3   *Relationships of association*

As noted above, certain language forms suggest relationships in which women are defined in terms of the men with whom they are associated, whereas the converse does not take place. Associations such as *man and wife*, but not *woman and husband*, or the more common use of the designation *Walt's wife* as opposed to *Marge's husband* have been interpreted as indicative of a relationship between the owner and the owned (Eakins and Eakins 1978). It has even been noted that the conventional placement of male before female in coordinate constructions (e.g. *husband and wife* but not *wife and husband*, or *host and hostess* but not *hostess and host*) indicates a pattern of male precedence. In fact, prescriptive grammarians writing as early as the mid-1600s indicated that the male gender should always be placed first because it is the "worthier" (Spender 1980:147).

Exercise 2

One of the exceptions to the ordering of masculine and feminine coordinate constructions (e.g. *husband and wife*) is found in the public address salutation, "Ladies and Gentlemen!" How might you explain this apparent exception to the more general pattern of placing the male first? Can you think of any other exceptions to the male-first pattern in coordinates?

7.9.4   *Labeling*

There are many instances of differential labeling that have been offered as evidence that unequal male–female power relations, as well as unequal levels of respect, are encoded in the English language. These include the scope of semantic reference covered by particular words, the emotive connotations of sex-paired words, and the patterns of derivation in lexical items. The age span typically covered by items such as *boy–girl* and *man–woman* illustrates that the semantic range of analogous lexical items is not always comparable for males and females. Older women are much more likely to be referred to as *girls* than older men are to be referred to as *boys*. A person might thus say, "I met this real nice girl" in reference to a 30-year-old female, but one would hardly say "I met this nice boy" to refer to a 30-year-old male. In virtually every instance of this type, males are favored. Thus, TV announcers still refer to the NCAA "girls' basketball tournament," while they never refer to the NCAA "boys' basketball tournament," even though both tournaments involve college students roughly between 18 and 22 years of age.

In paired masculine and feminine lexical items, it has been noted that the feminine member of the pair often undergoes SEMANTIC DEROGATION (Schulz 1975). That is, the feminine member of the pair often acquires connotations of subservience or diminished importance, as, for example, in such word pairs as *mister/mistress*, *governor/governess*, and *bachelor/spinster*. In many cases, the feminine item may also acquire connotations of improper sexual behavior, as in the case of *mistress*. Even when feminine items are directly derived from masculine items via the addition of a suffix, as in *bachelorette* or *poetess*, the new word often takes on connotations of lessened significance or respectability. In cases where gender is indicated through the addition of a suffix, the burden is typically carried by the feminine item rather than the masculine (e.g. *Carla* is derived from *Carl* or *Paulette* from *Paul*, etc.), suggesting a male norm for lexical items. Furthermore, one survey of dictionary items (Nilsen 1977) shows that masculine words outnumber feminine words by a ratio of three to one, and masculine words denoting prestige are six times as frequent as feminine words with prestige.

Finally, there are drastic differences in specialized vocabularies which are clearly indicative of the longstanding "double standard" which society has maintained for male and female behavior. For example, Julia P. Stanley (1977) found only 20 items describing promiscuous men (e.g. *animal*, *letch*), some of which even carried some positive connotations, such as *stud* and *Casanova*. By the same token, Stanley stopped counting when she reached 220 labels for promiscuous women (e.g. *whore*, *slut*, *tramp*). There are also comparable disparities in metaphorical labeling, as women tend to be labeled with reference to consumable items such as foods (e.g. *peach*, *sugar*, *cheesecake*, etc.) but men do not.

7.10   The Question of Language Reform

The linguistic manifestations of inequality and stereotyping based on sex are hardly disputable. The question that remains is whether changing the language will alter the unequal position of men and women in society or whether achieving increased social equality must precede increased linguistic equality. One answer might be that language simply mirrors sociocultural patterns: If a society treats women as unequal, then language will simply provide the symbolic mechanism for displaying society's underlying discriminatory base. Changing to alternate, more neutral forms will not really stop underlying sex stereotyping, as items characteristically undergo semantic derogation when associated with a feminine referent. After all, at one point, words like *mistress* and *governess* were neutral counterparts of their male equivalents *mister* and *governor*. So changing language-use patterns may simply be a linguistic cosmetic for an underlying problem of social inequality. From this vantage point, language dutifully follows a symbolic course set for it by the established social system; language can hardly be blamed for the more fundamental social inequity to be confronted.

However, it must be noted that just as language mirrors the prevailing social order, the use of language may reinforce and perpetuate the acceptance of these social conditions. Thus, whereas it may seem pointless to begin using *he or she* in place of generic *he* or to change one's title from *Mrs* or *Miss* to *Ms*, there is a sense in which if we do not make these changes, we continue to endorse the notion that women don't "count" as much as men and that women can only be defined in relation to the men who surround them. There is an obvious interdependence between language as a reflection of social differences and language as a socializing instrument. Changing language-use patterns may thus go hand-in-hand with changing social conditions. In other words, language reform may actually serve as an impetus for social change.

While there remains some discussion among linguists and other scholars of language concerning what constitutes "realistic" language reform with respect to sex reference in English, there seems to be a consensus on a number of proposed reforms. In fact, the Linguistic Society of America, the most influential organization for language scholars in the United States, has adopted a clear policy statement regarding non-sexist language usage, which includes the following strategies for avoiding sexist language:

1 Whenever possible, use plurals (*people, they*) and other appropriate alternatives, rather than only masculine pronouns and "pseudo-generics" such as *man*, unless referring specifically to males.
2 Avoid generic statements which inaccurately refer only to one sex (e.g., "Speakers use language for many purposes – to argue with their wives . . ." or "Americans use lots of obscenities but not around women").
3 Whenever possible, use terms that avoid sexual stereotyping. Such terms as *server, professor*, and *nurse* can be effectively used as gender neutral; marked terms like *waitress, lady professor*, and *male nurse* cannot.

(from the Linguistic Society of America Guidelines for Nonsexist Usage, approved by the LSA Executive Committee, May 1995)

Because guidelines such as the above have been so widely accepted, we don't believe we are being overly optimistic in claiming that most linguists take a strong and unified position favoring non-discriminatory language use.

Exercise 3

A critical notion in debates over reforming sexist language use is the determination of what constitutes "realistic" reform. Suggestions for reform have ranged from fairly radical proposals, such as changing words like *history* to *herstory*, to more modest proposals such as changing address forms (e.g. using *Ms* for women regardless of marital status) and altering generic noun and pronoun reference (e.g. using *people* instead of *man* and *he/she* instead of *he*). Are there any general guidelines we might follow in determining what constitutes a "realistic" reform in this area? For example, one principle might be that we should only change items of clear masculine association. In other words, we know that speakers are apt to associate generic *he* with males, but they may not associate *history* with *his story* (vs. *her story*); thus, we should change generic *he* to something like *he/she*, but we do not need to alter a word like *history*. What general principles can you think of to guide non-discriminatory language use? Are there principles based on practical considerations, such as the likelihood that a change will be adopted? As a point of reference, you might consider an actual set of guidelines set forth by a newspaper, a professional organization, or some other agency.

7.11   Further Reading

Bergvall, Victoria L., Janet M. Bing, and Alice F. Freed (eds) (1996) *Rethinking Language and Gender Research: Theory and Practice*. New York: Longman. This important collection presents current research which challenges a number of assumptions which traditionally have pervaded the field of language and gender study. Among these assumptions are the belief that sex-based language differences are more striking than other types of differences because men and women are inherently different, that women use more prestige language forms than men, and that one's identity as "male" or "female" takes precedence over other facets of personal identity. The use of language to perpetuate gender stereotypes and the oppression of women and minorities is also discussed. Of particular interest is the introductory chapter by Bing and Bergvall, "The question of questions: beyond binary thinking," which demonstrates the artificiality of the traditional male–female dichotomy.

Eckert, Penelope (1989) The whole woman: Sex and gender differences in variation. *Language Variation and Change* 1:245–67. This article outlines some of the shortcomings of approaches to language and gender which are grounded in traditional dialect study and proposes ways of reshaping dialect study so that "gender" may be examined as a social construct rather than a biological attribute.

Frank, Francine, and Frank Anshen (1983) *Language and the Sexes*. Albany: State University of New York Press. This work provides a readable introduction to empirical research in all areas of language and gender study. The work is important in that it marks a crucial shift from the study of "women's language" (as typified in Lakoff's article) to "language and gender." Further, Frank and Anshen move beyond Lakoff by including examinations of language and gender in different ethnic groups and countries.

Freed, Alice F. (1992) We understand perfectly: A critique of Tannen's view of cross-sex communication. In Kira Hall, Mary Bucholtz, and Birch Moonwomon (eds),

Locating Power: Proceedings of the Second Berkeley Women and Language Conference, Volume 1, 144–52. Berkeley: Berkeley Women and Language Group. This article provides a critique of Deborah Tannen's popular works on language and gender for non-experts.

Johnson, Sally, and Ulrike Hanna Meinhof (eds) (1997) *Language and Masculinity*. Oxford/Cambridge, MA: Blackwell. This collection of articles is devoted to the investigation of men's language as gendered language. Of particular interest to those who are new to language and gender studies is the overview article by Sally Johnson (chapter 1, "Theorizing language and masculinity: A feminist perspective").

Labov, William (1990) The intersection of sex and social class in the course of linguistic change. *Language Variation and Change* 2:205–54. This article provides a comprehensive summary of male–female language differences which have been observed in the course of dialect study.

Lakoff, Robin (1973) Language and women's place. *Language in Society* 2:45–80. Although many of the findings and interpretations in this presentation have now been challenged and denounced, this article stands as a pioneering effort in the history of language and gender studies. Some of the observations initially made by Lakoff served to inspire a generation of empirical research on language and gender issues.

Roman, Camille, Suzanne Juhasz, and Cristanne Miller (eds) (1994) *The Women and Language Debate: A Sourcebook*. New Brunswick: Rutgers University Press. This extensive collection of articles is divided into three parts, the third of which focuses on empirical studies on language and gender. Included in this section are articles by such important figures as Robin Lakoff, Marjorie Harness Goodwin, Penelope Brown, Nancy M. Henley, Cheris Kramarae, Susan Gal, Penelope Eckert and Sally McConnell-Ginet. Of special interest is the overview chapter by Cristanne Miller which introduces the section on empirical research on language and gender.

Tannen, Deborah (ed.) (1993) *Gender and Conversational Interaction*. New York/ Oxford: Oxford University Press. This collection of articles includes a section on competitiveness and cooperation in conversational interaction, a section on the relativity of discourse strategies (such as interruptions and silence), and a very useful section consisting of reviews of the numerous empirical studies that have been conducted on women, men, and interruptions (James and Clarke) and on amount of talk by women and men (James and Drakich).

8

Dialects and Style

Most of us have noticed that people speak very differently on different occasions. For example, we may notice that a friend speaks a certain way when talking with a supervisor in the workplace or with a professor at school but sounds quite different when chatting with friends over lunch or speaking with children at home. We may even notice that we change our own speech when we're in different settings or talking with different people. In particular, people who no longer live in their hometown may find themselves switching back into their home dialect when visiting home or even when talking on the phone with a family member back home.

In this chapter, we shift our focus from language variation across different groups of speakers to variation in the speech of individual speakers, or language STYLE. The study of language style is quite important to linguists who study language variation – with good reason. Research has proven that variation in speech style is just as pervasive as regional, social class, ethnic, and gender-based language variation. There are no single-style speakers. Even speakers who live in relative isolation from speakers of other language varieties display a considerable range of speech styles, or a considerable amount of what may be termed STYLE SHIFTING. Thus, if we hope to achieve a full understanding of language variation and of human language in general, then we have to include in our investigations not only variation across speakers but variation within individual speakers as well.

8.1   Types of Style Shifting

There are several different types of style shifting that may occur. First, we may notice speakers shifting from less formal to more formal speech, as for example when a group of co-workers talking casually among themselves suddenly switch to more formal speech when their boss walks in. Shifts from casual to formal speech may be marked by the reduction in the percentage use of certain casual speech features, such as the pronunciation of the *-ing* ending as *in'*, as in *walkin'*. These shifts may also be marked by the complete elimination of other features, such as double negatives (for example, *She don't know nothing*) and slang or taboo lexical items (for example, *That's cool, I can't get this damn copier to work*). In addition, speakers may add features which they consider to be formal, such as Latinate vocabulary words (for example, *erudite* instead of *smart*) or the pronoun *whom*, as in *I don't know for whom this gift is intended*. Speakers may also shift in the opposite direction – from formal to casual speech; this type of shift is characterized by an increase in casual speech features and a decrease in formal speech features.

It is important to note that stylistic variation along the formality–informality dimension is by no means confined to the levels of phonology, grammar, lexicon, and semantics. Rather, it also encompasses pragmatics (language use) and discourse – that is, the level of language organization which has to do with groups of utterances (e.g. an entire conversation) rather than with single utterances, words, or pronunciations. Thus, speakers who are shifting from formal to casual speech will not only increase their usage levels of casual pronunciation features but also may adopt a general conversational style which is more casual in nature. For example, they may open the conversation with a casual rather than formal greeting and may engage in more conversational overlap than they would in a formal context.

We also might observe speakers shifting from one dialect into another. For example, a Midwestern comedian may shift into "Southern" speech while on stage, or an African American may shift into Anglo-sounding speech when talking with a group of Anglo Americans. While speakers sometimes shift into other dialects in order to imitate or make fun of someone else, this is not always the case. Recent research indicates that speakers shift into other dialects (or other languages) for a number of reasons, some of them quite complex (e.g. Rampton 1995). For example, Anglo American teenagers may shift into African American Vernacular English (AAVE) in order to indicate that they are familiar with (and would like to be a part of) African American youth culture. Younger Anglo Americans may also shift into AAVE in a symbolic attempt to erase (or at least re-draw) longstanding ethnic boundaries. The term CROSSING has been applied to cross-dialectal (or cross-linguistic) shifts. Recent research suggests that crossing may be quite widespread and may have important implications for the study of second-language learning, language change in multi-ethnic communities, and language change in general.

Exercise 1

Based upon an audio recording of speeches to diverse audiences, examine stylistic variation in the speech of a person well known for the ability to bridge different cultures (for example, Jesse Jackson or Martin Luther King, Jr). Compare speeches made to members of minority cultures with those presented to members of cultural majorities. Are there any qualitative differences in linguistic form (for example, phonology, grammar)? What kinds of differences are there in language-use conventions when different audiences are addressed (for example, speaker–audience interplay, salutations)? Are there particular socially diagnostic features that the speaker might be manipulating (for example, multiple negation)? What kinds of socially diagnostic features do *not* appear to be manipulated? (For example, are socially diagnostic irregular verbs shifted?)

It is not always easy to classify a given style shift as either a shift in formality or a shift into an entirely different dialect. For some speakers, shifting to a more or less formal style might entail adopting the dialect of another speech community. For example, a speaker of AAVE may shift into an Anglo American variety in order to sound more formal or educated. Conversely, Anglo American teenagers who want to indicate that they are "cool" and casual might adopt features of AAVE rather than simply adding more double negatives or slang words to their own speech variety. Because it is not always easy to say whether a given style shift represents stylistic shifting within a given language variety or a shift to a different language variety, we do not make too much of this division in our discussion to follow.

A final type of style shifting may occur when speakers shift from one clearly recognized speech REGISTER to another. In general, a register is held to be a readily identifiable speech variety which individuals use in specific, well-defined speech situations. For example, when talking to babies or young children, adults often use a register known as "babytalk" or "motherese." This register is characterized by such features as high pitch, exaggerated intonational contours, and the use of words with diminutive /i/ endings (as in *tummy* for 'stomach') and double or REDUPLICATED syllables, as in *boo-boo* for 'injury' or *din-din* for 'dinner'. Another readily recognizable register is "legalese," the dense, often incomprehensible prose which typifies legal documents, particularly when you get to the "fine print" section. Again, it is not always easy to determine exactly what counts as a shift in register vs. a shift in formality or a shift in dialect variety. For example, if a student is sitting at his or her desk talking on the phone with his or her best friend and then hangs up and begins writing a term paper, not only is he or she shifting into an academic register (as well as into a written vs. spoken register), but he or she is becoming more formal as well. The student may even feel that he or she is shifting into an entirely different language variety, especially if his or her native dialect is very different from standard English or if the student is unfamiliar with the conventions of academic writing. While we may have an intuitive sense that shifting into different registers is somehow different from shifting into different dialects or from becoming more of less formal, the more closely we examine stylistic variation, the more these intuitive divisions break down.

Exercise 2

One of the language registers that has been examined by sociolinguists is the "math register" – the particular use of language associated with mathematics. In the following items, typical of language use in math problems, identify some of the specialized uses of language that might be a part of the math register. What parts of speech seem to be especially affected in this register?

1 Does each real number x have a subtractive inverse?
2 The sum of two integers is 20 and one integer is 8 greater than the other. Find the integers.
3 Find two consecutive *even* integers such that the sum of the first and third is 134.
4 Find three consecutive *odd* integers such that the sum of the last two is 7 less than three times the first.
5 From downtown a suburban phone call costs 15 cents more than a local call. One month Dr Thorn's phone bill showed 30 local calls and 42 suburban calls, and the total bill was $14.22. What is the cost of one local call?

In a book on dialect differences and math failure, *Twice as Less: Black English and the Performance of Black Students in Mathematics and Science*, Eleanor Wilson Orr (1987) suggests that the roots of the math difficulties experienced by many working-class black students are found in the grammatical differences that distinguish African American Vernacular English from standard English. Having examined the typical kinds of language uses in math in the above examples, react to this conclusion. Are there special features of the math register that are common to *all* students studying math? How does the use of language in math differ from "ordinary" language use? Are these differences unique to the field of mathematics? Do you think dialect differences pose special obstacles to learning math? Why or why not?

8.2   The Patterning of Stylistic Variation

The first sociolinguist to examine in detail the patterning of stylistic variation
was Labov (e.g. 1966). In order to study the patterning of language variation
and the progress of language change in New York City English in the mid-
1960s, Labov devised interview questionnaires which were designed to elicit
speech of several different styles, positioned along an axis of formality. The
bulk of the typical sociolinguistic interview was designed to yield conversational speech, which could be classified as either CASUAL or CAREFUL in style.
Casual speech was held to occur in such contexts as extended discussions
which were not in direct response to interview questions, remarks by the
interviewee to a third party rather than to the interviewer, and discussions of
highly emotional topics, such as near-death experiences. Speech was held to be
more careful when less emotionally charged topics were discussed or when the
interviewee provided direct responses to interview questions. Labov also turned
to cues surrounding speech itself, or PARALINGUISTIC CHANNEL CUES, to separate
casual from formal speech. For example, features such as increased speech
tempo, higher pitch, laughter, and heavier breathing were held to be indicators
of a shift into casual style.

In Labov's original study, a third type of stylistic context in the formality
continuum was established by including a reading passage as a part of the
interview. Labov believed that speakers would use a more formal style in this
reading passage than in the conversational interview because reading is usually
associated with more formal occasions than speaking. Finally, speakers were
asked to read lists of words in isolation. Some of the words were further set
apart by being MINIMAL WORD PAIRS – that is, words that are phonetically
identical except for one sound, such as *bet* and *bat*. According to Labov, these
latter two tasks should yield highly formal speech, since speakers should become
more and more formal in style as they focus increasing attention on *how* they
are speaking rather than on *what* they are speaking about.

Once interview speech was classified into different styles, Labov then investigated the incidence of certain features of New York City speech in each stylistic context by examining, in each context, the occurrence of a given dialect
feature in relation to the number of potential occurrences of the feature. For
example, if a speaker uttered 50 words which normally contain *r* after a vowel
and before a consonant, as in *work* or *farm*, and pronounced 20 of these words
without the *r*, as in *fahm* for 'farm', then the degree of *r*-lessness was said
to be 40 percent. Using this methodology, Labov found that speakers used
stigmatized dialect features, such as *r*-lessness or the pronunciation of [t] or
[tθ] for [θ] (as in [tru] or [tθu] for 'through' [θru]), at lower and lower percentage rates as they moved from casual style to minimal pair style. This patterning
mirrors the patterning of stigmatized features as one moves from the lowest to

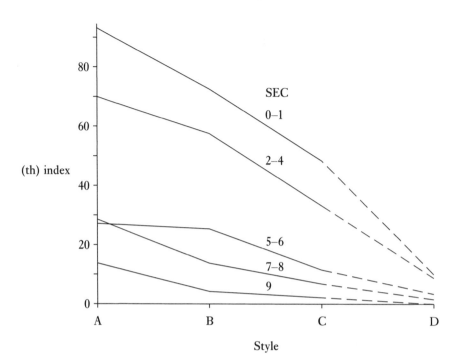

Socioeconomic class (SEC) scale: 0–1, lower class; 2–4, working class; 5–6, 7–8, lower middle class; 9, upper middle class. A, casual speech; B, careful speech; C, reading style; D, word lists.

Figure 8.1 Stylistic and social class differences in [t]/[tθ] usage in New York City English (adapted from Labov 1972b:113).

highest socioeconomic class. The intersection of stylistic and social class variation in the use of [t] or [tθ] for [θ] in New York City English is depicted in figure 8.1.

Figure 8.1 reveals that social class distinctions in the percentage use of stigmatized features tend to be preserved in each speech style. In other words, although all speakers decrease their percentage use of stigmatized features as they move from casual to formal speech, speakers in lower socioeconomic classes show higher levels of stigmatized features in each speech style than speakers of higher classes.

Sometimes, as speakers become more formal in style, members of lower social classes – usually the upper working class or lower middle class – will actually use stigmatized features at a lower rate (and prestige features at a higher rate) than members of higher social classes. Labov terms this "crossover" pattern HYPERCORRECTION, since speakers who exhibit this patterning are speaking in a hyper-"correct" or hyper-standard style. Labov maintains

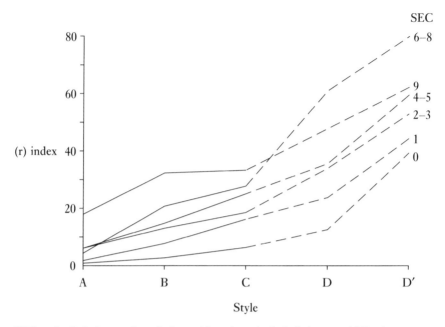

SEC scale: 0–1, lower class; 2–3, working class; 4–5, 6–8, lower middle class;
9, upper middle class. A, casual speech; B, careful speech; C, reading style;
D, word lists; D′, minimal pairs.

Figure 8.2 Class and style stratification for postvocalic *r* (adapted from Labov
1972b:114).

that lower-middle-class and upper-working-class speakers are more prone to
hypercorrection than members of other socioeconomic classes because, as we
have mentioned in previous chapters, they are more concerned with raising
their socioeconomic status than members of other class groups. Perhaps this is
because members of classes lower than the lower middle and upper working
classes cannot envision rising to a higher socioeconomic level, while those in
higher classes simply do not have as far to rise. Because of their concern with
achieving the next higher level of status, speakers in the lower middle class
attempt to talk like members of the upper middle class. In their attempts, they
sometimes go too far and end up utilizing prestige features at a greater rate, or
stigmatized features at a lower rate, than those they are trying to emulate. This
is particularly likely to occur in formal styles, where the focus on language is
greater than in casual styles. Figure 8.2 depicts hypercorrection in the use of
r-ful pronunciations (as in *farm* rather than *fahm* for 'farm') in New York City
by members of the lower middle class (social classes 4–8). Speakers in this
group display a higher rate of usage for this prestigious feature than speakers

of the upper middle class (class 9) in the formal "word list" and "minimal pair" styles (styles D and D').

Another form of hypercorrection involves the use of variants which are not typically found in one's language variety at all, at any percentage rate, as, for example, when a speaker of American English pronounces the "silent" *l* in *salmon* or the *t* in *often*. Hypercorrect pronunciations such as these, based on the spellings of words, are referred to as SPELLING PRONUNCIATIONS.

Hypercorrection can also involve using a feature in linguistic contexts where we don't usually expect it, as for example when a speaker says *Whom is it?* or *She's going with you and I*. Cases of hypercorrection which involve adding features or extending the boundaries of linguistic patterns are sometimes referred to as STRUCTURAL HYPERCORRECTION, whereas the type of hypercorrection which involves using features at a different rate than expected is known as STATISTICAL HYPERCORRECTION.

Exercise 3

One of the grammatical forms which is most commonly affected by hypercorrection is the reflexive pronoun. Based on the following examples, identify the reflexive pronoun form most affected by hypercorrection and the types of constructions in which hypercorrect reflexive forms are typically used.

1 David and myself often work together.
2 Please give the ticket to myself.
3 Between Marge and myself, we should be able to raise the kids.
4 This book was really written by the students and ourselves.
5 I arranged for myself to leave early.
6 He brought the project to myself for review.
7 The students often give a party for the other faculty and myself.

Another form of style shifting which is relatively self-conscious involves a speech style which we call PERFORMANCE SPEECH. We define performance speech as that register associated with speakers' attempting to display for others a certain language or language variety, whether their own or that of another speech community. Speakers may employ this register in the sociolinguistic interview, since this speech event is characterized by a focus, whether overt or covert, on how people speak rather than what they say. The performance register also occurs in natural conversations, as demonstrated, for example, in studies of dialect imitation (e.g. Butters 1993; Preston 1992, 1996). And anthropology-based studies of communicative patterns show that performance speech may even play a central role in the daily speech patterns of certain communities, particularly communities whose languages or dialects are receding in the face of encroaching languages or language varieties. In such communities, the dying language is often reduced from the primary vehicle of daily communication to a mere object of curiosity, or OBJECT LANGUAGE (Tsitsipis 1989), and so it is often performed for outsiders.

We have found that performance speech indeed is an important component of the endangered dialect of Ocracoke Island, North Carolina. Here we have encountered a number of speakers who purposely "put on" their unusual dialect for the benefit of tourists and prying sociolinguists, even though these speakers may not sound all that unusual in normal conversation. These speakers have even developed several rote phrases which highlight a number of the features of the traditional Ocracoke dialect. For example, one classic phrase, "It's hoi toide on the sound soid" ('It's high tide on the sound side'), showcases the well-known island /ay/ vowel (which sounds similar to [ɔɪ]) as well as the lesser-known but nonetheless important /aʊ/ vowel, which traditionally is realized as something like [æɪ] (as in *dane* for *down*) on Ocracoke.

Researchers who have investigated speakers' shifts into dialects other than their own have found that, for the most part, these shifts are not very accurate or complete (e.g. Bell 1992; Preston 1996). Speakers tend to use only a select few dialect features in depicting a language variety different from their own, and they often don't use these features in the same way as native speakers. For example, when Anglo Americans imitate AAVE, they seize on certain features such as invariant *be* (as in *He be late for school*) while completely ignoring other features of the dialect, such as possessive -*s* absence (as in *Jason book is on the desk*). In addition, Anglo American speakers often use invariant *be* in all sentences in which they would use *am*, *is*, or *are* rather than in only those sentences in which African Americans would use invariant *be*. As we have discussed in previous chapters, African Americans use invariant *be* to indicate habitual or recurrent action, as in *He always be late for school*, but do *not* use the form in other contexts, as in *He be late for school right now* or *He be nice*.

Even though speakers often do poorly in their productions of non-native dialects, this is not always the case. For example, speakers may accurately produce pronunciation features when the features are closely connected with certain lexical items. Non-Southerners who are attempting to sound Southern may use Southern monophthongal /ay/ (that is, [a]) in words or phrases with which this pronunciation is frequently associated, such as *nice white rice* [nas hwat ras], even if they don't use [a] for /ay/ in other words, such as *advice* or *slice*. Similarly, speakers may produce more complete versions of non-native dialects in set phrases than in other contexts, as, for example, when they utter the phrase *Y'all come back now, ya hear?* in imitation of Southern speech.

In addition, it has been shown that speakers give much better renditions of other dialects when they give animated "dialect performances" than when they merely try to produce isolated features or utter sentences in a dry manner. For example, Dennis Preston (1996) found that when a group of Anglo American speakers were given the task of reading a list of sentences in AAVE, they included more dialect features when they adopted what they perceived to be an African American persona and performed the sentences than when they attempted to produce dialect features analytically while reading the sentences in a straightforward way. Further, we have found that speakers who attempt to perform relatively "pure" versions of their own dying (and hence diluted) dialects display a remarkable degree of accuracy, down to the level of minute phonological detail. For example, in our investigation of the speech perform-ances of an Ocracoke fisherman, we discovered that this speaker's /ay/ vowels were closer to /ɔɪ/ (as in *boy*) in pre-voiced contexts (as in *tide* or *rise*) than in pre-voiceless contexts (e.g. *sight*, *nice*). This patterning parallels that which we have found for the traditional "hoi toide" vowel in non-performance speech in Ocracoke, since speakers show higher usage levels for the "hoi toide" vowel in pre-voiced environments than in pre-voiceless contexts.

In addition to the fact that social class distinctions are usually preserved across speech styles (except in cases of hypercorrection), Labov's studies of speech style also point to several other intriguing patterns. First, as noted by Allan Bell (1984), for any feature which shows differentiation along both social class and stylistic lines, the degree of stylistic differentiation is almost always less than the degree of social class differentiation. For example, if the highest social class in a community shows 20 percent *r*-lessness, as in *fahm* for 'farm', and the lowest social class 80 percent (a difference of 60 percent), then the percentage difference in *r*-lessness between the most formal and most casual styles will be less than 60 percent. This patterning suggests that stylistic varia-tion is derivative of social class variation – in other words, that a given feature is available for stylistic manipulation only if it carries some sort of social meaning in a given speech community.

Second, Labov observed that the speech style whose patterning is most regular and most reflective of the general patterning of a given language variety is the casual speech style. For example, in his studies of the vowel system of New York City English, Labov found that speakers' vowel systems in casual speech were more symmetrical and more closely aligned with what he had determined the general New York City system to be than were their vowel systems in more formal speech styles. In other words, speech spoken in casual contexts can be said to more closely approximate the "native" language variety, or the "vernacular," of a given community than speech spoken in other con-texts. This view is expressed in Labov's VERNACULAR PRINCIPLE, which holds that "the style which is most regular in its structure and in its relation to the evolution of the language is the vernacular, in which the minimum attention is paid to speech" (1972b:112).

Finally, Labov observed that the New York City vowel system was changing over time and that speakers' vowel systems in casual speech were more similar to the new New York City vowel system than were their vowels in more formal speech. In other words, casual speech seems to give a truer picture of language change in progress than more careful speech styles.

Labov's findings have had an enormous impact on sociolinguistic study over the past three decades. Because of his insistence that casual speech yields the most accurate information on language variation and change, subsequent researchers have focused on obtaining speech which is as casual and vernacular as possible, based on Labov's definition of casual style as that style in which minimal attention is paid to speech. Sometimes, the desire to obtain and investigate such speech has led to the neglect of the numerous other types of speech styles which also comprise everyday conversational interaction. However, it cannot be denied that Labov's emphasis on vernacular speech has yielded a vast body of casual speech data which might otherwise not have been obtained.

8.3   Explanations for Style Shifting

Showing that style shifts may correlate with social and situational factors and identifying the factors associated with style shifting is certainly an important aspect of describing stylistic variation. But it does not explain *why* speakers adjust their speech in the presence of various situational and other factors. Even if we come up with an exhaustive list of contextual factors that correlate with variation (e.g. Hymes 1962; Biber 1994; Brown and Fraser 1979), we are left with the question of why speakers vary their language in the presence of these factors. Are there underlying principles about communication or human behavior that can take us beyond the simple observation that speech styles correlate with particular sets of contextual factors? Several different proposals have been offered to explain why speakers adjust their speech in various ways – explanations that attempt to take us beyond the simple listing of contextual variables that correlate systematically with stylistic variation.

8.3.1   The "attention to speech" model

As we have already mentioned above, one of the earliest attempts to explain style shifting related to the amount of attention paid to speech. Under the ATTENTION TO SPEECH model, speakers are held to shift into more formal styles when they pay more attention to speech itself rather than to the subject matter of conversation and into less formal styles when they pay less attention to their speech. Degree of attention to speech is determined by such factors as the type of speech activity currently being engaged in (for example, question–answer pairs vs. an extended narrative), the subject matter of the conversation (for example, danger of death), and the paralinguistic channel cues discussed above. While sociolinguists usually equate "formal" speech with speech which more closely approximates the standard or prestigious language variety and "casual" speech with speech which is farther removed from the standard, we shall see below that it is possible to conceive of a number of different types of speech which fit these two designations.

The attention to speech model has been criticized for a number of reasons. First, researchers have pointed to the unreliability of Labov's channel cues as indicators of casual speech. For example, laughter may very well be indicative of increased nervousness (and increased attention to speech) rather than increased relaxation and decreased focus on one's speech. In addition, there is the question of how closely associated with a given stretch of speech a channel cue needs to be in order for the speech to count as truly casual: Does laughter which comes a few seconds before a given utterance indicate that the utterance is casual, or does the laughter have to occur simultaneously with the utterance?

Another reason Labov's model has been criticized is because of the difficulty of quantifying attention to speech. Experimentation with aural monitoring of speech suggests that there is a covariation of language forms with speakers' ability to hear their own speech. For example, speakers may produce more standard variants when they are able to aurally monitor their own speech than when this ability is blocked via "white noise" fed through headphones. However, the results and interpretation of such experiments are subject to important qualifications. Further, while some experiments indicate a correlation between increased aural monitoring and increased use of standard variants (e.g. Mahl 1972), other experiments show just the opposite – that speakers use forms which are *less* standard when they are better able to hear their own speech than when they are forced to speak under "noisy" conditions (e.g. Moon 1991).

Finally, the attention to speech model has been criticized for its unidimensionality. Under this model, all speech styles must be classified according to the single criterion of degree of formality. This means that sometimes speech styles which we intuitively recognize as quite different must be classed as similar styles. For example, the very different speech styles which occur when a speaker reads a passage provided by an interviewer and when the speaker discusses academic matters must be treated as similar styles since both are formal in nature. Similarly, the very different styles that occur when a speaker becomes emotionally involved in a political discussion and when the speaker tells an animated narrative about a near-death experience must be labeled simply as casual or informal style.

In addition, there are some speech styles that just don't seem to fit neatly along a formality–informality continuum at all. For example, when a speaker performs a rote phrase in order to demonstrate a dialect variety (for example, *Y'all come back now, ya hear?*, in imitation of Southern speech), a great deal of attention is focused on speech itself, and so we must classify such speech as "formal." Certainly, rote performance phrases are formal, in the sense that they conform to pre-set forms. However, dialect performances typically are characterized by exaggerated nonstandardness rather than the heightened standardness which characterizes the type of speech which linguists – and non-linguists – usually consider to be formal.

Even in controlled interview situations in which speakers do indeed become increasingly standard as they focus more and more attention on their speech, we are still faced with the question of whether reading style can be said to exist on the same plane as spoken styles. Furthermore, one can argue that the re-citation of isolated words will bring forth a specialized CITATION FORM REGISTER of pronunciation (i.e. the special pronunciation of a word when spoken in isolation) rather than speech which differs from conversational speech only in degree of formality.

In sum, the attention to speech model, which was developed as a convenient means of categorizing speech styles within the sociolinguistic interview, seems to be too restricted to offer a full account of stylistic variation in real-life conversational situations. However, the model does remain useful for investigating stylistic variation in connection with large-scale dialect surveys conducted via the sociolinguistic interview.

8.3.2   Speech accommodation theory

A more expansive explanation for stylistic variation, referred to as SPEECH ACCOMMODATION THEORY (SAT), has been proposed by the social psychologist Howard Giles and his colleagues (Giles and Powesland 1975; Giles 1984). In this model, style is explained primarily on the basis of a speaker's social and psychological adjustment to the ADDRESSEE – that is, the person(s) being addressed by the speaker. The most common pattern of adjustment is CONVERGENCE, in which the speaker's language becomes more like that of the addressee. The tendency to shift speech toward the addressee is summarized as follows:

> People will attempt to converge linguistically toward the speech patterns be-lieved to be characteristic of their recipients when they (a) desire their social approval and the perceived costs of so acting are proportionally lower than the rewards anticipated; and/or (b) desire a high level of communication efficiency, and (c) social norms are not perceived to dictate alternative speech strategies. (Beebe and Giles 1984:8)

Put simply, the model is rooted in the social psychological need of the speaker for social approval by the addressee, but the speaker must weigh the costs and rewards of such behavior in shifting speech to converge with that of the addressee.

The other side of the accommodation model is DIVERGENCE, in which speakers choose to distance themselves from addressees for one reason or another. Speakers will diverge linguistically from addressees under the following kinds of conditions:

> [when speakers] (a) define the encounter in intergroup terms and desire positive ingroup identity, or (b) wish to dissociate personally from another in an interindividual encounter, or (c) wish to bring another's speech behavior to a personally acceptable level. (Ibid.)

As we would expect from a model grounded in theories of social psychology, both the motivations of the individual speaker and the social relations among speakers and addressees are central to this explanation for stylistic shifting. A number of different experiments by Giles and others (e.g. Giles, Coupland, and Coupland 1991) have shown how speakers converge, and, in some cases, diverge with respect to speech-related phenomena such as rate of speech, content, pausing, and what is loosely referred to as "accent." Accent is the parameter most closely aligned with dialect variation as we discuss it in this book, but, unfortunately, socially diagnostic linguistic structures as discussed here are not very carefully delimited in most of the studies. Furthermore, the original accommodation model, rooted fairly simply in social approval, has now been subjected to considerable revision as different kinds of data have been examined. We return to this point below, when we discuss more recent social psychological-based investigations of style shifting.

8.3.3   The "audience design" model

One of the most widely accepted models for style shifting is the AUDIENCE DESIGN MODEL, originally proposed by Bell (1984). As with Speech Accommodation Theory, this model assumes that speakers adjust their speech primarily on the basis of attributes of the speech audience: Speakers adjust their speech toward their audiences if they wish to express or achieve solidarity with audience members; they adjust away from their audience if they wish to express or create distance. However, the audience design model extends the speech accommodation model in two very important ways: (1) by articulating in detail the different kinds of audiences which affect speaker convergence/divergence, and (2) by applying Speech Accommodation Theory to the quantitative investigation of specific linguistic variables rather than relying on general discussions of differences in "accent" across speech style.

The audience, as defined by Bell, includes not only those directly addressed, or ADDRESSEES, but also participants of various sorts who are not directly addressed. Speakers make the greatest adjustments in their speech in relation to their direct addressees, but they may also alter their speech based on non-addressed participants, with the degree of adjustment determined by such factors as whether the speaker is aware of the participants' presence and whether participants are ratified (i.e. sanctioned to participate in the conversation). Ratified but non-addressed participants are called AUDITORS, non-ratified parties of whom the speaker is aware are called OVERHEARERS, and other parties – that is, those whose presence is unknown and unratified – are called EAVESDROPPERS. Non-personal factors such as topic and setting may also affect style shifting under the audience design model, but these derive from audience-based considerations. For example, when speakers discuss a topic such as education, they may commonly shift into more standard speech, but this is because this topic is associated with a certain type of audience – namely, a high-status, standard-speaking audience – rather than because of the nature of the topic *per se*.

Under the audience design model, style shifts are usually undertaken in response to elements in the speaker's environment, particularly the make-up of the speaker's audience. However, they may also be initiated from within speakers themselves in an attempt to alter the existing situation. Bell calls such shifts INITIATIVE STYLE SHIFTS. He maintains that they occur when speakers shift their focus from the immediately present audience to an absent person or persons with whom they wish to identify. For example, a speaker who is being interviewed by a standard-speaking linguist may suddenly shift from relatively standard speech into highly vernacular speech because she wishes to identify with fellow speakers in her community rather than with the standard-speaking outsiders whom the linguist represents. The non-present group with whom speakers attempt to identify when they engage in initiative style shift is called the REFEREE GROUP; REFEREE DESIGN is the term applied to the component of the audience design model that focuses on these referee groups and initiative style shifting. The various components of the audience design model for style shifting are diagrammed in figure 8.3.

Bell has conducted detailed studies of style shifting in radio announcers who address a range of audiences and has also compiled evidence from a wide array of language variation studies to demonstrate the relative roles of addressees, auditors, and overhearers. The audience design model has gained wide acceptance, but a number of problems with the model have been pointed out over the years. For example, like the attention to speech model, the audience design model has been criticized for its unidimensionality, since it attributes nearly all style shifting to a single factor: the make-up of the speaker's audience. Matters such as topic, setting, and even the different types of social relationships which may exist among speakers and audience members (for example, family, employer/employee, etc.) are treated in only a cursory manner. Further, even if we agree that audience attributes should be our primary focus, it is not clear *which* attributes speakers accommodate toward or diverge from when they engage in style shifting. As Bell notes, there are three increasingly specific possibilities:

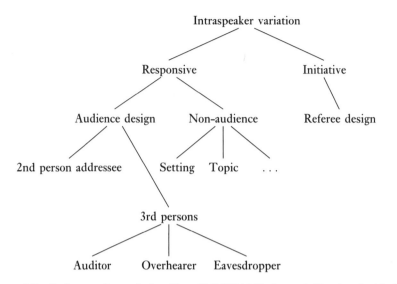

Figure 8.3   Style as audience design (from Bell 1984:162, figure 6. Reprinted with the permission of Cambridge University Press).

(1) Speakers assess the personal characteristics of their addressees and design their style to suit.

(2) Speakers assess the general level of their addressees' speech and shift relative to it.

(3) Speakers assess their addressees' levels for specific linguistic variables and shift relative to these levels.
    (Bell 1984:167)

Bell does not attempt to determine definitively which of these three possibilities holds true for most cases of style shifting and in fact maintains that speakers most likely respond to audiences on all three levels when they engage in style shifting. It is quite clear that speakers do indeed respond on level (1). For example, Fasold (1972) noted that the AAVE speakers he studied in Washington, DC, used vernacular variants more frequently with African American than Anglo interviewers, even though most of the African American interviewers were speakers of standard English. However, to claim that speakers respond to the personal characteristics of their audience members is to say nothing about *what* characteristics they are responding to: When someone speaks in a more vernacular manner with one interviewer than with another, is it primarily because of ethnicity, or perhaps because of some other factor, such as relative age, familiarity (perhaps the speaker has known one informant longer than another), gender, or even how friendly the interviewer is?

It is even more difficult to tease apart levels (2) and (3), since, as Bell puts it, "the general speech impression of level (2) largely derives from the combined assessment of many individual variables" (1984:168). In one of the few studies that has been conducted in an attempt to test whether (2) or (3) is the more likely case, John Rickford and Faye McNair-Knox (1994) show that it is possible for speakers to adjust their speech based on the general usage level of certain linguistic variants (level 2); however, speakers are *not* able to make more fine-grained adjustments (level 3). Further, Rickford and McNair-Knox note that not all variables stand an equal chance of figuring in style shifting: Features which are used frequently (for example, invariant *be* in AAVE in the 1990s, as in *He always be late for school*) are far more likely to be manipulated in stylistic variation than features with a low frequency of occurrence (for example, possessive *-s* absence, as in *Janet book is on the table*).

In our own studies, we have shown that the social meaning of dialect features influences whether they can be differentially used across different speech styles. For example, when Outer Banks speakers perform their unique dialect for outsiders, they produce exaggerated versions of the "hoi toide" vowel for which they are widely known. However, they do not produce exaggerated pronunciations of other, lesser-known vowel sounds which nonetheless are characteristic of traditional Outer Banks speech. For example, the best-known Outer Banks performance phrase, "It's hoi toide on the sound soid," contains an /aw/ vowel (in the word *sound*), which is typically pronounced as more of an [æɪ] (as in *signed* for 'sound') in Outer Banks English. This unusual pronunciation is not exaggerated in performance style, most likely because it has little social meaning for Outer Bankers. Thus, it appears that while /ay/ is a SOCIAL STEREOTYPE (see chapter 5) in Outer Banks English, /aw/ may be confined to mere SOCIAL INDICATOR status, since it does not appear to figure in style shifting – at least not in shifts into performance style. In Bell's original formulation (1984), the audience design model for style shifting leaves little room for the consideration of the social meaning of dialect features in the explanation for their patterning across different speech styles, since its focus is on audience attributes rather than the attributes of particular linguistic features. More current versions of the audience design model (e.g. Bell forthcoming) have begun to take into account the social meaning of language features.

Another limitation of the audience design model is that, in its emphasis on speakers' achieving solidarity with audience members through convergence, it is easy to overlook the fact that there may be any number of linguistic strategies for "identifying with" audience members besides attempting to talk like them. Although Bell has shown that radio announcers may seek solidarity with listening audiences through convergence of speech style, other studies of radio announcers indicate that announcers may achieve solidarity with their audiences through a variety of means (e.g. Coupland 1985). For example, an announcer might "grab" his or her audience by adopting the persona of a well-known cultural figure (whether mythical or real), even though this figure's speech style may be very different from that of either the announcer or the audience. Thus, a radio announcer in a metropolitan area in the South might perform the dialect of a country farmer to achieve solidarity with a relatively non-vernacular audience, since the announcer and audience share a common image of the "typical" (or stereotypical) rural Southern resident.

Perhaps the biggest shortcoming of the audience design model as it was originally formulated has to do, not with audience design *per se*, but with referee design. Originally, Bell maintained that initiative shifts were but a small component of the overall picture of style shifting, since, he claimed, most style shifts were based on audience design rather than referee design, and most referee-designed shifts were quite short-lived in nature. In addition, referee design was seen as derivative of audience design, since referee design involves convergence with non-present referee groups – in effect, non-present audience members. However, recent study indicates that the initiative dimension of the audience design model was not as fully developed as it should have been in the original formulation of the model and that the more closely we examine style shifting, the more pervasive initiative shifting seems to be.

8.3.4   "Speaker design" models for style shifting

In order to investigate style shifting in as much detail as possible, researchers have increasingly turned to individual and small-group studies, since small-group studies allow for the detailed examination of the conversational contexts and personal identificational considerations surrounding stylistic variation. These small-group studies seem to support Bell's belief that initiative style shifting plays a far greater role in everyday conversational interaction than had previously been supposed. In fact, there is a growing belief that *all* style shifts are essentially initiative, even those which appear to be clear cases of accommodation toward an immediately present audience.

The movement toward viewing style shifting as primarily initiative rather than responsive, or proactive rather than reactive, has led researchers to develop a renewed interest in social psychological approaches to style shifting. After all, if we maintain that speaker-internal factors play an important role in style shifting in addition to environmental factors, then it stands to reason that we investigate these speaker-internal factors (i.e. speakers' internal motivations for style shifting) in as much detail as possible. We might even follow Coupland in referring to current models for style shifting as SPEAKER DESIGN models, in contrast to audience design-based approaches.

Under "speaker design"-based models, style shifts are viewed, not merely as a means of responding to the attributes of audience members, but as a means of projecting one's own attributes – that is, one's personal identity. It is crucial that we understand that researchers who investigate "speaker design" do not view identity merely as the static intersection of various demographic categories, such as age, social class, and race. Rather, identity is seen as a dynamic notion which may change from conversational encounter to conversational encounter, as well as within a single conversational interaction. Thus, a speaker may project one particular identity while speaking with a small child but quite another identity (or another facet of a single identity) while reprimanding an employee. It is almost as if, while we converse, we are acting in a play, taking on certain *roles* in certain conversational situations and other roles in other interactions. These roles may be derived in part from social relations which are relatively permanent, as, for example, in the case of a mother conversing with her child or a supervisor talking with an employee. They may also have to do with more transient expressions of identity, as, for example, in the case of a mother who acts as playful friend to her child one moment, and so speaks in a lighthearted, conversational style, and as an authority figure the next, when she assumes a commanding tone. Of course, personal identity is not independent of audience-based considerations, since we may choose to project different aspects of our identity to different types of audiences (e.g. co-workers vs. children). In this regard, personal identity is to be viewed in terms of *relational* as well as *identificational* considerations (Coupland forthcoming).

If we view style shifts as shifts in role relationships rather than mere convergence with or divergence from audience members, present or absent, we can account for certain cases of stylistic variation which do not fit neatly into audience design-based approaches. For example, we can explain cases in which speakers appear to be seeking solidarity through divergence rather than convergence by pointing to the specific role which the diverging speaker is taking on. Thus, a radio announcer may achieve solidarity with an audience through taking on the role of a familiar persona rather than merely attempting to sound like audience members. Similarly, a fieldworker conducting an interview with an informant who is hesitant to speak might attempt to achieve solidarity with the informant by adopting the role of a chatty friend rather than by trying to match the reticent style of the informant.

We can also view speakers' shifts into performance style as shifts in role relationships rather than mere convergence/divergence. When our Outer Banks speakers give exaggerated performances of their "quaint" dialect, most likely it is not because they wish to sound like someone else (perhaps islanders from the past), but because they are taking on the role of "dialect performer." Residents of the Outer Banks are accustomed to visitors, including linguists, asking for samples of the dialect; they are also accustomed to visitors expressing disappointment when they listen to islanders engaged in daily conversation and realize that the dialect is not "British English" or "Australian English" or "Elizabethan English," as they have been led to believe. In fact, islanders have reported to us that visitors sometimes inform islanders that they are not "talking right," because their dialect isn't quite exotic enough. In order to keep tourists happy, it seems best not to speak or act "naturally" but to adopt the role of the quaint islander, complete with quaint island dialect.

Our in-depth analysis of style shifting in the speech of a fisherman from the Outer Banks island of Ocracoke seems to confirm that such role-playing underlies shifts into performance style. This speaker, a well-known islander named Rex O'Neal, shifts into performance speech only at certain points in our conversational interviews with him – namely, when the technical matters of tape-recording (such as turning over a tape) have to be attended to. In other words, he shifts into performance style whenever he shifts his focus from the interviewer with whom he is having a friendly, one-on-one conversation to the much wider audience for whom the interview is really being conducted – the linguists who will analyze the tape-recorded interview once it is completed. Although Rex O'Neal acts as a friendly conversational partner in relation to the fieldworker, it seems likely that he views himself as more of a depersonalized "dialect performer" in relation to the non-present linguists. In order to best fulfill this new role, he decides to give the linguists a sample of the "quaint" dialect he believes they want to hear, and so he shifts into performance style.

It is important to keep in mind that role shifts do not have to be responsive. Thus, while it appears that Rex O'Neal shifts into performance style *in response to* his focus on the non-present audience of linguists, his shift is not really reactive, because he could just as easily shift into exaggeratedly standard speech as exaggeratedly vernacular speech when he shifts his focus to a new audience. In fact, the expected reaction to the realization that our speech is being examined is to shift toward the standard variety rather than away from it. In other words, Rex O'Neal's shift is not *determined by* his audience; he shifts into performance speech because this is what he *opts* to do.

Researchers have even proposed that shifts which clearly involve convergence with audience members are proactive rather than reactive, because speakers must choose to converge rather than to diverge in some way. As Nikolas Coupland puts it, "From a self-identity perspective, shifts that are 'appropriate' [i.e. convergent] are nevertheless creative in the sense that speakers opt to operate communicatively within normative bounds" (forthcoming). It is a small step to go from claiming that all style shifts are proactive – that all style shifts involve adopting particular roles – to maintaining that all speech styles are performative, since each time we adopt a speech style, we take on a role. Thus, not only are speakers performing when they imitate other dialects (or exaggerate their own), but they are performing when they discuss work matters with their colleagues, when they gossip with friends over lunch, and when they talk intimately with family in the evening. The notion that all speech is performance may be new to sociolinguists, but it is certainly nothing new to students of literature. Such a belief has been expressed in the writings of the Russian critical theorist Mikhael Bakhtin (e.g. 1981), and we even find echoes of it in the famous quote from Shakespeare: "All the world's a stage, / And all the men and women merely players: / They have their exits and their entrances; / And one man in his time plays many parts, / His acts being seven ages" (*As You Like It* II.vii.139–43).

8.4 Future Directions for the Investigation of Stylistic Variation

Focusing on the speaker-internal motivations for style shifting has certainly increased our understanding of intra-speaker language variation; however, such approaches are not without their limitations. First, there is the question of reliability and reproducibility. Models based on "speaker design" allow for a range of post-hoc interpretations for any given style shift, since speakers' motivations are not directly observable and can only be inferred. In addition, there is the question of generalizability: Can we determine the personal identificational motivations which underlie stylistic variation in the speech of an individual speaker and then make general statements regarding identity projection and style shifting for an entire community? And is it the case that speakers are free to choose from among an unlimited set of personal identities during the course of their daily communicative interactions? Or, as seems more intuitively satisfying, do we want to maintain that each speaker has a single coherent identity which underpins her or his choice of stylistic varieties? Finally, if style shifting is largely an individualistic phenomenon, then where do speech styles get the meanings that enable individuals to use them in order to project certain identities?

Even though speech styles may be manipulated in very individualistic ways, it is likely that they derive the meanings that make such manipulation possible from speech differences which exist across large groups of speakers. For example, although we may shift into more standard speech than usual in order to project a highly authoritative individual identity, the authoritative connotations which our highly standard speech carries most likely derive from the fact that those with the most authority in our society speak standard English. The belief that stylistic meaning is derived from social meaning is directly reflected in the quantitative patterning of stylistic variation *vis-à-vis* social class variation, as discussed above: The amount of variation in a given feature across different speech styles is almost always less than the amount of variation in this feature across speakers of different social classes.

Further, speech styles carry personal identification meaning not only because they are closely associated with certain social classes but because they tend to be associated with certain conversational contexts. In other words, even though style shifting may indeed be highly idiosyncratic, it is not without norms: For example, we can expect with some certainty that a couple of good friends who are speaking casually will shift into more formal style if an authority figure whom they are trying to impress joins the conversation. Thus, even though current research suggests that we should increase our focus on the internal motivations for style shifting, we should not neglect the external factors which often *can* be correlated with style shifts, even if we no longer maintain that such external factors actually *trigger* these shifts.

Although researchers continue to work diligently to answer the question, "What do people do with style?," more research is needed to address what is perhaps a more fundamental question: "What exactly is speech style?" Investigating the composition of various speech styles is by no means new to sociolinguistics. However, this sort of approach usually falls outside the quantitative tradition of the investigation of speech style and within the more qualitatively based tradition of the analysis of speech register or genre (Gregory and Carroll 1978). Several sociolinguists are currently working to bring together the two traditions. Among them are Edward Finegan and Douglas Biber, who have conducted several large-scale, computer-based investigations of the different types of features that comprise different speech styles, including both spoken and written styles (1994). One of Finegan and Biber's chief findings is that features which may be considered to be "elaborated" in form (for example, full forms vs. contractions) tend to cluster together in speech registers/styles which are typically considered to be more formal and/or of higher social prestige, such as academic lectures and news broadcasts. Conversely, variants which are less elaborate and more "economical" in form tend to cluster together in more casual registers such as spontaneous conversations among friends. For example, non-contracted forms such as *Ann will not go* and *Walt is going to finish this book* will cluster together in prestige registers, while contracted forms such as *Ann won't go* and *Walt's gonna finish this book* will cluster together in non-prestige speech styles.

Based on their findings, Finegan and Biber have proposed a model for stylistic variation in which social class variation is viewed as derivative of stylistic variation rather than vice versa, as in such approaches as Labov's and Bell's. According to this view, the reason that members of different social classes speak different language varieties is that they have access to, and typically utilize, registers with different characteristics. Members of higher social classes have access to the elaborated registers which characterize formal writings and pre-planned speech events, such as lectures, while members of lower classes are relegated to using the more economical registers associated with casual, face-to-face conversational interaction, since they do not participate in as many planned speech events as upper-class speakers.

Finegan and Biber's model has been criticized for a number of reasons. For example, it does not seem possible, under their model, to account for Bell's observation that the degree of stylistic variation for a given variant is usually less than the degree of social class variation. In addition, the model cannot account for why, with just a few moments' thought, we can readily come up with a fairly lengthy list of economical variants which are associated with higher classes (e.g. *r*-lessness in prestige British speech, as in *fahm* for 'farm'), as well as a long list of elaborated variants that are associated with lower classes (e.g. multiple negation in a number of vernacular American varieties). Further, Finegan and Biber have been criticized for relying on data from Western speech communities when one can fairly readily point to non-Western speech communities in which prestige registers are characterized by non-elaborated forms and non-prestige registers by more elaborateness of form. For example, Judith Irvine (1996) discusses a rural Wolof community in Senegal in which economical language forms are so highly valued that members of the ruling caste employ members of a lower caste to speak *for* them in certain highly formal situations, so that the rulers need barely utter any linguistic forms at all, let alone any elaborated forms.

A more serious problem with Finegan and Biber's claim that elaborated forms are associated with prestige social classes and economical forms with non-prestige social groups is that this view sounds dangerously similar to the notion that speakers of low prestige varieties such as African American Vernacular English possess an impoverished communication system, incapable of expressing elaborate sentiments, subtle nuances, or even straightforward logical thought. Labov dispelled this notion a couple of decades ago in his ground-breaking article "The logic of nonstandard English" (1972a), in which he demonstrated the logic underlying several discussions by a speaker of African American Vernacular English. Further, as we have discussed throughout this book, linguists have shown – and continue to show – that *no* language variety is linguistically inferior to any other language variety.

Despite criticisms of Finegan and Biber's approach to register and style variation, there is growing concern with broadening the scope of stylistic variation study to include the investigation of the co-occurrence of language features within speech styles. In addition, researchers are moving beyond simply investigating linguistic variables, such as contracted vs. full forms or *r*-lessness vs. *r*-fulness, to examining other types of features which are associated with particular speech styles. These features may include certain types of linguistic features which have not yet been widely studied, such as intonation or voice quality, or they may be completely non-linguistic; for example, researchers may investigate how style of dress correlates with styles of speaking. Finally, in the search for an answer to the question "What is style?," researchers are turning toward the investigation of what speakers themselves perceive as "style." For example, it is unclear whether speakers consider a certain style to be formal because it is characterized by a low percentage of informal variants, such as -*in'* for -*ing* (e.g. *swimmin'* for *swimming*) or for some other reason, such as a relatively flat intonational contour. Similarly, we do not really know exactly how many variants or other features need to cluster together – and how distinctive these variants need to be – in order for speakers to view a given speech variety as a separate style or register. The search for the answers to these types of questions is already yielding intriguing findings, and it is certain to add greatly to our ever-increasing understanding of the linguistic, social, and psychological underpinnings of stylistic variation.

8.5 Further Reading

Bell, Allan (1984) Language style as audience design. *Language in Society* 13:145–204. This article is one of the most comprehensive attempts to explain the dynamics of style shifting. As indicated in the title, the model gives primacy to the speaker's audience in its account of stylistic variation.

Biber, Douglas, and Edward Finegan (eds) (1994) *Sociolinguistic Perspectives on Register*. New York: Oxford University Press. This collection of articles includes a number of recent investigations of stylistic variation from several different perspectives, ranging from the Labovian variationist perspective to Finegan and Biber's comprehensive register-based approach. Among the important works in this collection are Rickford and McNair-Knox's "Addressee- and topic-influenced style shift," in which they investigate the relative effects of addressee and topic on stylistic variation, and Finegan and Biber's "Register and social dialect variation," in which they outline an approach to style shifting in which social class variation is viewed as derivative of stylistic variation rather than vice versa.

Giles, Howard, Justine Coupland, and Nikolas Coupland (eds) (1991) *Contexts of Accommodation: Developments in Applied Sociolinguistics*. Cambridge: Cambridge University Press. This collection provides a current and comprehensive treatment of Speech Accommodation Theory, one of the most well-known and widely applied explanations for stylistic variation.

Labov, William (1972b) *Sociolinguistic Patterns*. Philadelphia: University of Pennsylvania Press. Chapter 2 in this collection describes a classic department store experiment carried out in New York City in which "casual" stylistic responses are contrasted with "emphatic" ones. It is worth reading for the ingenuity of the field technique. Chapter 3 reports one of the earliest attempts to incorporate stylistic variation into the study of social dialectology. The approach to stylistic variation set forth in this chapter has heavily influenced dialectologists' approach to stylistic variation, although it now has been replaced by more comprehensive models.

Rampton, Ben (1995) *Crossing: Language and Ethnicity among Adolescents*. London/New York: Longman. In this work, Rampton presents an in-depth study of a language phenomenon he terms *crossing* – that is, the use of an alien dialect or language for such purposes as establishing identity with another cultural group or redefining boundaries between cultural groups. Rampton demonstrates that crossing may have important implications for the study of second-language learning, language change in multi-ethnic communities, and language change in general.

Schilling-Estes, Natalie (1998) Investigating "self-conscious" speech: The performance register in Ocracoke English. *Language in Society* 27:53–83. This article examines performance speech in the Outer Banks island community of Ocracoke, North Carolina. In particular, it provides an in-depth look at the speech performances of one islander from the perspectives of acoustic phonetics, quantitative sociolinguistics, and discourse analysis.

9

The Patterning of Dialect

According to popular belief, dialect patterns are quite simple: All members of one group always use a particular dialect variant while members of a different group use another one. Thus, outsiders may assume that all speakers from Pittsburgh pluralize *you* as *you'ns* and use the lexical term *gumband* for *rubberband*, while speakers from other areas never do. Similarly, the popular view holds that vernacular dialect speakers always pronounce *-ing* words such as *swimming* as *swimmin'* and always use multiple negatives such as *They didn't do nothing* while speakers of a standard variety never use these forms. As we have seen already at various points in the previous chapters, this "all or nothing" perspective often veils the actual ways in which dialect forms may be manifested. Some of these patterns are quite obvious, but many of them are revealed in more subtle and complex ways. In this chapter, we examine in more detail some of the distributional patterns that dialectally diagnostic forms may take among different groups of speakers. As used here, the term DIALECTALLY DIAGNOSTIC refers to any dialect feature that has the potential to differentiate social groups of various types, whether defined on the basis of region, status, ethnicity, or some other social factor.

9.1 The Social Distribution of Dialect Forms

The pattern of dialect distribution which most closely matches the popular perception of dialect differences is referred to as GROUP-EXCLUSIVE USAGE, where one community of speakers uses a variant but another community never does. In its ideal form, group-exclusive usage means that all members of a particular community of speakers use the dialect form whereas no members of other groups ever use it. This ideal pattern, however, is rarely if ever manifested in American English dialects. As we have seen in previous chapters on dialect variation based on region, gender, and ethnicity, the kinds of social groupings that take place in American society are just too complex for this pattern to work out so neatly. In many cases, distinctions between groups exist on a continuum rather than in discrete sets. Furthermore, the definition of a social group is usually multidimensional rather than unidimensional. And, as we have seen, dialects are dynamic and not static systems, so that they are constantly undergoing change – change which is distributed disproportionately even within sharply defined speech communities. Thus, when considering the speaker from Ocracoke Island who may or may not pronounce words like *time* and *tide* as something like *toim* and *toid* on any given occasion, we have to take into account the different sociocultural, psychological, and linguistic factors that we discussed in previous chapters. These factors work together in such complex ways that we cannot determine precisely who will use what dialect features and when they will use them. The best we can do is to come up with a profile of the kind of Ocracoker who is most likely to use certain dialect features and the types of occasions in which these features most likely will occur.

The essential aspect of group-exclusive dialect forms is that speakers from other groups do not use these forms rather than the fact that all the members of a particular group use them. Not all people who are native to Pittsburgh use *you'ns* and *gumband*, but it is a safe bet that someone who is native to San Francisco or Seattle does not use these forms. Group-exclusive usage is therefore easier to define negatively than positively. Viewed in this way, there are many dialect features on all levels of language organization which show group-exclusive distribution. On a phonological level, many of the regional vowel productions we discussed in previous chapters, such as the pronunciation of the vowels in *caught* and *cot* as the same vowel or the pronunciation of the /ay/ in *time* as [a] (as in *tahm*), show group-exclusive distribution across regions. There are similar examples in morphology, such as the absence of the -*s* plural on nouns of weights and measures as in *four acre, five pound*, and the pluralization of *you* as *youse, y'all*, or *you'ns*. In syntax, the use of positive *anymore* as in *They go to the movies a lot anymore* and verbal complements such as *The kitchen needs remodeled*, or *The dog wants out* are examples of group-exclusive usage patterns, while in the lexicon there are numerous examples such as *gumband* for *rubberband*, *garret* for *attic*, *meehonkey* for *hide and seek*, as well as thousands of words found in the *Dictionary of American Regional English* (Cassidy 1985, 1991, 1996).

According to Philip M. Smith (1985), group-exclusive dialect features may exhibit SATURATED or UNSATURATED patterning. A feature shows saturated patterning if it is used by the vast majority of speakers within a particular regional or social group, while it shows unsaturated patterning if it is less pervasive but still group-exclusive. For example, among younger working-class African Americans, habitual *be*, as in *They usually be going to the movies*, might be considered a saturated form since the majority of speakers in this group use this form at one time or another. Note that the definition of the group in this case must include at least ethnicity, status, and age. By the same token, speakers of other varieties of English do not typically use this construction. In contrast, the resultative *be done* construction, as in *The chicken **be done** jumped out the pen* as found within the same population of working-class speakers, might be considered an unsaturated, group-exclusive form. Few speakers of African American Vernacular English have been found to use this construction, but no speakers of other varieties seem to use it.

Descriptive qualifications such as "saturated" and "unsaturated" group-exclusive usage are useful general labels, but they have not yet been defined with any rigor. That is, the classification of a form as saturated or unsaturated is not determined on the basis of a specific proportion of speakers sampled within a given population (e.g. more than 75 percent of the speakers in a representative sample use the form in saturated usage and fewer than 20 percent of the speakers use the form in unsaturated usage). Thus, these designations are imprecise and limited, although admittedly convenient as informal characterizations of dialect patterns.

Group-exclusive dialect forms may be taken for granted in one dialect while, at the same time, they are quite noticeable to speakers from other dialect areas. In American English, speakers from other regions may thus be quick to comment on how strange forms like *you'ns*, *The house needs painted*, and *gumband* seem to them when visiting Pittsburgh, much to the surprise of the lifetime resident of Pittsburgh who has assumed that these dialect features were in common use. With increased interaction across dialect groups, however, speakers may become aware of some of their own group-exclusive uses. As consciousness about these forms is raised, some of the forms begin to serve as symbolic markers of regional or social group identity. Sometimes, they even form the basis of the stereotypes of particular regional and ethnic dialects which are found in popular caricatures. However, it is important to remember that such caricatures are often not linguistically faithful to the actual use of dialect features by speakers from the particular community.

In contrast to group-exclusive forms, GROUP-PREFERENTIAL forms are distributed across different groups or communities of speakers, but members of one group are more likely to use the form than members of another group. For example, highly specific color terms (e.g. *mauve*, *plum*, etc.) are often associated with women as opposed to men, at least among middle-class Anglo speakers, but there are certainly many men who make similar distinctions, and, of course, there are women who do not use such refined color designations. The association of a finely graded color spectrum with women is statistically based, as more women make these distinctions than men. We thus refer to the use of highly specific color terms as a group-preferential pattern rather than a group-exclusive one. We would not expect group-preferential patterns to be as socially meaningful as group-exclusive dialect features, although popular stereotypes of group-preferential dialect patterns sometimes treat them as if they were group-exclusive. The popular characterization of vernacular speakers as saying *dese*, *dem*, and *dose* is such an instance where the stereotype of group-exclusive behavior actually obscures a fairly complex pattern which is really group-preferential and also highly variable.

Exercise 1

Suppose your approach to dialect patterning started with the classification of speakers on the basis of linguistic distribution rather than social classification. In other words, you started your analysis of *you'ns* or habitual *be* by separating everyone who used this form into one group and those who did not use it into another group. What would be the implication of this approach for the notions of group-exclusive and group-preferential distributional patterns as discussed above?

9.2   Linguistic Variability

As we have already observed in earlier chapters, the careful examination of dialect forms shows that dialects may sometimes be differentiated on the basis of how frequently particular forms are used rather than whether or not a variant is used. In other words, individual speakers may fluctuate in their use of variants, sometimes using one form and sometimes using an alternate. Furthermore, the relative frequencies of usage may help differentiate dialects. For example, consider the following excerpt showing the fluctuation of *-ing* and *-in'* within the speech of a single speaker during a single speech event.

> We were walk*in'* down the street and we saw this car go*ing* out of control. The driver looked like he was sleep*ing* at the wheel or someth*in'*. The next thing I knew the car was turn*in'* around and just spinn*ing* around. I thought the car was com*in'* right at me and I started runn*in'* like crazy. I was so scared, think*ing* the car was gonna hit me or someth*in'*.

In the ten examples of the form *-ing* in this passage, four cases end in *-ing* and six in *-in'*. According to the linguistic "rule" governing this process, which states that *-ing* in unstressed syllables may become *-in'*, all ten cases of *-ing* should be realized as *in'*, yet only six of them occur as *in'*. This kind of variation, where a speaker sometimes produces one variant and sometimes an alternate one, is referred to as INHERENT VARIABILITY. The term inherent variability reflects the fact that this fluctuation is an internal part of a single linguistic system, or dialect, and should not be considered to be the result of importations from another dialect or of speech errors. In other words, there is no evidence that the speaker fluctuating between *-ing* and *-in'* is switching between two dialects, one exclusively using *-ing* and another exclusively using *-in'*. Instead, the speaker is using a single dialect system – one with two pronunciation variants of this ending – and the speaker sometimes uses one form and sometimes the other. This kind of fluctuation has long been recognized within linguistics, where certain processes are considered "optional" because they may or may not be applied. For example, in standard English, there is an optional process which permits a speaker to place the particle *up* after a noun phrase rather than directly after the verb, so that *She looked up the number* may alternatively be realized as *She looked the number up*. Linguists do not say that each of these sentences belongs to a distinctly different dialect, and that a speaker switches between the dialects. Instead, we say that both of these sentences are options within a single system. Similarly, we may say that the *-in'* and *-ing* forms are alternating variants within one dialect system for most English speakers. The notion of inherent variability, then, is just an extension of this commonly recognized pattern of fluctuation between variants within a system.

9.3 The Conversational Interview and Inherent Variability

The basis for studying the kind of fluctuation that is essential to the study of linguistic variation is the conversational interview. This is particularly true in the field of social dialectology, where the primary focus is on variable phonological and grammatical structures. Even in a conversational interview focused on relatively neutral topics of discussion, the fact that a person is being interviewed and tape-recorded is a formidable obstacle to obtaining ordinary, everyday speech – the kind of speech that is so central to most studies of dialect variation. This problem has become known in sociolinguistics as the OBSERVER'S PARADOX, which Labov formulated thus: "To obtain the data most important for linguistic theory, we have to observe how people speak when they are not being observed" (Labov 1972c:113). A lot of attention in social dialect studies has been given to developing strategies for overcoming the inherent constraints of a tape-recorded interview with a relative stranger, ranging from concern with the personal characteristics of interviewers to the best physical locations for conducting these interviews and the kinds of questions to be asked in the interview.

The underlying goal of most conversational interviews is quite straightforward: to get as much naturalistic speech as possible from the interviewee, that is, speech that represents how the interviewee speaks in ordinary, everyday conversation when language is not directly under examination. This is sometimes easier said than done, but various dialect studies have used some rather ingenious strategies to bring this about. Over the years, a fairly good range of "safe" topics for discussion by fieldworkers has emerged, and most social dialect surveys now start with a traditional set of conversational questions. These questions are then modified based on the unique cultural and social differences characteristic of each community under study. Quite typically, the interview includes questions about childhood games (e.g. "Tell me about the kinds of games you played as a kid"), leisure activities such as TV and movies (e.g. "Tell me about some of your favorite TV programs or movies"), peer-group activities (e.g. "What kinds of things do you do with your friends?"), descriptions of life experiences (e.g. "Have you ever been in a situation where you thought you were going to die?"), and other items of personal interest that might produce extended conversation. In most cases, cues about items of interest are picked up by the fieldworker and pursued with a series of follow-up questions that will encourage the interviewee to develop themes of interest into a comfortable conversation focused on the topic of the conversation rather than the kind of speech the subject is producing.

One of the overriding considerations in the conversational interview is the need to avoid questions that might arouse suspicions about hidden intentions in interviewing. Interviewees often find it hard to believe that an interviewer is interested in finding out about culture and language simply for the sake of knowing such information, and they often are on guard for some disguised motive. Questions about social conditions and politics from an interviewer often can arouse these suspicions, even when touchy subjects are introduced by the interviewee rather than the fieldworker.

Many surveys of vernacular dialects now employ fieldworkers from the community itself, and some of the richest sources of data we have collected over the years come from interviews conducted by indigenous fieldworkers. Of course, outsiders may also possess the personal characteristics that help make a person a good fieldworker. Thus, it is often the case that people with empathetic, non-threatening conversational styles end up getting better interviews than fieldworkers who are carefully selected to match the status, age, and gender characteristics of the interviewee. Other things being equal, however, indigenous interviewers certainly possess the highest potential for tapping the natural use of vernacular forms, and there are some sociolinguists who feel that the deepest, most authentic forms of a vernacular variety are truly accessible only through the use of community fieldworkers. The role of rapport and empathy in an effective conversational interview may be discussed at length, but ultimately such qualities cannot be programmed. Nonetheless, good field-workers are invaluable to any significant dialect study, and it seems advisable that community members be involved in this process to some extent.

Although a fieldworker cannot control the elicitation of particular diagnostic forms when the focus of the interview is simply upon obtaining reasonable amounts of conversation, it is possible to include certain kinds of questions which raise the potential for targeted structures to occur. Thus, interview questions may be designed to yield narratives of past experiences or of movie plots in order to obtain significant numbers of past tense verb forms. Similarly, descriptions of different attributes (e.g. "What does he look like?") may raise the potential for predicate adjective constructions to occur (e.g. *He's tall and he's kinda thin . . .*).

The kinds of questions that promote the potential for certain structures are, of course, determined only after pilot trials with various formats and, in some cases, only after some of the analysis has begun. For example, in our early studies of Detroit speech (Wolfram 1969), we found that many of the occurrences of habitual *be* (e.g. *They be tagging somebody when they catch them*) among children occurred during their descriptions of traditional game activities, since such speech events call for the description of regularly occurring, or habitual, activities. Such information not only aided us in the analysis of the invariant form of *be* (Fasold 1969), it also helped researchers studying this form to devise questions that might bring out the use of *be* (Bailey and Maynor 1987). Care may therefore be given in a conversational interview to the kinds of questions that might elicit sufficient data for analysis, the kinds of linguistic structures that certain questions are likely to call forth, and the cultural topics that are relevant to the community. When these considerations are taken into account, the demands of the conversational interview may present a significant challenge. These concerns also point to the need for extensive pilot testing before widescale surveys are conducted. The success of particular topics in eliciting conversation varies considerably from community to community and from subject to subject, and the actual interview sometimes strays far from the structured topics as the fieldworker follows the interviewee's interests.

Exercise 2

Suppose that you are interested in examining the use of third person, singular present tense forms in a study of a dialect (e.g. *She goes to the store*). Think of some conversational questions that might produce these forms. Try out these questions in a brief, tape-recorded interview with a subject. When finished with your interview, review the recording and count the number of times a third person singular verb form was used by the subject. Was your questioning strategy successful in producing the form?

It is difficult to say how much conversation is necessary for meaning-ful analysis of dialect data, since this is subject to the kinds of structures that are being considered and the type of analysis being undertaken. For frequently occurring units in the phonology, a limited interview of fifteen minutes might provide adequate tokens of the sound unit for analysis, while for grammatical structures, considerably more conversation usually is required. Most studies relying on individual conversation interviews set minimal time limits of between 45 minutes and one hour, although there is certainly no hard and fast rule.

There are limitations to the single-interviewee conversational interview, just as there are limitations to other data-elicitation formats. Although this tech-nique provides access to a kind of naturalistic language data, it is not always successful in overcoming the observer's paradox, as speakers still may be con-scious that their speech is being "examined." In most cases, there are interludes where the attention to speech is sublimated, but it is never far away from the interviewee's consciousness. These kinds of interviews typically provide informal but somewhat careful conversational style.

The single-interviewee conversational interview also tends to be restricted in terms of the kinds of conversational discourses it elicits. For example, an interviewer may be able to elicit a narrative account of a past time event, but it will typically not be the kind of "performed narrative" that the subject might recount for a group of friends. Thus, some of the linguistic structures that occur in narrative performances may not be found in the stories that are told during the sociolinguistic interview. In a similar way, subjects' use of question forms within a conversation tend to be underrepresented, since the interviewer typically asks most of the questions.

Given the underlying concern with obtaining sufficient amounts of con-versation, there is no assurance that certain forms will be included as a part of the interview, even with considerable forethought to the kinds of structures that certain questions might encourage. Unfortunately, there are instances where the most critical structures for resolving a certain descript-ive or explanatory issue occur quite infrequently. For lexical differences, the situation is even more drastic, given the hundreds of possible dialect items. In fact, it is difficult to conceive of any significant study of lexical differences that relies exclusively upon conversational interviews of approximately an hour per subject.

Finally, there is the issue of comparability. It is difficult to ensure compar-ability in language structures even when subjects talk about similar topics for approximately the same length of time. For example, we have tabulated poten-tial multiple negative usage (i.e. negative sentences with indefinites such as *She didn't go no/anywhere*) for speakers with similar quantities of conversation only to find that one speaker had over 50 instances of potential multiple negation and another speaker had fewer than five instances. Given the flexibility that must be built into a meaningful conversational interview, it is difficult to ensure comparability for different subjects in a given study, to say nothing of comparability with other studies. Unfortunately, we cannot be certain whether particular structures are absent from an interview because there were no occasions for their occurrence or because they were legitimately not part of the speaker's linguistic system.

Obviously, there are many advantages found in gathering dialect data through the use of a conversational interview for the study of systematic variability, but there are significant limitations as well. As with other types of data-collection techniques, these limitations must be kept in mind as the researcher designs data-collection procedures to meet the goals of a particular dialect study.

9.4 Systematic Variation

One of the important discoveries to emerge from the detailed study of dialects over the past several decades, particularly social class dialects, was that dialects are sometimes differentiated not by the discrete, or categorical, use or non-use of forms, but by the relative frequency with which different variants of a form occur. In fact, it can be shown for a number of phonological and grammatical features that dialects are more typically differentiated by the extent to which a particular feature occurs, its relative frequency, rather than by its complete absence or categorical presence.

Table 9.1 displays the frequency levels of *-in'* for *-ing*, a phonological variable, and the syntactic variable of pronominal apposition (e.g. *My mother, she's*

Table 9.1 Relative frequency of variable phonological and grammatical features in four social groups in Detroit

	Upper middle class	Lower middle class	Upper working class	Lower working class
Mean percentage of *-in'* forms	19.4	39.1	50.5	78.9
Mean percentage of pronominal apposition	4.5	13.6	25.4	23.8

Adapted from Shuy, Wolfram, and Riley (1967)

coming to school as opposed to *My mother's coming to school*) in four different
social status groups of Detroit speakers (adapted from Shuy, Wolfram, and
Riley 1967). Although the figures represent the mean scores for each social
group, all of the individual speakers also exhibit variability between *-ing* and
-in', as well as between *my mother, she . . .* and *my mother . . .* Frequency levels
were computed for individual speakers by first noting all those cases where a
form like *-in'* might have occurred – namely, in unstressed syllables ending in
-ing. Then, the number of cases in which *-in'* actually occurred was counted.
For example, in the sample passage given above, there are ten cases where *-in'*
could have occurred, but only six of them, or 60 percent, were actually produced with the *-in'* form. This tabulation procedure follows a fairly standard
format for determining frequency levels of dialect forms, which can be indicated in the simple formula:

$$\frac{\text{No. of cases where a given form occurs}}{\text{No. of cases where the form might have occurred}} \times 100$$

In other words, we calculate the proportion of actual cases out of potential
cases (i.e. 0.6) and multiply by 100 to arrive at a percentage score (60 percent).

The fact that there is fluctuation between forms such as *-ing* and *-in'* does
not mean that the fluctuation is random or haphazard. Although we cannot
predict which variant might be used in a given instance, there are factors that
can increase or decrease the likelihood that certain variants will occur. These
factors are known technically as CONSTRAINTS ON VARIABILITY. The constraints
are of two major types. First, there are various social factors such as social class
(as in table 9.1) which systematically correlate with an increase or decrease in
the likelihood that a particular variant will occur. In other words, looking at
table 9.1, we can say that a speaker from the lower working class is more likely
to use both *-in'* for *-ing* and pronominal apposition than speakers from other
classes.

Not all of the systematic influences on variation, however, can be accounted
for simply by appealing to the various social factors discussed in previous
chapters. There are also aspects of the linguistic system itself that may affect
the variability of particular forms. Particular kinds of linguistic contexts, such
as the kinds of surrounding forms or the type of construction in which the
form occurs, may also influence the relative frequency with which these forms
occur. Because the linguistic influences on variation operate apart from the
social factors that correlate with variability, these are sometimes referred to as
INDEPENDENT LINGUISTIC CONSTRAINTS on variability. Linguistic constraints on
variability will be discussed in further detail below; our discussion of social
variables in previous chapters has already set forth some of the social constraints on variability.

9.5   Linguistic Constraints on Variability

The effect of linguistic factors on the relative frequency of particular forms can best be understood by looking at a particular case of phonological variation. Let us consider the process of word-final consonant cluster reduction that may affect sound sequences such as *st*, *nd*, *ld*, *kt*, and so forth. When this process operates, items such as *west*, *wind*, *cold*, and *act* may be pronounced without the final member of the cluster, as *wes'*, *win'*, *col'*, and *ac'*, respectively. The incidence of cluster reduction is quite variable, but certain linguistic factors systematically favor or inhibit the operation of the reduction process. These factors, or constraints, include whether the following word begins with a consonant or a vowel (more precisely, a non-consonant) and the way in which the cluster is formed.

With respect to the sound that follows the cluster, the likelihood of reduction is increased when the cluster is followed by a word beginning with a consonant. This means that cluster reduction is more frequent in contexts such as *west coast* or *cold cuts* than in contexts like *west end* or *cold apple*. An individual speaker might, for example, reveal consonant cluster reduction in 75 percent of all cases when the cluster is followed by a word beginning with a consonant (as in *wes' coast*) but show only 25 percent consonant cluster reduction when the cluster is followed by a non-consonant (as in *wes' end*). The important observation is that reduction may take place in both kinds of linguistic contexts, but it is regularly *favored* in those contexts where the word following the cluster begins with a consonant.

Exercise 3

In the following passage, tabulate the incidence of cluster reduction for all the underlined word-final clusters. Observe whether the cluster is reduced or not, as indicated by the phonetic content in the brackets following the underlined cluster. For example, gue<u>st</u>[s] would indicate a reduced item since the final [t] has been omitted, and gue<u>st</u>[st] would not. For the time being, ignore consonant clusters that are not underlined. Tabulate the items by setting up two columns, one for clusters followed by consonants and one for clusters followed by non-consonants. Items at the end of a sentence should be considered to be followed by non-consonants. For each cluster, first identify whether it is followed by a consonant or non-consonant and then enter it under the relevant category and identify in some way whether it is reduced or non-reduced. After extracting the first couple of items, your tabulation sheet might look like the following:

Clusters followed by a consonant	**Clusters followed by a non-consonant**
0 e.g. be<u>st</u>[st] movie	0 e.g. mo<u>st</u>[st] of
1 e.g. la<u>st</u>[s] year	1 e.g. coa<u>st</u>[s]. It
. . .	. . .

1 = reduced cluster
0 = unreduced cluster

After you have finished entering all the items under the appropriate category, calculate the percentage of cluster reduction for each category by dividing the total number of clusters in the category into the number of clusters that are actually reduced and multiply by 100. This will give you a percentage of cluster reduction for clusters followed by consonants and clusters followed by non-consonants. What can you say about the influence of the following context on cluster reduction based on this calculation?

Passage for word-final cluster reduction tabulation
La<u>st</u>[s] year I saw the be<u>st</u>[st] movie. It seemed silly but it was serious too. It was about this detective who lived in California, but he traveled up and down mo<u>st</u>[st] of the coa<u>st</u>[s]. It seemed like he was always one step ahead of the cops and one step behi<u>nd</u>[n] the bad guys at the same time. Nobody really liked him, and it seemed like he was almo<u>st</u>[s] killed every time he left the house. Mo<u>st</u>[s] of the time, he was running from both the criminals and the police. In fa<u>ct</u>[kt] both sides were totally confused by him.
    One time, the police set up a scam bu<u>st</u>[s] by pretending to smuggle in some drugs off the coa<u>st</u>[st]. When they smuggled the stuff inla<u>nd</u>[n] they wanted to sell it to the dealers. But the detective wasn't told so he thought it was a chance for a real bu<u>st</u>[st] on the dealers. Ju<u>st</u>[s] as he jumped in to make an arre<u>st</u>[s] a couple of dealers showed up, and he had to a<u>ct</u>[k] like he was one of them. So the police thought he was part of the dealers and the dealers thought he was part of the police. Both sides jumped in and he was trying to a<u>ct</u>[k] as if he was with the other side. He told a policeman to go along with him 'cause he was making a bu<u>st</u>[st] and he told a drug dealer to go along with him and he would get the drugs. Both sides were so confused by him they ju<u>st</u>[s] went along with the a<u>ct</u>[kt] and followed his lead. As it turned out, some of the police had gone undergrou<u>nd</u>[n] and some of the dealers had turned evidence to the police. He was so confused himself he didn't know who to arre<u>st</u>[st]. Finally, he ju<u>st</u>[s] left both groups shooting at each other. He ju<u>st</u>[s] couldn't figure out who was bad and who was good.

Cluster reduction is also influenced by the way in which the cluster is formed. Clusters that belong to a single morpheme, as in the case of root words such as *wind* and *guest*, are more likely to undergo reduction than clusters that are created through the addition of an *-ed* suffix, as in *guessed*, which ends phonetically in [st] ([gɛst]), and *pinned*, which ends in [nd] ([pɪnd]). Again, fluctuation between reduced and full pronunciation takes place with both types of clusters, but reduction takes place more frequently when the cluster is an inherent part of a word rather than the result of *-ed* suffix addition.

Exercise 4

Using the passage from Exercise 3, repeated below, now tabulate the incidence of final consonant cluster reduction for clusters formed through the addition of the *-ed* suffix. As with Exercise 3, the clusters formed through the addition of *-ed* are underlined and the phonetic content indicated within the phonetic brackets that follow the underlined item. In order to control for the influence of the linguistic environments we already tabulated in Exercise 3, the tabulation will need to separate those *-ed* clusters that are followed by a consonant (e.g. *They guessed five*) from those that are followed by a non-consonant (e.g. *They guessed at the answer*). Along with your figures from Exercise 3, you should now have figures for the incidence of cluster reduction in four different categories: (1) base word cluster followed by a consonant, (2) base word cluster followed by a non-consonant, (3) *-ed* cluster followed by a consonant, and (4) *-ed* cluster followed by a non-consonant. This table should look something like the following:

Root word followed by consonant	Root word followed by non-consonant	*-ed* cluster followed by consonant	*-ed* cluster followed by non-consonant
best[st] movie	most[st] of	seemed[m] silly	lived[vd] in
0	0	1	0
. . .	. . .	. . .	. . .

1 = reduced cluster
0 = unreduced cluster

Last year I saw the best movie. It see<u>med</u>[m] silly but it was serious too. It was about this detective who li<u>ved</u>[vd] in California, but he trave<u>led</u>[l] up and down most of the coast. It see<u>med</u>[md] like he was always one step ahead of the cops and one step behind the bad guys at the same time. Nobody really li<u>ked</u>[kt] him, and it see<u>med</u>[m] like he was almost ki<u>lled</u>[ld] every time he le<u>ft</u>[f] the house. Most of the time, he was running

from both the criminals and the police. In fact both sides were totally con-
fu<u>sed</u>[z] by him.

One time, the police set up a scam bust by pretending to smuggle in some
drugs off the coast. When they smug<u>gled</u>[l] the stuff inland they wanted to
sell it to the dealers. But the detective wasn't to<u>ld</u>[ld] so he thought it was a
chance for a real bust on the dealers. Just as he jum<u>ped</u>[pt] in to make an
arrest a couple of dealers showed up, and he had to act like he was one of
them. So the police thought he was part of the dealers and the dealers
thought he was part of the police. Both sides jum<u>ped</u>[pt] in and he was
trying to act as if he was with the other side. He to<u>ld</u>[ld] a policeman to go
along with him 'cause he was making a bust and he to<u>ld</u>[l] a drug dealer to
go along with him and he would get the drugs. Both sides were so confu<u>sed</u>[z]
by him they just went along with the act and followed his lead. As it
tur<u>ned</u>[n] out, some of the police had gone underground and some of the
dealers had tur<u>ned</u>[nd] evidence to the police. He was so confu<u>sed</u>[zd]
himself he didn't know who to arrest. Finally, he just le<u>ft</u>[f] both groups
shooting at each other. He just couldn't figure out who was bad and who
was good.

When we compare the relative effect of different linguistic factors on the
cluster reduction pattern, we find that some linguistic influences are greater
than others. In some dialects of English, the influence of the following segment
(consonant vs. non–consonant) is more important than the cluster formation
type (not *-ed* vs. *-ed* cluster). When one factor is more influential than others it
is referred to as the FIRST ORDER CONSTRAINT. The next most important factor
is the SECOND ORDER CONSTRAINT, the third most important the third order
constraint and so forth. The ordering of constraints may be likened to the
relative effect of different social factors, where social status, age, and gender
may all influence the relative incidence of cluster reduction, but not in equal
proportions.

In some cases, linguistic constraints on variability can be ordered differently
across varieties of English. Table 9.2 presents a comparison of word-final
cluster reduction for some different dialects of English, based upon a sample of
speakers in each population. As seen in this table, all of the varieties of English
represented here show clusters to be systematically influenced by the following
phonological context and the cluster formation type, but the ordering of constraints may differ. In some cases, such as standard English and Appalachian
Vernacular English, the influence of the following consonant is more important than the cluster type, whereas in other cases, such as Southern Anglo
American working-class speech and Southern African American working-class
speech, the cluster type is a more important constraint than the following
phonological context.

Table 9.2 Comparison of consonant cluster reduction in representative vernacular dialects of English

Language variety	Followed by consonant		Followed by non-consonant	
	Not -ed % reduced	-ed % reduced	Not -ed % reduced	-ed % reduced
Standard English	66	36	12	3
Northern Anglo American working class	67	23	19	3
Southern Anglo American working class	56	16	25	10
Appalachian working class	74	67	17	5
Northern African American working class	97	76	72	4
Southern African American working class	88	50	72	36
Chicano working class	91	61	66	22
Puerto Rican working class (NYC)	93	78	63	23
Italian American working class (Boston)	67	39	14	10
Native American Puebloan English	98	92	88	81
Vietnamese English	98	93	75	60

From Wolfram (1986)

Exercise 5

As noted above, the influence of the following consonant (i.e. a following word that begins with a consonant vs. one that does not) is more important than the influence of the cluster type (i.e. root word vs. -ed) for standard English and Appalachian Vernacular English. At the same time, we observed that for Southern Anglo American working-class and Southern African American working-class varieties, the cluster type is more important than the following consonant.

The ordering of constraints in relation to one another can be determined through a rather simple procedure. First, the scores for all logically possible linguistic contexts are listed in progressively descending (or ascending) order with each environment labeled alongside the frequency level. For example, for standard English and Appalachian Vernacular English, we find the following arrangement.

	Standard English	Appalachian Vernacular English
Followed by C, not -*ed*	66 (high score)	74
Followed by C, -*ed*	36	67
Not followed by C, not -*ed*	12	17
Not followed by C, -*ed*	3 (low score)	5

To determine the higher order constraint of the two constraints investigated here, we simply look for the factor which is common to the two highest scores. In this case, "followed by C" is common to both and so we conclude that the constraint "followed by C or non-C" is the highest order constraint. If we apply this procedure to the cases of Southern Anglo American working-class and Southern African American working-class varieties represented here, we get the following progression:

	Southern Anglo American working class	Southern African American working class
Followed by C, not -*ed*	56	88
Not followed by C, not -*ed*	25	72
Followed by C, -*ed*	16	50
Not followed by C, -*ed*	10	36

Notice that in this listing, it is the "not -*ed*" factor that is common to the two highest scores for each variety rather than "followed by C"; hence, "-*ed* vs. not -*ed*" is the more important constraint.

Using the figures given in table 9.2, apply this procedure to determine which linguistic constraint is more important for the following varieties: (1) Puerto Rican working-class English, (2) Chicano working-class English, (3) Italian American working-class English. Is the following consonant or not -*ed* (i.e. root word cluster) more important?

The analysis of linguistic constraints on variability can get much more sophisticated than the frequency tabulations and comparisons introduced here, as there now exist computerized statistical procedures for determining the relative influences of different kinds of constraints on variable linguistic processes such as consonant cluster reduction. These programs can take the analyst considerably beyond the level of statistical precision provided through raw tabulations. In technical studies of language variation, a multivariate statistical program known as VARBRUL is often used to determine the relative contribution of different factors to the overall variability of fluctuating forms, but other multivariate statistical procedures may also be used in detailed technical analysis. An extended discussion of these procedures is beyond the scope of this text, but the serious researcher interested in variation studies is obligated to learn such programs. For our purposes here, it is sufficient to recognize several fundamental insights about the nature of linguistic variation that have come from such systematic approaches to the study of language patterning.

First, we see that dialect differences are sometimes reflected in quantitative differences and the systematic patterning of variable differences rather than merely in more readily observable qualitative differences. Thus, in describing a dialect, we must be careful to note ways in which it differs quantitatively from other varieties as well as ways in which it differs qualitatively. We must also recognize that there are important constraints on the relative incidence of dialect forms based upon linguistic structure. Particular contexts will favor or inhibit the occurrence of a particular linguistic variant. It is important to take these systematic effects into account in our investigation of language variation. Thus, when we talk about the absence of the copula in varieties such as African American Vernacular English or Southern Anglo American Vernacular English, it is important to note that this phenomenon is much more common in contexts in which standard English has *are* (e.g. *You ugly, They ugly*) than those in which it has *is* (e.g. *He ugly, The bird ugly*), even though copula absence may be observed in both types of contexts.

Finally, our studies show that not all linguistic constraints have equal weight, as their effects may be ordered with respect to each other. In other words, some constraints are more important than others in their effect on the fluctuation of forms. In most cases of systematic linguistic variation, there are only a couple of major linguistic constraints on variability. Extensive analysis may reveal a number of fine-grained constraints, but the effects of such constraints are diminished as the constraints become more refined. The analysis of word-final consonant clusters we presented above has been extended to include linguistic constraints other than following environment and cluster type as discussed here. For example, linguists have investigated the effects of consonant type on cluster reduction (e.g. nasal + stop as in [nd] vs. stop + stop as in [pt]); they have also investigated the effects of syllable stress.

For example, is the [kt] of *act* more likely to be reduced than the [kt] of *contact*? However, these additional constraints tend to be much less significant by comparison with the primary constraints described here. The investigation of linguistic constraints on variability reveals the subtle and complex ways in which dialect differences are systematically structured. This complexity is, of course, a far cry from the common popular perception that dialects are rather haphazard and that vernacular speakers randomly "drop consonants" when they talk.

Before concluding our discussion of inherent variability, we should note that variability may combine with invariance in a number of ways. Forms that fluctuate in one linguistic environment may be invariant, or categorical, in another one. For example, while speakers may fluctuate between copula absence and presence for *is* and *are* in African American Vernacular English, they never exhibit absence for *am*. Thus, the same speaker who fluctuates between saying *he ugly* and *he's ugly* would never say *I ugly*, only *I'm ugly*. In a similar way, *-in'* and *-ing* may fluctuate for some words in a person's dialect, while *-ing* is categorically used with other words and *-in'* is used categorically with still another set of lexical items. Thus, a speaker may use only *-ing* with certain "formal" words (e.g. *reciting, pursuing*) and only *-in'* with certain other "informal" words (e.g. *somethin'*); for a third set of words, the speaker may show fluctuation between *-in'* and *-ing* as set forth earlier. Forms which occur in particular linguistic environments, as well as particular words, may show an invariant pattern at the same time that other words and forms in other environments show variability. An authentic description of dialect patterning must therefore separate special conditions of invariance from regular fluctuation influenced by linguistic and social constraints.

9.6   Systematic Relationships

The quantitative analysis of the systematic variability of a particular language feature is not the only way in which relationships among dialects can be viewed. Another way of looking at relations within and among varieties is through investigating the arrangements of language structures in relation to each other. Different language forms are not necessarily distributed randomly; instead, there may be systematic relations between items. In particular, we often find that the existence of one form implies the existence of another.

An IMPLICATIONAL RELATION in language holds when the presence of a particular characteristic of language implies the presence of another characteristic, but the converse does not necessarily hold. If form B is always present when-

Table 9.3 Implicational relationship between *is* and *are* absence

Language variety	is *absence*	are *absence*
Standard English	0	0
Southern Anglo American Vernacular English	0	1
African American Vernacular English	1	1

ever form A is present, we say that "A implies B." However, in an implicational relationship, the converse is not true, so that B may exist with or without the presence of A. This relationship may be expressed in the logical formula "if A, then B."

As an example of an implicational relation, consider again the case of copula absence mentioned above. Varieties of American English not only differ in the extent of copula absence they show; they also may exhibit a systematic implicational relationship between copula absence in *is* and *are* contexts. Copula absence in *is* contexts necessarily implies its absence in *are* contexts, but the converse is not true. In other words, if a variety of English shows the absence of *is* in sentences such as *He ugly*, it will also show absence in sentences with *are*, such as *You ugly*. However, a variety may have sentences such as *You ugly* without having sentences such as *He ugly*. A display of this patterning, called an IMPLICATIONAL ARRAY, is given in table 9.3. In this table, 1 stands for the presence of the characteristic, in this case, the absence of copula, and 0 the absence of the characteristic. The implicational relationship is indicated by setting up the table so that the value 1 in a column implies the presence of 1 in columns to the right of it. Thus, a 1 in the *is* deletion column implies a 1 in the *are* deletion column to the right of it as well. Each row represents a different variety of English in terms of the implicational relationships; these include a variety of African American Vernacular English, Southern Anglo American Vernacular English, and standard English, which has neither *is* nor *are* deletion.

The display in table 9.3 shows that there are varieties of English which indicate neither *is* nor *are* absence (many standard English varieties), that there are varieties that have both *is* and *are* absence (African American Vernacular English), and that there are still other varieties (some Southern Anglo American varieties) which indicate *are* deletion but not *is* deletion. There are, however, no varieties that have *is* deletion but not *are* absence, as indicated by the way the 1's and 0's are set up in the table.

The Patterning of Dialect

Table 9.4 Implicational array for different types of multiple negation in some selected varieties of English

English variety	Multiple negation type		
	c	*b*	*a*
Standard English	0	0	0
Some Northern Anglo American Vernacular varieties	0	0	X
Other Northern Anglo American Vernacular varieties	0	X	X
Some Vernacular Southern Anglo and African American English varieties	X	X	X
Other varieties of African American Vernacular English	X	X	1

The implicational relationships that hold between structures in the dialects of American English can sometimes be much more complex than the simple case presented in table 9.3. To give a slightly more extended case, we can look at the implicational relations that hold among different kinds of multiple negation. For our purposes here, we will identify three types of multiple negation: (a) the use of negative indefinites following a negativized verb phrase (e.g. *They **didn't** do **nothing** because they were too tired*); (b) the use of negative indefinites before a negativized verb phrase (e.g. ***Nobody can't** do it 'cause it's too hard*); and (c) the "inversion" of a negativized verb phrase and a negativized subject (e.g. ***Can't nobody** do it 'cause it's too hard*).

In table 9.4, three values are given with respect to the use of multiple negation: 1 indicates the categorical presence of multiple negation (that is, the multiple negative is used whenever it can be used), 0 indicates the categorical absence of multiple negation, and X indicates fluctuation between presence and absence. X's may also have an implicational relationship with other X's in that an X in a given column may be used to imply that a higher frequency level of the variant will be indicated in those X's to the right of the column. Various dialects of American English are delimited in terms of the types of multiple negation they contain, as indicated in the rows in table 9.4.

This implicational array indicates that if a variety has type c multiple negation (e.g. *Can't nobody do it*), then it will have type b (e.g. *Nobody can't do it*), and if a variety has type b, it will also have type a (e.g. *She didn't do nothing*). However, the converse does not hold, so that a does not imply the existence of b, nor does b imply c.

Exercise 5

There are a number of different types of regularization of subject–verb agreement patterns in English that show implicational relations. For example, if a dialect has (a) regularization of present tense *be* forms, as in *We is here*, it will also have (b) regularization of past tense *be* forms, as in *We was here*. Furthermore, if a variety has past tense *be* regularization, it will have (c) regularization with the existential form *there* as in *There's five of them*. (For convenience here, just label these types a, b, and c, as we did above.) However, the converse is not true, as it is possible for a dialect to have regularization with the existential (e.g. *There's five of them*) but not regularization with past tense *be* (e.g. *We was here*), and so forth. Show this implicational relationship by setting up a table as we have done above. For the sake of this exercise, use only the value 1 for the presence of a particular regularization pattern and the value 0 for the absence of the regularization pattern.

Several observations should be made about the application of implicational analysis to dialect patterning. First, we should note that not all speakers in a given speech community will conform to the ideal pattern. The fit between the ideal implicational pattern and the actual cases of language patterning is referred to as the SCALABILITY, or "reproducibility" of the implicational array. In the most simple computation, scalability is determined by first creating an array in which values (i.e. 1, 0, X) for all relevant features are given for all speakers in the particular study. In this array, each point of intersection between rows and columns is called a CELL. Then, the number of non-deviant cells is divided by the total number of filled cells and multiplied by 100 in order to arrive at a percentage score. Consider in table 9.5 a hypothetical case in which we have a sample of ten speakers and three different features, arrayed so that c implies b, and b implies a. In this table, the deviant cases are marked with an asterisk.

Since there are ten speakers and three features, we have 30 cells. Three of the cells are deviant in their implicational relation, thus giving the implicational array a scalability rating of 90 percent. A score above 85 or 90 percent scalability is usually considered a reasonable level for establishing a valid implicational relationship.

We can also observe that implicational relationships among dialect structures are more systematic when the items included in the set represent subtypes of a single structure rather than totally unrelated structures. Thus, different types of copula absence show implicational relationships with each other, and subtypes of multiple negation show implicational relationships with each other, but copula absence may not show any real implicational relationship with multiple negation, as these represent unrelated structural sets.

Table 9.5   Scalability rating for an implicational array

Speaker	Feature a	Feature b	Feature c
1	0	0	1
2	0	1	1
3	1	1	1
4	1	*0	1
5	0	1	1
6	1	1	1
7	0	1	*0
8	0	1	1
9	0	0	1
10	1	*0	1

Despite some limitations, the consideration of implicational relationships provides a couple of important insights about dialect patterning. First of all, this model establishes a systematic basis for looking at how closely related different dialects are to one another. For example, our implicational analysis of copula absence reveals the relative degree of distance among current standard English, Southern Anglo American English, and African American Vernacular English. As we saw in table 9.3, African American Vernacular English is closer to Southern Anglo American Vernacular English than it is to standard English in its use of copula absence, while Southern Anglo American Vernacular English is closer to standard English than African American Vernacular English.

The second insight provided by implicational analysis relates to language change. As we have mentioned at various points in previous chapters, language change is an ongoing process that usually takes place in orderly stages. One way of observing various stages in the process of change is to look at implicational relationships. Typically, the implicational array captures the systematic sequencing of stages in the change, so that we can observe what steps may have preceded or what steps are likely to follow in the progression of the change. For example, consider the case of *h* loss in words such as *hit* [hɪt] for *it* [ɪt] and *hain't* [hent] for *ain't* [ent], forms still found to some extent in isolated regions of the United States such as Appalachia, the Ozarks, and some Eastern coastal islands. At one point, *h* was always found in these items whether the word occurred in a stressed syllable (e.g. *Hit's the one I like*) or an unstressed syllable (e.g. *I like hit*). The occurrence of *h* in these items then began to fluctuate (sometimes *h* occurred and sometimes it didn't) in unstressed syllables while it was still retained categorically in stressed syllables. Next, the *h* was variably lost in both unstressed and stressed syllables, but it was more frequently lost in unstressed syllables, where the change first started. Through time, the *h* was completely lost in unstressed syllables while it was still maintained variably in

Table 9.6 Stages for language change in the loss of *h* in *(h)it* and *(h)ain't* in American English

Stage of change		Unstressed syllables	Stressed syllables
Stage 1	Earliest stage of English, before undergoing change	1	1
Stage 2	Earlier stage of English, at start of *h* loss	X	1
Stage 3	Change in full progress, *h* still exhibited by some older speakers in isolated dialect areas	X	X
Stage 4	Change progressing towards completion, *h* exhibited in restricted environment by some speakers in isolated dialect areas	0	X
Stage 5	Completed change, includes most English outside of isolated regions	0	0

stressed syllables. And finally, *h* was lost in most dialects in both stressed and unstressed syllables categorically. The stages of this change are summarized in table 9.6, using 1 to indicate the categorical presence of *h*, X to indicate variable presence, and 0 to indicate categorical absence. The implicational relationships among a given column and columns to the right hold as we have presented them in our other implicational arrays.

Among American English dialects today, stages 3 and 4 are still represented in various isolated vernacular varieties, and stage 5 is standard English usage, where the loss of *h* is complete. As we see in this example, some dialect differences may represent ongoing change at different stages in its progression. Although our depiction of the stages of *h* loss is a simplified picture, given the social and linguistic complexities surrounding all language changes, it provides a model of the progressive steps that so typically characterize language change.

Our survey of systematic patterning in dialects has been brief and, believe it or not, relatively non-technical. It is sufficient, however, to demonstrate that dialect patterning within and across dialects is very systematic and often rather intricate. Simplistic, categorical characterizations cannot come close to capturing the organizational detail that accounts for the myriad constellations of structures that comprise the dialects of American English.

9.7   Further Reading

Bayley, Robert, and Dennis R. Preston (eds) (1996) *Second Language Acquisition and Linguistic Variation.* Philadelphia/Amsterdam: John Benjamins. The introductory chapter by Dennis Preston in this volume provides a clear exposition of the development of variation analysis as a subfield of study in sociolinguistics, while the appendix by Richard Young and Robert Bayley demonstrates how to run the VARBRUL program on both Macintosh and DOS platforms. The appendix is the most extensive published documentation for this software program available.

Chambers, J. K. (1995) *Sociolinguistic Theory.* Cambridge, MA: Blackwell. This book offers an overview of the tenets of linguistic variation and the kinds of variables that correlate with fluctuating dialect forms. The first chapter outlines how the traditional view of language as an invariant phenomenon conflicts with the variationist model.

Fasold, Ralph W. (1970) Two models of socially significant linguistic variation. *Language* 46:551–63. This article was an early attempt to reconcile "implicational analysis" and "variable rules" as models for describing systematic variation in language. Although dated, it remains one of the more readable discussions of these models.

Guy, Gregory R. (1993) The quantitative analysis of linguistic variation. In Dennis R. Preston (ed.), *American Dialect Research.* Philadelphia/Amsterdam: John Benjamins, 223–49. Guy's chapter in the collection of readings compiled to commemorate the centennial of the American Dialect Society outlines the steps of quantitative analysis, with emphasis on so-called "variable rule analysis." It presents the procedural steps taken in VARBRUL, the multivariate statistical analysis program often used by variationists, but does not provide documentation for running the program.

Labov, William (1969) Contraction, deletion and inherent variability of the English copula. *Language* 45:715–62. As the initial presentation of the systematic variation of linguistic processes, this article is historically significant in its launching of variation theory, although many of the original details of this formulation have been revised substantially over the years. The article is also revised and reprinted as chapter 3 in Labov's *Language in the Inner City* (1972a).

Language Variation and Change. New York: Cambridge University Press. This journal is dedicated to the description and understanding of variability of all types. New developments in variation study are routinely published in this journal.

Wolfram, Walt (1993b) Identifying and interpreting variables. In Dennis R. Preston (ed.), *American Dialect Research.* Philadelphia/Amsterdam: John Benjamins, 193–221. This chapter discusses the notion of the linguistic variable, a fundamental construct in carrying out variation analysis. Both theoretical and practical considerations for conducting quantitative analysis of linguistic variation are reviewed.

10

On the Applications of
Dialect Study

10.1 Applied Dialectology

In and of themselves, dialects are highly fascinating, and many dialectologists are content to spend their lives collecting and cataloging examples of dialect forms. However valid this reason for studying dialects may be, many people still ask a basic utilitarian question: "What good is all this information on dialects anyhow?" Educators may, for example, want to know what value such information may have in their educational setting. Or parents may want to know how this information is relevant to their children's welfare. It is not even exaggerated to think that leaders on various levels may want to know how such information bears on sociopolitical issues related to language and society.

The relatively short history of social dialectology has shown that it is quite possible to combine a commitment to the objective description of sociolinguistic data and a concern for social issues relating to dialect. According to Labov (1982), there are two primary principles that may motivate linguists to take social action, namely, the PRINCIPLE OF ERROR CORRECTION and the PRINCIPLE OF DEBT INCURRED. These are articulated as follows:

Principle of error correction
A scientist who becomes aware of a widespread idea or social practice with important consequences that is invalidated by his [*sic*] own data is obligated to bring this error to the attention of the widest possible audience. (Labov 1982:172)

Principle of debt incurred
An investigator who has obtained linguistic data from members of a speech community has an obligation to use the knowledge based on that data for the benefit of the community, when it has need of it. (Labov 1982:173)

There are several outstanding instances in the history of social dialectology where these principles have been applied. In the 1960s, sociolinguists in the United States took a strong pro-difference stance in the so-called DEFICIT–DIFFERENCE CONTROVERSY that was taking place within education and within speech and language pathology (Baratz 1968; Labov 1969). Consonant with the principle of error correction, sociolinguists took a united stand against the classification and treatment of normal, natural dialect differences as language deficits or disorders. There is little doubt that sociolinguists played a major role in pushing the definition of linguistic normalcy toward a dialect-sensitive one, although the practical consequences of this definition are still being worked out in many clinical and educational settings (Wolfram, Christian, and Adger 1998).

In keeping with the principle of debt incurred, social dialectologists also rose to the occasion in a legal case referred to as the Ann Arbor Decision (1979). Linguistic testimony was critical to the judge's ruling in favor of the African American children who brought suit against the Ann Arbor, Michigan, Board of Education for not taking their dialect into account in reading instruction. In effect, the judge ruled that the defendants had failed to take appropriate action to overcome language barriers, in violation of federal anti-discrimination laws. In compliance with the judge's ruling, a series of workshops was conducted to upgrade awareness about language variation and to demonstrate how to apply sociolinguistic expertise in reading instruction.

Linguists were also quite active in their support of the resolution by the Oakland Unified School District Board of Education in 1996 and 1997, affirming the legitimacy of African American Vernacular English as a language system. Linguists attempted to explain to the American public why such a resolution was appropriate and even testified on behalf of the Oakland School Board at a US Senate subcommittee hearing on the status of this variety and its role in education. Some linguists have thus been fairly active in combining their objective examination of language variation with a social commitment to apply their knowledge to social and educational problems related to language.

There is another level of social commitment that sociolinguistic investigators might strive for in the communities in which they conduct their dialect research. This level is more positive and proactive, in that it involves active pursuit of ways in which linguistic favors can be returned to the community. Wolfram (1993a:227) encapsulates this level of involvement in an additional principle of social commitment called the PRINCIPLE OF LINGUISTIC GRATUITY.

Principle of linguistic gratuity
Investigators who have obtained linguistic data from members of a speech community should actively pursue positive ways in which they can return linguistic favors to the community.

This principle dictates that linguists must be committed to the creative implementation of community-based collaborative programs to return linguistic favors. These programs may range from service to community organizations to the production of language-related products on behalf of the community.

In this and the final chapter, we will take up several different areas of APPLIED DIALECTOLOGY. First, we examine the issue of dialect diversity and language assessment, one of the most critical areas for the application of dialect knowledge. Then we examine the issue of teaching standard English, a persistent concern raised by educators when confronted with dialect diversity. In the final chapter, we consider the application of information about dialects to language arts, including reading and the representation of dialects in literature. We discuss the impact of dialects not only upon the development of particular skills such as reading and writing, but also in terms of collaborative dialect awareness programs that involve researchers in the communities that have provided them with data for their dialect studies.

10.2 Dialects and Testing

The importance that mainstream American society places upon testing is fairly obvious; in fact, standardized testing probably could be added to the small list of inevitables in our society, such as taxes and death. Many standardized tests directly tap students' knowledge of and skill with language form and use, but language issues with respect to testing extend considerably beyond test items focused on language *per se*. The language in which directions are given, the language register used to tap information in other content areas, and even the language used in the interaction between test administrators and test takers establish an essential sociolinguistic dimension for tests regardless of the subject area. No area of testing is really free of language-based concerns.

A sociolinguistic perspective informs us about three critical dimensions of testing: (1) the definition of "correctness," or the normative linguistic behavior that serves as a basis for evaluating responses to test items; (2) the particular way in which language is used as a medium to tap different kinds of knowledge or skill; and (3) the sociolinguistic situation or context in which testing takes place. The first area involves an understanding of dialect differences since standardized tests use norms taken from some dialect of English, usually the standard dialect. The second area more typically involves an understanding of specialized language uses, as the focus is on language as a medium to access data. The third area involves more broadly based issues of language socialization and underlying sociolinguistic values. In the overall effect on test performance, all three dimensions may play a significant role, although differences in structural form tend to be the most transparent when it comes to dialect and testing.

The identification of a "correct," or normative, response is essential to success in most types of standardized tests. In some cases, this definition of linguistic correctness is based upon response data collected from sample populations used to standardize testing instruments – traditionally middle-class majority populations who use a variety of standard English. In other cases, the definition of correctness is not based on data obtained from sample populations at all, but is based instead upon the opinions of prescriptive language authorities who determine what the ideal standard form is to be – usually formal standard English as discussed in chapter 1. There is considerable latitude in classifying "incorrect" responses, but the traditional notion of correctness used in standardized testing instruments has usually been restricted to items characterizing a standard dialect in its real or ideal state.

10.2.1 Language achievement

One of the clearest examples of the impact of dialect differences on standardized test instruments comes from the kinds of achievement tests given to students at regular intervals in their educational progress. For example, consider how the notion of correctness is defined in several examples taken from the "Language Use" section of an achievement test. The examples in this case come from a disclosed version of the *California Achievement Test* given to third-graders. The directions for choosing a response instruct the student simply to identify one of the items in the brackets that "you think is correct."

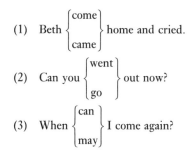

(1)   Beth $\left\{\begin{array}{c} \text{come} \\ \text{came} \end{array}\right\}$ home and cried.

(2)   Can you $\left\{\begin{array}{c} \text{went} \\ \text{go} \end{array}\right\}$ out now?

(3)   When $\left\{\begin{array}{c} \text{can} \\ \text{may} \end{array}\right\}$ I come again?

In each of these three cases, the "correct" form is the standard English form. The incorrect choice, however, is a "distractor," which may be of several different kinds. In question (1), the choice is between a standard dialect variant and a vernacular dialect variant. The use of the "bare root form" *come* as an irregular past tense form is quite common in a number of vernacular dialects (e.g. *Beth come home and cried*), whereas *came* is the standard dialect past tense form. In this sentence, incorrect is simply defined as a vernacular dialect form.

In sentence (2), the choice is between a form which is acceptable in both standard and vernacular dialects and one which is unacceptable in both varieties. In other words, *Can you go out now?* is a well-formed standard and vernacular dialect form and *Can you went out now?* is unacceptable in both types of varieties. In this case, the choice is between a linguistically well-formed, or

GRAMMATICAL, sentence and a linguistically ill-formed, or UNGRAMMATICAL, sentence, regardless of the dialect.

The differentiation between a correct and incorrect response in sentence (3), unlike (1) and (2), seizes upon the distinction between a formal standard variant and an informal standard one. In informal spoken standard English, most speakers would say *When can I come again?* In the case of sentence (3), the contrast is therefore between an ideal prescriptive standard English form (*may*) and an informal spoken standard English form.

What do these different notions of correctness and incorrectness mean for speakers of different dialects, in particular, for speakers of vernacular vs. standard dialects? For sentence (1), vernacular speakers relying on unconscious knowledge of their language rules may choose the "incorrect" response, whereas a standard speaker relying on this same type of knowledge would make the "correct" choice. In this regard, an awareness of the rules of vernacular dialects, such as those found in the appendix, can help us understand why vernacular speakers might systematically select "incorrect" answers. In order to make the "correct" choice for this sentence, the vernacular speaker must make a counter-intuitive linguistic choice and select a socially acceptable standard English structure instead of a linguistically well-formed vernacular structure. In this respect, we see that there may be very different tasks involved in responding to this item for a native vernacular dialect speaker and a native standard English speaker. Perhaps more importantly, the confusion between linguistic acceptability and social acceptability brings us back to the erroneous assumption about vernacular dialects widely held in some educational circles: Forms that do not agree with the rules of standard English violate fundamental rules of linguistic well-formedness – that is, they are "ungrammatical." We see that this mythology about the nature of dialect differences, discussed originally in chapter 1, has worked its way into the definition of correctness built into standardized language achievement tests.

For sentence (2), reliance upon knowledge of language rules should result in a correct response for both the vernacular and standard speaker, other things being equal, since the incorrect item is linguistically unacceptable across dialects. For sentence (3), however, reliance upon such knowledge would lead to an incorrect response by both a vernacular and standard speaker, since the item involves a prescribed formal structure which is not a regular part of informal standard or vernacular varieties. In this case, both standard and vernacular test takers would have to resort to explicitly learned knowledge about formal standard English to obtain the correct response.

A survey of representative language achievement tests given to students in early schooling shows that many of the test items focus on the first notion of correctness – the simple distinction between vernacular and standard dialect forms. In the *California Achievement Test* from which the examples above were taken, 14 out of 25 total sentences in the section titled "Language Usage" focus exclusively on this distinction. The distinction between formal and informal standard (sentence (3) above) is not so critical in early achievement testing, but it becomes much more prominent as students proceed to the higher levels of education; it is rampant in tests such as the *Scholastic Aptitude Test*.

Exercise 1

Following are some additional items from an achievement test. Identify the focus of each item in terms of the three dimensions of correctness discussed above: (1) standard vs. vernacular sentence structure, (2) grammatical vs. ungrammatical structure regardless of dialect, and (3) formal standard English vs. informal standard English sentence structure.

1   My sister $\left\{ \begin{matrix} am \\ is \end{matrix} \right\}$ six years old.

2   She will give me $\left\{ \begin{matrix} them \\ these \end{matrix} \right\}$ dolls.

3   I $\left\{ \begin{matrix} shall \\ will \end{matrix} \right\}$ go there tomorrow.

4   I $\left\{ \begin{matrix} am \\ are \end{matrix} \right\}$ a good pupil.

5   There $\left\{ \begin{matrix} was \\ were \end{matrix} \right\}$ no ducks on the lake.

6   Is George going to eat with $\left\{ \begin{matrix} us \\ we \end{matrix} \right\}$?

7   Father and $\left\{ \begin{matrix} they \\ them \end{matrix} \right\}$ are going on a trip.

The examination of standardized language achievement tests clearly shows that such tests are often heavily weighted toward the recognition of standard English forms. Assessing whether or not a student can recognize standard English is not, in itself, an issue, especially if an educational system incorporates the systematic introduction of the standard dialect into its educational curriculum. It is, however, problematic as an overall measure of "achievement," since it may measure different things for different groups of speakers. For a standard speaker, an achievement test may measure what the student, for the most part, already brings to school from the home community – inner language knowledge of the standard dialect. For a student from a vernacular dialect introduced to the standard dialect, it actually may measure an aspect of achievement – the ability to recognize standard English forms after the student has been introduced to them in the classroom. The underlying problem, then, is in the comparison of standard and vernacular speakers as if both groups started from the same linguistic baseline.

One of the recurring questions that surfaces with language tests of all types centers on the matter of CONTENT VALIDITY: Does the testing instrument measure the content area it claims to measure? As we have seen, a test might measure quite different language capabilities for different dialect groups. Thus, vernacular speakers who have learned to recognize some forms in the standard dialect may have made significant educational progress yet still score well below standard English speakers who get credit for achievement when they are simply resorting to language knowledge they brought to school to begin with. Those who construct such tests and those who interpret the scores of these tests must be careful to determine what the test actually measures in relation to what it claims to measure, particularly since "language usage" tests so often emphasize the standard–vernacular distinction.

10.2.2 Speech and language development tests

As children develop, they are routinely assessed in a number of areas of behavior, including "speech and language." The purpose of such testing is fairly straightforward – to determine if children are acquiring their language at a normal rate of development. Virtually all children are screened initially for speech and language development before entering school for the first time, and, on that basis, they are recommended for more extensive diagnosis and subsequent classification as "normal" or "disordered." If they are judged as disordered, they are typically enrolled in a speech and language therapy program, so that the consequences of the diagnostic procedure can be quite significant. Because of such widescale assessment of children for speech and language, there are many formal standardized test instruments which have been developed to measure the normalcy of linguistic development. Unfortunately, the definition of normal development traditionally has been based upon the norms of the standard English-speaking population, as middle-class samples of children typically have been used to arrive at developmental norms.

The definition of normative responses exclusively in terms of standard English structures holds considerable potential for DIALECT DISCRIMINATION, where a normative response in a non-standard English dialect is erroneously classified as an unacquired standard English form. For example, various popular tests of language development (e.g. the *Illinois Test of Psycholinguistic Ability* (*ITPA*), the *Clinical Evaluation of Language Fundamentals-Revised* (*CELF-R*), and the *Test of Language Development* (*TOLD*)) use a type of sentence-completion task called "grammatic closure" to determine children's mastery of English morphology. In this assessment procedure, the examiner points to appropriate pictures while reading a statement, stopping at the point where the child is to fill in the missing word(s). For example, the child may be shown two picture frames, one with one bed and another with two beds, while the examiner says, "Here is a bed, and here are two _____." The child then completes the utterance, with a correct response in this case being the plural form *beds*. In scoring the test according to the procedures set forth in most test manuals, only standard English forms are considered as "correct" responses. Many of the items inadvertently focus on differences between standard and vernacular dialect forms. For example, if vernacular-speaking children are given a stimulus such as "This is a foot. Here are two ____," they might legitimately respond *foots* or *feets*, applying a regularization process which characterizes their dialect. However, since the scoring only recognizes *feet* as a correct response, the authentic dialect response would be considered incorrect. Similarly, given a stimulus such as "The boy is opening the gate. The gate has been _____," speakers who respond with *open* rather than *opened* because of the application of the consonant cluster reduction process discussed in chapter 9 would be penalized despite their use of a dialect-appropriate cluster-reduced form. As with the achievement tests discussed above, an understanding of dialect differences reveals that many of the forms scored as "incorrect" constitute linguistically well-formed structures in terms of vernacular dialect norms.

Exercise 2

Following are five more items from the *ITPA* grammatic closure subtest. Based upon the kinds of dialect rules found in the appendix, predict which of these items might have legitimate dialect alternates. What are the variant dialect forms? Refer to the dialect rules in the appendix in your responses. In each case, the response(s) considered correct according to the test manual is (are) given in italics.

Item 9. The boy is writing something. This is what he *wrote/has written/did write*.
Item 15. This horse is not big. This horse is big. This horse is *bigger*.
Item 19. This is soap, and these are *soap/bars of soap/more soap*.
Item 22. Here is a foot. Here are two *feet*.
Item 29. The boy has two bananas. He gave one away and he kept one for *himself*.

In some cases, the effects of imposing standard norms of development on vernacular speakers can be quite severe. For example, in the case of one grammatic closure subtest, over 20 of the 33 items have legitimate dialect variants. If the test is scored at face value, a normally developing child who uses dialect variants where possible would look like a linguistically delayed standard English speaker. A normally developing ten-year-old vernacular speaker may, in fact, be assessed as having the linguistic development of a child less than five years of age. On the basis of such a discrepancy between chronological and mental age, vernacular-speaking children commonly have been enrolled in therapy, even though they are developing quite normally in terms of their community dialect. The stakes for the assessment of children's language development can be quite severe if legitimate dialect differences are not recognized for language development tests.

10.2.3   Predicting dialect interference

The type of language analysis typically used to determine the specific impact of dialect diversity on the assessment of language development is called CON-TRASTIVE LINGUISTICS. In its simplest version, contrastive linguistics places the rules of language variety X and language variety Y side by side and, on the basis of comparing similarities and differences in the systems, points out areas of potential conflict for a speaker of X confronted with the norms of Y. This is the procedure we employed above when we compared the correct responses of a test normed on standard English speakers with the rules of vernacular varieties and determined where alternate responses might be expected due to differences between systems. Over the past two decades, a number of major language assessment instruments have been examined from this perspective. However, it is necessary to balance ideal predictions of dialect interference with actual studies of speakers' performance. In this type of empirically based ERROR ANALYSIS, some of the predicted structures show up much more frequently than others. Furthermore, there are some "incorrect" responses that may be attributed to dialect differences in an indirect way. And there may be items that turn up that are not predictable based upon a simple side-by-side comparison of language varieties.

There are a couple of reasons why not all predicted dialect variants may occur in the assessment procedure. Many of the predicted dialect alternates may be variable structures rather than categorical ones, as discussed in chapter 9. For example, we might predict plural -s absence for AAVE speakers in a formal test, but vernacular speakers typically show plural absence levels of only 10 to 20 percent when actual levels of absence are tabulated in relation to those cases where a plural form might be absent. Certainly, we would expect this inherent variability to have an effect on test responses; presumably, a low-frequency dialect item will have a lower probability of occurring as an alternate than a high-frequency one. It is also possible that the formality of the testing situation may bring forth responses not directly predictable, as speakers may shift away from their native forms in sometimes erratic ways. For example, test takers sensitive to the social stigmatization of a vernacular verb agreement pattern such as *We was there* might compensate by extending *were* usage beyond its specified limits, thus using constructions such as *I were there* in a testing situation even though they do not use such structures in everyday speech. For most American dialects, this form follows neither standard nor vernacular dialect rules, as most vernacular dialects found in the US generalize *was* to cover both *was* and *were*, not *were* for *was* and *were*. This is a case of hyper-correction, as discussed in chapter 8, due no doubt to the formality of the testing situation. Indirectly, we may attribute this usage to the vernacular dialect, but not as a case of simple transfer of a vernacular dialect form to the standard dialect.

Although all predicted dialect forms will not occur in an actual test, studies of the incidence of dialect forms in relation to predicted forms indicate that these dialect variants may still account for a significant portion of "incorrect" responses. In one empirical study, for example, over 50 percent of predicted dialect alternates were found to occur (King 1972).

10.3   Testing Language

The concern for dialect differences in language testing actually raises deeper questions about the conventional tests used to assess language capability. Most standardized language assessment instruments focus on restricted domains or levels of language, raising the question of content validity mentioned earlier. In the case of tests constructed to assess language development, we may ask if the selective language capability measured by the instrument adequately represents the language content it proposes to measure. For example, consider how a traditional assessment instrument like the *Peabody Picture Vocabulary Test* (*PPVT*) measures a particular aspect of "word knowledge." In the *PPVT*, "knowing a word" is defined by the test taker's ability to associate a word label given by a test examiner with a picture of the object or activity, given a multiple choice of pictures (e.g. "Show me *toboggan*"). This notion of word knowledge involves a passive recognition task limited to items that are some-times culturally specific and dialectally restricted. From a broader linguistic perspective, however, knowing a word involves at least the following: (1) syntactic constraints – how to use the word in phrases and sentences; (2) semantic constraints – knowing appropriate ideas conveyed by the word and how the word relates to associated ideas; (3) stylistic constraints – knowing appropriate settings and styles of speaking for using the item; (4) morphological information – knowing what words the item is related to and how it attaches to other forms; (5) pragmatic constraints – knowing what the word entails, presupposes, and implies; and (6) phonological information – knowing how the word is pronounced. Compared to the expansive linguistic nature of word knowledge, the *PPVT* measures a very restricted aspect of knowledge.

Many language assessment instruments focus on the more superficial aspects of language rather than the underlying categories and relationships that constitute the deeper basis of language organization. Word inflections (e.g. plural suffixes, possessive suffixes) and more superficial grammatical structures (e.g. the *be* copula, negative indefinite forms) are often examined rather than the deeper conceptual basis of language capability such as the underlying categories of negation, possession, and identity. The limitations of traditional tests in this regard have led to reservations about using such instruments for any speaker, but their impact is even more significant given the ways in which the dialects of English typically differ from each other. Most comparisons of vernacular and standard varieties of English indicate that the majority of differences are found on the more superficial levels of language organization. The deeper the language level, the more similar the different dialects of English tend to be. We therefore may offer the following hypothesis about language testing and dialect differences:

> The more superficial and limited the scope of language capability tapped in a testing instrument, the greater the likelihood that the instrument will be inappropriate for speakers beyond the immediate population upon which it was normed.

10.3.1   Using language to access information

Although differences in linguistic form are the most transparent dimension of dialect differentiation in standardized testing, dialect differences also come into play when subject areas other than language itself are being examined. All tests are replete with language-based tasks which range from interpreting test directions to determining appropriate strategies for arriving at correct responses. Since language is used as a medium for providing and tapping data in a broad range of content areas, sociolinguistic differences may therefore affect the results of tests which, at first glance, have very little to do with language.

Test directions call for the establishment of a common frame of reference for test takers. Obviously, the desired goal of directions is clarity – the unambiguous understanding of what activity is to be performed by all test takers. It cannot be assumed, however, that all test takers interpret directions in the same way, despite the fact that methods of standardization can sometimes be quite elaborate. Even the most "simple" and "obvious" directions may be laden with the potential for misinterpretation. This misinterpretation may involve a particular item or the overall format in which directions are presented. For example, our observation of a simple instruction to "repeat" a sentence shows the word *repeat* to have different possible interpretations. In some communities, we have found that this simple direction may be interpreted as a paraphrasing task rather than a verbatim repetition task. We found that some children embellish stimulus sentences such as *The car is in the garage* by paraphrasing it, so that the original sentence might be rendered as *That little old car just sitting in the garage*. Obviously, such children are attempting to succeed at the task, but their creative paraphrase in this instance would only lead to reduced scores, since tests are based on the assumption that "repeat" is to be interpreted as verbatim repetition.

There are many ways of testing students' skill and knowledge levels, and most standardized tests rely upon special language uses to access the desired information. In fact, close scrutiny of the language of testing suggests that there is a special language register that guides those who write test items. In part, the language of test taking is based on a version of formal written language, but it is often more than that. For example, a "question" may be defined as an incomplete declarative statement, as in the following: "To prevent scum from forming in a partly used can of paint, one should _____" (from *Arco's Practice for the Armed Forces Tests*, p. 23). In addition to the specialized definition of a question as a completion task, the impersonal pronoun *one* and the infinitive at the beginning of the sentence set apart this sentence from everyday language usage. Note how this sentence differs from a common everyday question such as "What do you do if you want to keep scum [i.e. *skin* in some dialects] from forming in a can of paint that's been opened?"

Exercise 3

Consider the following questions, taken from training manuals for the Armed Forces Vocational Aptitude Battery and the *Scholastic Aptitude Test*. First translate these items into ordinary spoken language style. Compare your spoken language version with the formal test version of the question and note the kinds of differences between the two types of language use. What differences may be attributable to the conventional distinction between spoken and written language and what usage patterns seem peculiar to the way language is used in test questions?

1   When measuring an unknown voltage with a voltmeter, the proper precaution to take is to start with the . . .

2   When a certain pitcher contains three cups of water, the pitcher con-
    tains half its capacity.
3   It can be inferred from the passage that all of the following are charac-
    teristic of the author's grandmother EXCEPT . . .
4   Unlike a patient with Wernicke's aphasia, a patient with Broca's aphasia
    can do which of the following?

In some cases, the language register of testing may even use sentence structures that are "ungrammatical" in ordinary conversation. For example, the specialized use of verb + -ing forms in a frame such as "*Show me digging!*" (from
the *Peabody Picture Vocabulary Test*) is not a grammatical sentence in spoken
or written standard English. In its grammatical form, this construction would
have to be formed something like "*Show me [a picture of] somebody [who is]
digging!*" Examples of unique formats for asking questions accumulate fairly
rapidly when actual language usage in formal testing instruments is examined.

Along with the specialized registers of language used in testing, it is important to understand that many tests rely upon particular METALINGUISTIC TASKS,
that is, special ways of organizing and talking about language apart from its
ordinary uses for communication. These peculiar ways of using and referring
to language may be critical to obtaining the relevant data for measurement.
For example, it may be necessary for test takers to complete metalinguistic
tasks involving word replaceability and opposition (i.e. selecting the correct
antonym) in order to access their knowledge of word knowledge. There is
certainly ample indication that all individuals can give approximate definitions
or uses of words, but this does not necessarily involve word replaceability or
opposition. In natural language use, words are more likely to be defined through
examples in which the words are used appropriately. In addition, notions such
as synonymy (sameness) and antonymy (opposition) may be interpreted in
several different ways in natural language use even though they are considered
to have only one "correct" interpretation in the testing situation. Thus, antonymy
may legitimately be interpreted as "very different from" rather than "in direct
opposition to," so that *tall* and *far* might be considered opposites just as readily
as *tall* and *short*.

In a similar way, the special use of rhyming or minimal word pairs (i.e.
where the words sound alike except for one sound difference, such as *pit* and
pet) to tap a person's ability to decode letters in reading or spelling involves
skills that have little or nothing to do with decoding *per se*. Yet, it is common
for reading and spelling tests in the early grades to use such tasks to measure
decoding capability, as in "Find the word that rhymes with *sad*" or "Find the
word that sounds the same as *too*." Minimal word pairs and rhymes, of course,
may be different across dialects. We have already seen that *pin* and *pen* are
homophonous rather than a minimal word pair in Southern dialects; *fine* and

mind rhyme in some dialects; and in the native Philadelphia dialect of the first author, *bad* rhymes with *mad*, but not with *sad*. The particular metalinguistic tasks used to determine decoding capability may turn out to be just as significant, and, in some cases, a more significant stumbling block in testing than transparent structural dialect differences, although the effects of the former may be more subtle and indirect than the effects of the latter.

10.3.2   The testing situation

Although the consideration of broad-based social situations might seem somewhat removed from the discussion of dialect structures in testing, we must remember that dialects are ultimately embedded in sociocultural differences. Tests do not take place in a contextually neutral social setting, although many tests implicitly make this assumption, or at least assume that it is possible to control the social situation so tightly that unwanted background factors do not influence performance in a significant way.

Testing calls for the test taker to enter the experimental frame created by the test constructor and administrator. If the test taker is unable or unwilling to "play the experimental game," the measurements resulting from the test cannot be valid. Test takers bring with them values and assumptions about language use, and different cultural orientations yield differences in language use in the test situation. For example, language usage may be guided by the status relationship between the test administrator and test taker. One ethnographic study of a rural African American Southern community concludes that "experience in interacting with adults has taught him [i.e. the child] the values of silence and withdrawal" (Ward 1971:88), values commonly expressed in the working-class dictum that "children should be seen and not heard." This cultural orientation toward language interaction with adults may influence how a child responds to an adult administrator; it may also determine a child's willingness to ask questions about directions when confused. Culturally determined responses and interactional patterns may ultimately end up affecting test scores, although such influences are considerably more difficult to pin down specifically than are structural dialect differences. Regardless of the pervasive influence of culturally determined language-use patterns, the experimental frame of testing may assume, and indeed demand, that participants divorce themselves from cultural orientations about status relationships, interactional norms, and the role of language use just for the sake of the test.

Labov (1976) has pointed out that some of the most innocuous-appearing procedures for eliciting data (for example, eliciting spontaneous conversation) may be fraught with sociolinguistic values. For example, a friendly invitation by an adult to a child to "tell me everything you can about the fire engine on the table" is laden with values about verbosity (the more you tell the better), obvious information (describe the object even though you know the adult knows all about it), and consequences about information sharing (what a child tells the adult will not be held against the child). Values about language use, however, are particularly difficult to change merely for the purpose of entering an experimental frame. For example, Heath (1983) reports that "labeling" obvious information, objects, and activities (e.g. responding to questions such as "What is this?" or "What are they doing?" when the questioner already knows the answer) is a sociolinguistic routine quite common in some communities but not in others. Thus, speakers from different communities might relate to this common "teacher routine" sometimes used in informal language assessment procedures in quite different ways.

Exercise 4

Following are some hints for taking a test, found in a US Department of Labor guide on tests. Examine these hints in terms of the social situation surrounding the testing environment. What kinds of social factors might affect the outcome of the test? What do these factors have to do with the capability being tapped in a test? Do any of the hints deal with underlying assumptions about language?

1   Get ready for the test by taking other tests on your own.
2   Don't let the thought of taking a test throw you, but being a little nervous won't hurt you.
3   Arrive early, rested, and prepared to take the test.
4   Ask questions until you understand what you are supposed to do.
5   Some parts of the test may be easier than others. Don't let the hard parts keep you from doing well on the easier parts.
6   Keep time limits in mind when you take a test.
7   Don't be afraid to answer when you aren't sure you are right, but don't guess wildly.
8   Work as fast as you can but try not to make mistakes. Some tests have short time limits.

10.3.3   Resolving the assessment dilemma

Given the potential bias that many assessment instruments have for non-mainstream groups, it is not surprising that a number of alternatives have been offered for reducing sociolinguistic bias in testing. Fay Vaughn-Cooke (1983) has identified seven alternative proposals for resolving the dilemma of test bias for nonmainstream dialect groups.

1 Standardize existing tests on non-mainstream English speakers.
2 Include a small percentage of minorities in the standardization sample when developing a test.
3 Modify or revise existing tests in ways that will make them appropriate for non-mainstream speakers.
4 Utilize a language sample when assessing the language of non-mainstream speakers.
5 Utilize criterion-referenced measures when assessing the language of non-mainstream speakers.
6 Refrain from using all standardized tests that have not been corrected for test bias when assessing the language of non-mainstream speakers.
7 Develop a new test which can provide a more appropriate assessment of the language of non-mainstream English speakers. (Vaughn-Cooke 1983:29)

Although some research has been undertaken on each of the alternatives, the development of unbiased instruments, according to Vaughn-Cooke (1983:33), still "reveals a rather dismal picture." This conclusion seems especially warranted when the overall sociolinguistic context of assessment is considered. A strategy of assessment which gives vernacular dialect speakers credit for acquiring a vernacular dialect form in a formal test of language development may neutralize one type of dialect discrimination, but it does not resolve the issue of how information on language development is most equitably tapped for speakers representing a wide range of cultural and sociolinguistic backgrounds. By the same token, the use of non-traditional procedures to obtain language data may improve the possibility of obtaining valid data, but this alternative does not meet the criteria necessary for the standardization process. Meanwhile, formal testing continues to flourish in American society, and there is little realistic hope of systematically dismantling the testing bureaucracy in the name of sociolinguistic equality. Even if the cry of those calling for a testing moratorium were heeded, it would not eliminate the need for accurate knowledge about language development and capability for different groups of speakers.

After a couple of decades of confronting testing from a sociolinguistic perspective, it has become clear that there is no "quick fix" solution. The best we can offer are some realistic ways of coping with the need for adequate assessment in a context which is heavily biased in favor of middle-class, standard English-speaking groups.

10.3.4 The language diagnostician

Specialists such as speech and language pathologists and English/language arts teachers often have little alternative but to assess the language capabilities of their clients or students. How can these professionals arrive at an authentic picture of the language of those who do not come from standard English-speaking communities? The answer to this question involves acquiring a knowledge base founded in descriptive sociolinguistics and applying this information to a language diagnostic in a practical way. As a starting point, such professionals must *know the descriptive linguistic characteristics of the local communities they serve.* A language specialist in Southern rural Appalachia must know the linguistic structures characterizing this community, just as a language specialist in a Northern African American urban context should know the dialect characteristics of this community. While descriptive sociolinguistic profiles of different communities are certainly not complete, there are now a number of dialect overviews available to specialists. In most cases, however, these general descriptions still need to be supplemented by active observation of the sociolinguistic particulars of local communities. The serious language diagnostician really needs to become an observer of community language behavior as well as a reader of available sociolinguistic profiles.

In cases where the selection of formal test instruments is outside the diagnostician's control, there is a critical need to bring sociolinguistic information to bear on subjects' responses. More than once, specialists have bemoaned the fact that they thought a particular language assessment test was unfair to vernacular dialect speakers but that they had no choice but to administer it. In these situations, it is necessary to be able to identify those particular linguistic responses that might be attributable to dialect differences and how these responses might affect the score. Of course, this kind of analysis can only be conducted when item-by-item responses are made available to the language specialist.

Where possible, language specialists should also *experiment with the administration of required standardized tests in a non-traditional, or nonstandardized manner.* A test can be given in standardized format first, then given in a way which might provide the client or student an opportunity to perform at a maximal level. Instructions can be reworded, additional time for responding can be given, and additional props can be used, among other nonstandard administration options. Where possible, it is also important to *ask test takers why particular responses were chosen.* Practitioners who do this may find the explanations quite insightful, often revealing different kinds of sociolinguistic processing. Some "wrong" answers turn out to be quite reasonable when the test taker explains how the answer was obtained.

When tests are given in a nonstandardized manner, this must be reported for the record, so that both a standard and alternative score are included in any report of the test, along with an explanation of how the scores were obtained. Such reports may provide important information on how different sociolinguistic tasks are interfering with the valid interpretation of test results.

In reality, it is not possible to obtain an accurate picture of language capability on the basis of formalized assessment instruments, since so many of these tests measure limited, superficial aspects of language ability. *Formal measures of language ability must be complemented with assessment strategies more focused on underlying language capabilities in realistic communicative contexts.* In some professions, such as speech and language pathology, there is increasing emphasis on the use of a language sample in assessment. As defined in this discipline, a LANGUAGE SAMPLE consists of data on language collected through natural conversational interviews instead of a technique in which language items are directly elicited. Such interviews are typically conducted by the diagnostician, but there is no reason why they cannot be conducted just as effectively by community members of some type (e.g. parents, peers, or other appropriate members of the community). Using language data from such interviews, those who devise and administer tests should be able to move away from more superficial aspects of language form toward a focus on underlying aspects of the communicative message. As mentioned previously, such an approach is less likely to penalize the vernacular dialect speaker, since the vast majority of structural dialect differences involve the relatively superficial levels of grammar and phonology. In their extensive study of children acquiring African American Vernacular English, Ida Stockman and Fay Vaughn-Cooke (1986) found very few differences from standard English speakers when the focus is upon underlying semantic content categories and relationships rather than surface grammatical form. For example, whereas the possessive meaning may not be indicated by a surface morpheme (i.e. -'s) in vernacular constructions such as *woman_ dress* ('woman's dress') or *Terry_ hat* ('Terry's hat'), the collocation of nouns certainly indicates the underlying category of "possession" quite adequately. This model neutralizes the effect of dialect in the assessment of language capability. It also provides a baseline for distinguishing those normally developing African American Vernacular English speakers from the small percentage of speakers who are genuinely disordered in their language development in terms of community language norms.

Finally, *it is essential to complement the assessment of language capabilities with ethnographic information about language use in a natural setting.* How is language used in a natural setting with peers, family members, and other community participants? To some extent, such information may be obtained by questioning relevant community participants. Since it is the community which sets norms, the community's perspective on speech may be critical for obtaining a true profile of language capability. But more than simple questioning of community members is involved if a true picture of language is to emerge. There is a sense in which the diagnostician must become an active observer of how language is used in its social settings – in the playground, on the bus, and in the classroom with teachers and other students. How does the student use language to communicate and interact socially? Whereas an ethnographic perspective may take a language diagnostician considerably beyond the clinic or classroom setting, it is imperative to extend the context of language observation if an accurate picture of language is to emerge. The insight from such an ethnographic perspective may not be as readily quantifiable as data obtained from standardized formal instruments, but it is invaluable for a true picture of language capability.

10.4 Teaching Standard English

Few people would deny that there are some social and educational advantages in knowing standard English. Nonetheless, there are several different dimensions that make the topic of spoken standard English controversial, and in some respects, also make it an elusive educational issue. One major issue involves the practical definition of standard English. What precisely is standard English in a given community context, and who speaks it? Another area of concern is the status of vernacular dialects in relation to the standard variety. What happens to vernacular dialects when they confront the standard variety in different settings? Can a delicate balance between the "appropriate" uses of a vernacular and standard dialect be achieved? Finally, there is the matter of methodology in teaching standard English. Can standard English really be taught effectively in an educational setting? Where and how is the standard variety best learned? Given the nature of the issues surrounding standard English, it is not surprising that discussions of this topic can become quite heated. Unfortunately, these popular discussions are often filled with sociolinguistic misconceptions about the nature and significance of dialect differences. In the discussion to follow, we examine the major issues involved in teaching and learning spoken standard English and set forth the sociolinguistic context surrounding these issues.

10.4.1   What standard?

We already noted in chapter 1 that the notion of standard English operates on both a formal and informal level. The formal standard is codified, prescriptive, and relatively homogeneous, whereas the informal standard is more subjective, somewhat flexible, and tends to exist on a continuum. Obviously, the formal standard is easier to define than the informal one, since we can simply appeal to established sources such as usage guides and established authorities on the English language for specific guidance. Even though there is no single central authority for the formal standard variety, there are not that many items over which there are persistent quibbles regarding standard conventions. The sphere of usage for the formal standard, however, is relatively restricted, largely confined to writing and specialized public presentations. On the other hand, the informal standard is more widely applicable, and relevant to the vast majority of everyday language interactions. Furthermore, it is the informal standard, rather than the formal one, that most consistently governs people's everyday evaluation of the social significance of dialect differences.

Given the real-world heterogeneity of the spoken standard, we may ask if there is any way we can unify this notion, at least for instructional purposes. In an effort to unify the notion of spoken standard English, the British linguist Peter Strevens, in the article "Standards and the standard language" (1985), separates ACCENT, which refers to features of phonology, from other levels of dialect. He notes that accent is highly localized and variant, whereas other components of a language, particularly grammar, are less localized and less variant in terms of social norms of standardness. Once accent is eliminated from the definition of the standard language, he maintains that there is one standard which may be paired with any local accent. According to this definition, standard English has no local base, and is the "only dialect which is neither localized in its currency nor paired solely with its local accent" (Strevens 1985:6).

There is certainly some merit to the separation of phonology from other aspects of dialect when talking about standard English, but Strevens's proposal oversimplifies the issues. For one, there are aspects of pronunciation alone which may mark a person as a vernacular speaker, such as the frequent use of *d* for voiced *th*, the stereotypical *dese*, *dem*, and *dose* pattern, and the use of *t* for voiceless *th*, as in *trow* for *throw* or *tink* for *think*. In fact, we have cases where speakers are classified as nonstandard on the basis of phonology alone. By the same token, one locale's normative grammar may sometimes be considered nonstandard in another context. Thus, the use of double modals, as in *You might could do it*, is fairly widespread among native residents of North Carolina regardless of social class, yet it is considered quite nonstandard in non-Southern contexts. So we see that phonology is not always excluded from the definition of the spoken standard, nor is grammar always generally applicable in judging standards across different regions. On the whole, however, grammar is less flexible than phonology across regional standard varieties, but it is a matter of degree rather than kind.

A couple of terms often used in reference to spoken standard English in the United States are STANDARD AMERICAN ENGLISH (SAE) and NETWORK STANDARD. The designation SAE is often used to distinguish this variety from other Englishes used throughout the world, such as Standard British English (so-called Received Pronunciation, or RP), Australian English, and so forth. It is the variety which is aimed at when teaching American English to speakers of other languages and is the model most often used as the basis for teaching standard forms to vernacular speakers. The Network Standard simply seems to be a concrete example of SAE; it is the model aimed for by TV and radio announcers whose audiences are national in scope, in much the same way that BBC English is an instantiation of RP pronunciation in the British Isles.

What exactly do people mean when they refer to SAE and Network Standard? Although these notions are difficult to pin down precisely, they typically refer to a variety of English devoid of both general and local socially stigmatized features, as well as regionally obtrusive phonological and grammatical features. This, however, does not eliminate dialect choices altogether. We have repeatedly noted that it is impossible to speak English without speaking some dialect of English. In those cases where dialect choices have to be made, the guiding principle calls for the selection of a form that will be least likely to call attention to itself for the majority of speakers outside of the area because of its dialect uniqueness. Items that have distinct regional connotations are therefore to be avoided in striving for SAE. Of course, the determination of what features are least likely to call dialect attention to themselves is somewhat subjective and tends to be a relative rather than absolute matter.

For example, speakers attempting to achieve the SAE pronunciation of the vowel in items like *caught* and *fought* would typically avoid a raised vowel quality (something closer to the [ʊ] of *put*) or a lowered quality (something like the [a] of *father*), since these are likely to be dialectally marked. Interestingly, in actual network announcing, the latter pronunciation is apparently becoming more acceptable, as the "low vowel merger" of *caught* and *cot* spreads among American dialects. Whatever the case, the choice of the pronunciation is hardly "dialect-free." However, given the alternative pronunciations, the [ɔ] pronunciation is the least likely to call attention to regionality; hence, it is most dialectally "unmarked." In this framework, some entire dialect areas will be considered more marked than others, so that entire regions (e.g. Southern, New England) may be singled out as dialects to be avoided in striving for the SAE ideal.

The attempt to "deregionalize" speech in SAE or Network Standard is, of course, easier said than done, and most speakers considered representatives of SAE still retain vestiges of their regional dialect. A comparison of nightly news programs will reveal that some network announcers are better than others at disguising their native regional dialect heritage; however, discerning dialectologists can usually still identify regional traces in pronunciation and lexical choice. In many cases, those who aspire to acquire this ideal standard have worked very hard to eliminate the most regionally obtrusive features. Manuals of instruction and so-called "accent reduction" training are available to help attain this goal, but in most instances, success in the SAE ideal is not complete.

Contrary to popular opinion, SAE is fairly limited in terms of the occasions and professions that call for its usage; it is also quite restricted in terms of who routinely uses it. On most speaking occasions, REGIONAL STANDARD ENGLISH is more pertinent than SAE, although the notion of regional standard English certainly receives much less public attention. Regional standard English refers to the variety which is recognized as standard for speakers in a given locale. This variety may contain regional features, particularly in pronunciation and vocabulary, but also some features of grammar and language use. At the same time, this standard differs from the regional vernacular in that it avoids both general and local socially stigmatized features of English. Most typically, it is associated with middle-class, educated native speakers of the region. In the local context, these speakers would be rated as standard English speakers by community members from different social strata within the community.

In a Southern setting such as Memphis, Tennessee, the regional standard may include a number of Southern regionalisms, such as the lack of contrast between [ɪ] and [ɛ] before nasals in *pin* and *pen*, the monophthongization of /ay/ in *time* or *Hi*, plural *y'all*, personal dative pronouns, as in *I got me a new outfit*, and so forth. The standard Philadelphia, Pennsylvania, variety would not, of course, have any of these features but might include the local "broad *a*" pronunciation (i.e. [ɛ^ɔ] or even [ɪ^ɔ] in items like *bad* and *pass*), the vowel [i] in items such as *att*[i]*tude* vs. *att*[ə]*tude* or *magn*[i]*tude* vs. *magn*[ə]*tude*), positive *anymore* (e.g. *Anymore we watch videos rather than go to the movies*), and pronoun absence in personal *with* phrases (e.g. *Are you coming with?*), among other features. In both locales, the standard dialects would share the avoidance of a general set of socially stigmatized features such as multiple negatives and different irregular verbs (e.g. *They seen it, They brang it to the picnic*), and so forth.

Regional standards are not necessarily transferable, so that the standard dialect for Memphis might not be considered standard in the context of Philadelphia, and vice versa. To a large extent, the acceptance of a regional standard outside of its indigenous locale is tied in with attitudes and stereotypical views of the region by speakers from other regions. The difficulty in transferring regional standards from one area to another has sometimes concerned educators who wish to teach a standard English, and, as mentioned above, there are some privately available instructional programs that are specifically geared towards teaching SAE as a replacement for a regional standard. These programs may work with individuals or with small, select groups, but it is doubtful whether SAE can replace regional standard varieties on a broad scale. One reason for this is that those who strongly influence the perpetuation of language, such as schoolteachers, tend to model their speech on regional standards rather than SAE. We will have more to say about the conflict between regional standards and SAE when we discuss the practical considerations for instructional programs in standard English. At this point, it is sufficient to understand the types of standard English relevant to the discussion of spoken language standards in an educational context.

10.4.2   Approaches to standard English

There are basically three different philosophical positions on the teaching of standard English. One position maintains that standard English should be taught as a REPLACIVE DIALECT, supplanting the dialect of vernacular-speaking students. This position, sometimes referred to as ERADICATIONISM, is the one manifested by educators who "correct" the nonstandard dialect forms of their students. Traditionally, much of the motivation for this position has been based on the conviction that vernacular dialects are simply linguistic corruptions of standard English, following the popular mythology we discussed in chapter 1. A more enlightened sociolinguistic viewpoint, however, still might maintain that the realities of present-day American society confer social stigma on speakers of a vernacular dialect in the mainstream marketplace, so even if a vernacular dialect is linguistically equal, it is not socially equal. Therefore, the vernacular variety should be replaced with the more socially acceptable, mainstream standard English variety.

Another position on teaching standard English maintains that standard English should be taught as an ADDITIVE DIALECT rather than a replacive one. This position is referred to as BIDIALECTALISM, by analogy with bilingualism, in which two separate languages are maintained. An educational curriculum with this goal is geared toward maintaining both standard and vernacular varieties for use in different social situations. For many community contexts, where the vernacular serves essential functions of social solidarity, the vernacular would be available, and for more formal, mainstream marketplace functions, the non-stigmatized standard variety would be available. Like the eradicationist position, the bidialectalism position recognizes the social stigmatization of vernacular dialects, but it rejects the notion that the vernacular dialect is an inferior linguistic system that needs to be replaced. Instead, it advocates the use of two different systems for different purposes within and outside the local community.

A more extreme position rejects the obligation to learn spoken standard English at all, maintaining that both the eradicationist and bidialectalism positions stand too ready to accommodate the dialect prejudices of American society. Rather than focusing on teaching standard English as a replacive or additive dialect, the DIALECT RIGHTS position devotes attention to attacking the underlying ethnocentrism and prejudice that are at the heart of dialect intolerance. In 1974, a subdivision of the nation's largest and most influential organization of English teachers, the National Council of Teachers of English (NCTE), adopted a quite strong position on students' dialect rights, as follows:

> We affirm the students' right to their own patterns and varieties of the language
> – the dialects of their nurture or whatever dialects in which they find their own
> identity and style. Language scholars long ago denied that the myth of a standard
> American dialect has any validity. The claim that any one dialect is unacceptable
> amounts to an attempt of one social group to exert its dominance over another.
> Such a claim leads to false advice for speakers and writers, and immoral advice
> for humans. A nation proud of its diverse heritage and its cultural and racial
> variety will preserve its heritage of dialects. We affirm strongly that teachers

must have the experiences and training that will enable them to respect diversity and uphold the right of the students to their own language. (Committee on College Composition and Communication Language Statement 1974:2–3)

Predictably, such a forceful position statement turned out to be quite controversial. It also proved to be somewhat vague in terms of its implications for teaching standard English. A number of discussions from within and outside NCTE have attacked this position, and subsequent discussion has attempted to modify it and clarify the meaning of critical phrases such as "the rights of students to their own language."

While the dialect rights position may seem overstated and unrealistic to some, it rightly points to the unequal burden placed upon vernacular speakers. The burden of linguistic adjustment is placed squarely upon vernacular speakers, when there should be an equally strong moral responsibility placed upon the mainstream population to alter its prejudices and respect dialect differences for what they are – a natural manifestation of cultural and linguistic diversity.

The dialect rights position may be morally right, but there is another issue to be confronted. Whether we like it or not, some type of language standardization seems inevitable in large diverse societies whose members must communicate with one another no matter what their dialect background. Standard languages exist throughout the world, not just in the United States or other English-speaking areas (see, for example, Fasold 1984). Given the fact that some kind of language standardization is bound to persist in English, as in other languages, the crux of the standard English debate ultimately seems to involve balancing the inevitabilities of dialect diversity and standardization with the sociopolitical realities that confer the status of "nonstandardness" on nonmainstream, vernacular-speaking groups.

10.4.3   Conditions for teaching standard English

The previous discussion ignored a practical but essential factor in the consideration of teaching standard English – the prospects for success. Is it really possible to teach spoken standard English on a broad-based scale? No one denies that there are individual cases in which students from vernacular-speaking backgrounds learn standard English, but there is no indication that this is happening for large groups of speakers in American schools. Furthermore, it may be questioned whether the majority of these individual success stories can be attributed to specific instructional programs. We have to remember that, in one form or another, the educational system has been attempting to impart standard English to its students for a long time, without apparent widescale success.

Why is it that so many students from vernacular-speaking backgrounds seem to resist efforts to teach them standard English? Although this question cannot be answered definitively, a couple of reasons for this resistance can be offered. Probably the most essential explanation is a sociopsychological one. Dialect is an integral component of personal and social identity. Despite the mainstream stigmatization of vernacular dialects, these varieties carry strong positive connotations for individuals and local groups. The acquisition of spoken standard English simply cannot be isolated from its social ramifications, as the acquisition of some other types of academic knowledge may be. There is an important difference between learning a set of facts about math or science, for example, and learning a standard English language structure. When peer influences dictate vernacular dialect use in the formation and projection of group solidarity, the use of standard English may lead to an identity crisis. Notwithstanding that there are different contexts in which standard and vernacular varieties may be appropriate, students are still often called upon to choose symbolically between one or the other, sometimes right in the classroom. For many students, group reference norms simply overrule the mainstream values of the classroom. To use standard English in the context of a roomful of vernacular-speaking peers may be an open invitation to ridicule by other students. In fact, we have collected many personal anecdotes about students being put down by their peers for using the standard variety, even in the context of the classroom.

There is also a dimension of language learning to consider in explaining why standard English forms may be difficult even for motivated students who want to learn the standard variety. When two systems are highly similar, with minor differences, it is sometimes difficult to keep the systems apart. In such cases of widescale overlap, more careful attention to the small differences is required – especially if one language has already been thoroughly habituated. In some ways, it may be easier to work with language systems that are drastically different, since the temptation to merge overlapping structures and ignore relatively minor differences is not as great. Naturally, dialectologists tend to emphasize differences rather than similarities between dialects, but in reality, standard and vernacular dialects show only minor differences, and these differences may be difficult for the learner to sort out.

Once a linguistic structure is entrenched, it is difficult to break out of the pattern without paying focused attention to the details of the pattern. The special attention needed to do this, referred to as MONITORING, is actually somewhat unnatural, given the fact that we do not ordinarily have to think about the structures of language in order to speak a language. In fact, excessive monitoring has its own set of problems. For example, too much monitoring can be disruptive to the normal fluency of relatively unmonitored speech, where we focus on what we are talking about rather than the structures we are using.

The previous discussion is not meant to discourage efforts to teach or acquire standard English, since students should have a right to this variety just as they have a right to their vernacular varieties. As the linguist James Sledd put it:

> Bureaucratic pretenses to the contrary notwithstanding, nobody has in fact opposed, or in any reason could oppose, the teaching of standard English, for the good ends and by good means, to students of any age who want to learn it. The question whether or not it should be taught is thus a spurious one. (Sledd 1976:236)

It may well be that the major issue surrounding standard English instruction is not whether it should be offered but rather how it should be taught – that is, under what conditions and by what means. These conditions should offer students a reasonable chance of succeeding at the same time they remain faithful to fundamental sociolinguistic premises underlying dialect diversity.

As a preliminary consideration, the *teaching of standard English must take into account the group reference factor*. The available evidence on second-language and second-dialect learning suggests a strong dependency upon the sociopsychological factor of group reference for success. Speakers who desire to belong to a particular social group will typically learn the language of that desired group, whereas those with no group reference can be stubbornly resistant to change. Thus, vernacular speakers will best achieve success in learning standard English if their social orientation is geared toward a standard English-speaking group.

The group reference dimension may be the most essential of all the factors affecting the learning of standard English, but it is also the most difficult to program into pedagogical materials. Values pertaining to social group membership and social aspirations are typically not under the control of the educational system, and efforts to motivate students in terms of vague future employment opportunities are often made in vain. Remember that the positive values of the standard dialect in mainstream culture are countered with a competing set of values for the vernacular – values that are often a lot more compelling for an adolescent than the pronouncements made by a classroom teacher. Programs with realistic hopes of success therefore have to mold peer and indigenous community influence into a constructive force endorsing the standard variety. This is, of course, easier said than done, but there may be some situations within the everyday lives of an indigenous peer group in which the use of standard English is advantageous, and these must be highlighted in outlining a rationale for the use of the standard variety.

At the very least, an instructional program in standard English should involve an honest, open discussion of the values of both vernacular and standard varieties of American English and some relevant, concrete scenarios that might underscore the utility of being able to command both types of varieties. The key here is to stress that there may be immediate needs for standard

English as well as the vernacular variety. Such discussions may seem to be mere preliminaries to actual instruction, but students must feel within themselves, and reinforce in one another, that standard English serves some useful purpose in their lives. The reasons for learning standard English must be examined closely from the perspective of the student, and, in some cases, such instruction could even be offered as an optional program for those students who feel a need for it.

Exercise 5

Think of some reasons why a junior high school student might want to know standard English apart from reasons given by traditional educators. Try to put yourself in the place of a junior high school student who is not really thinking about future educational success and distant employment opportunity. What might standard English do for students right now, in terms of people they interact with? Looking at it from such a vantage point, what do you conclude about the utility of standard English at this point in the students' lives?

Once a program in standard English is adopted, *the goals for teaching standard English should be clearly recognized in the instructional program.* There are obviously quite different goals that might be incorporated into a standard English program, ranging from the ability to use standard English in a restricted real-world context (e.g. service encounters) to the ability to use both standard and vernacular English in a full set of conversational encounters. The goals of a particular program should be transparent in the materials, and the pedagogical strategies should be consistent with these goals. Thus, if the stated goal of a program is functional bidialectalism in which both the standard and vernacular are maintained to serve different social purposes, then the materials should integrate this perspective pedagogically in a meaningful way. The program should incorporate some language scenarios which start with the vernacular and move to the standard variety and others that start with the standard and move to the vernacular. In this regard, it is interesting to note that many current instructional programs articulate the goal of bidialectalism as an educational objective but never support the notion with truly bidialectal instructional materials. Just as there are social contexts in which standard English may be more appropriate, there are contexts in which vernacular dialects serve essential social functions, and the existence of these differential social contexts must be squarely faced and made evident in the materials if they are to capture the real-life significance of dialects in students' lives. How a focus on true bidialectalism is to be manifested is a matter for the creative instructor, who may choose to have students engage in role-playing or in real-life activities that reveal the value of dialectal diversity. The bottom line consideration, however, is a program in which underlying educational goals and pedagogical strategies are in harmony.

Another principle that must be considered in teaching standard English is *the need to couple information about the nature of dialect diversity in American society with pedagogical instruction in standard English*. Given the level of misinformation and dialect prejudice existing in our society, there is a strong need to incorporate basic sociolinguistic information into instructional materials. This information should include some basic notions of the nature of dialect diversity, as well as an introduction to the sociolinguistic conditions that lead to the development of dialects. Students should know that the reason they are learning standard English is not related to the inherent inadequacy of their linguistic system or their presumed failure to learn "the English language." In all fairness, they have a right to understand that all dialects, including their own vernacular dialect, are systematic and patterned, and that the dialects of English differ from each other in systematic ways. Students can never gain genuine linguistic self-respect unless they realize the sociopolitical basis of dialect inequality rather than simply assuming that the basis for dialect differences lies in some inherent linguistic deficiency.

An understanding of basic sociolinguistic principles related to dialect differences can do several things for a student. First, it can provide a proper perspective on dialect diversity to counteract the popular misconceptions that presently abound. Instructors are just as fully obligated to present factual information about languages and dialects as they are to provide students with accurate information about such subjects as chemistry and biology in the face of some erroneous myths surrounding these subject areas.

A second reason for incorporating information about the nature of dialect diversity into standard English instruction is related to its high interest level. Learning about dialect differences piques a natural curiosity about cultural differences. Presented properly, language variety is a fascinating subject in its own right. Whether or not students choose to learn standard English, they deserve the opportunity to learn about English dialects as a part of general education. It is not a frivolous or tangential study, but one which presents a unique laboratory for scientific inquiry as well as social science and humanities study. We will discuss the scientific rationale for studying dialects in more detail in chapter 11.

Third, there is now some indication that students who feel more positive and confident about their vernacular dialect are more successful in learning the standard one. So there is also a pedagogical reason for presenting to students an accurate perspective on their own dialect.

Another consideration in teaching standard English is the *focus on systematic differences between standard and non-standard English forms*. Teaching standard

English is not identical to teaching a foreign language, where a speaker starts with no knowledge of the language. We have already noted that the similarities between the dialects of English far outnumber the differences, and this fact cannot be ignored in instructional materials on standard English. Given the similarities and differences between standard and vernacular forms, it seems reasonable to organize materials in such a way as to highlight this systematic relationship between standard and nonstandard forms. Students do not need to learn the "English language"; they need to learn some standard English correspondences for particular socially stigmatized forms. Materials should take into consideration the systematic differences between standard and nonstandard correspondences, including the nature of the differences, the relative social significance of the differences, and even how frequently particular stigmatized forms might be expected to occur. In other words, the program should take advantage of current sociolinguistic descriptions of vernacular dialects. This contrastive base should underlie all programs for teaching standard English regardless of the type of instructional method used.

Although dialectologists tend to focus on the structural linguistic differences between standard and vernacular varieties, the teaching of standard English cannot be limited to grammatical and phonological structures. *Conventions for language use also enter into the consideration of standard English*, and this dimension must be incorporated into an effective program of instruction in standard English. In fact, many of the concerns about language expressed by those in the workplace turn out to be focused on *how* language is used rather than on *what* particular nonstandard structures are used. How people answer the telephone or engage in service encounters in the workplace is a vital concern to employers, and such matters often become central issues in cross-cultural and cross-regional interactions. Regional and social differences in conventions for communicative encounters tend to bear greater responsibility for interpersonal conflict than linguistic structures *per se*, so that discussions of these conventions have to be included in standard English instruction along with more narrowly defined linguistic structures. Conventional language routines such as greetings, leave-taking, turn-taking, and so forth, as well as particular speech acts such as denial, refusal, and so forth, have to be considered as important components of programs which teach standard English. To underscore the significance of these conventions in the workplace, we often ask educators and employers which is preferable, a person who responds to an inquiry about a boss's whereabouts by saying, "She's not here. What do you want?" or a person who replies with, "I'm sorry, she not in now. She be back this afternoon." In practically every case, people prefer a person who comes across as "polite but vernacular" to one who uses standard English forms without adopting the appropriate conventions for carrying out various mainstream language functions. A program for teaching standard English probably cannot be very successful without considering the broader conventions of language use and behavior. Such a program may move closer to a prescription for "appropriate" appearance than some sociolinguists feel comfortable with, but in order to fully understand the overall context in which standard English forms exist, one cannot naively disregard the full set of behavioral complements that go along with language form, including norms for carrying out various communicative functions.

Exercise 6

Suppose you were asked to design a standard English program specifically for receptionists whose primary responsibility is to answer the telephone and take messages. What particular functionally based routines and specialized language-use conventions have to be included in this program? Are there any particular structural features that you might anticipate occurring fairly regularly in such a situation? In order to answer these questions, you will have to envision the kinds of interactions that ordinarily occur in this interactional situation. Better yet, try observing some actual telephone conversations between receptionists and clients in order to accumulate real data.

In determining standard English norms, it is important to point out that *the standard variety taught in an instructional program should be realistic in terms of the language norms of the community*. We have pointed out repeatedly that the definition of spoken standard English is a flexible one, sensitive to regional variation, stylistic range, and other social variables. The notion of general Standard American English is not going to prove very useful to a classroom of students who speak Delta Southern or Eastern New England dialects in varying degrees of vernacularity, particularly if this class is likely to be instructed by a teacher who speaks a standard version of the local regional variety. It seems ludicrous for an instructor in the South to attempt to get schoolchildren to make the distinction between [ɪ] and [ɛ] in *pin* and *pen* if the instructor, a standard Southern dialect speaker, does not maintain the distinction. Similarly, we have witnessed a New England speaker pontificating about the need to "put in your *r*'s" while pronouncing "*r*'s" without the postvocalic *r* (saying [az] for *r*'s). Apart from the difficulty instructors may have in teaching students to use dialect features they do not use themselves in their regional standard, it seems futile to attempt to rid vernacular speakers of local standards on a widescale basis. There is very little realistic hope of success for a program in Charleston, South Carolina, which sets out to make standard English speakers sound like they come from Ohio. And the few speakers who might successfully complete such a program would obviously run the risk of coming across as pretentious and "phony" in their native region.

The admission of local standard norms in a program of instruction does not necessarily rule out generally applicable materials, since there are many aspects of social differentiation in grammar that cut across regional varieties. A focus on local norms, however, implies that the vernacular items selected for replacement by standard features should represent the broadest-based socially stigmatized items possible. At the same time, the instructional program should allow for regional flexibility. This flexibility will naturally be greatest with respect to pronunciation, but it may also apply to some dimensions of grammar, vocabulary, and language use as well.

Finally, materials in standard English instruction *should take into account our current understanding of how a second dialect is acquired.* At this point, there is considerable debate about how a second dialect is acquired, as well as the extent to which an alternate dialect can actually be mastered once the native dialect has been acquired. Our knowledge about acquiring a second language is much more advanced than our knowledge of second-dialect acquisition, so that we might turn to studies of second-language acquisition for models. In doing so, however, we must keep in mind the clear-cut differences that exist between second-language and second-dialect acquisition. Programs for teaching a standard dialect have been heavily influenced by second-language instructional models and methods in recent decades, but most standard English materials have not kept up to date with the rapid development of second-language acquisition models in very recent years. For example, many current standard English programs rely heavily on contrastive drills – that is, drills which highlight the sometimes subtle differences between standard and vernacular varieties. One such drill is a discrimination drill in which a standard structure is contrasted with a nonstandard one so that students can clearly detect the difference between the standard and nonstandard variant. Sentence pairs are given, and subjects are asked simply to identify the sentences as the same or different. A typical drill for -*s* third person would look something like the following:

Stimulus pair	Student response
She works hard. She work hard.	different
She play after school. She play after school.	same
She comes home late. She comes home late.	same

For a motivated student, this kind of drill certainly raises the level of consciousness about the structural differences between standard and nonstandard variants. There are, however, some practical and theoretical concerns that have to be raised about these kinds of drills. On a practical level, they can be very boring and students lose interest rapidly unless they are highly motivated to begin with. Certainly, the level of self-motivation this kind of activity must assume precludes its usage in a regular classroom situation. Even when complemented with higher-interest activities, the routine of the drills can become monotonous in a hurry. In most cases, then, the practical limitations of these drills are quite severe.

Research in second-language acquisition also indicates that contrastive drills are not necessarily a very effective language-learning strategy. In this regard, an important distinction is made between language acquisition and language learning (Krashen 1982; Krashen, Scarcella, and Long 1982). LANGUAGE ACQUISITION involves tacit or implicit knowledge of language rules and tends to come forth automatically, whereas LANGUAGE LEARNING involves the explicit knowledge of rules, which tends to come forth under certain conditions associated with increased awareness or monitoring of speech. Acquisition, rather than learning, leads to fluency in a second language, and too much explicit learning of language rules can, in fact, interfere with second-language fluency, as a speaker may tend to "overmonitor" speech. The difference between language learning and language acquisition seems to have important implications for second-dialect acquisition. Contrastive drills tend to rely upon explicit learning rather than the tacit rule knowledge characteristic of acquisition. The drill approach may serve a person adequately when speech is being heavily monitored, as in language testing or deliberative writing, but it may break down in less monitored, more natural situations. Thus, a heavy dose of more naturalistic uses of language which incorporates standard English forms might prove to be more effective in the acquisition of standard English than reliance upon the kind of explicit learning that takes place in structural drills. Of course, we cannot assume that acquiring a second dialect is identical to acquiring a second language, and it may well be that the overwhelming similarities of two dialect systems leave little alternative but to focus on the finer points of differentiation that are targeted through these kinds of drills.

Unfortunately, we do not have exhaustive research data on the ideal conditions under which a standard variety is acquired as a second dialect. Case studies of native vernacular speakers who have acquired a standard variety, however, underscore the motivational factor rather than pedagogical technique, and the set of strategies which have been shown to lead to successful acquisition range from "immersion" in a standard English-speaking context, mimicry of personal and impersonal standard English models, explicit drill techniques, and even traditional prescriptive "correction."

We also do not have solid research data on the optimal age for learning another dialect. Some programs, taking a cue from the apparent naturalness of second-language acquisition during the pre-adolescent period, feel that standard English instruction should focus on children in their early years of schooling. Certainly, there is evidence that native-like control of a language, particularly with respect to phonology, is realistically achieved only prior to the "critical period" of development, the pre-pubescent period. The study of second-dialect acquisition (Payne 1980) also shows a similar cut-off period for dialect shift, although some adjustment apparently takes place after this period. At the same time, there is evidence that standard English grammar certainly can be acquired after this period, and selective changes in socially stigmatized phonological features can also take place. Thus, the CRITICAL AGE HYPOTHESIS, which maintains that true language mastery can only take place during the pre-pubescent age period, is not nearly as relevant for the acquisition of standard English as the acquisition of another language or even another regional variety of English.

A strong argument against teaching standard English in the earliest years of a child's education comes from the sociopsychological considerations examined in this chapter. Children may learn some standard English forms when presented with them in primary education, but will these forms persist in the face of strong peer pressure as these children move into adolescence? There is a good chance that the speech of a student's peers will pre-empt other considerations in the formative adolescent years of dialect development, regardless of what took place in school prior to this time.

Due to the significance of the sociopsychological factors involved in dialect acquisition, some sociolinguists feel that success in teaching spoken standard English will only come if and when a person realizes the utility of this dialect on a very personal level. In most cases, this heightened personal awareness of the uses of standard English in the broader marketplace does not take place until early adulthood. After years of investigating students' progress in informal and formal programs to teach spoken standard English, there is still no evidence that this variety can really be imposed against a student's will. However, where there's a will, there are probably a number of different ways to attain this dialect goal. Thus, the role of instructional programs in the acquisition of standard English seems to be to facilitate the process for motivated students by providing systematic and relevant opportunities to move toward the desired standard English goal. This observation is not meant to denigrate the many well-intended programs that currently exist, but simply to place them in their proper sociolinguistic perspective. A guaranteed pedagogical strategy has not yet emerged in teaching standard English. We would, however, expect a reasonable instructional approach to be consistent with the fundamental sociolinguistic premises we have discussed at various points in this book.

10.5   Further Reading

Fasold, Ralph (1990) *The Sociolinguistics of Language.* Oxford: Blackwell. The final chapter of this book, "Some applications of the sociolinguistics of language," covers a number of educational implications that result from the consideration of language variation. The approach to the application of sociolinguistic knowledge is quite similar to that found in this treatment.

Labov, William (1976) Systematically misleading data from test questions. *Urban Review* 9:146–69. In this article on the general question of language assessment and cultural and linguistic divergence, Labov examines the broad sociolinguistic context of interviewing and the interpretation of test data.

Milroy, James, and Lesley Milroy (1985) *Authority in Language: Investigating Language Prescription and Standardisation*. London: Routledge and Kegan Paul. This book offers historical and contemporary commentary on the problem of prescription and "correctness" in English. The presentation shows how the notion of standard language has affected a wide range of practical matters in society.

Terrell, Sandra L. (ed.) (1983) *Nonbiased Assessment of Language Differences: Topics in Language Disorders*, No. 3. Rockville: Aspen. This special issue of the periodical *Language Disorders* is devoted to the question of assessing the language capabilities of linguistically diverse populations in a non-biased manner. The articles are of most immediate concern to speech and language pathologists involved in assessing vernacular dialect speakers, but also have broader application.

Vaughn-Cooke, Anna Fay (1983) Improving language assessment in minority children. *Asha* 25:29–34. Vaughn-Cooke discusses the strategies that have been offered in an effort to neutralize the traditional bias of standardized testing instruments toward vernacular-speaking children. It is an insightful, concise overview.

Wolfram, Walt, Donna Christian, and Carolyn Adger (1998) *Dialects in Schools and Communities*. Mahwah: Lawrence Erlbaum. This work directly deals with the most common educational concerns about dialects and standards, including dialect and writing, dialect and reading, and dialect and classroom behavior. It is intended primarily for practitioners who confront the practical manifestations of dialect divergence in an educational context.

11

Dialect Awareness in the School and Community

In this final chapter, we continue our examination of the role of dialect differences in the school and community. We have already discussed the possible effect of dialect diversity on testing and the issue of teaching standard English. We now turn to the effect of dialect on basic educational skills such as reading and writing. How might dialect differences influence the fundamental process of learning to read? Is there a legitimate role for dialects in general education? How about informal education regarding dialect in the context of the broader community? We begin our discussion by considering the role of dialect in language arts education and conclude by considering how dialect researchers may work collaboratively with local communities in establishing dialect awareness programs. We use the term DIALECT AWARENESS PROGRAMS here to refer to activities that are intended to promote an understanding of and appreciation for language variation. Following the principle of linguistic gratuity introduced in chapter 10, we maintain that these programs should be collaborative and proactive, as linguists work with community members and educators to foster an appreciation for the role of dialect in community life.

11.1 Dialects and Reading

Certainly there are many factors that correlate with reading achievement, ranging from students' nutritional problems to the number of books in the home of the student. Among these potential factors is the spoken dialect of the reader. Given the correlation between vernacular speech and reading failure, it is important to understand how language variation affects the reading process so we can determine whether or not dialect in its own right may cause reading difficulties.

One process in reading which may be affected by dialect is DECODING. By decoding, we mean the process whereby written symbols are related to the sounds of language. In English, of course, this process refers to the ways in which the letters of the spelling system, or orthography, systematically relate to the English sound system, along with ways in which syntax and morphology are represented in writing. Whereas different approaches to reading rely on decoding skills to varying degrees, and some approaches de-emphasize a basic decoding model of reading, reliance to some extent on the systematic "sounding out of letters" referred to as the PHONICS APPROACH has been utilized for over half a century now. As students proceed in the acquisition of reading skills, the significance of decoding may diminish drastically, but it is still a rudimentary skill that plays a significant role in the beginning stages of many reading programs.

A reading teacher engaged in decoding tasks with students must recognize that there are systematic differences in the symbol–sound relationships from dialect to dialect. For example, consider how a speaker of a vernacular dialect might decode the passage "There won't be anything to do until he finds out if he can go without taking John's brother." A modified orthography is used here to indicate the pronunciation differences for the vernacular speaker.

An example of vernacular dialect decoding
Deuh won't be anything to do until he fi*n*' out if he can go wi*f*out taki*n*' John— bro*vuh*.

We see that decoding differences affect a number of symbol–sound relationships in the example, such as the final consonant of *find*, the *th* of *without*, the *th* and final *r* of *brother*, and so forth. These differences are no greater than variant regional decodings of the vowel *au* of *caught* (e.g. [ɔ] or [a]) or the *s* of *greasy* (e.g. [s] or [z]), except that they involve a couple of socially disfavored variants. The variant decoding becomes a problem only if an instructor does not recognize dialectally appropriate sound–symbol relationships and classifies these differences as errors in decoding. Imagine the confusion that might be created for a dialect speaker if an accurate dialect decoding such as the pronunciation of the *th* as [f] or as [v] in *without* and *brother*, respectively, is treated as a problem analogous to the miscoding of *b* as [d] or *sh* as [s]. The potential impact of dialects on the decoding process can be minimized if reading instructors are able to separate dialect-appropriate renderings of sound–symbol relationships from genuine miscodings of sound–symbol relationships such as the pronunciation of *d* as [b].

The next version of the passage considers the possible mismatch between dialect-based grammatical differences and the standard English grammar of reading texts.

An example of grammatical mismatch in written text and spoken vernacular dialect
It won't be *nothing* to do till he find— out *can he* go without taking John— brother.

The use of existential *it* for *there*, multiple negation, the absence of inflectional
-s, and the inverted question order of *can he go* are all instances of mismatch
between the spoken vernacular variety and the written word that might occur
if the reader were processing the language in a vernacular dialect. The original
passage is relatively close to the spoken form of standard English, so that the
mismatch between spoken and written language is greater for a vernacular
speaker than it is for a standard dialect speaker.

From the standpoint of simple linguistic processing, it is reasonable to hypothesize that the greater the mismatch between the spoken and written word,
the greater the likelihood that processing difficulties will occur in reading.
But the real issue is whether dialect differences are great enough to become a
significant barrier to linguistic processing. At this point, there are no carefully
designed experimental studies that have examined this important research
question in detail, but several observations are relevant. First of all, there is
some indication that vernacular dialect speakers are capable of processing most
spoken standard English utterances whether or not they produce this variety
themselves. In other words, they have receptive if not productive ability in
standard English. Although receptive and productive capability in language
may not transfer to the reading process in the same way, we would certainly
expect considerable carryover from this receptive capability in spoken standard
English to the reading process, which is itself a receptive language activity.

It is also erroneous to assume that standard English speakers confront written language that is identical to the way they speak, and vernacular speakers
do not. In reality, all readers encounter written text that differs from spoken
language to some extent. Even in early reading, sentences such as *Over and
over rolled the ball* or *Up the hill she ran* represent a written genre that differentiates written from spoken language for all speakers of English.

Admittedly, the gap between written language and spoken language will be
greater for vernacular dialect speakers than it is for speakers of standard varieties. But is this gap wide enough to cause problems on the basis of linguistic
differences alone? Again, carefully controlled experimentation designed to resolve this issue is lacking. However, we are reminded of the fact that there are
situations in the world where the gap between spoken dialect and written text
is quite extensive but does not result in significant reading problems. In northern Switzerland, for example, texts are written in standard German although
much of the population speaks Swiss German, yet the Swiss population does
not reveal significant reading failure. Although it is difficult to measure "degree
of dialect difference" in a precise way, Swiss German is certainly as different
from standard written German as many vernacular dialects of English are from
standard written English. Pointing to linguistic mismatch as the primary basis
for reading failure among vernacular speakers thus seems suspect. Differences
in the written and spoken language may have to be taken into account by an
aware reading instructor, but it is doubtful that the neutralization of these

differences in reading material would alleviate the reading problems associated with various vernacular-speaking populations.

Another area of language variation that may impact on the reading process involves the broader sociolinguistic base of language, including differences in cultural background. In most current models of the reading process, the application of background knowledge is essential for comprehension. Readers need such background in order to derive meaning by inference; they may also need to apply knowledge about the world in order to process some literal content. For example, imagine the differences in how a third grader from California and one from New York City might interpret the following passage on the age of giant redwood trees. Incidently, this item appeared in the *Metropolitan Achievement Test* designed for third graders.

> They are so big that roads are built through their trunks. By counting the rings inside the tree trunk, one can tell the age of the tree. (from Meier 1973)

Deborah Meier (1973:15) reports that some of the children in New York conjured up fairy-tale interpretations of this passage that included, among other things, pictures of golden rings lying inside trees. The fairy-tale interpretation was certainly fostered by images of cars driving through giant holes in trees. On the other hand, children who live near a redwood forest in California would interpret the passage quite differently, since its literal content would match their knowledge of the world. There is certainly the potential for students to expand their range of experience through reading, but background information is critical for comprehension. Thus, community-specific language and cultural experiences may actually affect reading comprehension in subtle but important ways.

Finally, we need to remember that dialect differences may have an effect on the assessment of reading skills. Early-level reading tests are particularly susceptible to the impact of dialect because they often rely on metalinguistic tasks that are sensitive to dialect-specific decoding differences. For example, the use of minimal word pair tasks or rhyming tasks to measure decoding skills might result in misclassifying cases of dialect-appropriate symbol–sound relationships as incorrect responses. Consider the following test items, taken from an actual reading achievement test, which includes word pairs as part of an attempt to determine early readers' specific decoding abilities.

> Choose the words that sound the same:
> *pin/pen*
> *reef/wreath*
> *find/fine*
> *their/there*
> *here/hear*

For speakers of some vernacular varieties, all of these items might legitimately sound the same. The "correct" responses, however, would be limited to *their/ there* and *here/hear*, based upon the non-Southern middle-class dialect norm. An informed perspective on language variation must therefore consider the ways in which reading skills are measured in testing along with other dimensions by which reading skills are acquired.

11.1.1   Dialect readers

At one stage in the consideration of dialects and reading, it was proposed that "dialect readers" be used in teaching vernacular-speaking children to read. A DIALECT READER is a text that incorporates the nonstandard grammatical forms typical of a vernacular-speaking community. For example, the following passages, taken from the *Bridge* reading materials developed by Simpkins, Simpkins, and Holt (1977), contrast African American Vernacular English and standard English versions of a passage.

African American Vernacular English version
No matter what neighborhood you be in – Black, White or whatever – young dudes be having they wheels. Got to have them. Well, anyway, there happen to be a young brother by name of Russell. He had his wheels. Soul neighborhood, you know. He had this old '57 Ford. You know how brothers be with they wheels. They definitely be keeping them looking clean, clean, clean.

Standard English version
Young guys, Black or White, love their cars. They must have a car, no matter how old it is. James Russell was a young man who loved his car like a baby loves milk. He had an old blue and white '59 Chevrolet. He spent a great deal of time keeping his car clean. He was always washing and waxing it. (taken from Rickford 1997:179)

Limited experimentation with dialect readers has shown that students tend to make gains in traditional reading achievement levels when using dialect readers as opposed to conventional reading materials (Rickford and Rickford 1995). For example, Gary C. Simpkins and Charlesetta Simpkins (1981) reported that students using the *Bridge* materials far exceeded the gains of students using regular reading materials on a standardized reading test (6.2 months of gain for a four-month period vs. 1.2 months for a four-month period for those using the regular reading materials).

Notwithstanding some positive preliminary results, dialect readers have proven to be highly controversial. One reason for the controversy relates to the deliberate use of socially stigmatized language forms in written material. This tactic is viewed by some as a reinforcement of nonstandard dialect patterns, thus flying in the face of traditional mainstream, institutional values endorsing standard dialects. Another reason for the controversy is the fact that this approach singles out particular groups of readers for special materials, namely, those who speak vernacular dialects. This selective process may be viewed as patronizing and, ultimately, racist and classist educational differentiation.

From a sociolinguistic vantage point, the use of dialect readers seems to be based on three assumptions: (1) that there is sufficient mismatch between the child's system and the standard English textbook to warrant distinct materials, (2) that the benefits of reading success will outweigh any negative connotations associated with the use of a socially stigmatized variety, and (3) that the use of vernacular dialects in reading will promote reading success. We have already considered whether the mismatch between spoken and written language is a significant problem; at this point, there simply is no good evidence for this strong position. Given children's socialization into mainstream attitudes and values about dialects at an early age, there is also little reason to assume that the sociopsychological benefits of using a vernacular dialect would outweigh the disadvantages. In fact, the opposite seems to be the case, as children reject nonstandard forms in reading, and parents and community leaders rail against their use in dialect readers. Although preliminary research has indicated some gains for children given these materials (Leaverton 1973; Simpkins and Simpkins 1981; Rickford and Rickford 1995), large-scale, substantive research on dialect readers is lacking. Due to the continuing controversy surrounding the use of dialect primers, this alternative now has been largely abandoned, although John Rickford and Angela Rickford (1995) have called for renewed and more extended experimentation with dialect readers.

Thus far, the most highly developed curriculum which uses dialect readers is found in *Bridge: A Cross-Cultural Reading Program* (Simpkins, Simpkins, and Holt 1977). This program is not designed for beginning readers but for older junior high and high school students who have experienced reading difficulty. The program limits the dialect text to passages representative of students' cultural background experiences so that the use of the vernacular is placed in an appropriate community context. It also makes a sincere effort to provide positive motivation and successful reading experiences for students. While this program is hardly free of controversy, its limitation of dialect passages to culturally appropriate contexts has made it less offensive than other approaches which use dialect passages without regard for their culturally appropriate settings. In some respects, the use of dialect passages in the *Bridge* program falls in line with a well-established tradition of representing dialect in literature. In this instance, the intent is to seize upon this literary tradition of dialect representation for the benefit of a reader who may identify with the dialect rather than the representation of a dialect assumed to be different from that of the reader.

Although there are some essential ways in which dialect may affect reading, most current approaches downplay simple linguistic differences as a primary factor in accounting for the high levels of reading failure found among vernacular-speaking populations. Instead, cultural values about reading, socialization into the activity of reading, and the mismatch between students' interests and the content of reading material have been considered more essential factors in accounting for high failure rates among nonmainstream populations. Focus on these other variables does not, however, excuse reading instructors from understanding the ways in which dialects may affect reading and from taking these factors into consideration in teaching literacy skills to speakers of vernacular dialects.

11.2 Dialect Influence in Written Language

When a rural schoolchild in Southeastern Pennsylvania writes a sentence like *Cow feed don't have jagers* ('Cow feed doesn't have thorns in it') or a phrase like *the corn got all* ('The corn is finished'), attention is drawn to the fact that such writing may reflect some aspect of the student's spoken language. In this case, a term like *jagers* (perhaps spelled more appropriately as *jaggers*) is a common label in this dialect region for 'thorns' and other objects capable of causing scratches. Similarly, the use of *don't* with a third person singular subject is a common vernacular agreement pattern, and the use of *got all* is a regional expression traceable to the influence of Pennsylvania German in the area (Wolfram and Fasold 1974:205). Obviously, spoken language can have some influence on written language. However, the relationship between spoken and written language is not always as simple and direct as examples of this type might lead us to believe. Writing, after all, is more than a simple reflection of spoken language, and very few people actually write exactly as they talk. With respect to dialects, the important question is how language variation may be manifested in written language style.

It is not particularly difficult to document cases of spoken language influence on writing such as that cited above, regardless of the vernacular dialect under review (e.g. Farr-Whiteman 1981). As we shall see below, we need to appeal to some general principles related to the process of acquiring writing skills as well as knowledge about dialects in order to explain some of the patterns of nonstandard writing that have been found.

One of the interesting findings about dialect and writing relates to the relative frequency with which certain nonstandard forms occur. For example, Farr-Whiteman (1981) identifies a few nonstandard structures that occur relatively frequently in writing and some others that occur infrequently, at least at certain stages in the process of acquiring writing skills. Among those forms frequently found in a sample of writing by eighth-grade students are the following: (1) verbal -*s* absence (e.g. *She go__*), (2) plural -*s* absence (e.g. *four mile__*), (3) possessive -*s* absence (e.g. *John hat*), (4) -*ed* absence resulting from consonant cluster reduction (e.g. *Yesterday they miss*), and (5) copula *is* and *are* absence (e.g. *We going to the game*). On the other side of the ledger are non-standard structures which appear relatively infrequently, including multiple negation, the use of *ain't*, and habitual *be*. In spelling, the orthographic reflection of *f* for *th* (e.g. *baf* for *bath*) and postvocalic *r* absence (e.g. *ca* for *car*) were also relatively rare in writing compared with their incidence in speech.

A partial explanation of the different frequency levels we find for different vernacular features in writing may relate to the social evaluation of forms. Items that are highly stigmatized and that affect relatively small sets of items are apparently the first to be corrected during the course of a child's schooling. By the time students are in eighth grade, as they were in the Farr-Whiteman study, shibboleths of nonstandard usage such as *ain't* may have been purged from writing. There is, then, a dimension of social evaluation that enters into the explanation of why some nonstandard structures are more susceptible to reflection in writing than others.

One of the most revealing aspects of spoken and written language relationships in the Farr-Whiteman study involves the comparison of the relative frequency of nonstandard forms in speech vs. writing, tabulated for both Anglo American and African American vernacular dialect speakers. In figure 11.1, the incidence of verbal -*s* and plural -*s* absence in spoken (S) and written (W) language is summarized for 32 Anglo American and African American eighth graders in Southern Maryland.

Figure 11.1 indicates relationships between spoken and written language that go beyond a simple DIRECT TRANSFER MODEL. Under the transfer model, the occurrence of a form in writing which is matched by one in the spoken dialect is interpreted as a direct carryover from a spoken language pattern to written language. That is, there is a straightforward causal relationship between spoken and written language variation. The figures in 11.1 do not support a simple version of this model. For example, Anglo Americans have a higher frequency of verbal and plural -*s* absence in their written language than they do in their spoken language. This pattern would hardly be predicted on the basis of their spoken language, since the Anglo American speakers do not have appreciable levels of suffix -*s* absence in their speech. Furthermore, we would normally expect a lower incidence of a socially stigmatized feature in the formal context of a written school essay than in spoken language.

Differences in the relative occurrence of suffixes in spoken and written language are also shown for the African American sample. Plural -*s* absence in spoken AAVE is relatively infrequent compared to verbal -*s* absence, yet both types of suffix absence are relatively high in writing. This pattern is confirmed

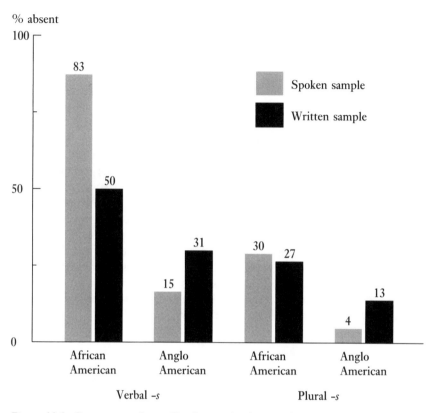

Figure 11.1 Percentage of -*s* suffix absence in the speech and writing of Anglo and African Americans (adapted from Farr-Whiteman 1981:158).

on the basis of a much more extensive examination of writing taken from the writing samples collected for the National Educational Assessment Profile (Whiteman 1976).

The pattern of suffix absence in writing is further confirmed by a pattern found for consonant cluster reduction. In writing, word-final cluster reduction affecting -*ed* forms (e.g. *miss* for 'missed') is much more frequent than it is for clusters that are part of the same morpheme (e.g. *mis* for 'mist'), quite the reverse of what it is for spoken language (see chapter 9). As Marcia Farr-Whiteman (1981:160) puts it, "these features (plural -*s*, verbal -*s*, and consonant -*ed*) seem to be omitted in writing at least in part simply because they are inflectional suffixes." In this regard, we note that inflectional suffixes are typically redundant markings, and that most words may stand as independent items in writing apart from the suffix. In other words, *miss* alone is a whole word whether or not the *-ed* is added; *mis* for *mist*, however, cannot stand alone in this way. All writers of English, regardless of their native dialect, seem to reveal some instances of suffix omission in the process of learning the written form of the language.

While generalized processes pertaining to the formative stages of writing may affect all writers to some extent, this does not nullify the effect of dialect on writing. Some forms may still be directly attributable to the spoken dialect; other spoken language forms, however, combine with different principles of writing to account for nonstandard written language forms. Inflectional *-s* absence may be revealed as part of the natural process of learning how to write regardless of the spoken dialect, but speakers of a dialect with substantial levels of suffix absence still tend to show a higher incidence of suffix omission in writing than writers of other dialects. The point that needs to be emphasized here is that dialect definitely can influence writing, but it is not solely responsible for the occurrence of nonstandard forms.

Writing failure, like reading failure, is a complex issue that goes far deeper than surface differences in dialect forms. Nonetheless, a writing instructor who is aware of the way in which dialect may surface in writing is certainly in a better position to improve writing skills than one who has no awareness of potential spoken language influences on the written medium.

Exercise 1

In the following sample composition, there are two types of digression from standard written English. First, there is a set of errors related to the mechanical conventions of written language. These include various mistakes in the application of arbitrary punctuation conventions and some types of spelling errors (e.g. *to* vs. *too*, *fair* vs. *fare*). The second set of nonstandard writing forms may reflect the influence of spoken language by a speaker of a vernacular dialect. Based on your knowledge of vernacular dialect features, differentiate the "error" types, labeling mechanical problems as **Type I** errors and spoken language influence as **Type II**. In the case of those forms classified as **Type II**, indicate what vernacular dialect feature may be the source of the spoken language influence. You may need to consult the appendix of dialect structures for this exercise.

> I tel you bout me and my fren basebal team. wen we together we do all kinds of things he play basketball and I play basebal. Las yere I seen the basketbal teme play and it look like I didnt have a chanc of making it. Im a pretty good baseball player tho and the coch knowed it. James the best player we miss him when he couldnt play last weak.

11.3   Writing Dialect for Literary Purposes

Not only do dialect forms sometimes inadvertently appear in writing, but they may also be used deliberately in literary works. Writers have attempted to portray characters through dialect for centuries. Such portrayals can be found everywhere from the daily comic strips in most newspapers to respected literary works going back as far as Chaucer. The representation of dialect in American literature arose, for the most part, in the nineteenth century and is now quite common in modern literature depicting characters of different regional background, social status, and ethnic group membership.

There are a number of reasons why an author would want to represent some aspect of dialect in a literary work. In one tradition, dialects have been used for comic effect, to poke fun at a character which the author feels superior to because of the character's lack of cultural sophistication or education. This tradition is manifested in various comic-strip characterizations of "hillbilly" speech. In another tradition, dialects are used for purposes of character development. It would be incongruous for Mark Twain's Huckleberry Finn to speak like a citified standard English-speaking adult when the viewpoint being developed is that of a rural Southern adolescent. Part of the development of a regional folkway may come from the portrayal of a nonmainstream, regional dialect.

Dialect writing may even be used as a kind of dramatic statement of identity on the part of a writer. The poet Paul Laurence Dunbar, writing at the turn of the twentieth century, wrote about one-fourth of all his poems in a vernacular dialect, in an apparent attempt to portray realistically the conditions of black life in America. From a somewhat different perspective, we find the text of Geneva Smitherman's *Talkin' and Testifyin'* (1977), an academic book about African American Vernacular English which strongly endorses its usefulness as a communicative system in the black community, deliberately sprinkled with doses of written AAVE. The written code-switching into AAVE at various points emphasizes important features of this dialect in a way that underscores the effectiveness and legitimacy of the variety. Different authors obviously use dialect for purposes which range from gross stereotyping to essential character development, so that the appropriateness of dialect in a particular literary work has to be evaluated in terms of what the writer is trying to accomplish through the representation of dialect rather than the use of literary dialect *per se*.

The representation of literary dialect is actually quite tricky from the perspective of a dialectologist, since balance must be maintained between presenting a credible version of a dialect and presenting readable text (Ives 1971). There are, of course, different levels of language variation that may be captured in literary dialect, but the most difficult level to represent is phonology, as it must be reflected through spelling modifications. Given the many obstacles to representing dialect phonology through spelling, most writers have resorted to a tradition which relies heavily on a selective and somewhat arbitrary set of spelling changes.

One of the traditional ways of representing dialect in spelling is through EYE DIALECT. Eye dialect typically consists of a set of spelling changes that have nothing to do with the phonological differences of real dialects. In fact, the reason it is called "eye" dialect is because it appeals solely to the eye of the reader rather than the ear, since it doesn't really capture any phonological differences. The spellings of *was* as *wuz*, *does* as *duz*, *excusable* as *exkusable*, or *wunce* for *once* do not represent any known aspect of phonological variation; these changes are just different ways of spelling common words to convey the impression that their speaker is an uneducated vernacular speaker.

Certain changes in spelling conventions may, on the other hand, be used to portray real phonological variation between a standard dialect and a nonmainstream variety of some type. A writer who spells *them* as *dem*, *fellow* as *feller*, *first* as *fust*, or *itch* as *eetch* is attempting to convey phonological differences in which a sound is changed (e.g. *them* becomes *dem*, *itch* becomes *eetch*), a sound is added (*fellow* becomes *feller*), or a sound is lost (*first* becomes *fust*) in a nonmainstream variety. Consonant changes are relatively easy to portray in writing but vowels are difficult, given the small phonetic details often involved in differentiating dialects. Furthermore, symbol–sound correspondences tend to be more varied for vowels than they are for most consonants. Nonetheless, writers may effectively use the spelling *ee* for *eetch* to symbolize the [i] rather than the [ɪ] sound usually associated with the *i* spelling (e.g. *bit, mitt*). Certain changes based on fairly widespread patterns of sound–symbol correspondence of this type have become fairly traditional in literary texts (e.g. *u* to symbolize a central vowel, as in *tuck*). Other cases exemplify specially created conventions for dialect writing. For example, an apostrophe is usually used in dialect writing to indicate that a sound or a syllable has been "lost" in the dialect by comparison with the standard variety, so that *mo'* for *more*, *ac'* for *act*, *'cause* for *because*, and *'cept* for *except* would all indicate an "absent" sound or syllable.

Of course, literary spelling conventions do not always differentiate clearly between eye dialect and real dialect differences, sometimes combining both traditions within the same word. Dialect spellings such as *wunst* for *once* and *'nuff* for *enough* combine eye dialect (the *wu* . . . of *wunst* and the . . . *uff* of *'nuff*) with genuine pronunciation differences, namely, the intrusive *t* of *once* and the deleted word-initial syllable of *enough*. For descriptive and practical reasons, it is virtually impossible to be faithful to dialect pronunciation in writing, although there are certainly different degrees of accuracy that distinguish writers.

In principle, it should be easier to represent dialect grammar and vocabulary than phonology, and some authors choose to represent dialect by ignoring phonology and concentrating on particular grammatical structures and vocabulary items. As it turns out, however, writers range widely in how accurate their portrayals of dialect grammar and vocabulary are, since these portrayals require a high degree of familiarity with the descriptive details of the dialects being depicted in order to remain faithful to the actual spoken dialects. Many writers resort to using selective grammatical and lexical features rather than attempting to use a comprehensive set of structures based upon descriptive dialectology. Consequently, many writers often lapse into stereotypes based upon a mixture of personal experience and a conventional set of structures taken from other authors' literary representations of dialect. Even for writers quite familiar with the representative dialects, it is virtually impossible to be completely faithful to a dialect in writing. This is especially true when we consider the variable dimension of dialects as discussed in chapter 9.

Based upon descriptive accounts of various dialects, it is quite possible for a dialectologist to evaluate how accurately different varieties are represented in literary works. For example, it is possible to evaluate the literary representation of regional dialects found in *The Adventures of Huckleberry Finn* (Rulon 1971) based upon descriptive knowledge of the dialects Twain intended to represent in his characters. It is also possible to compare how different writers represent the same dialect, as Constance W. Weaver (1970) has done for the literary representations of AAVE in several different works. Detailed tabulations of dialect features which include both a qualitative and quantitative dimension show considerable variation and degrees of faithfulness among authors. Some authors are obviously more skilled at portraying dialect details than others. For example, although Claude Brown's (1965) portrayal of AAVE in *Manchild in the Promised Land* shows discrepancies between his literary representation and the dialect as it is typically used in Northern urban communities, the author manipulates the relative frequency of nonstandard structures in the main character's passage from adolescence to adulthood and in shifting between different speaking styles in a subtle but effective way, according to Weaver's (1970) sociolinguistic analysis.

As we consider the question of accuracy in literary dialect, we also have to consider the matter of artistry. Just as writers of literature do not necessarily seek to portray people exactly as they exist in real life, so too is it sometimes necessary for artistic purposes to depart from complete accuracy in dialect representation. Sometimes this departure is based on sheer practicality. As we have been discussing, it is impossible to portray every dialect detail on all levels and still end up with a text that is readable to the non-linguist. At other times, departures from dialect accuracy may be undertaken for effect. For example, just as descriptive detail pertaining to a character's physical appearance or surroundings may be downplayed at moments where other matters are more crucial, so too are there moments where obtrusive dialect differences must take a back seat to other facets of character or plot development. Thus, it is not always the case that apparent dialect "inaccuracies" from a sociolinguistic point of view necessarily reflect a lack of knowledge about dialect patterning or an inability to portray these patterns on the part of the writer who uses dialect in literary texts.

Exercise 2

Examine the following passage from Richard Wright's *Native Son*. The passage portrays the vernacular dialect of an African American preacher. Answer the following questions, based on the passage, which is taken from page 263 of a 1961 publication of this work. The original work was published in 1941.

1 What forms seem to be simple examples of eye dialect?
2 What cases of spelling change represent actual phonological differences?
3 What kinds of grammatical details are included in the passage?
4 Are there phonological and grammatical differences that you might expect but do not appear in the passage?

"fergit ever'thing but yo' soul, son. Take yo' mind off ever'thing but eternal life. fergit what the newspaper say. Fergit yuh's black. Gawd looks past yo' skin 'n inter yo' soul, son. He's lookin' at the only parta yuh tha's *His*. He wants yuh 'n' He loves yuh. Give yo'se'f t' 'Im, son. Lissen, lemme tell yuh why yuh's here; lemme tell yuh a story tha'll make yo' heart glad."

11.4   Proactive Dialect Awareness Programs

It is easy to argue that educators who deal with dialectally diverse groups of students should know something about the dialects of their students. But what about such knowledge for the students themselves? And what about dialect awareness for community members who are no longer involved in formal education? We maintain that both formal and informal educational programs on dialects hold appeal for all sorts of people in the community, from elementary school students to retired citizens with an interest in local history. In the following sections, we first discuss dialect awareness programs in formal education and then discuss broader, community-based programs.

Most educational systems claim to be committed to a fundamental search for the truth about laws of nature and matter. When it comes to dialects, however, there is an educational tolerance of misinformation and folklore that is matched in few subject areas. Remember, from our original presentation in chapter 1, that there is an entrenched mythology about dialects that pervades our understanding of this topic, particularly with respect to the nature of standard and vernacular varieties. In its own way, the popular understanding of dialects is probably akin to a modern geophysicist's maintaining that the planet Earth is flat. Furthermore, the factual misinformation is not all innocent folklore, as we saw in our discussion of dialects and testing. At the very least, then, the educational system and society at large should assume responsibility for replacing the entrenched mythology about dialects with factual information.

Operating on erroneous assumptions about language differences, it is easy for students and community members to fall prey to the perpetuation of unjustified stereotypes about language as it relates to class, ethnicity, and region. Equity in education is hardly limited to how educators view students. It also affects how students feel about other students and themselves. Students who speak mainstream varieties may view their vernacular-speaking peers as linguistically deficient, just as the broader-based educational system often does. Worse yet, the stereotypes that evolve from the mythology about dialects affect how people view themselves, so that vernacular speakers may actually come to view their own linguistic behavior as "proof" that they are just as "stupid" as their language varieties are held to be.

The equity issue with respect to dialect does not stop with perceptions and attitudes; the failure to recognize dialect differences may lead to a kind of discrimination that is as onerous as other types of discrimination based upon race, ethnicity, gender, or class. As Milroy and Milroy (1985:3) note:

> Although public discrimination on the grounds of race, religion and social class is not now publicly acceptable, it appears that discrimination on linguistic grounds is publicly acceptable, even though linguistic differences may themselves be associated with ethnic, religious and class differences.

Dialect discrimination cannot be taken more lightly than any other type of potential discrimination, and there is now a precedent for litigation based upon such discrimination.

From a humanistic standpoint, the reasons for endorsing dialect awareness programs given thus far are probably a sufficient rationale for introducing the study of dialects into the educational curriculum and promoting dialect awareness among the population at large. There is, however, another rationale related to the nature of intellectual inquiry. The study of dialects affords us a fascinating window through which we can see how language works. Certainly, an important aspect of understanding language in general, and the English language in particular, is the development of an appreciation for how language changes over time and space and how various dialects arise. Studying dialects formally and informally provides a wealth of information for examining the dynamic nature of language. Given the inherent public interest in dialects, this type of study has great potential for piquing students' and community members' interest in how language works. Furthermore, the inner workings of language are just as readily observed in examining dialects and their patterning as through the exclusive study of a single standard variety.

The study of dialects offers another enticement. Language, including dialects, is a unique form of knowledge in that speakers know a language simply by virtue of the fact that they speak it. Much of this knowledge is not on a conscious level, but it is still open to systematic investigation. Looking at dialect differences provides a natural laboratory for making generalizations drawn from carefully described sets of data. We can hypothesize about the patterning of language features and then check our hypotheses on the basis of actual usage patterns. This, of course, is a type of scientific inquiry. Such a rationale for studying dialects may seem a bit esoteric at first glance, but hypothesizing about and then testing language patterns is quite within the grasp even of younger students. In fact, we have led classes of students in the middle elementary grades through the steps of hypothesis formation and testing by using exercises involving dialect features. For example, the exercise on *a*-prefixing that was included in chapter 1 actually comes from an eighth grade curriculum on dialects that we have taught in North Carolina for several years now.

Finally, there is a utilitarian reason for studying dialects. Information about dialects should prove helpful to students as they work to develop the language skills required as a part of the educational process, including the use of the standard variety. Vernacular dialect speakers may, for example, apply knowledge about dialect features to composing and editing skills in writing. We have personally witnessed students who studied *-s* third person absence in a unit on dialects transfer this knowledge to their writing when called upon to write standard English. The studying of various dialects hardly endangers the sovereignty of standard English in the classroom. In fact, if anything, it enhances the learning of the standard variety through the heightened sensitivity to language variation.

11.5   A Curriculum on Dialects

Although it is beyond the scope of this book to present actual lesson plans for a curriculum on dialects in the schools, it is reasonable to introduce some of the major themes that might be covered in such a unit of study, especially since dialect study is a relatively novel idea at the elementary and secondary levels of education. Our own experimentation has focused on a middle-school curriculum, but similar units can be designed for an upper-level elementary language arts curriculum as well.

A unit on dialects certainly needs to focus on the fundamental naturalness of dialect variation in American society. Students need to confront stereotypes and misconceptions about dialects, and this is probably best done inductively. An easy method of doing this involves having students listen to representative speech samples of regional, class, and ethnic varieties. Students need to hear how native standard English speakers in New England, the rural South, and urban North compare to appreciate the reality of diverse regional spoken standards, just as they need to recognize different vernacular varieties in these regions. And students in "standard"-speaking regions need to consider some of the features of their own dialect as it compares with others in order to understand that everyone really does speak a dialect. Although most tape-recorded collections of dialect samples are personal ones that are not commercially available, video productions like *American Tongues* (Alvarez and Kolker 1987) can be used to provide an entertaining introduction to dialects while, at the same time, exposing basic prejudices and myths about language differences.

It is also important for students to examine cases of dialect variation from their own community as a basis for seeing how natural and inevitable dialects are. For starters, students should at least be able to offer regional names for short order, over-the-counter foods (e.g. *sub/hoagie/hero*, etc.) and drinks (e.g. *soda/pop*, etc.). Virtually all communities have some local and regional lexical items that can be used as a starting point for examining dialect diversity. For example, in some of our dialect awareness materials (Wolfram, Schilling-Estes, and Hazen 1997; Wolfram, Dannenberg, and Messner 1997), we have developed exercises on local lexical items such as the following, which is taken from our dialect curriculum titled *Dialects and the Ocracoke Brogue* (Wolfram, Schilling-Estes, and Hazen 1997).

Ocracoke dialect vocabulary game: How to tell an O'cocker from a Dingbatter

Fill in the blanks in the sentences below, choosing your answer from the list provided. You only have five minutes to complete the worksheet, and you **may not** look at the lexicon or share answers. At the end of five minutes, you will swap your book with a neighbor to check each other's work. For each correct answer, you will receive 1 point, and for each question missed, you will receive **no** points. Good luck.

WORD LIST: across the beach, buck, call the mail over, dingbatter, doast, goaty, good-some, meehonkey, miserable 'n the wind, mommuck, O'cocker, pizer, quamished, Russian rat, say a word, scud, smidget, slick cam, to, up the beach, yaupon, young 'uns

1 They went _____ to Hatteras to do some shopping.
2 That _____ is from New Jersey.
3 That place sure was smelling _____.

4   Elizabeth is _____ the restaurant right now.
5   I put a _____ of salt on my apple.
6   We took a _____ around the island in the car.
7   They're always together because he's his _____.
8   At night we used to play _____.
9   The ocean was so rough today I felt _____ in the gut.
10   Last night she came down with a _____.
11   I saw a big _____ in the road.
12   They sat on the _____ in the evening.
13   When Rex and James Barrie get together they sure can _____.
14   You can't be an _____ unless you were born on the island.
15   The sea was real rough today; it was _____ out there.
16   When they _____ I hope I get my letter.
17   She used to _____ him when he was a child.
18   There was no wind at all today and it was a _____ out there on the sound.
19   There was a big, dead shark that they found _____.
20   _____ don't act like they used to back then.

Put a 1 by all the correct answers and an X by all the incorrect answers. Add up all of the correct answers and place the total in the blank. Hand the workbook back to its owner.

How did you score?
        16–20: O'cocker   6–10: educable dingbatter
        11–15: honorary O'cocker   0–5: uneducable dingbatter

[Answers: 1 *up the beach*; 2 *dingbatter*; 3 *goaty*; 4 *to*; 5 *smidget*; 6 *scud*; 7 *buck*; 8 *meehonkey*; 9 *quamished*; 10 *doast*; 11 *Russian rat*; 12 *pizer*; 13 *say a word*; 14 *O'cocker*; 15 *miserable 'n the wind*; 16 *call the mail over*; 17 *mommuck*; 18 *slick cam*; 19 *across the beach*; 20 *young 'uns*]

Students themselves can take an active role in the construction of dialect vocabulary exercises by helping to collect local lexical items. In the process, they learn to document and compile dialect items and determine the ways in which their local dialect is similar to and different from other varieties. In fact, in our studies of lexical items, community members have often taken leading roles in the collection and compilation of community-based lexical inventories (e.g. Locklear, Schilling-Estes, Wolfram, and Dannenberg 1996). Certainly, such collections underscore the naturalness of dialect diversity and seize upon the natural curiosity that all people seem to have concerning "different word uses."

Another essential type of activity concerns the acquisition of knowledge about the patterning of dialect. As we saw in chapter 1, the popular stereotype is that various dialects, particularly vernacular varieties, are simply imperfect attempts to speak the standard variety. In addition, people tend to think of "grammar rules" as prescriptive dicta that come from books rather than from natural language usage. An inductive exercise on the systematic nature of dialects, such as the *a*-prefixing exercise in chapter 1, can go a long way towards dispelling such notions. It also can set the stage for generating a non-patronizing respect for the complexity of systematic differences among dialects. The advantage of the *a*-prefixing exercise in particular is that it involves a form whose patterning is intuitive to both those who use the form in their vernacular dialect and those who do not (Wolfram 1982). This fact makes the exercise appropriate for students regardless of their native dialect. Exercises of this type are an effective way of confronting the myth that dialects have no rules of their own; at the same time, such exercises effectively demonstrate the underlying cognitive patterning of language.

Following is an example of a dialect patterning exercise that illustrates how students can uncover the intricate patterns that underlie dialect forms. This exercise involves the merger of the vowels [ɪ] and [ɛ] in items like *pin* and *pen*, a well-known and widespread Southern pronunciation pattern.

A Southern vowel pronunciation

In some Southern dialects of American English, words like *pin* and *pen* are pronounced the same. Usually, both words are pronounced as *pin*. This pattern of pronunciation is also found in other words. List A has words where the *i* and *e* are pronounced the SAME in these dialects.

List A: i *and* e *pronounced the same*
1   *tin* and *ten*
2   *kin* and *Ken*
3   *Lin* and *Len*
4   *windy* and *Wendy*
5   *sinned* and *send*

Although *i* and *e* in **List A** are pronounced the SAME, there are other words where *i* and *e* are pronounced differently. **List B** has word pairs where the vowels are pronounced **DIFFERENTLY**.

List B: i *and* e *pronounced differently*
1   *lit* and *let*
2   *pick* and *peck*
3   *pig* and *peg*
4   *rip* and *rep*
5   *litter* and *letter*

Is there a pattern that can explain why the words in **List A** are pronounced the SAME and why the words in **List B** are pronounced DIFFERENTLY? To answer this question, you have to look at the sounds that are next to the vowels. Look at the sounds that come after the vowel. What sound is found next to the vowel in all of the examples given in **List A**?

Use what you know about the pronunciation pattern to pick the word pairs in **List C** that are pronounced the SAME and those that are pronounced DIFFERENTLY in some Southern dialects. Mark the word pairs that are pronounced the same with **S** and the word pairs that are pronounced differently with **D**.

List C: same or different?
___ 1 *bit* and *bet*
___ 2 *pit* and *pet*
___ 3 *bin* and *Ben*
___ 4 *Nick* and *neck*
___ 5 *din* and *den*

Exercise 3

Work through the following exercise as if you were a student in a dialect awareness program. What might a student learn about grammatical rules pertaining to vernacular dialects from this exercise? The exercise is from Wolfram, Schilling-Estes, and Hazen (1997).

Plural absence on nouns

In English, we form a regular plural by adding an *-s* sound, so that we say *one dog* but *two dogs* or *a cat* but *two cats*. In the traditional dialect of Ocracoke English, there is a set of nouns that do not take *-s* endings. **List A** gives some of the nouns that do not need to add a plural *-s*. As you look at the sentences in **List A**, answer the following questions:

• What kinds of things do the nouns in **List A** refer to? Is there a common topic for these nouns?
• What kinds of words occur before the noun?

List A: nouns without plural -s
1 We caught *two hundred pound_* of flounder.
2 How *many bushel_* does he have?
3 There are *two pint_* sitting in the back yard.
4 There are *lots of gallon_* of water.
5 They have *three acre_* for building.
6 It's about *six mile_* up the road.

List B: nouns with plural -s

In **List B** the nouns in the sentences MUST take a plural -*s* ending. What is the difference in the type of nouns in **List A** and **List B** that might explain why some nouns MUST have the -*s* and why others do not need it? Look at the differences in the meaning of the nouns in **List A** and **List B**.

1 We caught *two hundred cats.*
2 How *many dogs* does he have?
3 There are *two chickens* sitting in the back yard.
4 They have *lots of ponies* down below.
5 They have *three sisters.*
6 It's about *six teachers.*

In **List C** the same nouns of **List A** are given, but as they are used in **List C** they MUST have the -*s* plural. What is the main difference that can explain when the -*s* is needed and when it is not needed?

List C: when the plural -s needs to be present
1 We had *pounds* of flounder that spoiled.
2 Sometimes people use *bushels* instead of *pounds.*
3 The *pints* of ice cream are in the freezer.
4 We had *gallons* of water in the skiff.
5 The best *acres* are owned by the government.
6 The beautiful beaches go for *miles.*

After examining the three lists of words, you should be able to figure out the rule or pattern for leaving off the -*s* plural. The rule has two parts. One part has to do with the meaning of the noun and the other part has to do with the kind of word that modifies the noun.

• State the exact pattern for -*s* plural absence based on your analysis of the nouns in **Lists A, B,** and **C.**
• Say which of the nouns in **List D** must have the -*s* and which do not need the -*s* ending and say why. If you have stated the rule for plural -*s* correctly, you should be able to do this without guessing.

List D: predicting -s plural absence
1 She had three pound__ of fish left.
2 She had pound__ of fish left.
3 It's forty inch__ to the top.
4 It's inch__ to the top.
5 There are six Russian rat__ in that yard.
6 There are Russian rat__ in the yard.

NOTE: The pattern of plural absence you looked at here is a dialect trait which can be found in various dialects in the United States and in the British Isles. For example, this pattern is prominent in the dialects spoken in the Appalachian and Ozark mountain ranges. It is also rather common in some parts of Northern Ireland and in the North of England.

The advantages of these types of exercises should be obvious, as students learn how linguists collect and organize data to formulate rules. Such exercises also provide students with a model for analyzing data that they might collect from their own community. In the best case scenario, students should record language data, extract particular examples from the data, and formulate linguistic rules themselves. In this way, students may learn on a firsthand basis about examining language in a scientific way.

In addition to seeing dialect study as a kind of scientific investigation, students should be encouraged to see how dialect study merges with the social sciences and the humanities. Dialect study can be viewed from the perspective of geography, history, or sociology; it also can be linked with ethnic or gender studies. Thus, the examination of dialect differences offers great potential for students to probe the linguistic manifestations of other types of sociocultural differences. For example, a student or group of students interested in history may thus carry out independent research to determine the contributions of various historical groups to a particular locale by researching the migratory routes of the first English-speaking inhabitants of the area, and showing how settlement history is reflected in the dialect. Similarly, a group of students interested in sociology may examine status differences in a community as manifested in language. Or, a group of students may probe the linguistic manifestations of in-group behavior by examining the way new vocabulary items are created and diffused in a group of speakers who share a common interest. The ways in which new words are formed, as discussed in chapter 3, can be examined through the investigation of the jargon surrounding some specialized activity (e.g. electronic mail, playground basketball) or through the investigation of slang as used by peer cohorts who hang out at the mall just as readily as it can through the study of how mainstream words have developed. Students can even create a new slang term and follow its spread among their peers to observe the social dynamics of language.

While it is possible to develop specific lessons relating dialect study to social science and the humanities, the true value of broad-based approaches to dialect study is realized by allowing groups of students to examine complementary topics and by having the groups share their investigations with other class members. There are a number of creative ways in which students can examine how language and culture go hand-in-hand.

As we have mentioned, one of the greatest advantages of a curriculum on dialects is its potential for tapping the language resources of students' indigenous communities. In addition to classroom lessons, students can learn by going into the community to collect live dialect data. In most cases, the language characteristics of the local community should make dialects come alive in a way that is unmatched by textbook knowledge. Educational models that treat the local community as a resource to be tapped rather than a liability to be overcome have been shown to be quite effective in other areas of language arts education, and there is no reason why this model cannot be applied in an analogous fashion to the study of community dialects. A model that builds upon community strengths in language, even when the language is different from the norm of the mainstream educational system, seems to hold much greater potential for success than one that focuses exclusively upon language conflicts between the community and school. In fact, the community dialect may just turn out to be the spark that ignites students' interest in the study of language arts. The study of dialects can, indeed, become a vibrant, relevant topic of study for all students, not just for those who choose to take an optional course on this topic at a post-secondary level of education.

11.6   Community-based Dialect Awareness

In the previous section, we examined the role of dialect studies in formal education. In this final section, we consider the role of dialect awareness in the broader context of the community. There are a number of roles dialectologists can take with respect to community-based, collaborative programs. Although dialectologists are not in a position to make decisions about the future of a dialect in a given area, they can work with community members (1) to ensure that the dialect is documented in a valid and reliable way, (2) to raise the level of consciousness within and outside the community about the traditional form of the dialect and its changing state, and (3) to engage representative community agents and agencies in an effort to understand the historic and current role of dialect in community life.

Our personal involvement with local communities on the Outer Banks of North Carolina, whose dialects are in a moribund, or dying, state (Wolfram and Schilling-Estes 1995), includes work with local institutions and a variety of community agents. For example, a summary of products we have produced and the activities we have undertaken for the Ocracoke community is given below. Also included is a partial listing of the media coverage which our programs have received.

Products for a community-based dialect awareness program
*   *Hoi Toide on the Outer Banks: The Story of the Ocracoke Brogue* (Wolfram and Schilling-Estes 1997). A book for non-experts made available at tourist sites on the Outer Banks, museums, and general interest bookstores throughout North Carolina.
*   *Ocracoke Dialect Vocabulary* (North Carolina Language and Life Project). A popular booklet for visitors to Ocracoke.
*   *Dialects and the Ocracoke Brogue* (Wolfram, Schilling-Estes, and Hazen 1997). A student text used for an eighth-grade social studies curriculum taught at the Ocracoke school.

- *Ocracoke Live.* An archival compact disc of select community speech samples.
- *The Ocracoke Brogue.* A video documentary on the history and state of the Ocracoke brogue (Blanton and Waters 1995).
- Presentations to the Ocracoke Preservation Society and to visitors' groups on the state of the Ocracoke brogue; book signings and presentations at popular bookstores.
- Design and distribution of "Save the Brogue" T-shirt in the community, at local stores, and the museum operated by the Ocracoke Preservation Society.
- Issue of the Ocracoke school newspaper dedicated to dialect awareness efforts, including articles and poems about the Ocracoke brogue.
- Construction of a permanent exhibit on the Ocracoke brogue at the museum operated by the Ocracoke Preservation Society.
- Grant writing on behalf of the community to raise funds for establishing programs and exhibits related to the Ocracoke dialect.
- News articles on endangered dialects and dialect awareness distributed by the Associated Press, including some with accompanying sound samples which readers may access by phone.
- International television and radio press coverage, including spots on BBC television and radio and articles in London newspapers such as *The Times* and the *Evening Standard.*

As indicated in the list, our involvement has included a broad range of products and activities. We have written a book for non-experts, compiled archival tapes, developed a dialect awareness program for the school, and produced a couple of documentary videos on Outer Banks sites where we have been collecting data. We even designed a commemorative "Save the Brogue" T-shirt that we have given to many members of the Ocracoke community and now sell through the Ocracoke Preservation Society.

Local institutions involved include the Ocracoke Preservation Society, the Ocracoke school, and various North Carolina museums. Key community members have also served as active participants in various phases of our program, including the president of the Ocracoke Preservation Society, community leaders, and students and teachers in the school.

The venues we use to disseminate information include both traditional and non-traditional agencies. For example, we have instituted experimental programs in the Ocracoke school and made presentations to the Ocracoke Historical Preservation Society and to various visitors' groups on Ocracoke. We also share royalties from the sales of our trade book with the Preservation Society in the hope that our programs and materials will be recognized as part of the society's preservation efforts. Along with these institutional efforts, we have even shown our documentary several times at the local bar and grill, Howard's Pub, where both residents and tourists typically congregate for informal socializing. These showings resulted in animated, positive discussions about the dialect by both Ocracoke residents and tourists. The endangered status of the

Ocracoke brogue has also been the subject of several local, regional, and even international television and radio news programs, and there were at least a dozen major feature articles in local and regional newspapers from 1993 to 1997 that focused on the state of the dialect and the threats to its survival. As noted above, several of these stories were accompanied by sound bites; readers were invited to call an advertised telephone number and listen to a recorded sample of the brogue for themselves. The *Virginian Pilot* newspaper reported that more readers called in to hear the sample of the brogue than any other sound bite they had yet made available to their readership.

Our community-based efforts have attempted to engage students, teachers, and community members in collecting and documenting dialect data. For example, several local community members routinely make observations and take notes for us about lexical items. In fact, one local school teacher, following one of our lessons, returned the following day with over two pages of lexical items and phrases elicited from her elderly relatives. On another occasion, she wrote a poem which includes many unique Outer Banks lexical items in celebration of the dialect, which we reproduce below. In this poem, the italicized words are particular lexical items which characterize the Ocracoke brogue.

The Ocracoke Brogue
by
Gail Hamilton

Ocracoke Tradition, Heritage and Such
For some *dingbatters* is really too much
What is a first cousin once-removed?
Does a trip *down below* have to be approved?

Mommuck, doset, and *miserable 'n the wind*
Is this *O'cock brogue* meant to offend?
When I see *wampus cat*, what do I see?
Hoi toid on the seund soid is Greek to me!

Hey, *puck* isn't used in the game of hockey.
Do *O'Cockers* "*hoid*" when playing *meehonkey*?
While on your *pizer*, do you sit for *a spell*?
If you go *down below*, do you got to . . . well?

Been a *whit* since I took a *scud across the beach.*
Things get *catawampus* if they're hard to reach.
Every *whipstitch* the *creek* gets *slick cam*
If you're not confused, well *pucker dog*, I am!

If I'm *Down Point* or *Up Trent*, Where'll I be?
Well, *Bucky*, it's still *good-some* to me!
Some may get *quamish* from the attention,
but this Brogue's too unique not to mention.

Perhaps the most significant aspect of this language arts teacher's involvement is the fact that it has transformed her from a teacher who once sought to stamp out dialect in her classrooms to a teacher who now understands and seeks to preserve the rich dialect heritage of her community.

As dialectologists and linguists, of course, we may not be able to save this or any other unique, endangered variety of a language. But we can at least chronicle the dialect for the historical record – for community members, curious outsiders, and academicians. In the process, we can seize on the natural curiosity all of us have about dialects as a basis for working with communities to celebrate language diversity as an integral part of a community's heritage. This seems to be the least we can do as dialect researchers who profit greatly from studying the rich variety of dialects and languages which lend so much to the cultural landscape of American society.

11.7   Further Reading

Farr, Marcia, and Harvey Daniels (1986) *Language Diversity and Writing Instruction.* Urbana, IL: National Council of Teachers of English. This reasoned treatment offers a theoretical framework, along with practical suggestions for educators who wish to improve the writing skills of students from vernacular-speaking communities.

Glowka, Wayne A., and Donald M. Lance (eds) (1993) *Language Variation in North American English: Research and Teaching.* New York: Modern Language Association. This collection of essays is devoted to the discussion of practical methods for presenting notions about language variation to students. Some of the articles offer helpful aids for getting students involved in the study of language variation.

Rickford, John R. (1997) Unequal partnership: Sociolinguistics and the African American speech community. *Language in Society* 26:161–98. Rickford discusses the responsibility of linguists to consider ways in which they can serve the communities which have provided rich data for descriptive and theoretical research.

Rickford John R., and Angela Rickford (1995) Dialect readers revisited. *Linguistics and Education* 7:107–28. This article discusses a recent attempt to experiment with dialect readers. It also reviews some previous experimentation with dialect readers and concludes that the abandonment of dialect readers was premature and empirically unwarranted.

Wolfram, Walt (1993a) Ethical considerations in language awareness programs. *Issues in Applied Linguistics* 4:225–55. This article addresses some of the underlying ethical considerations that attend dialect awareness programs, including some of the issues surrounding the kind of dialect awareness programs proposed in this chapter.

Wolfram, Walt and Natalie Schilling-Estes (1997) *Hoi Toide on the Outer Banks: The Story of the Ocracoke Brogue.* Chapel Hill/London: University of North Carolina Press. The book is written for non-experts, including tourists on the Outer Banks, residents of the local community, and other readers curious about Outer Banks dialects. The final chapter details the community-based collaborative dialect awareness programs that have been adopted by the Ocracoke community and the Ocracoke school.

Appendix: An Inventory of Socially Diagnostic Structures

The following inventory summarizes many of the dialect structures of American English mentioned in the text; it also introduces some structures not covered in the preceding chapters. It is limited to phonological and grammatical structures. For each of the structures, a brief general comment is given about the linguistic patterning of the structure, as well as a statement about its dialect distribution. We emphasize items that are socially significant in terms of the standard–vernacular continuum rather than those that are strictly regional, although many of the structures are both socially and regionally meaningful. To the extent possible, traditional orthography is used in representing forms, but this is not possible in all cases.

Phonological Structures

Consonants

Final cluster reduction
Word-final consonant clusters ending in a stop can be reduced when both members of the cluster are either voiced (e.g. *find, cold*) or voiceless (*act, test*). This process affects both clusters which are a part of the base word (e.g. *find, act*) and those clusters formed through the addition of an *-ed* suffix (e.g. *guessed, liked*). In standard English, this rule may operate when the following word begins with a consonant (e.g. *best kind*), but in vernacular dialects, it is extended to include following words beginning with a vowel as well (e.g. *best apple*). This pattern is quite prominent in AAVE and in dialects of English that retain influence from other languages, such as Hispanic English and Vietnamese English. It is not particularly noticeable in other American English dialects.

Plurals following clusters
Words ending in *-sp* (e.g. *wasp*), *-sk* (e.g. *desk*), and *-st* (e.g. *test*) may take an *-es* (phonetically [ɪz]) plural in many vernacular varieties, following the reduction

of their final clusters to -*s*. Thus, items such as *tes'* [tɛs] for *test* and *des* [dɛs] for *desk* will be pluralized as *tesses* and *desses*, respectively, much as words ending in *s* or other *s*-like sounds in standard English (e.g., *bus, buzz*) are pluralized with an -*es* ending (*buses, buzzes*).

In some historically isolated varieties of English such as Appalachian and Southeastern coastal varieties, the -*es* plural may occur even without the reduction of the final cluster to -*s*, yielding plural forms such as *postes* and *deskes*. Such forms are considerably rarer in AAVE and seem to be a function of hypercorrection.

Intrusive t
A small set of items, usually ending in *s* and *f* in the standard variety, may be produced with a final *t*. This results in a final consonant cluster. Typical items affected by this process are *oncet, twicet, clifft*, and *acrosst*. Intrusive *t* is primarily found in Appalachian varieties and other rural varieties characterized by the retention of older, or relic, forms.

A quite different kind of intrusive *t* involves the "doubling" of an -*ed* form. In this instance, speakers add an -*ed* ending (phonetically [ɪd]) to verbs which are already marked with an -*ed* ending pronounced *t* (e.g. [lʊkt] 'looked'). This process yields forms such as *lookted* for *looked* and *attackted* for *attacked*.

th *sounds*
There are a number of different processes that affect *th* sounds. The phonetic production of *th* is sensitive to the position of *th* in the word and the sounds adjacent to it. At the beginning of the word, *th* tends to be produced as a corresponding stop, as in *dey* for *they* ([d] for [ð]) and *ting* for *thing* ([t] for [θ]). These productions are fairly typical of a wide range of vernaculars, although there are some differences in the distribution of stopped variants for voiced vs. voiceless *th* ([ð] vs. [θ]). The *t* use of *t* in *thing* (voiceless *th*) tends to be most characteristic of selected Anglo- and second-language-influenced varieties, whereas the use of *d* in *they* (voiced *th*) is spread across the full spectrum of vernacular varieties.

Before nasals, *th* participates in a process in which a range of fricatives, including *z, th*, and *v*, may also become stops. This results in forms such as *aritmetic* for *arithmetic* or *headn* for *heathen*, as well as *wadn't* for *wasn't, idn't* for *isn't*, and *sebm* for *seven*. This pattern is typically found in Southern-based vernacular varieties, including Southern Anglo and African American Vernacular Varieties.

In word-final position and between vowels within a word (that is, in intervocalic position), *th* may be produced as *f* or *v*, as in *efer* for *ether, toof* for *tooth, brover* for *brother*, and *smoov* for *smooth*. This production is typical of AAVE, with the *v* for voiced *th* [ð] production more typical of Eastern varieties of the vernacular. Some Southern-based Anglo dialects, as well as some varieties influenced by other languages in the recent past, also have the f production in *tooth*.

Some restricted Anglo varieties use a stop d for intervocalic voiced *th* as in *oder* for *other* or *broder* for *brother*, but this pattern is much less common than the use of a stop for *th* in word-initial position.

r *and* l

There are a number of different linguistic contexts in which r and l may be lost or reduced to a vowel-like quality. After a vowel, as in *sister* or *steal*, the r and l may be reduced or lost. This feature is highly regionally diagnostic and is quite typical of traditional Southern speech and Eastern New England speech.

Between vowels, r also may be lost, as in *Ca'ol* for *Carol* or *sto'y* for *story*. Intervocalic r loss is more socially stigmatized than postvocalic r loss and is found in rural, Southern-based vernaculars.

Following a consonant, the r may be lost if it precedes a rounded vowel such as u or o, resulting in pronunciations such as *thu* for *through* and *tho* for *throw*. Postconsonantal r loss may also be found if r occurs in an unstressed syllable, as in *p'ofessor* for *professor* or *sec'etary* for *secretary*. This type of r-lessness is found primarily in Southern-based varieties. Before a bilabial sound such as p, l may be lost completely, giving *woof* for *wolf* or *hep* for *help*. Again, this is characteristic only of Southern-based varieties.

Sometimes r-lessness causes one lexical item to converge with another. Thus, the use of *they* for *their* as in *theyself* or *they book* apparently derives from the loss of r on *their*, even though speakers who currently use *they* in such constructions no longer associate it with r-less *their*.

There are also occasional instances in which an intrusive r may occur, so that items such as *wash* may be pronounced as *warsh* and *idea* as *idear*. Certain instances of intrusive r are the result of a generalized pronunciation process, whereby r can be added onto the ends of vowel-final words (e.g. *idear*), particularly when these words precede vowel-initial words (*the idear of it*). Other cases (e.g. *warsh*) seem to be restricted to particular lexical items and are highly regionally restricted as well.

Initial w *reduction*

In unstressed positions within a phrase, an initial w may be lost in items such as *was* and *one*. This results in items such as *She's* [šiz] *here yesterday* for *She was here yesterday* and *young 'uns* for *young ones*. This appears to be an extension of the process affecting the initial w of the modals *will* and *would* in standard varieties of English (e.g. *he will* → *he'll*; *he would* → *he'd*). This process is found in Southern-based vernaculars.

Unstressed initial syllable loss

The general process of deleting unstressed initial syllables in informal speech styles of standard English (e.g. *because* → *'cause*; *around* → *'round*) is extended

in vernacular varieties so that a wider range of word classes (e.g. verbs such as
'member for *remember* or nouns such as *'taters* for *potatoes*) and a wider range of
initial syllable types (e.g. *re-* as in *'member* for *remember*, *su-* as in *'spect* for
suspect) are affected by this process.

Initial h *retention*

The retention of *h* on the pronoun *it* [hɪt] and the auxiliary *ain't* [hent] is
still found in vernacular varieties retaining some older English forms, such as
Appalachian English and Outer Banks English. This form is more prominent
in stressed positions within a sentence. The pronunciation is fading out among
younger speakers.

Nasals

There are a number of processes that affect nasal sounds; there are also items
that are influenced by the presence of nasals in the surrounding linguistic
environment.

One widespread process in vernacular varieties is so-called "*g*-dropping," in
which the nasal [ŋ], represented as *ng* in spelling, is pronounced as [n]. This
process takes place when the *ng* occurs in an unstressed syllable, as in *swimmin'*
for *swimming* or *buyin'* for *buying*. Linguists refer to this process as "velar
fronting" since it involves the fronting of the velar nasal [ŋ], produced toward
the back of the mouth, to [n], a more fronted nasal sound.

A less widespread phenomenon affecting nasals is the deletion of the word-
final nasal segment in items such as *man*, *beam*, and *ring*, particularly when the
item is in a relatively unstressed position within the sentence. Even though
the nasal is deleted, the words still retain their final nasal character, because
the vowel preceding the *n* has been nasalized, through an assimilation process
common to all varieties of English. Thus, *man*, *beam*, and *ring* may be pronounced as *ma'* [mæ̃], *bea'* [bĩ], and *ri'* [rĩ], respectively, with the vowel
carrying a nasal quality. Most frequently, this process affects the segment *n*,
although all final nasal segments may be affected to some extent. This process
is typical of African American Vernacular English.

The phonetic quality of vowels may be affected before nasal consonants, as
in the well-known merger of the contrast between [ɪ] and [ɛ] before nasals as in
pen and *pin*. Some Southern dialects restrict this merger to a following *n*,
whereas others extend it to following *m* (e.g. *Kim* and *chem*) and [ŋ] as well.

Other consonants

There are a number of other consonantal patterns that affect limited sets of
items or single words. For example, speakers have used *aks* for *ask* for over a
thousand years and still continue to use it in several vernacular varieties,
including AAVE. The form *chimley* or *chimbley* for *chimney* is also found in a
number of Southern-based vernaculars. The use of *k* in initial *(s)tr* clusters as

in *skreet* for *street* or *skring* for *string* is found in AAVE, particularly rural Southern varieties. Such items are quite socially obtrusive but occur with such limited sets of words that they are best considered on an item-by-item basis.

Vowels

There are many vowel patterns that differentiate the dialects of English, but the majority of these are more regionally than socially significant. The back vowel [ɔ] of *bought* or *coffee* and the front vowel [æ] of *cat* and *ran* are particularly sensitive to regional variation, as are vowels before *r* (e.g. compare pronunciations of *merry*, *marry*, *Mary*, *Murray*) and *l* (compare *wheel*, *will*, *well*, *whale*, etc.). Although it is not possible here to indicate all the nuances of phonetic difference reflected in the vowels of American English, several major patterns of pronunciation may be identified.

Vowel shifts

There are several shifts in the phonetic values of vowels that are currently taking place in American English. The important aspect of these shifts is the fact that the vowels are not shifting their phonetic values in isolation but as rotating systems of vowels. One major rotation is the "Northern Cities Vowel Shift." In this rotation, the phonetic values of two series of vowels are affected; the low long back vowels are moving forward and upward, and the short front vowels are moving downward and backward. For example, the /ɔ/ vowel, as in *coffee*, is moving forward toward the /a/ of *father*. The low vowel in a word like *pop* or *lock*, in turn, moves towards the [æ] of *bat*, which, in turn, moves upward toward the vowel [ε] of *bet*. At the same time, another rotation moves the short vowel [ɪ] of *bit* toward the [ε] of *bet*. The [ε], in turn, moves backward toward the mid vowel of *but* [ʌ], which is then pushed back. Short vowels and long vowels tend to rotate as different subsystems within the overall vowel system. Diagrammatically, the shift may be represented as shown in figure A.1. In this chart, front vowels appear to the left of the chart and high vowels towards the top. For convenience, "key words" in terms of idealized Standard American English phonemes are given. The arrows point in the direction of the phonetic rotations taking place in the shift.

Regionally, the pattern of vowel rotation represented in figure A.1 starts in Western New England and proceeds eastward into the northern tier of Pennsylvania, Northern Ohio, Indiana, Illinois, Michigan, and Wisconsin. It is more concentrated in the larger metropolitan areas. More advanced stages of this change can be found in younger speakers in the largest metropolitan areas in this Northern region, such as Buffalo, Albany, Cleveland, Detroit, and Chicago. Minority groups in these metropolitan areas tend not to participate in this phonetic shift.

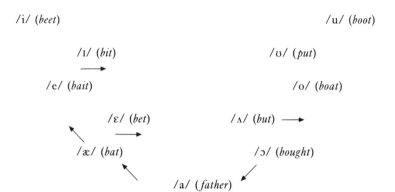

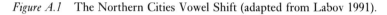

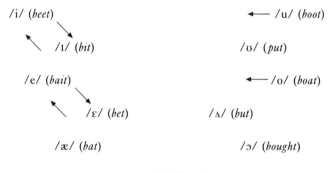

Figure A.1 The Northern Cities Vowel Shift (adapted from Labov 1991).

/i/ (*beet*)   ← /u/ (*boot*)

\   /ɪ/ (*bit*)   /ʊ/ (*put*)

/e/ (*bait*)   ← /o/ (*boat*)

\   /ɛ/ (*bet*)   /ʌ/ (*but*)

/æ/ (*bat*)   /ɔ/ (*bought*)

/a/ (*father*)

Figure A.2 The Southern Vowel Shift (adapted from Labov 1991).

The Southern Shift is quite different from the Northern Cities Shift. In this rotation pattern, the short front vowels (the vowels of words like *bed* and *bid*) are moving upward and taking on the gliding character of long vowels. In Standard American English, a vowel like the long *e* of *bait* actually consists of a vowel nucleus [e] and an upward glide into [ɪ], whereas a vowel like the short *e* [ɛ] of *bet* does not have this gliding character, at least not in the idealized standard variety. In the Southern Vowel Shift, the vowel of *bed* takes on a glide, becoming more like *beyd* [bɛɪd]. Meanwhile, the long front vowels (the vowels of *beet* and *late*) are moving backward, and the back vowels (the vowels of *boot* and *boat*) are moving forward. This phonetic rotation is illustrated in figure A.2.

Low back vowel merger
One of the major regional pronunciation processes affecting vowels is the merger of the low back vowels /a/ and /ɔ/. This merger means that word pairs

like *cot* and *caught*, or *hawk* and *hock*, are pronounced the same. This regional merger radiates from two centers, one in Eastern New England, centered near the Boston area, and one centered in Western Pennsylvania in the Ohio Valley. Its western extension covers a large portion of the American West, excluding major metropolitan areas such as Los Angeles and San Francisco.

Other vowel mergers

There are a number of vowel mergers or "near mergers" that take place when vowels occur before certain kinds of consonants. The following mergers may occur before *r*, *l*, and the nasal segments.

- /i/ and /ɪ/, as in *field* and *filled* (Texas and the South)
- /e/ and /ɛ/ before /l/, as in *sale* and *sell* (Texas and the South)
- /u/ and /ʊ/, as in *pool* and *pull* (Texas and the South)
- /e/, /ɛ/, /æ/, /ʌ/ before /r/, as in *Mary*, *merry*, *marry*, *Murray*
- /ɪ/ and /ɛ/ before nasals, as in *pin* and *pen* (South)

Different dialects naturally may be distinguished by the kinds of mergers in which they participate. Thus, some varieties in the South and some other areas of the United States merge the vowels of *Mary*, *merry*, and *marry*, while the regional dialect of Southeastern Pennsylvania and New Jersey that encompasses Philadelphia merges *merry* and *Murray* while keeping these items distinct from *Mary* and *marry*.

Other dialects may indicate vowel shifts in which a vowel moves so close to another vowel that speakers from other dialect areas may think the two sounds have merged. In reality, a subtle distinction between the two sounds is maintained. For example, the backed and raised /ay/ vowel of the Outer Banks of North Carolina in words like *tide* may seem quite similar to /oy/ (as in *boy*), but it is maintained as distinct. Similarly, the /ɪ/ vowel (as in *bit*) may be raised so that it sounds almost like /i/ (as in *beet*), particularly before palatals such as *sh* and *tch*, so that people may hear *feesh* for *fish* and *reach* for *rich*. Just as with /ay/ and /oy/, though, a distinction between /ɪ/ and /i/ is preserved. This near merger is also found in some mainland Southern varieties, including the Upper Southern variety of Appalachian English. Isolated varieties may also retain a lower vowel production of /æ/ before *r* so that *there* may sound like *thar* and *bear* like *bar*.

æ raising

The vowel of words such as *back* or *bag* may be heightened from its typical phonetic position so that it is produced closer to the [ɛ] of *beg* or *bet*. The feature is found in a number of Northern areas and is an integral part of the Northern Cities Vowel Shift.

Variants of aw

The vowel nucleus of words like *out*, *loud*, and *down* may be produced in a number of different ways. In one pronunciation, which is sometimes referred to as CANADIAN RAISING because of its prominence in certain areas of Canada, the nucleus of /aw/ is raised to a schwa quality so that a phrase such as *out and about* sounds like *oat and about* [əʊt n əbəʊt]. This pronunciation is found in coastal Virginia and North Carolina, as well as some scattered dialect regions in Northern areas. Other dialect areas (e.g. Philadelphia, Pittsburgh) pronounce /aw/ with a fronted nucleus [æ], as in [dæʊn] for *down*; and we sometimes find that /aw/ may be produced with little or no glide as well, so that items like *down* and *Dan* may sound quite similar.

In a somewhat different production, the glide of /aw/ may be fronted as well as the nucleus, so that *brown* [bræɪn] may actually be confused with *brain* and *house* [hæɪs] may be confused with *highest*. This production is concentrated in the coastal dialects of the Southeastern US, such as those of Smith Island and Tangier Island in the Chesapeake Bay and the North Carolina Outer Banks.

Variants of ay

Several different processes may affect the diphthong /ay/ in words such as *time*, *tide*, and *tight*. The /ɪ/ glide which forms the second half of this diphthong (made up of [a] + [ɪ]) may be lost, yielding pronunciations such as [tam] for *time* and [tad] for *tide*. This glide loss, or UNGLIDING, is characteristic of practically all Southern-based vernaculars and is not particularly socially significant in the South. The absence of the glide is more frequent when the following segment is a voiced sound (e.g. *side*, *time*) than when it is a voiceless one (e.g. *sight*, *rice*), and only certain Anglo Southern varieties exhibit extensive ungliding of /ay/ before voiceless sounds.

Another process affecting some varieties of American English involves the raising of the nucleus of /ay/ so that *tide* and *tight* may be produced as [təɪd] and [təɪt]. This process often parallels the raising of the nucleus in /aw/ and also may be referred to as Canadian Raising because of its widespread presence in Canada. In the US, this type of /ay/ raising is found in the Tidewater Virginia area and other Eastern coastal communities. It is especially common before voiceless sounds (e.g. [təɪt] 'tight').

The nucleus of /ay/ may also be backed and/or raised (that is, /ay/ is pronounced as something like [ʌˀɪ]) so that it sounds quite close to the /oy/ of *toy* or *boy*. This backing and raising is associated with the Outer Banks of North Carolina, where speakers are referred to as "hoi toiders" for *high tiders*, but a number of dialects of American English use a backed nucleus for /ay/, including New York City English and some mainland Southern varieties.

Final unstressed ow

In word-final position, standard English *ow*, as in *hollow* or *yellow*, may become *r*, giving *holler* or *yeller*, respectively. This "intrusive *r*" also occurs when suffixes are attached, as in *fellers* for *fellows* or *narrers* for *narrows*. This production is characteristic of Upper Southern varieties such as those found in Appalachia or the Ozarks, although it is found to some extent in Southern rural varieties as well.

Final unstressed ə *raising*

Final unstressed *a* (phonetically [ə]), as in *soda* or *extra*, may be raised to a high vowel [i] giving productions such as *sody* (phonetically [sodi]) and *extry* [ɛkstri]). Again, this production is found in rural vernaculars of the Upper and Lower South.

ire/our *collapse*

The sequence spelled *ire*, usually produced in standard English as a two-syllable sequence which includes the [aɪ] diphthong (i.e. [taɪ.ɚ] 'tire'; [faɪ.ɚ] 'fire'), can be collapsed into a one-syllable sequence when /ay/ is unglided to [a]. This process yields pronunciations such as *far* for *fire* and *tar* for *tire*. It affects not only root words like *fire* but also /ay/ + *er* sequences formed by the addition of an -*er* suffix, as in *buyer* [bar]. A similar process affects -*our/ower* sequences which phonetically consist of a two-syllable sequence involving the [aʊ] diphthong and *r*, as in *flower* [flaʊ.ɚ] or *hour* [aʊ.ɚ]. These sequences may be reduced to a single syllable, so that *flower* sounds like *fla'r* [flar] and *hour* like *a'r* [ar].

Grammatical Structures

The verb phrase

Many of the socially significant grammatical structures in American English varieties involve aspects of the verb phrase. Some of this variation is due to the principles of readjustment discussed in chapter 2, but there are also some items that have their roots in the historical origins of different dialect varieties.

Irregular verbs

There are five ways in which irregular verbs pattern differently in standard and vernacular dialects of English. For the most part, these different patterns are the result of analogy, but there are also some retentions of patterns that have become obsolete in standard varieties. These differences are as follows:

1   past as participle form
      I *had went* down there.
      He may *have took* the wagon.
2   participle as past form
      He *seen* something out there.
      She *done* her work.
3   bare root as past form
      She *come* to my house yesterday.
      She *give* him a nice present last year.
4   regularization
      Everybody *knowed* he was late.
      They *throwed* out the old food.
5   different irregular form
      I *hearn* something shut the church house door.
      Something just *riz* up right in front of me.

Different dialects may differ according to which of the above patterns are found in the variety. The majority of vernaculars in the North and South indicate patterns 1, 2, and 3. Some rural vernaculars in the South may exhibit pattern 5 in addition to the first three. Varieties subject to the influence of second-language-learning strategies (e.g. Vietnamese English) will often reveal a higher incidence of regularization pattern 4 than other varieties.

Co-occurrence relations and meaning changes
There are a number of different types of constructions which can vary from dialect to dialect based on the types of structures that can co-occur with certain verbs or meaning changes which affect particular verbs. These constructions include the following types:

1   shifts in the transitive status of verbs (i.e. whether or not the verb is required to take an object)
      If we *beat*, we'll be champs.
2   types of complement structures co-occurring with particular verbs
      The kitchen *needs remodeled*.
      The students *started to messing* around.
      I'll *have* him *to do* it.
      The dog *wanted out*.
      Walt *called himself dancing*.
3   verb plus verb particle formations
      He *happened in* on the party.
      The coach *blessed out* his players.
4   verbs derived from other parts of speech (e.g. verbs derived from nouns)
      Our dog *treed* a coon.
      We *doctored* the sickness ourselves.

5 broadened, narrowed, or shifted semantic reference for particular verb forms

> He *carried* her to the movies.
> My kids *took* the chicken pox when they were young.
> I been *aimin'* to go there.

For the most part, differences related to meaning changes and co-occurrence relations between verbs and other sentence elements have to be dealt with on an item-by-item basis. All vernaculars, and many regional varieties, indicate meaning shifts and co-occurrence relations not found in standard English to some extent.

Special auxiliary forms

There are a number of special uses of auxiliary forms that set apart vernacular dialects of English from their standard counterparts. Many of these auxiliaries indicate subtle but significant meanings related to the duration or type of activity indicated by verbs, or "verb aspect."

Completive done

The form *done* may mark a completed action or event in a way somewhat different from a simple past tense form, as in a sentence such as *There was one in there that done rotted away* or *I done forgot what you wanted*. In this use, the emphasis is upon the "completive" aspect or the fact that the action has been fully completed. The *done* form may also add intensification to the activity, as in *I done told you not to mess up*. This form is typically found in Southern Anglo and African American vernaculars.

Habitual be

The form *be* in sentences such as *Sometimes my ears be itching* or *She usually be home in the evening* may signify an event or activity distributed intermittently over time or space. The predominant construction for habitual *be* involves a form of *be* + verb *-ing*, as in *My ears be itching*. The unique aspectual meaning of *be* is typically associated with African American Vernacular English, although isolated and restricted constructions with habitual *be* have been found in some rural Anglo varieties.

Be + s

In some restricted parts of the South (e.g. areas of the Carolinas where the historic influence of Highland Scots and Scots Irish is evident), *be* may occur with an *-s* third person suffix as in *Sometimes it bes like that* or *I hope it bes a girl*. However, *bes* is not restricted to contexts of habitual activity and thus is different from habitual *be* in AAVE. *Bes* is also distinguished from *be* in contemporary AAVE by the inflectional *-s*; further, *bes* is obviously a receding form, while *be* in AAVE is quite robust.

Remote time béen
When stressed, *béen* can serve to mark a special aspectual function, indicating that the event or activity took place in the "distant past." In structures such as *I béen had it there for about three years* or *I béen known her*, the reference is to an event which took place, literally or figuratively, in some distant time frame. This use, which is associated with AAVE, is dying out in some varieties of the vernacular, but is still prominent in those varieties more closely aligned with the apparent creole predecessor of AAVE, in which the form most likely was used much more extensively.

Fixin' to
The use of *fixin' to* (also produced as *fixta, fista, finsta,* and *finna*) may occur with a verb with the meaning of 'about to' or 'plan to'. Thus, in a sentence such as *It's fixin' to rain,* the occurrence of rain is imminent. In a construction such as *I was fixin' to come but I got held up,* the speaker is indicating that he or she had intended to come. This special use of *fixin' to* is found only in the South, particularly in the South Atlantic and Gulf states.

Indignant come
The use of the form *come* as an auxiliary in sentences such as *She come acting like she was real mad* or *He come telling me I didn't know what I was talking about* may convey a special sense of speaker indignation. It is a CAMOUFLAGED FORM, in the sense that it appears to be much like a comparable standard English use of *come* with movement verbs (e.g. *She came running home*), but it does not function in the same way as its standard counterpart. It is found in AAVE.

A-prefixing
An *a-* prefix may occur on *-ing* forms functioning as verbs or adverbs, as in *She was a-comin' home* or *He starts a-laughin' at you.* This form cannot occur on *-ing* forms that function as nouns or adjectives. Thus, it cannot occur in sentences such as *He likes a-sailin'* or *The movie was a-charmin'.* The *a-* is also restricted phonologically, in that it occurs only on forms whose first syllable is accented; thus, it may occur on *a-fóllowin'* but not *a-discóverin'.* The *a-* prefix is also preferred on items beginning with a consonant (e.g. *Kim was a-drinkin'*) over those beginning with a vowel (e.g. *Kim was a-eatin'*). As currently used by some speakers, the *a-* prefix may be used to indicate intensity, but it does not appear to have any unique aspectual marking analogous to habitual *be* or completive *done.* It is quite characteristic of vernacular Appalachian English but is found in other rural varieties as well.

Double modals
Double modals are combinations of two MODAL verbs, or verbs expressing certain "moods" such as certainty, possibility, obligation, or permission. Possible

combinations include *might could, useta could, might should, might oughta,* and so forth. Sentences such as *I might could go there* or *You might oughta take it* are typically Southern vernacular structures; in Northern varieties, modal clustering occurs only with *useta,* as in *He useta couldn't do it.* Double modals tend to lessen the force of the attitude or obligation conveyed by single modals, so that *She might could do it* is less forceful than either *She might do it* or *She could do it.* In some Southern states such as the Carolinas, double modals are quite widespread and not particularly stigmatized.

Liketa *and* (su)poseta
The forms *liketa* and *(su)poseta* may be used as special verb modifiers to mark speakers' perceptions of significant events that were on the verge of happening. *Liketa* is a COUNTERFACTUAL, in that it is used in a non-literal way to indicate that an impending event did not occur. In a sentence such as *It was so cold, I liketa froze to death, liketa* conveys the meaning not only that the speaker did not freeze to death, but also that the speaker was never in any real danger of freezing. *(Su)poseta,* in sentences such as *You (su)poseta went there,* parallels the standard English construction *supposed to have.*

Absence of be *forms*
Where contracted forms of *is* or *are* may occur in standard English, these same forms may be deleted in some vernacular varieties. Thus, we get structures such as *You ugly* or *She taking the dog out* corresponding to the standard English structures *You're ugly* and *She's taking the dog out,* respectively. It is important to note that this absence only takes place on "contractible" forms; thus, it does not affect *they are* in a construction such as *That's where they are* since *they are* cannot be contracted to *they're* in this instance. Furthermore, the absence of *be* does not usually apply to the *am* form, so that sentences such as *I ugly* do not occur. The deletion of *are* is typical of both Southern Anglo and AAVE varieties, although the absence of *is* is not very extensive in most Anglo varieties. A more general version of *be* absence which includes *am* is sometimes found in varieties developed in the process of learning English as a second language (e.g. Vietnamese English).

Subject–verb agreement
There are a number of different subject–verb agreement patterns that enter into the social and regional differentiation of dialects. These include the following:

1 agreement with existential *there*
    There was five people there.
    There's two women in the lobby.
2 leveling to *was* for past tense forms of *be*
    The cars was out on the street.
    Most of the kids was younger up there.

3   leveling to *were* with negative past tense *be*
    It weren't me that was there last night.
    She weren't at the creek.
4   leveling to *is* for present tense forms of *be*
    The dogs is in the house.
    We is doing it right now.
5   agreement with the form *don't*
    She don't like the cat in the house.
    It don't seem like a holiday.
6   agreement with *have*
    My nerves has been on edge.
    My children hasn't been there much.
7   *-s* suffix on verbs occurring with third person plural noun phrase subjects
    Some people likes to talk a lot.
    Me and my brother gets in fights.
8   *-s* absence on third person singular forms
    *The dog stay_* outside in the afternoon.
    *She usually like_* the evening news.

Different varieties exhibit different patterns from the list above. Virtually all vernacular varieties show patterns 1, 2, and 5 above (in fact, standard varieties are moving towards the pattern found in 1), but in different degrees. The patterns illustrated in 6 and 7 above are most characteristic of rural varieties in the Upper and Lower South, and that found in 8 are most typical of AAVE. The leveling of past *be* to *weren't* in 3 appears to be regionally restricted to some coastal dialect areas of the Southeast and a few historically isolated Southern dialect areas.

Past tense absence
Many cases of past tense *-ed* absence on verbs (e.g. *Yesterday he mess up*) can be accounted for by the phonological process of consonant cluster reduction found in the discussion of phonology. However, there are some instances in which the use of unmarked past tense forms represents a genuine grammatical difference. Such cases are particularly likely to be found in varieties influenced by other languages in their recent past. Thus, structures such as *He bring the food yesterday* or *He play a new song last night* may be the result of a grammatical process rather than a phonological one. Grammatically based tense unmarking tends to be more frequent on regular verbs than irregular ones, so that a structure such as *Yesterday he play a new song* is more likely than *Yesterday he is in a new store*, although both may occur. In some cases, both phonological and grammatical processes operate in a convergent way.

    Tense unmarking has been found to be prominent in varieties such as Vietnamese English and Native American Indian English in the Southwest. In the latter case, unmarking is favored in habitual contexts (e.g. *In those days, we play a different kind of game*) as opposed to simple past time (e.g. *Yesterday, we play at a friend's house*).

Historical present
In the dramatic recounting of past time events, speakers may use present tense verb forms rather than past tense forms, as in *I go down there and this guy comes up to me. . . .* In some cases an *-s* suffix may be added to non-third person forms, particularly with the first person form of *say* (e.g. *so I says to him . . .*). This structure is more prominent in Anglo vernaculars than in AAVE.

Perfective be
Some historically isolated varieties of American English may use forms of *be* rather than *have* in present perfect constructions, as in *I'm been there before* for 'I've been there before' or *You're taken the best medicine* for 'You have taken the best medicine'. This construction occurs most frequently in first person singular contexts (e.g. *I'm forgot*) but can also occur in the first person plural and in second person contexts as well (e.g. *we're forgot, you're been there*). Occasionally, the perfect tense can even be formed with invariant *be*, as in *We be come here for nothing* or *I'll be went to the post office*. Perfective *be* derives from the historic formation of the perfect with *be* rather than *have* for certain verbs (e.g. *He is risen* 'He has risen') and is restricted to historically isolated dialect areas.

Adverbs

There are several different patterns that distinguish adverb usage among vernacular varieties. These involve differences in the placement of adverbs within the sentence, differences in the formation of adverbs, and differences in the use or meaning of particular adverbial forms.

Adverb placement
There are several differences in terms of the position of the adverb within the sentence, including the placement of certain time adverbs within the verb phrase, as in *We were **all the time** talking* or *We watched **all the time** the news on TV*. These cases do not hold great social significance and are not particularly socially stigmatized. More socially marked is the change in order with various forms of *ever*, as in *everwhat, everwho,* or *everwhich* (e.g. ***Everwho** wanted to go could go*). These older English forms are generally found only in vernaculars retaining relic forms of English, but even in these contexts they are currently dying out.

Comparatives and superlatives
Most vernacular varieties of English indicate some comparative and superlative adjective and adverb forms which are not found in standard varieties. Some

forms involve the regularization of irregular forms, as in *badder* or *mostest*, while others involve the use of *-er* and *-est* on adjectives of two or more syllables (e.g. *beautifulest*, *awfulest*), where the standard variety uses *more* and *most*. In some instances, comparatives and superlatives are doubly marked, as in *most awfulest* or *more nicer*. As we discuss in chapter 2, both regularization and double marking are highly natural language processes.

-ly *absence*

In present-day American English, some adverbs which used to be formed by adding an *-ly* suffix no longer take *-ly*. Thus, in informal contexts, most standard English speakers say *They answered wrong* instead of *They answered wrongly*. The range of items affected by *-ly* absence can be extended to various degrees in different vernacular dialects. These items may be relatively unobtrusive (e.g. *She enjoyed life awful well*) or quite obtrusive (e.g. *I come from Virginia original*). The more obtrusive forms seem to be more prominent in Southern-based vernacular varieties than Northern dialects, particularly Upper Southern varieties such as Appalachian and Ozark English.

Intensifying adverbs

In some Southern-based vernaculars, certain adverbs can be used to intensify particular attributes or activities. In standard English, the adverb *right* is currently limited to contexts involving location or time (e.g. *He is **right** around the corner*). However, in Southern-based vernaculars, *right* may be used to intensify the degree of other types of attributes, as in *She is **right** nice*. Other adverbs, such as *plumb*, serve to intensify attributes in totality, as in *The students fell **plumb** asleep*. Additional intensifying adverbs found in these varieties include items such as *big old*, *little old*, *right smart*, and *right much*, among others.

A special function of the adverb *steady* has been described for AAVE. In this variety, *steady* may be used in constructions such as *They be **steady** messing with you* to refer to an intense, ongoing activity.

Other adverbial forms

There are a number of other cases in which the adverbial forms of vernacular varieties differ from their standard counterparts. Some of these involve word class changes, as in the use of *but* as an adverb meaning "only," as in *He ain't **but** thirteen years old*, or the item *all* in *The corn got **all***. In many Midland dialects of American English, *anymore* may be used in positive constructions with a meaning of 'nowadays', as in *She watches a lot of videos **anymore***.

Some vernacular dialects contain adverbial lexical items not found at all in standard varieties (e.g. *yonder*, as in *It's up **yonder***), while other adverbial differences come from the phonological fusion of items, as in *t'all* from *at all* (e.g. *It's not coming up **t'all***), *pert' near* (e.g. *She's **pert' near** seventy*), or *druther* (e.g. ***Druther** than lose the farm, he fought*). Again, such differences must be considered on an item-by-item basis.

Negation

The two major vernacular negation features of American English are the use of so-called "double negatives," or the marking of negative meaning at more than one point in a sentence, and the use of the lexical item *ain't*. Other forms, resulting directly from the acquisition of English as a second language (e.g. *He no like the man*), are found in the speech of people learning English as a second language but do not seem to be perpetuated as a continuing part of the vernacular English variety of such speakers once they have completed the transition to English. An exception may be the negative tag *no* as found in some Hispanic English varieties, as in *They're going to the store, no?*

Multiple negation

There are four different patterns of multiple negative marking found in the vernacular varieties of English:

1. marking of the negative on the auxiliary verb and the indefinite(s) following the verb
   The man *wasn't* saying *nothing*.
   He *didn't* say *nothing* about *no* people bothering him or *nothing* like that.
2. negative marking of an indefinite before the verb phrase and of the auxiliary verb
   Nobody didn't like the mess.
   Nothing can't stop him from failing the course.
3. inversion of the negativized auxiliary verb and the pre-verbal indefinite
   Didn't nobody like the mess.
   Can't nothing stop him from failing the course.
4. multiple negative marking across different clauses
   There *wasn't* much that I *couldn't* do (meaning 'There wasn't much I could do')
   I *wasn't* sure that *nothing wasn't* going to come up (meaning 'I wasn't sure that anything was going to come up')

Virtually all vernacular varieties of English participate in multiple negation of type 1 in the above inventory; restricted Northern and most Southern vernaculars participate in 2; most Southern vernaculars participate in 3 above; and restricted Southern and African American Vernacular English varieties participate in 4.

ain't

The item *ain't* may be used as an alternate for certain standard English forms, including the following:

1   forms of *be* + *not*
     She *ain't* here now.
     I *ain't* gonna do it.
2   forms of *have* + *not*
     I *ain't* seen her in a long time.
     She *ain't* gone to the movies in a long time.
3   *did* + *not*
     He *ain't* tell him he was sorry.
     I *ain't* go to school yesterday.

The first two types are found in most vernacular varieties, but the third type, in which *ain't* corresponds with standard *didn't*, has only been found in AAVE.

Past tense wont
The form *wont*, pronounced much like the negative modal *won't*, may occur as a generalized form for past tense negative *be* – that is, *wasn't* and *weren't*. Thus, we may find sentences such as *It wont me* and *My friends wont the ones who ate the food*. Although the form probably arose through the application of phonological processes to forms of *wasn't* and *weren't*, *wont* now seems to serve as a past tense analogue of *ain't*, since both *ain't* and *wont* have a single form for use with all persons and numbers (as opposed to standard forms of *be* + *not*, which vary quite a bit by person and number). Its use is restricted to rural Southern varieties, particularly those found in the South Atlantic region.

Nouns and pronouns

Constructions involving nouns and pronouns are often subject to socially significant dialect variation. The major types of differences involve the attachment of various suffixes and the use of particular "case" markings, or markings which indicate the role which nouns and pronouns play in the particular sentences in which they occur.

Plurals
There are several different ways in which plurals may be formed which differentiate them from plurals found in standard varieties of English. These include the following:

1   general absence of plural suffix
     Lots of *boy__* go to the school.
     All the *girl__* liked the movie.
2   restricted absence of plural suffix with measurement nouns
     The station is four *mile__* down the road.
     They hauled in a lotta *bushel__* of corn.

3 regularization of various irregular plural noun forms
They saw the *deers* running across the field.
The *firemans* liked the convention.

Plural absence of type 1 is found only among varieties where another language was spoken in the recent past and, to a limited degree, in AAVE. In category 2, plural suffix absence is limited to nouns of weights (e.g. *four pound*, *three ton*) and measures (e.g. *two foot*, *twenty mile*), including some temporal nouns (e.g. *two year*, *five month*); this pattern is found in Southern-based vernaculars, particularly in historically isolated areas. Category 3 includes regularization of plurals that are not marked overtly in standard English (e.g. *deers*, *sheeps*), forms marked with irregular suffixes in the standard (e.g. *oxes*), and forms marked by non-suffix plurals (e.g. *firemans*, *snowmans*). In the last case, plurals may be marked with both plural forms, as in *mens* or *childrens*. Some kinds of plurals in category 3 are quite widespread among the vernacular varieties of English (e.g. regularizing non-marked plurals such as *deers*), whereas others (e.g. the double marking in *mens*) are more limited.

Possessives
There are several patterns involving possessive nouns and pronouns, including the following:

1 the absence of the possessive suffix
The *man_ hat* is on the chair.
John_ coat is here.
2 regularization of the possessive pronoun *mines*, on the basis of analogy with *yours*, *his*, *hers*, etc.
Mines is here.
It's *mines*.
3 the use of possessive forms ending in *-n*, as in *hisn* or *yourn*. Such forms can only be found in phrase- or sentence-final position, as in *It is hisn* or *It was yourn that I was talking about*; *-n* forms do not usually occur in structures such as *It is hern book*.
Is it *yourn*?
I think it's *hisn*.

The first two types of possessives are typical of AAVE, and the third type is found in vernacular Appalachian English and other rural varieties characterized by the retention of relic forms, although it is now restricted to older speakers in these varieties.

Pronouns
Pronoun differences typically involve regularization by analogy and rule extension. The categories of difference include the following:

1 regularization of reflexive forms by analogy with other possessive pronouns
   He hit *hisself* on the head.
   They shaved *theirselves* with the new razor.
2 extension of object forms to coordinate subjects
   Me and him will do it.
   John and them will be home soon.
3 adoption of a second person plural form to "fill out" the person-number paradigm
   a *Y'all* won the game.
      I'm going to leave *y'all* now.
   b *Youse* won the game.
      I'm going to leave *youse* now.
   c *You'uns* won the game.
      I'm going to leave *you'uns* now.
4 extension of object forms to demonstratives
   Them books are on the shelf.
   She didn't like *them* there boys.
5 a special PERSONAL DATIVE use of the object pronoun form
   I got *me* a new car.
   We had *us* a little old dog.

The first four types of pronominal difference are well represented in most vernacular dialects of English. The particular form used for the second person plural pronoun (type 3) varies by region; 3a, of course, is the Southern form and 3b the Northern form, with some specific regions (e.g. Western Pennsylvania, Southern Appalachia) using 3c. The so-called personal dative illustrated in 5 is a Southern feature, but it is not particularly stigmatized in the South.

Other pronoun forms, such as the use of an object form with a non-coordinate subject (e.g. **Her in the house**) and the use of subject or object forms in possessive structures (e.g. *It is she book*; *It is he book*), are quite rare in most current vernaculars, except for those still closely related to a prior creole state. The use of possessive *me*, as in *It's me cap*, is occasionally found in historically isolated varieties which have some Scots-Irish influence.

Relative pronouns
Differences affecting relative pronouns (e.g. *who* in *She's the one who gave me the present*) include the use of certain relative pronoun forms in contexts where they would not be used in standard varieties and the absence of relative pronouns under certain conditions. Differences in relative pronoun forms may range from the relatively socially insignificant use of *that* for human subjects (e.g. *The person that I was telling you about is here*) to the quite stigmatized use of *what*, as in *The person what I was telling you about is here*. One form which is becoming more common, and spreading into informal varieties of standard

English, is the use of the relative pronoun *which* as a coordinating conjunction (i.e. *and*), as in *They gave me this cigar, which they know I don't smoke cigars.*

In standard English, relative pronouns may be deleted if they are the object in the relative clause, so that *That's the dog that I bought* can alternately be rendered as *That's the dog I bought.* In most cases where the relative pronoun is the subject, however, the pronoun must be retained, as in *That's the dog that bit me.* However, a number of Southern-based varieties may sometimes delete relative pronouns in subject position, as in *That's the dog bit me* or *The man come in here is my father.* The absence of the relative pronoun is more common in existential constructions such as *There's a dog bit me* than in other constructions.

Existential it/they

As used in sentences such as *There are four people in school* and *There's a picture on TV*, the standard English form *there* is called an EXISTENTIAL, since it indicates the mere existence of something rather than specific location (as in *Put the book over there*). Vernacular varieties may use *it* or *they* for *there* in existential constructions, as in *It's a dog in the yard* or *They's a good show on TV*. *They* for *there* seems to be found only in Southern-based vernaculars; *it* is more general, and appears to be spreading.

Other Grammatical Structures

There are a number of additional structures which we have not included in this overview of vernacular grammatical constructions. Some of the forms we have not included are those which were once thought to be confined to vernacular varieties but have been shown, through empirical sociolinguistic study, to actually be quite common in informal standard varieties. For example, we did not include the structure known as "pronominal apposition," in which a pronoun is used in addition to a noun in subject position, as in *My father, he made my breakfast*, because this feature is found in practically all social groups of American speakers, even though it is often considered to be a vernacular dialect feature. Furthermore, it is not particularly obtrusive in spoken language. It has also been found that the use of inverted word order in indirect questions, as in *She asked could she go to the movies*, is becoming just as much a part of informal spoken standard English as indirect questions without inverted word order, as in *She asked if she could go to the movies*. Other differences, such as those affecting prepositions, have to be treated on an item-by-item basis and really qualify as lexical rather than grammatical differences. Thus, forms such as *of a evening/of the evening* ('in the evening'), *upside the head* ('on the side of the head'), *leave out of there* ('leave there'), *the matter of him* ('the matter with him'), *to* for *at* (e.g. *She's to the store right now*), and so forth have to be treated individually. In most cases, their social significance is also secondary to their regional significance, so that we have not treated them in detail. Traditional *Linguistic Atlas* surveys and the *Dictionary of American Regional English* give much more adequate detail about these forms than could be given in this overview.

Glossary

absolute position   The position at the end of a clause or sentence; for example, *his* is in absolute position in *The book is **his***, but not in ***His** book is here*.

accent   (1) A popular label for dialect, with particular reference to pronunciation. (2) Speech influenced by another language (e.g. "She speaks with a French accent"). (3) See **stress**.

acronym   A word formed by combining the initial sounds or letters of words, for example *NATO* or *UN*.

additive dialect   See **bidialectalism**.

address form   The name used in speaking to or referring to a person; for example, *Ms Jones, Chris, Professor Smith*.

addressee   A person to whom speech is directed.

affix   A morpheme that attaches to the base or root word; in *retells*, *re-* and *-s* are affixes.

agreement   A co-occurrence relationship between grammatical forms, such as that between the subject and verb of a sentence; in the following sentence, the third person singular subject agrees with the verb because it is marked with the morpheme *-s*: ***She likes dialectology***.

alveolar   A sound produced by touching the blade of the tongue to the small ridge just in back of the upper teeth.

analogy   The application of a pattern to forms not previously included in a set, as in the regularization of the plural *ox* to *oxes* or the formation of the past tense of *bring* as *brang* on the basis of *sing* and *sang* and *ring* and *rang*.

    four-part analogy; also **proportional analogy**   The changing of irregular forms for words on the basis of regular patterns (e.g. *cow* : *cow* :: *ox* to *oxes*).

    minority pattern analogy   The changing of a form on the basis of an irregular pattern; for example, the formation of the past tense of *bring* as *brang* on the basis of *sing/sang* rather than the regular *-ed* past tense pattern.

    leveling   The reduction of distinct forms within a grammatical paradigm, as in the use of *was* with all subject persons and numbers for past tense *be* (e.g. *I/you/ (s)he/we/you/they was*).

Anglicist hypothesis   The contention that African American Vernacular English is derived historically from dialects found in the British Isles.

apex   A dialect pocket, or the regionally restricted extension of one dialect area into an adjacent one; for example, the Hoosier apex is an extension of Southern speech in Southern Indiana and Illinois.

applied dialectology   The application of knowledge from the study of dialects to social and educational issues.

argot   A specialized vocabulary or jargon, typically used in such a way as to conceal the subject of conversation from outsiders; often used with reference to criminal activity.

aspect   A grammatical category pertaining to verbs which indicates type or duration of activity; for example *has written* (perfect aspect) vs. *has been writing* (imperfect aspect). Compare **tense** and **mood**.

aspiration   A puff of air after the production of a stop, as in the pronunciation of *p* in *pie* [pʰaɪ]; usually indicated by a raised [ʰ] after the sound.

assimilation   The modification of sounds so that they become more like neighboring sounds; for example, the negative prefix *in-* assimilates to *il-* when preceding an *l* (e.g. *illogical*).

attention to speech   The model for **style shifting** which maintains that style shifting is directly related to the amount of attention given to speech: The more attention paid to speech, the more formal the style will become.

audience design model   The model for **style shifting** which maintains that speakers adjust their speech based primarily upon the attributes of people in their audience of listeners.

auditor   A person in a speech situation who is considered to be a legitimate participant in the conversational interaction but is not directly addressed.

auxiliary   A form occurring with a main verb, traditionally referred to as a "helping verb"; for example, *has* in *has made*, *done* in *done tried*.

back formation   The creation of a shorter word from a longer word based on the removal of what appears to be an affix but is in reality part of the original word; for example, *burgle* from *burglar*, *orientate* from *orientation*.

back vowel   A vowel produced with the tongue toward the back of the mouth; for example, the [u] of *Luke*, the [o] of *boat*.

backchanneling   The linguistic and extralinguistic strategies used by a listener to indicate that the speaker may continue with an extended conversational turn; for example, *uhmm* and *right* may serve as backchanneling devices.

bare root   The root form of a verb. With certain verbs, may be used to indicate past tense in vernacular dialects; for example, *give* may be used as a past tense form in sentences such as *Yesterday they give me a present*.

bidialectalism   The position in teaching standard English that maintains that the standard should co-exist with a vernacular variety rather than replace it.

bilabial   See **labial**.

blending The creation of a new word by combining portions of different words; for example, words such as *smog* (*smoke* + *fog*) or *twirl* (*twist* + *whirl*) were formed through blending.

borrowing A language item that is taken from another language; for example, *arroyo* 'gully' from Spanish.

bound morpheme A morpheme that cannot stand alone as a separate word but must be attached to another item; for example, the -*s* in *boys*. Compare **free morpheme**.

breaking See **vowel breaking**.

broad *a* A non-technical label for the vowel found in words such as *bat* and *back*.

broadening See **semantic broadening**.

bundle of isoglosses A set of isoglosses that cluster together and serve to set apart dialect areas on a map.

camouflaged form A form in a vernacular variety that looks like a standard counterpart but is used in a structurally or functionally different way; for example, constructions such as *They come here talking that nonsense* in AAVE appear to be like standard structures such as *They come running* but actually carry a unique meaning of speaker indignation.

Canadian Raising The raising of the nucleus of the /ay/ and /aw/ diphthongs to [ə], as in [rəɪt] for *right* or [əʊt] for *out*.

careful style A speech style which occurs during relatively formal moments of a conversational sociolinguistic interview, such as during question and answer exchanges. Compare **casual style**.

cascade diffusion The spread of language features from areas of denser population to areas of sparser population. Also called **hierarchical diffusion**. See **gravity model**. Compare **contagious diffusion**, **contrahierarchical diffusion**.

case A form that indicates the role of a noun or pronoun in a sentence. For example, *I* is the subject of the sentence in *I hate cheaters* and therefore is in **subjective case**; *me* is the object of the verb in *Dogs hate me* and thus is in **objective case**.

casual style A speech style which occurs during relatively informal moments of a conversational sociolinguistic interview, such as during animated narratives. Compare **careful style**.

cell In an implicational array, any point where a row and column intersect.

chain shifting The shifting of a series of vowels in phonetic space in order to preserve phonetic distinctiveness among the vowel sounds. See **vowel rotation**.

change from above A change in a language form of which speakers are consciously aware.

change from below A change in a language form of which speakers are not aware on a conscious level.

change from outside   A language change that takes place due to borrowing from other language or dialect groups.

change from within   A change that is initiated from within the language itself, due to the internal dynamics of the linguistic system.

channel cues   Features accompanying speech that are indicative of the style of speaking in which a speaker is engaging; for example, laughter or increased tempo may be a channel cue for more casual speech style. Also called **paralinguistic channel cues**.

citation form   The way a word is produced when recited in isolation; for example, the pronunciation of *photograph* as an isolated word vs. its pronunciation in normal conversation.

clipping   The formation of a new word through the removal of syllables, such as *dorm* for *dormitory*.

coining   The creation of a new word not based on any previous form; for example, *meehonkey* for 'hide and seek' on the island of Ocracoke, North Carolina.

colloquial   Forms associated with informal language usage.

communication network   A group of people who are linked together via lines of communication.

complement   A word, phrase, or clause that completes a predicate; structures co-occurring with particular verbs (e.g. *painting* in *The house needed painting*, the clause *the house was dirty* in *I told him that the house was dirty*).

completion task   A format used to elicit an item in which the interviewee completes an incomplete sentence (e.g. "The hard inside of a peach is called a_____."). Also known as "fill-in-the-blank."

completive   A form signaling that an action has been completed at a previous time, with emphasis upon the completion; for example, 'completive' *done* in *He **done** took out the garbage* or *You **done** messed up this time*.

compound   A word created by combining two or more words, as in *lighthouse* from *light + house*.

concord   See **agreement**.

consonant   A sound produced by momentarily blocking airflow in the mouth or throat; for example, [b] and [t] in *bat*.

consonant cluster   The sequencing of two or more consecutive consonants without an intervening vowel; for example, [st] in *stop* or [ld] in *wild*.

consonant cluster reduction   The elimination of a consonant in a cluster; for example, the [st] in *mist* [mɪst] may become [s], as in *mis'* [mɪs].

constraint (on variability)   A linguistic or social factor that increases or decreases the likelihood that a given variant in a fluctuating set of items will occur. For example, the voicing of the following consonant is a constraint on the variability of /ay/ in Southern speech, since /ay/ is more likely to be pronounced as [a] when the following sound is voiced than when it is voiceless.

contagious diffusion　The spread of language features from a central point outward in geographic space. See **wave model**.

content validity　The extent to which a test measures the content area it claims to measure.

content word　A word having referential meaning, such as the noun *dog* or the adjective *blue*. Compare **function word**.

contraction　The shortening of words by omitting sounds, often resulting in the attachment of the contracted word to another word; for example, *is* + *not* contracts to *isn't*, *she will* contracts to *she'll*.

contrahierarchical diffusion　The spread of language features from sparsely populated areas to those of denser population. Compare **cascade diffusion, contagious diffusion**.

contrastive drill　A language-learning drill in which structures from two different languages or dialects are placed side by side to focus on the contrast between forms; for example, a sentence pair such as *The man nice* vs. *The man's nice* focuses on the contrast between copula absence and presence.

contrastive linguistics　The study of different languages or dialects by comparing structures in each of the varieties to determine points of similarity and difference between the varieties.

convergence　(1) In **Speech Accommodation Theory**, the notion that speakers will adjust their speech to become more like that of their addressees. Compare **divergence**. (2) The adjustment of a language variety over time to become more like another dialect or other dialects. Compare **divergence hypothesis**.

conversion　The creation of a new word by using an existing word as a different part of speech; for example, the verb *run* may be used as a noun in *They scored a run*.

copula　The form used to "link" a subject with a predicate; in English, a form of *be* when used as a linking verb, as in *She is nice, Tanya is the boss*.

copula deletion　The absence of the copula, as in *You ugly* for *You're ugly*; the term usually is extended to auxiliary uses of *be* forms as well, as in *He writing a book* for *He's writing a book*.

counterfactual　A form used to indicate that a situation is hypothetical rather than real. For example, counterfactual *liketa* (e.g. *I liketa froze to death*) is used to refer to a situation that didn't occur and was never likely to occur.

covert prestige　Positive value ascribed to language forms which is based on the local social value of the forms rather than their value in larger society. See **overt prestige**.

creolist hypothesis　The contention that African American Vernacular English developed historically from an ancestral creole language.

creole language　A special contact language in which the primary vocabulary of one language is superimposed upon a specially adapted, somewhat restricted grammatical structure; this language system may be used as a native language. See **pidgin language**.

critical age hypothesis   The hypothesis that true language mastery can only occur during a given age period, namely, during the prepubescent period.

crossing   The use of a non-native dialect or dialect features.

cultural difference theory   An approach to language and gender that views differences in men's and women's speech as a function of differential socio-cultural experiences by men and women. Compare **deficit theory, dominance theory**.

dative   The grammatical case in which forms occur when they function as the indirect object of a sentence; for example, *Terry* in *Todd gave the ball to Terry*, *Howard* in *They made a glossary for Howard*. See **personal dative**.

debt incurred   See **principle of debt incurred**.

decoding   The process of breaking down the written word letter by letter and relating it to the sound units or phonemes of spoken language.

decreolization   The process whereby a historical creole language loses the distinguishing features of its creole predecessor, usually through contact with a standard variety of the language.

deficit–difference controversy   A controversy which took place in the 1960s and 1970s in which linguists argued with educators that vernacular varieties of English should be considered as different dialects of English rather than deficient versions of standard English.

deficit theory   With reference to language and gender studies, the theory that considers female language traits as deficient versions of male language. Compare **dominance theory, cultural difference theory**.

definition by ostentation   The indication of knowledge about a language feature by demonstrating its use.

density   The extent to which members of a social network all interact with one another; if there is a high degree of interaction (i.e., if "everyone knows everyone else"), the network has **high density**, if not, it has **low density**. See **social network**.

derivational morpheme   A prefix or suffix that changes the basic meaning and/or word class of an item; for example, the *-er* in *buyer* changes the form from a verb to an noun.

devoicing   The phonetic change of voiced sounds to their voiceless counter-parts, as in [d] to [t] (e.g. *bad* to *bat*) or [z] to [s] (*buzz* to *bus*).

dialect   A variety of the language associated with a particular regional or social group.

dialect awareness programs   Activities conducted by linguists and community members that are intended to promote an understanding of and appreciation for language variation.

dialect discrimination   In testing, penalizing speakers of vernacular variet-ies on the basis of dialect differences; for example, in language-acquisition testing, treating the use of a dialect form as evidence that the standard form has not been acquired.

dialect endangerment See **endangered dialect**.

dialect reader A reading text that incorporates the speech of a vernacular-speaking community.

dialect rights A position advocating that students should not be asked to give up their dialect, either by replacing it or by adding a standard variety.

dialectally diagnostic With reference to language features, serving to differentiate social and regional groups from one another.

diffusion The spread of language features; typically used with reference to regional spread but may also be used with reference to spread across social groups. See **cascade diffusion, contagious diffusion, contrahierarchical diffusion**.

diphthong A "two-part" vowel consisting of a main vowel, or **nucleus**, followed by a secondary vowel, or **glide**; for example, the [aɪ] of *bite* and the [ɔɪ] of *boy* are diphthongs.

diphthongization See **vowel breaking**.

direct transfer model A model accounting for dialect influence in writing on the basis of direct carryover from spoken to written language.

directive A speech act in which the speaker directs the listener to do something; for example, *Take the garbage out*.

discrimination drill A drill in which two forms or structures are given side by side and the listener judges the form as either the "same" or "different"; for example, *She run* vs. *She runs*.

dissimilation Changing similar sounds so that they become more distinctive from one another; for example, the first *l* of *colonel* has been changed to [r] to make it less like the final *l*.

divergence (1) In **Speech Accommodation Theory**, the notion that speakers may adjust their language to distance themselves from addressees. Compare **convergence**. (2) The development of a language variety or language structure so that it becomes more dissimilar from other varieties or structures.

divergence hypothesis The contention that contemporary African American Vernacular English is becoming increasingly dissimilar from corresponding vernacular Anglo varieties.

dominance theory With respect to language and gender, the consideration of male–female language differences as the result of power differences between men and women. Compare **deficit theory, cultural difference theory**.

double modal The co-occurrence of two or even three modal forms within a single verb phrase, as in *They might could do it* or *They might oughta should do it*.

double negation See **multiple negation**.

dropped *r* See ***r*-lessness**.

eavesdropper   A person who is not known to be part of a speaker's audience but who may be listening in on a conversational exchange.

elicitation frame   A question designed to lead an interviewee to produce a word or structural item (e.g. *What is the hard inside part of a peach called?*).

endangered dialect   A dialect characterized by the sharp recession of longstanding dialect features in the face of the encroachment of features from other varieties.

environment   See **linguistic environment**.

eradicationism   The position on teaching standard English that maintains that the standard dialect should be taught in place of a vernacular one, thus "eradicating" the vernacular variety.

error analysis   An analytical procedure which starts with the set of actual non-normative responses produced by a speaker rather than non-normative responses which are predicted on the basis of a structural comparison of the varieties.

error correction   See **principle of error correction**.

existential   A form used to indicate existence but having no referential meaning of its own; for example, the form *there* in *There are four students taking the course*. Also called **expletive**.

expletive   (1) An interjection, often used with reference to profane words (e.g. *Damn!*). (2) See **existential**.

extension   See **rule extension**.

eye dialect   The use of spelling to suggest dialect difference; the spelling does not reflect an actual dialect difference; for example, *wuz* for *was*.

fine stratification   See **gradient stratification**.

first order constraint   The factor that has the greatest systematic effect on the variability of an item; the second most important factor is referred to as the **second order constraint**.

flap   A sound made by rapidly tapping the tip of the tongue to the **alveolar** ridge, as in the usual American English pronunciation of *t* in *Betty* [bɛDi] or *d* in *ladder* [læDɚ].

floor   The right to speak, as in *holding the floor*.

focal area   A regional area at the center of dialect innovation and change; changes radiate from this area outward.

focusing   The selection of only a few dialect features to mark an entire language variety.

folk etymology   Altering words so that they are transparent in terms of known meanings and forms, as in *cold slaw* for *cole slaw* or *old timer's disease* for *Alzheimer's disease*.

Formal Standard English   The variety of English prescribed as the standard by language authorities; found primarily in written language and the most formal spoken language (e.g. spoken language which is based on a written form of the language).

fossilized form   A form that occurs during the learning of a second language and persists while other forms continue their development toward the second-language norm.

four-part analogy   See **analogy.**

free morpheme   A morpheme that can occur alone as a word; for example, *boy* in *boys*. Compare **bound morpheme.**

fricative   A sound produced with a continuous flow of air through a narrow opening so that there is "friction" at the point of articulation (e.g. [f], [s], [θ]).

front vowel   A vowel produced toward the front of the mouth, as in the [i] of *beet* or the [æ] of *bat*.

function word   A word used to indicate grammatical relations between elements of a sentence rather than referential meaning; for example, articles such as *the/a*, prepositions such as *to/at*. Compare **content word.**

g-dropping   The production of *ng* in unstressed syllables as *n'* (e.g. *swimmin'* for *swimming*); in spelling, this is usually indicated by *n'*, but the actual phonetic shift involves the change from the back nasal [ŋ] to a front nasal [n].

Geechee   See **Gullah.**

gender   The complex of social, cultural, and psychological factors that surround sex; contrasted with sex as biological attribute.

general social significance   The social evaluation of a form that holds regardless of the geographical area in which it is found.

generic *he*   The use of the masculine pronoun *he* for referents which can be either male or female; for example, *If a student wants to pass the course, **he** should study*. The noun *man* historically has also been used as a generic, as in *Man shall not live by bread alone*.

glide   The secondary vowel of a **diphthong** (e.g. [ɪ] in *bite* [baɪt]). So called because speakers glide from the main vowel or **nucleus** to the secondary vowel in the production of the diphthong.

glottal stop   A rapid opening and closing of the vocal cords that creates a kind of "popping" sound. In some dialects, a glottal stop may occur instead of a [d] or [t] in *bottle* [baʔl].

gradient stratification   The distribution of socially significant linguistic structures among members of different social groups along a continuous scale rather than on the basis of discrete breaks between adjacent social groups. Also referred to as **fine stratification.**

grammar   The organization of words into sentences. Also called **syntax.**

grammatical   (1) Sentences and forms that conform to the unconscious rules of a language or dialect; linguistically "well formed" as opposed to "ill formed." (2) In popular usage, language forms and constructions that conform to norms of social acceptability; in this usage, "grammatical" constructions may or may not be linguistically well formed; conversely, linguistically well-formed constructions may or may not be socially acceptable. Compare **ungrammatical**.

grammaticalization   The encoding of a unique meaning onto a form; for example, in AAVE, the invariant form of *be* has become uniquely associated with habituality in sentences such as *You always be acting weird*.

gravity model   A model of dialect diffusion which holds that linguistic features spread via **cascade** or **hierarchical diffusion**.

group-exclusive   With reference to language forms or patterns, confined to one particular group of speakers.

group-preferential   With reference to language forms or patterns, concentrated in a certain group of speakers but found to an extent among other speakers.

group reference   Identification with a particular group in terms of socio-psychological self-definition.

Gullah   A creole language spoken primarily by African Americans in the Sea Islands off the coast of South Carolina and Georgia. Also called **Geechee**.

habitual   An activity that takes place at intermittent intervals over time (e.g. as signaled by the use of *be* in the AAVE structure *When I come home, I usually be taking a nap*).

hierarchical diffusion   See **cascade diffusion, gravity model**.

high vowel   A vowel made with the tongue in high position in the mouth, as in the [i] of *beet* or the [u] of *boot*.

historical present   A present tense form used in the recounting of a past time event, as in *Yesterday, I go down there and this guy comes up to me . . .*; generally used for dramatic vividness.

homophones/homophonous words   Different words that are pronounced the same, as in *dear* and *deer*; in some Southern dialects of English *pin* and *pen* are homophones.

Hoosier apex   See **apex**.

hypercorrection   The extension of a language form beyond its regular linguistic boundaries when a speaker feels a need to use extremely standard or "correct" forms. See **statistical** and **structural hypercorrection**.

implicational array   A display indicating **implicational relations** among language forms. In an implicational array, the feature X implies the presence of the feature Y, but the converse does not hold.

implicational relation   A condition in which one dialect form implies the existence of another; for example, if a speaker has copula absence for *is* (e.g. *He ugly*), then the speaker also has copula absence for *are* (e.g. *You ugly*).

independent linguistic constraint   See **linguistic constraint**.

indirect speech act   A speech act used to accomplish another type of speech act; for example, a statement such as *The garbage is overflowing* when used to request a person to empty the garbage.

inflectional morpheme In English, a suffix that augments a word without changing its basic meaning or its word class, as in -*s* in *dogs*, -*er* in *bigger*).

Informal Standard English The spoken variety of English considered socially acceptable in mainstream contexts; typically characterized by the absence of socially stigmatized linguistic structures.

inherent variability Variability between items within a single dialect system; speakers sometimes produce one variant and sometimes another. For example, sometimes speakers say *drinking* and at other times they say *drinkin'* in the same social context.

initiative style shift A shift in speech style motivated by the speaker's attempt to alter the existing situation in some way.

interdental A sound produced by placing the tongue tip between the upper and lower teeth; sounds such as the [θ] of *think* and the [ð] of *the* are interdentals.

interruption "Breaking into" the speech of the person holding the floor without waiting for a signal which indicates that the speaker is ready to relinquish the floor.

intervocalic Occurring between vowels; for example, *r* in *Mary*, *t* in *butter*.

intonation The pitch contours that accompany phrases and sentences; for example, question intonation on *Are you going?* vs. statement intonation of *You are going.*

intransitive verb A verb that does not take an object; for example, the verb *jog* in *The students jogged* is intransitive.

intrusive Additional, as in the additional *t* of *acrosst* or the *r* of *marsh*.

intuition In linguistics, the ability of native speakers to judge the well formedness of particular kinds of sentences. With reference to vernacular dialects, judgment of well formedness, or **grammaticality**, may be in opposition to judgments of social acceptability. For example, the sentence *Sometimes my ears be itching* is a well-formed, grammatical sentence as judged by native speaker intuitions but is socially unacceptable.

inversion A reversal of the "typical" order of items; for example, *Are you going?* vs. *You are going*, or *Can't nobody do it* vs. *Nobody can't do it.*

irregular form An item that does not conform to the predominant pattern; for example, the -*en* plural of *oxen*, the past tense of *come* (*came*). Compare **regular form**.

isogloss A line on a map indicating a boundary between the use and non-use of a particular linguistic feature. See also **bundle of isoglosses**.

isoglossal layering See **layering**.

jargon A particular vocabulary characteristic of a group of speakers who share a certain interest; for example, computer jargon, sports jargon.

labial A sound produced primarily with the lips; the [p] in *pit* is **bilabial**, involving both lips, while the [f] in *four* is **labiodental**, since it involves the lower lip and upper teeth.

labiodental   See **labial**.

language acquisition   The unconscious learning of language rules which results in implicit knowledge of language.

language learning   The conscious learning of rules of language which results in more explicit knowledge of language.

language register   See **register**.

language sample   Language data based on conversational interviews, as opposed to the direct elicitation of items.

language transfer   See **transfer**.

lax vowel   A vowel produced with comparatively little muscular tension; the [ɪ] of *bit* is a lax vowel compared with the [i] of *beet*, which is a "tense" vowel. See **short vowel**.

layering   A hierarchical arrangement of dialect features in which successive areas show differing levels of shared dialect forms. See **primary, secondary, tertiary dialect area**.

leveling   See **analogy**.

lexicographer   A person who compiles a dictionary or **lexicon**.

lexicon   The vocabulary of a language, including words and morphemes.

linguistic constraint   A linguistic factor, such as a type of linguistic environment or structural composition, which systematically affects the variability of fluctuating forms. Also referred to as **independent linguistic constraint**.

linguistic environment   The linguistic context that surrounds a form, such as the sounds that occur next to a given sound.

linguistic geography   The study of dialects in terms of their regional distribution.

linguistic gratuity   See **principle of linguistic gratuity**.

linguistic inferiority principle   The principle which holds that the language of a socially subordinate group is linguistically deficient compared to the more standard variety spoken by the superordinate social group.

linguistic marketplace   Those aspects of the socioeconomic realm that most directly relate to linguistic variation; for example, a receptionist may use standard language forms due to considerations of the linguistic marketplace. A **linguistic market index** is a scale which measures the importance of standard English in various jobs.

linguistic rule   (1) An unconscious pattern which governs the occurrence of a particular language form. For example, *a-* prefixing is governed by a rule which states that the *a-* prefix may be attached to *-ing* forms which act as verbs but not as nouns or adjectives (as in *The women went a-hunting* vs. *The women like hunting*). (2) An explicit statement about the patterning of linguistic forms; a precise statement describing where a form may occur structurally.

linguistic variable   A varying linguistic structure (e.g. *-ing/in'*) which may correlate with social factors such as region or status, or with other linguistic factors, such as linguistic environment.

long vowel   In English, a tense vowel, as in words such as *feet*, *bait*, *boot*, and *vote*. No longer corresponds with actual temporal length in English. Compare **short vowel**.

low back merger   The merger of the vowels in word pairs like *cot* and *caught*.

low vowel   A vowel produced with the tongue in a lowered position in the mouth; for example, vowels such as the [a] of *father*, the [ɔ] of *caught*, or the [æ] of *bat*.

marker   See **social marker**.

meaning shift   A change in word meaning so that a word can now be used to refer to an entirely different class of referents than previously (e.g. *bead* used to mean 'prayer' but now refers to a type of jewelry).

merger   The elimination of contrast between sounds; for example, *caught* and *cot* in some English dialects. Also called **neutralization**.

metalinguistic task   A task that involves talking about language rather than simply using language. Usually performed to give researchers insight into the structure and function of language forms.

metaphorical extension   The extension of the meaning of a word to refer to items which are quite different from its original referents but which share a meaning feature with the original set of referents. For example, *submarine* has been metaphorically extended to apply to a type of sandwich which is similar in shape to the seafaring vessel.

metathesis   The rearrangement of sounds in a sequence, as in [æks] for *ask*.

mid vowel   A vowel produced with the tongue in the middle range of tongue height, as in the [ɛ] of *bet*, the [ʌ] of *but*, or the [o] of *boat*.

minimal word pair   A pair of words that are identical except for one sound; word pairs such as *bit* and *pit* or *bit* and *bet* are minimal word pairs.

minority pattern analogy   See **analogy**.

modal   An auxiliary verb which expresses certain "moods" related to permission, obligation, suggestion, or the speakers' attitude toward the truth of her or his assertions; for example, *can, may, will, shall, must*. See also **double modal**.

monitoring   The act of paying attention to how one is speaking during the production of speech.

monophthongization   The reduction of a two-part vowel, or diphthong, to a one-part vowel, or monophthong, through the elimination of the glide, as in [tam] for *time* or [bɔl] for *boil*.

monosyllabic   Consisting of one syllable, as in *go* or *but*.

mood   A grammatical category which pertains to speakers' attitudes toward the truth of their assertions (e.g. possibility, probability) or to speakers' expressions of obligation, permission, and suggestion. Mood is usually indicated in English through **modal** verbs, such as *must, should*, and *may*.

moribund dialect   A dialect which is no longer spoken by the younger speakers in the speech community.

morpheme The smallest meaningful unit of language; for example, in *dogs*, *dog* and *-s* are morphemes.

morphology The level of language which concerns words and their meaningful components, or **morphemes**.

morphosyntactic Pertaining to the marking of a syntactic relationship through a particular morpheme; for example, third person *-s* in *Tyler works hard* indicates a relationship between the subject and verb.

multiple negation The marking of negation at more than one point in a sentence (e.g. *They didn't do nothing about nobody*). Also called **double negation, negative concord**.

multiplex network A social network characterized by the interaction of individuals in a social network in a number of different spheres, such as work, leisure, and neighborhood. See **social network**.

multiplexity See **multiplex networks**.

narrowing See **semantic narrowing**.

nasal A segment produced by allowing air to pass through the nasal cavity, as in the *m* of *mom* or the *n* of *no*.

naturalistic speech Speech that represents how people talk under normal, ordinary circumstances.

negative concord See **multiple negation**.

Network Standard A variety of English relatively free of marked regional characteristics; the ideal norm aimed for by national radio and television network announcers. See **Standard American English**.

neutralization see **merger**.

nonstandard With reference to language forms, socially stigmatized through association with socially disfavored groups.

nonstandard dialect A socially disfavored dialect of a language; used synonymously with **vernacular dialect** in this book.

Northern Cities Vowel Shift A vowel shift or rotation in which the low back vowels are moving forward and upward and the short front vowels are moving downward and backward; found predominantly in Northern metropolitan areas.

nucleus The core or base of a vowel sound; in a word like *bike* [baɪk], the [a] is considered the vowel nucleus.

object language A language variety which has been reduced to a mere object of curiosity rather than a primary vehicle for communication.

objective case The form which a noun or pronoun takes when it is the object of a verb (e.g. *me* in *Tanya likes me*). See **case**.

observer's paradox A widely accepted tenet in sociolinguistics which holds that the best speech for analysis is that which occurs when people are not being observed.

open *o* The [ɔ] vowel; occurs in words such as *caught* or *song*, as produced in some dialects of English.

orthography The spelling system of a language.

overhearer A member of a speaker's audience whose presence is known to the speaker but who is not considered to be a participant in the conversational exchange.

overt prestige Positive value ascribed to language forms which is based on the value of the forms in mainstream society. See **covert prestige**.

paradigm A set of items that relate to a particular base form, as in the subject pronouns (e.g. *I, you, he/she/it, we, you, they*).

paralinguistic channel cues See **channel cues**.

participle A word derived from a verb, having qualities of an adjective or noun as well as a verb; for example, *charming* in *He was charming, taken* in *It was taken.*

perceptual dialectology The study of how non-linguists classify different dialects.

performance speech The type of speech used when speakers are attempting to display for others a certain language variety.

personal dative A pronoun in dative case which refers back to the noun in subject position and is used to emphasize a particular state or action; for example *I got me a dog, She ate her some lunch.* Typically found in Southern dialects of American English.

phoneme A basic unit of contrast, or meaning difference, in phonology. Usually established on the basis of "minimal word pairs." For example, /p/ and /b/ are considered to be different phonemes in English because they can be used to make meaning differences, as in *pit* and *bit*.

phonemic brackets The slashes / / surrounding sounds which are used to indicate that the enclosed symbols represent phonemes rather than phonetic or orthographic elements.

phonetic brackets The symbols [ ] which are used around sounds to indicate that they are being presented in their phonetic form, particularly as opposed to their phonemic or orthographic form.

phonetic space The area in the mouth in which language sounds, particularly vowels, are produced.

phonics An approach to reading based upon the letter-by-letter processing of written symbols; letters are "sounded out" and combined with each other to decipher words.

phonology The sound system of a language.

phrase timing The timing of syllables in which stressed syllables in phrases are held longer and unstressed ones shortened by comparison.

pidgin language A language used primarily as a trade language among speakers of different languages; has no native speakers. The vocabulary of a pidgin language is taken primarily from a superordinate language, and the grammar is drastically reduced.

possessive An item indicating possession, such as the suffix -*s* in *John's hat* or the pronoun *his* in *his hat.*

postconsonantal   Occurring immediately after a consonant, as in the *r* of *brought*.

post-insular   Formerly isolated. Used in reference to languages or language varieties whose speakers have lived in relative isolation for an extended period of time but have subsequently emerged from such isolation or are in the process of becoming less isolated. Also **post-isolated**.

post-isolated   See **post-insular**.

postvocalic *r*   The sound *r* when it follows a vowel, as in the *r* of *poor*.

pragmatics   The level of language organization pertaining to language use; takes into account such matters as speakers' and hearers' beliefs, attitudes, and intentions.

prefix   An affix attached to the beginning of a word base, such as *re-* in *retell*.

preposing   The shift of an item to the beginning of a sentence; for example, *Yesterday* in **Yesterday Marge ran**, as opposed to *Marge ran yesterday*.

Prescriptive Standard English   The variety deemed standard by grammar books and other recognized language "authorities." See **Formal Standard English**.

prestigious   See **socially prestigious**.

primary dialect area   That portion of a dialect area which exhibits the greatest concentration of shared dialect features.

principle of debt incurred   The sociolinguistic tenet which holds that linguists should use knowledge gained from their research to correct errors about language in society and education.

principle of error correction   The sociolinguistic tenet which holds that linguists should use data from their research to benefit the community that provided them with data.

principle of linguistic gratuity   The tenet which holds that linguists should proactively seek ways to use data from their research to benefit the community that provided linguistic data.

pronominal apposition   The use of a co-referential pronoun in addition to a noun in subject position; for example, *mother* and *she* in *My **mother**, **she** came home early*.

proportional analogy   See **analogy**.

prosody, prosodic   The aspects of pitch, intensity, and timing that accompany the segments of spoken language.

raising   Pronouncing a vowel with a higher tongue position; for example, the **Northern Cities Vowel Shift** is characterized by the raising of /æ/ to near /ɛ/ position, and Tidewater Virginia speech is characterized by the raising of the nucleus of /ay/ to **schwa** position.

recutting   Reanalyzing words into component parts different from the original parts; for example, *a napron* historically was recut into *an apron*, and *an other* is currently being recut into *a + nother*, as in *a whole nother*.

reduplication The repetition of a word or part of a word, as in *teensy-weensy*, *boo boo*.

referee design The component of the audience design model for **style shifting** that focuses on referee groups and initiative style shifting.

referee group A non-present group with whom speakers attempt to identify when they engage in an initiative style shift.

regional standard English A variety considered to be standard for a given regional area; for example, the Eastern New England standard or the Southern standard.

register A specialized use of language for a well-defined situation or occasion; for example, the math register or the "babytalk" register.

regular form An item conforming to the predominant pattern, such as the regular plural form *cats* or the regular past tense form *missed*. Compare **irregular form**.

regularization The process in which irregular forms are changed to conform to the predominant or "regular" pattern; for example, *oxen* becomes *oxes* or *grew* becomes *growed*.

relative clause A clause that modifies a noun; in *The man who took the course was demented, who took the course* is a relative clause.

relative pronoun A pronoun that introduces a relative clause, such as *who* in *The woman who liked the class was a linguist*.

relic area An area where older language features survive after they have disappeared from other varieties of the language.

relic form An older language form which has been retained in certain dialects but lost from most varieties of a language; for example the *h* of *hit* for 'it' is a relic form still found in Appalachian English.

replacive dialect See **eradicationism**.

retroflex A sound produced with the tip of the tongue curled upward; the consonant sound *r* in *run* and the vowel sound *ir* in *bird* are retroflex language sounds.

r-lessness The absence or reduction of the *r* sound in words such as *car* and *beard*.

rule See **linguistic rule**.

rule extension The expansion of a rule of limited application to a broader set of items.

saturated With reference to language features, used by the vast majority of speakers within a given speech community. Saturated features contrast with **unsaturated features**, or those used by only a few speakers in the speech community.

scalability The extent to which an ideal implicational array is matched by the actual patterning of the data. Computed by dividing the number of non-deviant cells by the total number of filled cells.

schwa   A mid central vowel symbolized as [ə]; for example, the first vowel in *appear* [əpir]. Generally occurs in unstressed syllables in English.

second order constraint   See **first order constraint**.

secondary dialect area   That portion of a dialect area showing the second highest concentration of shared dialect features.

semantic broadening   Meaning shift in which words can be used to refer to a more general class of items than previously. For example, *holiday* has been broadened to refer to all days off from work rather than just "holy days," or days of religious significance.

semantic derogation   Meaning shift in which words take on more negative connotations or denotations. For example, the word *mistress* was once the female counterpart of *mister* but has taken on negative meanings not matched by its male counterpart.

semantic narrowing   Meaning shift in which words come to refer to a less general class of items than previously. For example, *girl* could once be used to refer to a young child of either sex; *deer* was once used to refer to all animals but now refers only to one specific type of animal.

semantic shift   See **meaning shift**.

semantics   The level of language organization which pertains to word meaning.

sharp stratification   A distributional pattern for socially significant language features characterized by a clear-cut division between social groups. Compare **gradient stratification**.

short vowel   In English, a "lax" vowel, as in *bit*, *bet*, and *put*. No longer corresponds with actual temporal duration in English.

sibilant   A sound produced with a groove in the middle of the tongue through which the air passes, creating a "hissing" sound; sounds such as the [s] of *see* and the [z] of *zoo* are sibilants.

slang   Words with special connotations of informality and solidarity that replace mainstream or "normal" words (e.g. *rad* for 'great'; *wasted* for 'drunk').

social dialectology   The study of language variation in relation to social status or other social relationships.

social indicator   A language feature whose usage correlates with social stratification but not speech style; speakers do not indicate awareness of such features or their social meaning.

social marker   A language feature whose usage correlates with both social stratification and speech style; speakers are aware of such forms and their social meaning but do not comment overtly upon them.

social network   The pattern of social relationships that characterizes a group of speakers.

social stereotype   A language feature that speakers are aware of and comment upon. May be stigmatized (e.g. *ain't*), prestigious (e.g. [vaz] instead of [veɪs] for 'vase'), or simply "unusual" (e.g. "hoi toide" for 'high tide').

social variable A social attribute or characteristic such as status, ethnicity, or gender that may correlate with linguistic variation.

socially diagnostic With respect to language features, serving to distinguish a certain social group of speakers.

socially prestigious Socially favored; with respect to language forms or patterns, items associated with high-status groups.

socially stigmatized Socially disfavored, as in a language form or pattern associated with low-status groups (e.g. *He didn't do nothing to nobody*).

sociolect A dialect defined on the basis of a social grouping, such as a social class or ethnic group, as opposed to a dialect defined primarily on the basis of region.

sociolinguistics The study of language in relation to society; the study of language in its social context.

Southern Vowel Shift A vowel shift or rotation in which the short front vowels are moving upward and taking on the gliding character of long vowels, the long front vowels are moving backward and downward, and the back vowels are moving forward.

speaker design model A model for **style shifting** that focuses on the speaker's internal motivations rather than factors external to the speaker, such as audience make-up.

Speech Accommodation Theory The model for **style shifting** which maintains that speakers shift style based on their social-psychological adjustment to the addressee; adjustment toward the addressee is **convergence**; adjustment away from the addressee is **divergence**.

speech act An utterance which accomplishes a social action. For example, *Take the garbage out!* is a directive speech act in which the speaker directs the hearer to perform an activity.

speech community A group of speakers united on the basis of their shared language characteristics; members of a speech community also tend to share social and regional attributes as well.

spelling pronunciation The pronunciation of an item based on its spelling rather than its conventional spoken form (e.g. *often* pronounced with [t]).

Standard American English A widely socially accepted variety of English that is held to be the linguistic norm and that is relatively unmarked with respect to regional characteristics of English. See **Network Standard**.

standard dialect The dialect associated with those socially favored in society; the dialect considered acceptable for mainstream, institutional purposes. See **Formal Standard English, Informal Standard English, Network Standard, regional standard English**.

statistical hypercorrection The quantitative overuse of a prestigious linguistic form; usually found among those groups attempting to emulate a higher social group, for example, the overuse of postvocalic *r* in New York City by the lower middle class in formal speech style.

stigmatized   See **socially stigmatized**.

stopping   The process of producing fricatives as stop consonants, as in *these* [ðiz] being pronounced as *dese* [diz].

stress   Force or intensity which is given to a syllable. Syllables spoken with such force are **stressed syllables**, those without such force are **unstressed syllables** (e.g. in *pity* [pɪ] is a stressed syllable, [ti] is unstressed).

structural hypercorrection   The extension of a linguistic boundary in the attempt to produce more standard or "correct" English; for example, the use of *whom* in *Whom is it*, where the objective form is extended to a subject function.

style   One of the speech varieties used by an individual; different speech styles tend to correlate with such factors as audience, occasion, degree of formality, etc.

style shifting   Variation within the speech of a single speaker; often correlates with such factors as audience, degree of formality, etc.

subjective case   The form which a noun or pronoun takes when it is in subject position in a sentence (e.g. *I* in *I like students*). See **case**.

substratal language effect   The influence of a language on another language variety after the former language has ceased to be a source for immediate transfer (e.g. the holdover effect of Italian vowels on "Italian English" even though Italian is no longer actively used in the community).

suffix   A form attached to the end of a base or root word, as in the *-s* of *bats*.

Superstandard English   Forms or styles of speech which are more standard than called for in everyday conversation (*It is I who shall write this*).

superstrate   A language spoken by a dominant group which influences the structure of the language of a subordinate group of speakers. Often used to refer to the dominant language upon which a **creole language** is based.

suprasegmental   Pertaining to elements of language such as stress and intonational contour that accompany the sound segments (e.g. consonants and vowels) of language.

swamping   The inundation of a longstanding dialect area with speakers from other dialect areas.

syllable timing   Timing of utterances in which each syllable in a phrase has approximately equal duration.

syntax   See **grammar**.

taboo word   A word having a social prohibition against its ordinary use, such as the "four-letter" words of English (e.g. *shit, damn*).

tag question   A special type of question formed by items attached to, or "tagged," onto the end of the sentence (e.g. *right* in *You're coming to class, right?* or *aren't you* in *You're coming to class, aren't you?*).

task interference   In testing, an impediment to valid testing due to the way language is used to obtain information.

tense (1) Produced with more muscular tension; for example, the sound [i] in *beet* is a "tense" vowel, whereas the [ɪ] of *bit* is a "lax" vowel. See **long vowel**. (2) The time reference of an activity or event (e.g. "past tense" in *Jason missed the lecture*).

tertiary dialect area The third-ranked, outer, area in the layered, hierarchical concentration of shared dialect features.

transfer The adoption of a form from another language, usually a form from a first language carried over into a second language in the process of acquiring the second language.

transitional zone An intermediate area existing between two established dialect areas.

transitive verb A verb that takes an object (e.g. *like* in *Students like movies*).

transparency principle The need for language to make meanings direct enough to avoid obscurity in meaning.

turn-taking Shifting from one speaker to another in a conversational exchange.

ungliding The loss or reduction of the glide, or second half of a diphthong; for example, in many Southern varieties, the /ay/ vowel in words such as *time* [taɪm] is unglided to [a], as in [tam].

ungrammatical (1) Outside the parameters of a given linguistic rule, usually indicated by placing an asterisk in front of the form or sentence (e.g. **She is tall very*). (2) Socially unacceptable (e.g. *I seen it*); although "ungrammatical" is often used in this sense by non-linguists, linguists do not generally use the term in this way, restricting its use to the technical sense given in 1.

uniplex network A social network characterized by the interaction of speakers on one sphere only (e.g. speaker A works with B but does not socialize with B; speaker B socializes with C but does not live near C, etc.).

unsaturated See **saturated**.

variant One of a set of alternating items; for example, *-ing* and *-in'* are variants.

velar Sounds produced by touching the back of the tongue against the "soft palate" or **velum** at the back of the mouth; the [k] of *cow*, the [g] of *go* and the [ŋ] of *sing* are velar sounds.

vernacular The indigenous language or dialect of a speech community. The term **vernacular dialect** is often used to refer to **non-standard** or non-mainstream varieties as opposed to the standard variety.

vernacular principle The contention that the speech style that is most regular in its structure and in its relation to community patterns of language change is the vernacular.

voiced sound A sound produced by bringing the vocal cords close together, causing them to vibrate when air passes through them in the production of speech sounds (e.g. [z] as in *zoo*, [v] as in *vote*).

voiceless sound   A sound produced with the vocal cords open and not vibrating, as in the [s] of *suit* or the [f] of *fight*.

vowel breaking   The process by which a one-part vowel, or **monophthong**, is divided, or "broken," into a two-part vowel, or **diphthong**, as in some Southern pronunciations of words like *bed* [bɛɪd] and *bid* [bɪɪd].

vowel nucleus   The segment that serves as the core or center of a **diphthong**, or two-part vowel.

vowel reduction   The change or neutralization of a vowel to the quality of a schwa [ə]; usually takes place in unstressed syllables (e.g. the second *o* of *photograph* [fotəgræf]).

vowel rotation   The systematic shifting of the phonetic values of a set of vowels, as in the **Northern Cities Vowel Shift** or the **Southern Vowel Shift**.

wave model   A model for the diffusion of language change which views change as radiating outward in a wavelike pattern from a central point, or **focal area**. See **contagious diffusion**.

weakening   Changing the pronunciation of sounds so that they involve less blockage of airflow in the mouth; for example, changing [t] to [θ] between vowels.

word-medial   Occurring in the middle of a word, as in the sound *k* of *baker*.

References

Alvarez, Louis, and Andrew Kolker (1987) *American Tongues*. New York: Center for New American Media.

Ann Arbor Decision, The: Memorandum, Opinion, and Order & The Educational Plan (1979) Washington, DC: Center for Applied Linguistics.

Arco's Practice for the Armed Forces Tests (1973) New York: Arco.

Bailey, Guy, and Marvin Bassett (1986) Invariant *be* in the Lower South. In Michael Montgomery and Guy Bailey (eds), *Language Variety in the South: Perspectives in Black and White*. University: University of Alabama Press, 158–79.

——, and Natalie Maynor (1987) Decreolization. *Language in Society* 16:449–74.

——, Natalie Maynor, and Patricia Cukor-Avila (eds) (1991) *The Emergence of Black English: Text and Commentary*. Philadelphia/Amsterdam: John Benjamins.

——, Tom Wikle, Jan Tillery, and Lori Sand (1993) Some patterns of linguistic diffusion. *Language Variation and Change* 5:359–90.

Bakhtin, Mikhael (1981) *The Dialogic Imagination*, ed. M. Holquist, trans. C. Emerson and M. Holquist. Austin: University of Texas Press.

Baratz, Joan (1968) Language in the economically disadvantaged child: A perspective. *ASHA* (April):143–5.

Bauer, Laurie, and Peter Trudgill (eds) (1998) *Language Myths*. New York: Penguin.

Baugh, John (1983) *Black Street Speech: Its History, Structure, and Survival*. Austin: University of Texas Press.

—— (1984) Steady: Progressive aspect in Black Vernacular English. *American Speech* 59:3–12.

—— (1988) Language and race: Some implications for linguistic science. In Frederick J. Newmeyer (ed.), *Linguistics: The Cambridge Survey*, Vol. IV. New York: Cambridge University Press, 64–74.

—— (1991) The politicization of changing terms of self-reference among American slave descendants. *American Speech* 66:133–46.

—— (1996) Perceptions with a variable paradigm: Black and white speech detection and identification based on speech. In Edgar W. Schneider (ed.), *Focus on the USA*. Philadelphia/Amsterdam: John Benjamins, 169–82.

Bayley, Robert (1994) Consonant cluster reduction in Tejano English. *Language Variation and Change* 6:303–26.

——, and Dennis R. Preston (eds) (1996) *Second Language Acquisition and Linguistic Variation*. Philadelphia/Amsterdam: John Benjamins.

Beebe, Leslie, and Howard Giles (1984) Speech-accommodation theories: A discussion in terms of second language acquisition. *International Journal of the Sociology of Language* 46:5–32.

Bell, Allan (1984) Language style as audience design. *Language in Society* 13:145–204.

——(1992) Hit and miss: Referee design in the dialects of New Zealand television advertisements. *Language and Communication* 12 (3/4):327–40.

——(forthcoming) Back in style: Reworking audience design. In John Rickford and Penelope Eckert (eds), *Style and Variation*. Cambridge/New York: Cambridge University Press.

Bergvall, Victoria L., Janet M. Bing, and Alice F. Freed (eds) (1996) *Rethinking Language and Gender Research: Theory and Practice*. New York: Longman.

Biber, Douglas (1994) An analytical framework for register studies. In Douglas Biber and Edward Finegan (eds), *Sociolinguistic Perspectives on Register*. New York: Oxford University Press, 31–56.

——, and Edward Finegan (eds) (1994) *Sociolinguistic Perspectives on Register*. New York: Oxford University Press.

Bing, Janet M., and Victoria L. Bergvall (1996). The question of questions: Beyond binary thinking. In Victoria L. Bergvall, Janet M. Bing, and Alice F. Freed (eds), *Rethinking Language and Gender Research: Theory and Practice*. New York: Longman.

Blanton, Phyllis, and Karen Waters (1995) *The Ocracoke Brogue*. Raleigh: North Carolina Language and Life Project.

Bodine, Ann (1975) Androcentrism in prescriptive grammar: Singular 'they', sex-indefinite 'he', and 'he' or 'she'. *Language in Society* 4:129–46.

Brasch, Ila Wales, and Walter Milton Brasch (1974) *A Comprehensive Annotated Bibliography of American Black English*. Baton Rouge: Louisiana State University Press.

Brend, Ruth M. (1975) Male–female intonation patterns in American English. In Barrie Thorne and Nancy Henley (eds), *Language and Sex: Difference and Dominance*. Rowley, MA: Newbury House, 84–7.

Brown, Claude (1965) *Manchild in the Promised Land*. New York: New American Library.

Brown, Penelope, and Colin Fraser (1979) Speech as a marker of situation. In Klaus Scherer and Howard Giles (eds), *Social Markers in Speech*. Cambridge: Cambridge University Press, 33–62.

——, and Stephen C. Levinson (1987) *Politeness: Some Universals in Language Usage*. New York: Cambridge University Press.

Butters, Ronald R. (1989) *The Death of Black English: Divergence and Convergence in White and Black Vernaculars*. Frankfurt: Lang.

——(1993) The imitation of dialect for illegal purposes: An empirical study. Paper presented at New Ways of Analyzing Variation 22, Ottawa, Canada, October 1993.

Callary, Robert E. (1975) Phonological change and the development of an urban dialect in Illinois. *Language in Society* 4:155–69.

Cameron, Deborah (1996) The language–gender interface: Challenging co-optation. In Victoria L. Bergvall, Janet M. Bing, and Alice F. Freed (eds), *Rethinking Language and Gender Research: Theory and Practice*. New York: Longman.

Carver, Craig M. (1987) *American Regional Dialects: A Word Geography*. Ann Arbor: University of Michigan Press.

Cassidy, Frederic G. (gen. ed.) (1985, 1991, 1996) *Dictionary of American Regional English*, Vols 1–3. Cambridge, MA: Harvard University Press, Belknap.

Cedergren, Henrietta (1973) The interplay of social and linguistic factors in Panama. Ph.D. dissertation, Cornell University.

Chambers, J. K. (1973) Canadian raising. *Canadian Journal of Linguistics* 18:113–35.

——(1995) *Sociolinguistic Theory*. Cambridge, MA: Blackwell.

Committee on College Composition and Communication Language Statement (1974) Students' rights to their own language. *College Composition and Communication* 25 (special issue, separately paginated). Champaign-Urbana: National Council of Teachers of English.

Crosby, Faye, and Linda Nyquist (1977) The female register: An empirical study of Lakoff's hypothesis. *Language in Society* 6:313–22.

Coupland, Nikolas (1985) "Hark, hark the lark": Social motivations for phonological style-shifting. *Language and Communication* 5 (3):153–71.

——(forthcoming) Language, situation and the relational self: Theorising dialect-style in sociolinguistics. In John Rickford and Penelope Eckert (eds), *Style and Variation*. Cambridge/New York: Cambridge University Press.

Dannenberg, Clare and Walt Wolfram (forthcoming) Ethnic identity and grammatical restructuring: *Bes* in Lumbee English. *American Speech*.

Dillard, J. L. (1972) *Black English: Its History and Usage in the United States*. New York: Random House.

Downes, William (1984) *Language and Society*. London: Fontana.

Dubois, Betty Lou, and Isabel Crouch (1975) The question of tag questions in women's speech: They don't really use more of them, do they? *Language in Society* 4:289–94.

Dumas, Bethany K., and Jonathan Lighter (1976) Is slang a word for linguists? *American Speech* 51:5–17.

Eakins, Barbara, and Gene Eakins (1978) *Sex Differences in Human Communication*. Boston: Houghton Mifflin.

Eble, Connie (1989) *College Slang 101*. Georgetown: Spectacle Lane Press.

——(1996) *Slang and Sociability: In-Group Language Among College Students*. Chapel Hill/London: University of North Carolina Press.

Eckert, Penelope (1989) The whole woman: Sex and gender differences in variation. *Language Variation and Change* 1:245–67.

——(1990) Cooperative competition in adolescent girl talk. *Discourse Process* 13:92–122.

——, and Sally McConnell-Ginet (1994) Think practically and look locally: Language and gender as community-based practice. In Camille Roman, Suzanne Juhasz, and Cristanne Miller (eds) (1992), *The Women and Language Debate: A Sourcebook*. New Brunswick: Rutgers University Press, 432–60. Reprinted from *Annual Review of Anthropology* 21:461–90.

Ewers, Traute (1996) *The Origin of American Black English:* Be-*Forms in the Hoodoo Texts*. Berlin/New York: Mouton de Gruyter.

Farr, Marcia, and Harvey Daniels (1986) *Language Diversity and Writing Instruction*. Urbana: National Council of Teachers of English.

Farr-Whiteman, Marcia (1981) Dialect influence in writing. In Marcia Farr-Whiteman (ed.), *Writing: The Nature, Development, and Teaching of Written Communication*, Vol. 1. Hillsdale: Lawrence Erlbaum Associates, 153–66.

Fasold, Ralph W. (1968) A sociolinguistic study of the pronunciation of three vowels in Detroit speech. Unpublished manuscript.

——(1969) Tense and the form *be* in Black English. *Language* 45:763–76.

——(1970) Two models of socially significant linguistic variation. *Language* 46:551–63.

——(1972) *Tense Marking in Black English: A Linguistic and Social Analysis.* Arlington: Center for Applied Linguistics.

——(1976) One hundred years from syntax to phonology. In Sanford Seever, Carol Walker, and Salikoko Mufwene (eds), *Diachronic Syntax.* Chicago: Chicago Linguistic Society, 79–87.

——(1981) The relation between black and white speech in the South. *American Speech* 56:163–89.

——(1984) *The Sociolinguistics of Society.* Oxford: Blackwell.

——(1990) *The Sociolinguistics of Language.* Oxford: Blackwell.

Feagin, Crawford (1979) *Variation and Change in Alabama English: A Sociolinguistic Study of the White Community.* Washington, DC: Georgetown University Press.

——(1987) A closer look at the Southern drawl: Variation taken to the extremes. In Keith M. Denning, Sharon Inkelas, Faye C. McNair-Knox, and John R. Rickford (eds), *Variation in Language: NWAVE-XV at Stanford* (Proceedings of the Fifteenth Annual Conference on New Ways of Analyzing Variation). Stanford: Stanford University, 137–50.

Ferguson, Charles A., and Shirley Brice Heath (eds) (1981) *Language in the USA.* New York: Cambridge University Press.

Finegan, Edward (1980) *Attitudes Toward English Words: The History of a War of Words.* New York: Teachers College Press.

——, and Douglas Biber (1994) Register and social dialect variation: An integrated approach. In Douglas Biber and Edward Finegan (eds), *Sociolinguistic Perspectives on Register.* New York: Oxford University Press, 315–47.

Fischer, John N. L. (1958) Social influences on the choice of a linguistic variant. *Word* 14:47–56.

Francis, Nelson W. (1983) *Dialectology: An Introduction.* New York: Longman.

Frank, Francine, and Frank Anshen (1983) *Language and the Sexes.* Albany: State University of New York Press.

Frazer, Timothy C. (1983) Sound change and social structure in a rural community. *Language in Society* 12:313–28.

Freed, Alice F. (1992) We understand perfectly: A critique of Tannen's view of cross-sex communication. In Kira Hall, Mary Bucholtz, and Birch Moonwomon (eds), *Locating Power: Proceedings of the Second Berkeley Women and Language Conference,* Vol. 1. Berkeley: Berkeley Women and Language Group, 144–52.

Galindo, Letticia D. (1987) Linguistic influence and variation on the English of Chicano adolescents in Austin, Texas. Ph.D. dissertation, University of Texas at Austin.

Gauchat, Louis (1905) L'unité phonétique dans le patois d'une commune. *Festschrift Heinreich Morf: Aus Romanischen Sprachen und Literaturen.* Halle: M. Niemeyer, 175–232.

Giles, Howard (ed.) (1984) *The Dynamics of Speech Accommodation* (special issue of the *International Journal of the Sociology of Language* 46).

——, and Peter F. Powesland (1975) *Speech Style and Social Evaluation.* London: Academic Press.

——, Justine Coupland, and Nikolas Coupland (eds) (1991) *Contexts of Accommodation: Developments in Applied Sociolinguistics*. Cambridge: Cambridge University Press.

Glowka, Wayne A., and Donald M. Lance (eds) (1993) *Language Variation in North American English: Research and Teaching*. New York: Modern Language Association.

Gold, David L. (1981) The speech and writing of Jews. In Charles A. Ferguson and Shirley Brice Heath (eds), *Language in the USA*. New York: Cambridge University Press, 273–92.

Goodwin, Marjorie Harness (1990) *He-Said-She-Said: Talk as Social Organization among Black Children*. Bloomington: Indiana University Press.

Graff, David, William Labov, and Wendell A. Harris (1986) Testing listeners' reactions to phonological markers of ethnic identity: A new method for sociolinguistic research. In David Sankoff (ed.), *Diversity and Diachrony*. Philadelphia/Amsterdam: John Benjamins, 45–58.

Grandgent, C. H. (1889) The first year of the American dialect society. *Dialect Notes* 1.

Gregory, Michael, and Suzanne Carroll (1978) *Language and Situation: Language Varieties and their Social Contexts*. London: Routledge and Kegan Paul.

Gumperz, John J. (1982) *Discourse Strategies*. New York: Cambridge University Press.

Guy, Gregory R. (1988) Language and social class. In Frederick J. Newmeyer (ed.), *Linguistics: The Cambridge Survey*, Vol. IV. New York: Cambridge University Press, 37–63.

——(1993) The quantitative analysis of linguistic variation. In Dennis R. Preston (ed.), *American Dialect Research*. Philadelphia/Amsterdam: John Benjamins, 223–49.

——, B. Horvath, J. Vonwiller, E. Daisley, and I. Rogers (1986) An intonational change in progress in Australian English. *Language in Society* 15:23–52.

Hannah, Dawn (1998) The copula in Samaná English: Implications for research on the linguistic history of African American Vernacular English. *American Speech*.

Harrison, Linda (1975) Cro-magnon woman – In eclipse. *The Science Teacher* (April): 8–11.

Hartman, James W. (1985) Guide to pronunciation. In Frederic G. Cassidy (gen. ed.), *Dictionary of American Regional English*, Vol. 1. Cambridge, MA: Harvard University Press, Belknap, xli–lxi.

Hazen, Kirk (1997) Past and present "be" in Southern ethnolinguistic boundaries. Ph.D. dissertation, University of North Carolina at Chapel Hill.

Heath, Shirley Brice (1976) A national language academy? Debate in the new nation. *International Journal of the Sociology of Language* 11:8–43.

——(1983) *Ways with Words: Language, Life and Work in Communities and Classrooms*. New York: Cambridge University Press.

Henley, Nancy M., and Cheris Kramarae (1994) Gender, power, and miscommunication. In Camille Roman, Suzanne Juhasz, and Cristanne Miller (eds), *The Women and Language Debate: A Sourcebook*. New Brunswick: Rutgers University Press, 383–406. Reprinted from N. Coupland, H. Giles, and J. M. Wiemann (eds) (1991), *Miscommunication and Problematic Talk*. Newbury Park: Sage Publications, 18–43.

Hock, Hans Henrich, and Brian D. Joseph (1996) *Language History, Language Change, and Language Relationship: An Introduction to Historical and Comparative Linguistics*. Berlin/New York: Mouton de Gruyter.

Horvath, Barbara M. (1985) *Variation in Australian English: The Sociolects of Sydney*. New York: Cambridge University Press.

Huffines, Marion Lois (1984) The English of the Pennsylvania Germans. *German Quarterly* 57:173–82.

——(1986) Intonation in language contact: Pennsylvania German English. In Werner Enninger (ed.), *Studies on the Language and the Verbal Behavior of the Pennsylvania Germans.* Wiesbaden: Franz Steiner Verlag, 26–36.

Hyatt, Harry Middleton (1970–8) *Hoodoo-Conjuration-Witchcraft-Rootwork,* Vols 1–5. Hannibal: Western Publishing.

Hymes, Dell (1962) The ethnography of speaking. In T. Gladwin and W. C. Sturtevant (eds), *Anthropology and Human Behavior.* Washington, DC: Anthropological Society of Washington. Reprinted in Joshua A. Fishman (1968) *Readings in the Sociology of Language.* The Hague: Mouton.

Illinois Test of Psycholinguistic Abilities (1968) Champaign-Urbana: University of Illinois.

Irvine, Judith (1996) Formality and informality in communicative events. *American Anthropologist* 81:773–90.

Ives, Sumner (1971) A theory of literary dialect. In Juanita V. Williamson and Virginia M. Burke (eds), *A Various Language: Perspectives on American Dialects.* New York: Holt, Rinehart, and Winston, 145–77.

James, Deborah (1996) Women, men and prestige speech forms: A critical review. In Victoria L. Bergvall, Janet M. Bing, and Alice F. Freed (eds), *Rethinking Language and Gender Research: Theory and Practice.* New York: Longman, 98–125.

——, and Sandra Clarke (1993) Women, men, and interruptions: A critical review. In Deborah Tannen (ed.), *Gender and Conversational Interaction.* New York/Oxford: Oxford University Press, 231–74.

——, and Janice Drakich (1993) Understanding gender differences in amount of talk: A critical review of research. In Deborah Tannen (ed.), *Gender and Conversational Interaction.* New York/Oxford: Oxford University Press, 281–312.

Jespersen, Otto (1922) *Language: Its Nature, Development, and Origin.* London: Allen and Unwin.

Johnson, Ellen (1996) *Lexical Change and Variation in the Southeastern United States.* Tuscaloosa, AL: University of Alabama Press.

Johnson, Sally, and Ulrike Hanna Meinhof (eds) (1997) *Language and Masculinity.* Oxford/Cambridge, MA: Blackwell.

Kiesling, Scott Fabius (1996) Language, gender, and power in fraternity men's discourse. Ph.D. dissertation, Georgetown University.

King, Pamela (1972) An analysis of the Northwestern syntax screening test for lower class black children in Prince George's County. Unpublished M.A. thesis, Howard University.

Kochman, Thomas (1981) *Black and White: Styles in Conflict.* Chicago: University of Chicago Press.

Krashen, Stephen D. (1982) *Principles and Practice in Second Language Acquisition.* Oxford: Pergamon Press.

——, Robin Scarcella, and Michael Long (eds) (1982) *Child–Adult Difference in Second Language Acquisition.* Rowley, MA: Newbury House.

Kretzschmar, William A. (1996) Quantitative areal analysis of dialect features. *Language Variation and Change* 8:13–40.

——, and Edgar W. Schneider (1996) *Introduction to Quantitative Analysis of Linguistic Survey Data.* Thousand Oaks: Sage Publications.

Kroch, Anthony (1978) Towards a theory of social dialect variation. *Language in Society* 7:17–36.

Kurath, Hans (1939) *Handbook of the Linguistic Geography of New England*. Providence: Brown University.

—— (1949) *Word Geography of the Eastern United States*. Ann Arbor: University of Michigan Press.

—— (1971) The origins of the dialectal differences in spoken American English. In Juanita V. Williamson and Virginia M. Burke (eds), *A Various Language: Perspectives on American Dialects*. New York: Holt, Rinehart, and Winston, 12–21.

——, and Raven I. McDavid, Jr (1961) *The Pronunciation of English in the Atlantic States*. Ann Arbor: University of Michigan Press.

Labov, William (1963) The social motivation of a sound change. *Word* 19:273–307.

—— (1966) *The Social Stratification of English in New York City*. Washington, DC: Center for Applied Linguistics.

—— (1969) Contraction, deletion and inherent variability of the English copula. *Language* 45:715–62.

—— (1972a) *Language in the Inner City: Studies in the Black English Vernacular*. Philadelphia: University of Pennsylvania Press.

—— (1972b) *Sociolinguistic Patterns*. Philadelphia: University of Pennsylvania Press.

—— (1972c) Some principles of linguistic methodology. *Language in Society* 1:97–120.

—— (1972d) The logic of nonstandard English. Ch. 5 in *Language in the Inner City: Studies in the Black English Vernacular*. Philadelphia: University of Pennsylvania Press, 201–40.

—— (1976) Systematically misleading data from test questions. *Urban Review* 9:146–69.

—— (1982) Objectivity and commitment in linguistic science. *Language in Society* 11:165–201.

—— (1984) The intersection of sex and social factors in the course of language change. Paper presented at NWAVE, Philadelphia.

—— (1985) The increasing divergence of black and white vernaculars: Introduction to the research reports. Unpublished manuscript.

—— (1987) Are black and white vernaculars diverging? Papers from the NWAVE XIV panel discussion. *American Speech* 62:5–12.

—— (1990) The intersection of sex and social class in the course of linguistic change. *Language Variation and Change* 2:205–54.

—— (1991) The three dialects of English. In Penelope Eckert (ed.), *New Ways of Analyzing Sound Change*. New York: Academic Press, 1–44.

—— (1994) *Principles of Linguistic Change: Internal Factors*. Cambridge, MA: Blackwell.

——, and Wendell Harris (1986) De facto segregation of black and white vernaculars. In David Sankoff (ed.), *Diversity and Diachrony*. Philadelphia/Amsterdam: John Benjamins, 1–24.

——, Sharon Ash, and Charles Boberg (1997) A national map of the regional dialects of American English. Unpublished manuscript. Philadelphia: University of Pennsylvania.

——, Paul Cohen, Clarence Robins, and John Lewis (1968) *A Study of the Non-Standard English of Negro and Puerto Rican Speakers in New York City*. United States Office of Education Final Report, Research Project 3288.

Laferriere, Martha (1979) Ethnicity in phonological variation and change. *Language* 55:603–17.

Lakoff, Robin (1973) Language and women's place. *Language in Society* 2:45–80.

Leap, William L. (1993) *American Indian English*. Salt Lake City: University of Utah Press.

Leaverton, Lloyd (1973) Dialect readers: Rationale, use, and value. In James L. Laffey and Roger W. Shuy (eds), *Language Differences: Do They Interfere?* Newark: International Reading Association, 114–26.

LePage, R. B., and Adrée Tabouret-Keller (1985) *Acts of Identity*. Cambridge: Cambridge University Press.

Lighter, Jonathan E. (1994) *Historical Dictionary of American Slang*, Vol. 1. New York: Random House.

Lippi-Green, Rosina (1997) *English with an Accent: Language, Ideology, and Discrimination in the United States*. London/New York: Routledge.

Locklear, Hayes Alan, Natalie Schilling-Estes, Walt Wolfram, and Clare Dannenberg (1996) *A Dialect Dictionary of Lumbee English*. Raleigh: North Carolina Language and Life Project.

Lourie, Margaret A., and Nancy Faires Conklin (eds) (1978) *A Pluralistic Nation: The Language Issue in the United States*. Rowley, MA: Newbury House.

McConnell-Ginet, Sally (1988) Language and gender. In Frederick J. Newmeyer (ed.), *Linguistics: The Cambridge Survey*, Vol. IV. New York: Cambridge University Press, 75–99.

McCrum, Robert, William Cran, and Robert McNeil (1986) *The Story of English*. New York: Elisabeth Sifton Books/Viking.

MacKay, Donald G. (1983) Prescriptive grammar and the pronoun problem. In Barrie Thorne, Cheris Kramarae, and Nancy Henley (eds), *Language, Gender, and Society*. Rowley, MA: Newbury House, 38–53.

McMillan, James B. (1978) American lexicology, 1942–1973. *American Speech* 53:141–63.

——, and Michael Montgomery (1989) *Annotated Bibliography of Southern American English*. Tuscaloosa: University of Alabama Press.

Mahl, G. F. (1972) People talking when they can't hear voices. In A. W. Siegman and B. Pope (eds), *Studies in Dyadic Communication*. New York: Pergamon, 211–64.

Maltz, Daniel, and Ruth Borker (1982) A cultural approach to male–female miscommunication. In John J. Gumperz (ed.), *Language and Social Identity*. Cambridge: Cambridge University Press, 195–216.

Martyna, Wendy (1978) What does 'he' mean? *Journal of Communication* 28 (Winter):131–8.

——(1980) The psychology of the generic masculine. In Sally McConnell-Ginet, Ruth Borker, and Nelly Furman (eds), *Women and Language in Literature and Society*. New York: Praeger, 69–77.

Meier, Deborah (1973) Reading failure and the tests. An Occasional Paper of the Workshop for Open Education, New York.

Mencken, H. L. (1962) *The American Language: An Inquiry into the Development of English in the United States*, Supplement I. New York: Alfred A. Knopf.

Miller, Cristanne (1994) Who says what to whom?: Empirical studies of language and gender. In Camille Roman, Suzanne Juhasz, and Cristanne Miller (eds), *The Women and Language Debate: A Sourcebook.* New Brunswick: Rutgers University Press, 265–79.

Milroy, James (1992) *Linguistic Variation and Change: On the Historical Sociolinguistics of English.* Oxford/Cambridge, MA: Blackwell.

Milroy, James, and Lesley Milroy (1985) *Authority in Language: Investigating Language Prescription and Standardisation.* London: Routledge and Kegan Paul.

Milroy, Lesley (1987) *Language and Social Networks*, 2nd edn. *Language in Society 2.* Oxford/Cambridge, MA: Blackwell.

Montgomery, Michael (ed.) (1989) Language. In Charles Reagan Wilson and William Ferris (eds), *Encyclopedia of Southern Culture.* Chapel Hill/London: University of North Carolina Press, 757–92.

——, and Janet Fuller (1996) Verbal -*s* in 19th-century African American English. In Edgar W. Schneider (ed.), *Focus on the USA.* Philadelphia/Amsterdam: John Benjamins, 211–30.

——, and Margaret Mishoe (forthcoming) "He bes took up with a Yankee girl and moved to New York, It's a shame in this world": The verb *bes* in the Carolinas and its history. *American Speech.*

——, Janet Fuller, and Sharon DeMarse (1993) The black men has wives and sweet harts [and third person -*s*] Jest like the white men: Evidence for verbal -*s* from written documents on nineteenth-century African American speech. *Language Variation and Change* 5:335–57.

Moon, Seung-Jae (1991) An acoustic and perceptual study of undershoot in clear and citation-form speech. Ph.D. dissertation, University of Texas at Austin.

Mufwene, Salikoko S. (1996) The development of American Englishes: Some questions from a creole genesis hypothesis. In Edgar W. Schneider (ed.), *Focus on the USA.* Philadelphia/Amsterdam: John Benjamins, 231–64.

——, John R. Rickford, Guy Bailey, and John Baugh (eds) (1998) *African American Vernacular English.* London/New York: Routledge.

National Council of Social Studies, Task Force on Ethnic Studies (1976) *Curriculum Guidelines for Multiethnic Education.* Arlington: National Council on Social Studies.

Nichols, Patricia (1983) Linguistic options and choices for black women in the rural South. In Barrie Thorne, Cheris Kramarae, and Nancy Henley (eds), *Language, Gender, and Society.* Rowley, MA: Newbury House.

Nilsen, Alleen Pace (1977) Sexism as shown through the English vocabulary. In Alleen Pace Nilsen, Haig Bosmajiian, H. Lee Gershuny, and Julia P. Stanley (eds), *Sexism and Language.* Urbana: National Council of Teachers of English.

Orr, Eleanor Wilson (1987) *Twice as Less: Black English and the Performance of Black Students in Mathematics and Science.* New York: Norton.

Payne, Arvilla C. (1980) Factors controlling the acquisition of the Philadelphia dialect by out-of-state children. In William Labov (ed.), *Locating Language in Time and Space.* New York: Academic Press, 143–78.

Peñalosa, Fernando (1980) *Chicano Sociolinguistics: A Brief Introduction.* Rowley, MA: Newbury House.

Pickering, John (1816) A vocabulary, or collection of words and phrases which have been supposed to be peculiar to the United States of America. In M. M. Mathews (ed.) (1931), *The Beginnings of American English: Essays and Comments*. Chicago: University of Chicago Press.

Poplack, Shana, and David Sankoff (1987) The Philadelphia story in the Spanish Caribbean. *American Speech* 62:291–314.

——, and Sali Tagliamonte (1989) There's no tense like the present: Verbal -*s* inflection in Early Black English. *Language Variation and Change* 1:47–84.

——, and —— (1991) African American English in the diaspora: Evidence from old-line Nova Scotians. *Language Variation and Change* 3:301–39.

Preston, Dennis R. (1986) Five visions of America. *Language in Society* 15:221–40.

——(1992) Talking black and talking white: A study in variety imitation. In Joan H. Hall, Nick Doane, and Dick Ringler (eds), *Old English and New: Papers in Honor of Frederic G. Cassidy on the Occasion of his 85th Birthday*. New York: Garland, 327–55.

——(1996) Whaddayaknow?: The modes of folk linguistic awareness. *Language Awareness* 5 (1):40–77.

Pyles, Thomas, and John Algeo (1982) *The Origins and Development of the English Language*. New York: Harcourt Brace Jovanovich.

Rampton, Ben (1995) *Crossing: Language and Ethnicity among Adolescents*. London/New York: Longman.

Rickford, John R. (1991) Grammatical variation and divergence in Vernacular Black English. In Marinel Gerritsen and Dieter Stein (eds), *Internal and External Factors in Language Change*. Berlin/New York: Mouton de Gruyter, 175–200.

——(1997) Unequal partnership: Sociolinguistics and the African American speech community. *Language in Society* 26:161–98.

——, and Renee Blake (1990) Copula contraction and absence in Barbadian English, Samaná English, and Vernacular Black English. *Berkeley Linguistics Society* 16:257–68.

——, and Lisa Green (1998) *African American Vernacular English*. New York: Cambridge University Press.

——, and Faye McNair-Knox (1994) Addressee- and topic-influenced style shift. In Douglas Biber and Edward Finegan (eds), *Sociolinguistic Perspectives on Register*. New York: Oxford University Press, 235–76.

——, and Angela Rickford (1995) Dialect readers revisited. *Linguistics and Education* 7:107–28.

Rogers, Everett M. (1983) *Diffusion of Innovations*, 3rd edn. New York: Free Press.

Roman, Camille, Suzanne Juhasz, and Cristanne Miller (eds) (1994) *The Women and Language Debate: A Sourcebook*. New Brunswick: Rutgers University Press.

Rulon, Curt (1971) Geographical delimitation of the dialect areas in *The Adventures of Huckleberry Finn*. In Juanita V. Williamson and Virginia M. Burke (eds), *A Various Language: Perspectives on American Dialects*. New York: Holt, Rinehart, and Winston, 215–21.

Sankoff, David, and Suzanne Laberge (1978) The linguistic market and the statistical explanation of variability. In David Sankoff (ed.), *Linguistic Variation: Models and Methods*. New York: Academic Press, 239–50.

Santa Ana, Otto (1991) Phonetic simplification processes in the English of the barrio: A cross-generational sociolinguistic study of the Chicanos of Los Angelos. Ph.D. dissertation, University of Pennsylvania.

——(1993) Chicano English and the Chicano language setting. *Hispanic Journal of Behavioral Sciences* 15:1–35.

Schilling-Estes, Natalie (1995) Extending our understanding of the /z/ → [d] rule. *American Speech* 70:291–302.

——(1996) The linguistic and sociolinguistic status of /ay/ in Outer Banks English. Ph.D. dissertation, University of North Carolina at Chapel Hill.

——(1997) Accommodation versus concentration: Dialect death in two post-insular island communities. *American Speech* 72:12–32.

——(1998) Investigating "self-conscious" speech: The performance register in Ocracoke English. *Language in Society* 27:53–83.

——, and Jessica Schrider (1996) The symbolization of islander identity: Sex- and gender-based variation in Ocracoke English. Paper presented at New Ways of Analyzing Variation 25, Las Vegas, October 1996.

——, and Walt Wolfram (1994) Convergent explanation and alternative regularization patterns: *were/weren't* leveling in a vernacular English variety. *Language Variation and Change* 6 (3):273–302.

—— and ——(1996) Symbolic identity and language change: /ay/ and /aw/ in two post-insular island communities. Paper presented at New Ways of Analyzing Variation 25, Las Vegas, October 1996.

Schneider, Edgar W. (1983) The origin of the verbal *-s* in Black English. *American Speech* 58:99–113.

——(1989) *American Earlier Black English: Morphological and Syntactic Variables.* Tuscaloosa: University of Alabama Press.

——(ed.) (1996) *Focus on the USA.* Philadelphia/Amsterdam: John Benjamins.

Schulz, Murial R. (1975) The semantic derogation of women. In Barrie Thorne and Nancy Henley (eds), *Language and Sex: Difference and Dominance.* Rowley, MA: Newbury House, 64–75.

Shuy, Roger W., and Frederick Williams (1973) Stereotyped attitudes of selected English dialect communities. In Roger W. Shuy and Ralph W. Fasold (eds), *Language Attitudes: Current Trends and Prospects.* Washington, DC: Georgetown University Press, 85–96.

——, Walt Wolfram, and William K. Riley (1967) *Linguistic Correlates of Social Stratification in Detroit Speech.* USOE Final Report No. 6–1347.

——, ——, and —— (1968) *Field Techniques in an Urban Language Study.* Washington, DC: Center for Applied Linguistics.

Simpkins, Gary C., and Charlesetta Simpkins (1981) Cross-cultural approach to curriculum development. In Geneva Smitherman (ed.), *Black English and the Education of Black Children and Youth.* Detroit: Wayne State University, 221–40.

——, ——, and Grace Holt (1977) *Bridge: A Cross-cultural Reading Program.* Boston: Houghton Mifflin.

Singler, John V. (1989) Plural marking in Liberian settler English, 1820–1980. *American Speech* 64:4–64.

——(1991) Liberian settler English and the ex-slave recordings: A comparative study. In Guy Bailey, Natalie Maynor, and Patricia Cukor-Avila (eds), *The Emergence of Black English: Text and Commentary.* Philadelphia/Amsterdam: John Benjamins, 249–74.

Sledd, James (1976) Language differences and literary values: Divagations from a theme. *College English* 38:224–31.

Smith, Philip M. (1985) *Language, The Sexes and Society*. New York: Blackwell.

Smitherman, Geneva (1977) *Talkin' and Testifyin': The Language of Black America*. Boston: Houghton Mifflin.

——(1991) What is Africa to me? Language ideology and *African American. American Speech* 66:115–32.

——(1994) *Black Talk: Words and Phrases from the Hood to the Amen Corner*. Boston: Houghton Mifflin.

Spears, Arthur K. (1982) The Black English semi-auxiliary *come. Language* 58:850–72.

Spender, D. (1980) *Man Made Language*. Boston: Routledge and Kegan Paul.

Stanley, Julia P. (1977) Paradigmatic woman: The prostitute. In David L. Shores and Carole P. Hines (eds), *Papers in Language Variation*. University: University of Alabama Press, 303–21.

Steinmetz, Sol (1981) Jewish English in the United States. *American Speech* 56:3–16.

Stockman, Ida J. (1986) Language acquisition in culturally diverse populations: The black child as a case study. In Orlando L. Taylor (ed.), *Nature of Communication Disorders in Culturally and Linguistically Diverse Populations*. San Diego: College-Hill Press, 117–55.

——, and Fay B. Vaughn-Cooke (1986) Implications of semantic category research for language assessment of nonstandard speakers. *Topics in Language and Language Disorders* 6:15–25.

Strevens, Peter (1985) Standards and the standard language. *English Today* 2 (April): 5–8.

Tannen, Deborah (1987) *That's Not What I Meant! How Conversational Style Makes or Breaks Relationships*. New York: Ballantine.

——(1990) *You Just Don't Understand: Women and Men in Conversation* New York: Ballantine.

——(ed.) (1993) *Gender and Conversational Interaction*. New York/Oxford: Oxford University Press.

Tarone, Elaine E. (1973) Aspects of intonation in Black English. *American Speech* 48:29–36.

Taylor, Orlando L. (ed.) (1986) *Nature of Communication Disorders in Culturally and Linguistically Diverse Populations*. San Diego: College-Hill Press.

Terrell, Sandra L. (ed.) (1983) *Nonbiased Assessment of Language Differences: Topics in Language Disorders*, No. 3. Rockville: Aspen.

Thomas, Erik (1993) Why we need descriptive studies: Phonological variables in Hispanic English. *Proceedings of the First Annual Symposium about Language and Society-Austin*. Austin: University of Texas Linguistics Department, 42–9.

Trudgill, Peter (1972) Sex, covert prestige, and linguistic change in the urban British English of Norwich. *Language in Society* 1:179–95.

——(1974) *The Social Differentiation of English in Norwich*. Cambridge/London: Cambridge University Press.

——(1983) *On Dialect: Social and Geographical Perspectives*. New York: New York University Press.

——(1990) *The Dialects of England*. Cambridge, MA: Blackwell.

Tsitsipis, Lukas D. (1989) Skewed performance and full performance in language obsolescence: The case of an Albanian variety. In Nancy C. Dorian (ed.), *Investigating*

Obsolescence: Studies in Language Contraction and Obsolescence. Cambridge: Cambridge University Press, 139–48.

Vaughn-Cooke, Anna Fay (1983) Improving language assessment in minority children. *Asha* 25 (June):29–34.

Viereck, Wolfgang (1988) Invariant *be* in an unnoticed source of American English. *American Speech* 63:291–303.

Ward, Martha Coonfield (1971) *Them Children: A Study in Language Learning*. New York: Holt, Rinehart, and Winston.

Weaver, Constance W. (1970) Analyzing literary representations of recent Northern urban Negro speech: A technique, with application to three books. Ph.D. dissertation, Michigan State University.

Weldon, Tracey (1996) Copula variability in Gullah: Implications for the Creolist Hypothesis. Paper presented at New Ways of Analyzing Variation 25, October 1996.

Whiteman, Marcia F. (1976) Dialect influence and the writing of black and white working class Americans. Ph.D. dissertation, Georgetown University.

Williams, Joseph M. (1975) *The Origins of the English Language: A Social and Linguistic History*. New York/London: The Free Press.

Wolfram, Walt (1969) *A Linguistic Description of Detroit Negro Speech*. Washington, DC: Center for Applied Linguistics.

——(1974a) The relationship of Southern White Speech to Vernacular Black English. *Language* 50:498–527.

——(1974b) *Sociolinguistic Aspects of Assimilation: Puerto Rican English in New York City*. Washington, DC: Center for Applied Linguistics.

——(1980) *A-* prefixing in Appalachian English. In William Labov (ed.), *Locating Language in Time and Space*. New York: Academic Press, 107–43.

——(1981) Varieties of American English. In Charles A. Ferguson and Shirley Brice Heath (eds), *Language in the USA*. New York: Cambridge University Press, 44–68.

——(1982) Language knowledge and other dialects. *American Speech* 57:3–18.

——(1984) Unmarked tense in American Indian English. *American Speech* 59:31–50.

——(1985) Variability in tense marking: A case for the obvious. *Language Learning* 35:229–53.

——(1986) Language variation in the United States. In Orlando L. Taylor (ed.), *Nature of Communication Disorders in Culturally and Linguistically Diverse Populations*. San Diego: College-Hill Press, 73–115.

——(1988) Reconsidering the semantics of *a-* prefixing. *American Speech* 63:247–53.

——(1991) *Dialects and American English*. Englewood Cliffs, NJ: Prentice Hall.

——(1993a) Ethical considerations in language awareness programs. *Issues in Applied Linguistics* 4:225–55.

——(1993b) Identifying and interpreting variables. In Dennis R. Preston (ed.), *American Dialect Research*. Philadelphia/Amsterdam: John Benjamins, 193–221.

——(1995) On the sociolinguistic significance of obscure dialect structure: NP$_i$ *call* NP$_i$ V-*ing* in African American Vernacular English. *American Speech* 69:339–60.

——(1996) Delineation and description in dialectology: The case of perfective *I'm* in Lumbee English. *American Speech* 71:5–26.

——, and Donna Christian (1976) *Appalachian Speech*. Washington, DC: Center for Applied Linguistics.

——, and Ralph Fasold (1974) *The Study of Social Dialects in the United States.* Englewood Cliffs, NJ: Prentice Hall.

——, and Natalie Schilling-Estes (1995) Moribund dialects and the endangerment canon: The case of the Ocracoke brogue. *Language* 71:696–721.

——, and —— (1997) *Hoi Toide on the Outer Banks: The Story of the Ocracoke Brogue.* Chapel Hill/London: University of North Carolina Press.

——, Donna Christian, and Carolyn Adger (1998) *Dialects in Schools and Communities.* Mahwah: Lawrence Erlbaum.

——, Clare Dannenberg, and Kyle Messner (1997) *Dialects and Appalachian English.* An 8th grade curriculum. Raleigh: North Carolina Language and Life Project.

——, Kirk Hazen, and Jennifer Ruff Tamburro (1997) Isolation within isolation: A solitary century of African American English. *Journal of Sociolinguistics* 1:7–38.

——, Natalie Schilling-Estes, and Kirk Hazen (1997) *Dialects and the Ocracoke Brogue.* An 8th grade curriculum. Raleigh: North Carolina Language and Life Project.

——, Erik Thomas, and Elaine Green (1997) Reconsidering the development of African American Vernacular English: Lessons from isolated speakers. Paper presented at New Ways of Analyzing Variation 26, Québec, Canada.

——, Natalie Schilling-Estes, Kirk Hazen, and Chris Craig (1997) The sociolinguistic complexity of quasi-isolated southern coastal communities. In Cynthia Bernstein, Tom Nunnally, and Robin Sabino (eds), *Language Variation in the South Revisited.* University: University of Alabama Press, 173–187.

Wright, Richard (1961) (originally published 1941) *Native Son.* New York: The New American Library.

Young, Richard, and Robert Bayley (1996) VARBRUL analysis for second language acquisition research. In Robert Bayley and Dennis R. Preston (eds), *Second Language Acquisition and Linguistic Variation.* Philadelphia/Amsterdam: John Benjamins, 253–306.

Index